SPEAK HINDI FROM DAY 1

Books By Kavita Kumar

- *Hindi for Non- Hindi Speaking People — main book*
- *Hindi for Non- Hindi Speaking People — (Companion Work Book)*
- *Hindi-English Phrasebook*

- *Namaste- Eine Einfeurung in die praktischen Gebrauch des Hindi*
- *Namaste- Eine Einfeurung in die praktischen Gebrauch des Hindi Arbeits Buch*
- Reise Begleiter –Hindi German Phrasebook
- *English for Hindi Speaking People in four volumes covering grammar, vocabulary, phrases, spoken English. Vol 1. — 4*

SPEAK HINDI FROM DAY 1

Kavita Kumar

Rupa . Co

First Published 2008
Second Impression 2010

Published by

Rupa . Co

7/16, Ansari Road, Daryaganj
New Delhi 110 002

Sales Centres:

Allahabad Bengalooru Chandigarh Chennai
Hyderabad Jaipur Kathmandu
Kolkata Mumbai

Printed in India by
Gopsons Papers Ltd.
A-14 Sector 60
Noida 201 301

CONTENTS

43. SITUATIONAL PHRASES

PREFACE

Speak Hindi from Day One is a complete course on learning Hindi as a foreign language. It is a highly user-friendly instructional tool for learners. Learning the Devanagri script is always advisable. However, with this book, it is no longer a necessity. It contains the text both in Devanagri as well as Roman script.

The book is designed with a learner in mind who wants to learn Hindi for travel or professional needs, but has no time to take short or long term formal courses at specific hours and at specific learning centers. The book helps you to learn Hindi effectively as a foreign language without straining your most valuable yet limited resource - TIME. The book has all that one needs to learn a language.

Committing words to memory is a very important part of learning a new language. This book gives you words and phrases and shows you how to put them together in a meaningful order just as the native speakers would do.

This is not just a phrasebook. It takes you deep into the subtleties of the language and helps you to advance from a basic level to a higher level of expertise and proficiency. It offers you a wide variety of learning material as you journey through it's four sections, G, S, D and P.

G provides the learner with basic grammar rules followed by clear explanations and plenty of examples from day-to-day life. The learner is gradually led to foray into the complex language structures by dynamically splitting them into smaller, easier to comprehend sentence models with varied verb conjugations in all possible tenses and moods. There are examples with detailed clear explanations. Every chapter contains several exercises with self check-answers.

S contains simple stories with detailed grammar analysis and cross references, thus giving the learner the opportunity to recapitulate and further fortify what has been learnt in section G.

D has dialogues based on situations encountered in day-to-day life. Natives everywhere tend to describe their point of view, their thoughts and impressions on personal, national, or global matters using idiomatic language. There is never any word-for-word translation for such expressions. Like any other language, Hindi has its own idiomatic expressions which reflect the culture and philosophical mind set of the speakers. These dialogues have been specially designed to expose the

the learner to the use of such idiomatic expressions and phrases.

P has a small bank of situational phrases. For more in this direction refer to the author's *Hindi English Phrasebook* .

For more on Hindi Grammar , it's usages and practice, refer to theauthor's *Hindi For Non Hindi Speaking People* and the accompanying Workbook.

January 14, 2008

Kavita Kumar
Varanasi

ABBREVIATIONS

adj.	adjective
adv.	adverb
aux.	auxiliary
compul. str.	Compulsion Structure
comp. v.i.	Compound verb intransitive
comp. v.t.	Compound verb transitive
cond. str.	Conditional structure
conj.	Conjunct
cont. comp.	Continuative compound
D	dialogues
f.pl.	feminine plural
f.sg.	feminine singular
fut.	future
G	gender; also used here as Grammar in numbering chapters of section one.
hon.	honorific
imper.	imperative
inc. comp.	inceptive compound
inf.	infinitive
Inform.	Informal
Int.	intimate
Inter.	interrogative
IPC	Imperfective Participial Constructions
m.pl.	masculine plural
m.sg.	masculine singular
N	number
nom. case	nominative case
obj.	object
obl.pl.	oblique case plural
obl.sg.	oblique case singular
pl.	plural

non-prox.	non-proximate
P	phrases
past. perf.	Present perfect
past hab.	Past habitual
pres. ind.	Present indefinite
pres. perf.	Present perfect
PPC	Past participle construction
pp_n	postposition
prog.	progressive
pron.	pronoun
prox.	proximate
refl. pron.	reflexive pronoun
S	stories
subj.	subject
subjunc.	subjunctive
v.i.	verb intransitive
v.r.	verb root
v.t.	verb transitive
'X'	any indefinite subject
⇛	changes to

Introduction

Hindi belongs to the Indo-European family of languages. In its long journey starting with Sanskrit, through Prakrit, Pali and Apăbhraṃś, it came across several linguistic influences from foreign traders and political invaders. As a result, some existing sounds and syntax were dropped, while some new sounds, verb conjugations and words were taken in.

Hindi uses Devanāgri script which is believed to have sprung from Prācīn Nāgrī — a derivative of Brāhmī script. The development of Devanāgri to its present form is believed to have begun sometime in 1000 AD.By 1200 AD the vowels, consonants and vowel symbols had become like Hindi. Some further changes by way of standardization continued to take place, and by the end of 1800, the script attained its present form. Unlike Sanskrit, Prakrit etc, the final 'a' अ ceased to be pronounced. Already words from Pashto, Arabic, Persian, and Turkish had become part of Hindi. Also, the use of compound verbs and the conjunct 'ki' कि had come into Hindi through the influence of Persian and Arabic.

Devanāgri script is written from left to right. It has all the features of an ideal script . All possible consonant and vowel sounds are contained in the Hindi alphabet which is classified in a scientific order. Vowels[1] and consonants[2] are listed separately. Long and short vowels are kept together. Each vowel, long or short, has a separate character as well as a symbol form to be used when combined with consonants. Consonants, classified on the basis of the area of articulation,

1. see page one. 2. see pg. 7.

begin with the velars, move forward through the prepalatals, palatals, dentals to the labials, followed by liquids, sibilants and glottal. Consonants in Hindi have five main classifications. The word used in Hindi for classification is 'varga'. Each 'varga' is named after the first letter contained in it. For instance, the first letter of the first classification is 'ka' क, hence it is called the 'ka' क-varga. Based on the first letter of the following classifications, they are called 'ca' च-varga, 'ṭa' ट-varga, 'ta' त- varga and 'pa' प-varga respectively.

All classifications have five letters each; the first and third letter of each classification is non-aspirate, the second and fourth letters are aspirates. The fifth letter is a nasal consonant.

In writing, the nasal consonant provided at the end of each classification can precede the remaining four of its group where required, either in its character form or as a dot above the preseding letter. For complete comprehension of use of nasal consonants, see pg. 17-18. The vowel 'a' अ is inherent in all the consonants. In writing, one vowel following a consonant is affixed to it in its symbol form. However if a word requires use of more than one vowel, the following vowels are written as character.

Hindi is a phonetic language and hence very easy to learn. It is read almost the way it is written. There are no silent letters; pronunciation ambiguities are rare. There are very few exceptions, and very few irregular verbs.

Hindi is an accurate, friendly and living language, generously taking into its fold new sounds as and when required. For instance, when new vocabulary came in with Muslim invaders requiring use of the sounds क़ *qa*, ख़ *kha*, ग़ *ga*, फ़ *fa*, ज़ *za* found in Arabic and Persian. Hindi rose to the occasion by modifying the already existing similar sounding consonants by affixing a dot underneath. Similarly, when English words came in the language, it introduced the use of a crescent-like symbol placed above the bar to assure correct pronunciation of English words such as college कॉलिज, doctor डॉक्टर etc. Apart from the full stop which is a dot in English but a vertical stroke in Hindi, it took all the other punctuation symbols used in English.

Since 1900, there have been considerable changes in word power and usage. Bhartendu Harish Chandra followed by several other scholars initiated the task of standardizing Hindi. This work has been being continued by the Central Hindi Institute, Delhi, and the Nagri Pracarni Sabha, Varanasi. There is growing use of *tatsam* words. Of the modified letters, use of क़ *qa*, ख़ *kha* and ग़ *ga* is becoming extinct. Instead क *qa*, ख *kha* and ग *ga* are used both in speech and script. The use of फ़ *fa*, ज़ *za* continues both in writing and speech since they are used in English too, which is the preferred language of the modern youth particularly, and of Indians in general. New vocabulary is continuously evolving to meet the needs of a technology-based world. The use of compound verbs which already by 1800, had found its way into Hindi through the Persian and Arabic influence, has gradually increased, further fortifying the power of expressing subtle meaning and finer nuances.

The Hindu view of time is cyclic and not linear as in Christianity. Christianity believes in an absolute beginning of the world order with God's word. God's word was the beginning and God's word (on the day of Judgement) will be the end.

Hindu view believes in the coexistence of world and Divine, and in repeated cyclic creations and dissolutions, without a beginning, with out end, each cycle leaving behind impressions(saṃskāras) based on previous karmas, out of which arises the next cycle. Thus goes on the entire cosmos, cycles of creation and dissolution, and not absolute creation.Time is perceived as an eternally revolving wheel without any beginning or end; hence the same words *kal* for tomorrow and yesterday, *parsoṁ* for day after tomorrow and day before yesterday, and *narsoṁ* for two days after tomorrow and two days before yesterday are used. Appropriate past or future verb endings leave no room for doubt regarding the timing of the event.

The Indian perception of life in every object is imbibed through the language; hence only two genders, masculine and feminine, are recognized grammatically. Foreign students are advised to learn the gender with every new noun-word, without which correct verb conjugation is not possible. The sound of a word is the master key to gender-determination.

The sages declared 'ego' as man's deadliest enemy. This, along with the basic Hindu belief which admits the supremacy and omnipotence of the creator of the universe, accepts Him as the doer of all activity and assumes for the people a humble, passive role as recipients of His grace or wrath, and is reflected in the language. Several sentence constructions have the subject in the dative case (i.e. subject followed by को) instead of the nominative case. For instance, while an English speaker says "I am hungry", "I hurt myself", or "I like it", the corresponding Hindi constructions are *mujhko bhūkh lagī hai, mujhko coṭ lagī hai, mujhko pasand hai* etc., meaning respectively, "To me hunger is", "To me injury is", or "To me pleasing is". Similarly, "I need" = *mujhko cāhie*, "I know"= *mujhko patā hai* or *mujhko ātā hai* etc. The underlying concept is that the subject is not actively doing the action but things are actually happening to him or coming to him.

Hindi has a separate catagory of causative verbs corresponding to the English 'have-passive' structure — a long syntactic formation to express the idea of getting something done by somebody. 'आ' (ā) or 'वा' (vā) is infixed between the existing transitive or intransitive verb roots and their 'ना' (nā) endings. This reflects the sociological setup with its ages-long, deeply-ingrained caste structure which has a class of people who have been recognized as existing mainly for providing service to those higher up in the caste hierarchy.

Students learning Hindi as a foreign language are bound to come across several constructions which if interpreted and understood in the religio-socio-philosophical background, are easily comprehended and mastered.

Hindi today is a fully-fledged, well accomplished language of the people, of journalism and literature, of law, science and business. It is the national language of India.

G 1 VOWELS (स्वर)

	1	2	3	4	5	6
	V	S	T	C+V	Position	Pronunciation
1.	अ		a	क ka	inherent in C	shut, hut
2.	आ	ा	ā	का kā	follows C	bar, car
3.	इ	ि	i	कि ki	precedes C	hit ,sit
4.	ई	ी	ī	की kī	follows C	seat, meet
5.	उ	ु	u	कु ku	subscript	put, full
6.	ऊ	ू	ū	कू kū	subscript	fool, pool
7.	ऋ	ृ	ṛ	कृ kṛ	subscript	trip,grip
8.	ए	े	e	के ke	superscript	tape, hate
9.	ऐ	ै	ai	कै kai	superscript	tap, hat
10.	ओ	ो	o	को ko	follows C	coal, pole
11.	औ	ौ	au	कौ kau	follows C	caught hot

V= Vowel; S= Symbol; T= transliteration; C= consonant ;

- The first vowel अ 'a' is inherent in all consonants for phonetic ease.

VOWELS

- The consonant without the inherent अ 'a', are written with a subscript stroke written left to right downwards क्
  The consonant क ka = क् k + अ a
- All Hindi vowels have their nasalized form. The air passes freely through the nasal cavity. The symbol used is a crescent with a dot above it. Since Hindi uses vowel symbols to join consonants and vowels, sometimes, to avoid crowding, only a dot instead of crescent and dot is used.
  अं ˙ / अँ ṁ **कं /कँ kaṁ**
- 'Visarga ':' is transliterated as 'ḥ'. It occurs mostly in loan words from Sanskrit.

  अः : ḥ कः kaḥ

Before doing the vowels and the consonants in detail, I would like you to know a couple of things about the Hindi (known as Devanāgrī) script.

- Devanāgrrī script requires a horizontal bar on most letters of the alphabet. Always begin by making a horizontal bar; draw it just long enough for the letter that you plan to write. This is important, since some letters have an opening and do not require the horizontal bar on top.
- Vowels in Hindi have an alternative symbol form too.
- The first vowel 'अ a' is inherent in all the consonants. It has no symbol. When required to be used independent of consonant, the character 'अ' is used.
- All other vowels have a symbol representing the character.
- In writing, one vowel following a consonant is affixed to it in symbol form. However if more than one vowel follow the consonant,you cannot add symbols to symbols; the remaining vowel or vowels are written as characters.

Hindi script provides for both long vowel and short vowel at the same time.

1. The first vowel is short अ।

Its pronunciation resembles the sound of the English vowel 'u' in words such as ' shut', 'hut', 'jug' etc as shown in row 1, column 6, page 1.

It has no symbol form. It is inherent in all the consonant.
For transliteration we use the English vowel 'a'

2. The second vowel is long आ।

It is written exactly like short अ followed by a vertical stroke.
Its pronunciation resembles the sound of the English vowel 'a'
as in words such as 'car', bar', 'jar' etc as shown in row 2, column 6, page 1.

Its symbol is a vertical stroke which follows any consonant as shown in row 2, column 4, page 1.

For transliteration we use the English vowel 'a' with a bar on it as shown in row 2, column 3, page 1.

3. The third vowel is short इ।

Its pronunciation resembles the sound of the English vowel 'i' in words such as ' sit', 'kit', 'it' etc.

Its symbol is a vertical stroke with a loop which precedes the consonant as shown in row 3, column 4, page 1.

For transliteration we use the English vowel 'i' as shown in row 3, column 3 , page 1.

For affixing the symbol for short 'इ ':
first make the vertical stroke on the left of the consonant;
next make the loop as shown.
Ideally, the hand should move from the upper end of the vertical stroke to the middle of the consonant. If the consonant has a vertical stroke as part of the character, then this loop should be extended to the upper end of this vertical stroke.

☞ In the case of two conjoined consonants, short 'इ 'symbol which actually belongs to the second member of the group is written before the first member but read between the two. **e.g.** शान्ति śānti. Here, as you see, the short 'इ ' symbol which belongs to the consonant त 'ta' is written to the left of **the consonant** न **'na'.**

4. The fourth vowel is long ई।

Its pronunciation resembles the sound of combinations of English vowels 'ea' or 'ee' , as, for example, in words ' heat', 'seat', 'meet' etc.

Its symbol is a vertical stroke with a loop which follows the consonant, as shown in row 4, column 4 , page 1.

For transliteration we use the English vowel 'i' with a bar on top' as shown in row 4, column 3, page 1.

For affixing the symbol for long ई ।
first make the vertical stroke on the right side of the consonant;
next make the loop as shown.
Ideally, the hand should move from the middle of the consonant to the upper end of this vertical stroke. If the consonant already has a vertical stroke as part of the character, then this loop should begin at the upper end of this vertical stroke and be extended to the upper end of the vertical stroke affixed to its right.

5. The fifth vowel is short उ।

Its pronunciation resembles the sound of English vowel 'u'. as, for example, in words such as ' full', 'bull', 'pull' etc.

Its symbol is a subscript. It is a kind of a small loop moving from right to left upwards, below the consonant, as shown in row 5, column 4, page 1.
For transliteration we use the English vowel 'u'. as shown in row 5, column 3, page 1.

6. The sixth vowel is long ऊ।

Its pronunciation resembles the sound of English vowels 'oo' as, for example, in words such as 'fool', 'pool' 'cool' etc.

Its symbol is a subscript. It is a kind of a small loop moving from left to right downwards, below the consonant, as shown in row 6, column 4, page 1.

For transliteration we use the English vowel 'u with a bar on it'. as shown in row 6, column 3, page 1.

7. The seventh vowel is short ऋ।

Its pronunciation resembles the combined sound of English consonant 'r' followed by the vowel 'i'. as, for example, in words ' grip', 'trip', etc.

☞ ऋ though similar in sound is s a vowel different from the consonant र 'ra'. The former has a vowel symbol, a subscript which resembles English letter 'c', affixed below the preceding consonant but pronounced after it, as shown in row 7, column 4, page 1.

र 'ra' has forms such as, ˏ , ʻ , ‸ etc. as shown on page 14.

For transliteration we use the English consonant 'r with a dot underneath', as shown in row 7, column 3, page 1.

8. The 8th vowel is ए।

Its pronunciation resembles the sound of English vowel 'a' as in 'fate' 'hate' or the combined sound of the vowels 'a' and 'i' as, for example, in words 'mail' 'sail' etc.

Its symbol is a kind of slanting stroke drawn from left to right downwards to meet the horizontal bar covering the consonant, as shown in row 8, column 4, page 1.

For transliteration we use the English vowel 'e'. as shown in row 8, column 3, page 1.

9. The 9th vowel is ऐ।

Its pronunciation resembles the sound of English vowel 'a', as, for example, ' fat', 'hat', 'mat' etc.

ऐ/ ै is alternatively pronounced with select words as 'a+i' where 'a' is like 'u' in shut and 'i' is like 'i' in sit. Examples भैया bha-i-yā, नैया na-i-yā:

Its symbol is two slanting strokes drawn from left to right downwards to meet the horizontal bar covering the consonant, as shown in row 9, column 4, page 1.

For transliteration we use the English vowels 'ai'. as shown in row 9, column 3, page 1.

10. The tenth vowel is ओ।

Its pronunciation resembles the sound of English vowels 'o' or 'ou', 'oa', such as ' hole', 'soul' 'coal' etc.

Its symbol is a combination of a vertical stroke on the right side of the consonant and a slanting stroke above the horizontal bar covering the consonant. as shown in row 10, column 4 page 1.

While writing, remember to make the vertical stroke to the right first, and then the superscript, moving the hand from the upper end downwards, joing the lower end of the superscript to the upper end of the vertical stroke.
For transliteration we use the English vowel 'o'. as shown in row 10, column 3, page1

11. The eleventh vowel is औ।

Its pronunciation resembles the sound of English vowels 'o', 'au', or 'ou', as, for example, in words ' hot', 'thought' 'caûght' etc.

औ/ ौ is alternatively pronounced with select words as 'a+u' where 'a' is like 'u' in shut and 'u' is like 'u' in full. Examples कौवा ka-u-vā.

Its symbol is a combination of a vertical stroke on the right side of the consonant and two slanting strokes above the horizontal bar covering the consonant as shown in row 11, column 4, page 1.

While writing, remember to make the vertical stroke to the right first, and then the superscripts, moving the hand from the upper end downwards, joining the lower end of the superscripts to the upper end of the vertical stroke.

For transliteration we use the English vowel 'au' as shown in row 11, column 3, page 1.

CONSONANTS

non-aspirate	aspirate	non-aspirate	aspirate	nasal
क	ख	ग	घ	ङ
ka	kha	ga	gha	ṅa (angaṁ)
च	छ	ज	झ	ञ
ca	cha	ja	jha	ña (añyāṁ)
ट	ठ	ड	ढ	ण
ṭ	ṭha	ḍa	ḍha	ṇa
		ड़	ढ़	
		ṛa	ṛha	
त	थ	द	ध	न
ta	tha	da	dha	na
प	फ	ब	भ	म
pa	pha	ba	bha	ma
य	र	ल	व	semi vowels
ya	ra	la	va	
श	ष	स		sibilants
śa	ṣa	sa		
ह ha				glottal

क्ष kṣa (It is a combination of क् + ष) conjuncts

त्र tra (It is a combination of त् + र)

ज्ञ jña'/ gya (It is a combination of ज् + ञ . Sanskritarians pronounce it as 'jña' where as Hindi speakers pronounce it as 'gya')

CONSONANTS

क ka- varga – Velars

Area of articulation , velar region

non-aspirate	aspirate	non-aspirate	aspirate	nasal
क	ख	ग	घ	ङ
ka	kha	ga	gha	ṅa (angaṁ)

'ka' and 'ga' are non-aspirates;
'kha' and 'gha' are aspirates;

'angaṁ' is a nasal consonant. It never comes at the beginning of a word.

ख kha and घ gha 'are not familiar sounds in English.

काका	काकी	कोआ	खाक	
kākā	kākī	koā	khāk	
खाकी	खाओ	गई	कंघी	गंगा
khākī	khāo	gaī	kaṅghī	gaṅgā

च ca- varga- Prepalatals.

च	छ	ज	झ	ञ
ca	cha	ja	jha	ña (añyāṁ)

'ca' is used as transliteration symbol for 'च', and corresponds to the sound 'ch' as in church or champion.

च ca, ज ja are non-aspirates.

छ cha, झ jha are aspirates.

ञ ña (añyāṁ) is nasal consonant. . It never comes at the beginning of a word.

छ cha, झ jha are unfamiliar in English.

चाचा	चाची	छाछ	गज	जाग
cācā	cācī	chāch	gaj	jāg

जीजी	जीजा	चख	काजू	चाकू
jījī	jījā	cakh	kājū	cākū

ṭ a- varga - Palatals/Retroflexes

Area of articulation : The tip of the tongue touches the hard palate.

ट	ठ	ड	ढ	ण
ṭ	ṭha	ḍa	ḍha	ṇ
	ड़	ढ़		Flaps
	ṛa	ṛha		

ट ṭ, ड ḍa nonaspirates.

ठ ṭha, ढ ḍha aspirates.

'ठ ṭha and ढ ḍha' are unfamiliar sounds in English. ढ ḍha can be used in all three places, the beginning, middle and end of a word. e.g. बुड्ढा buḍhā, ढाई, ḍhāī, बेढब beḍhab.

ड़ ṛa, ढ़ ṛha were not part of Devanagri alphabet in Sanskrit. These are typical Hindi sounds, not found almost in all other Indian languages. They are found at the end or in the middle. e.g. पड़ना paṛnā, पड़ paṛ, पढ़ना paṛhnā, गढ़ gaṛh These never come at the beginning of a word.

For pronouncing ड़ ṛa, ढ़ ṛha the tongue touches the hard palate and is rolled at the same time to produce these sounds which , again,, are unfamiliar in English.

ण ṇa is a nasal consonant. Tongue is rolled to pronounce this nasal consonant. It never comes at the beginning of a word.

टाटा	डैडी	ठक-ठक	काठ	डाक
ṭaṭa	ḍaiḍī	ṭhak-ṭhak	kāṭh	ḍāk
अण्डा	चोटी	झाड़ू	झाड़ो	झाड़िए
aṇḍā	coṭī	jhāṛū	jhāṛo	jhāṛie

CONSONANTS

त ta-varga- Dentals

Tip of the tongue touches where the upper hind teeth meet the gums.

त	थ	द	ध	न
ta	tha	da	dha	na

'त ta and द da' are non-aspirates.

'थ tha and ध dha' are aspirate.

'त ta and ध dha''unfamiliar sound in English.

'थ tha and ध dha' not fully covered on top.

छाता	ताज	ताज़ा	चखना		छकना	छूना
chātā	tāj	tāzā	cakhnā		chaknā	chūnā
कान	नाक	नोक	कोन	तन	तनु	जीनत
kān	nāk	nok	kon	tan	tanu	jīnat
नाद	थन	छाती	तीज	जाना	जीना	दान
nād	than	chātī	tīj	jānā	jīnā	dān

प pa-varga- Labials

The point of articulation is lips.

प	फ	ब	भ	म
pa	pha	ba	bha	ma

प pa and ब ba are non aspirates.

फ pha and भ bha are aspirates

भ bha is open on top.

फ pha and भ bha sounds are unfamiliar in English.

पापा	फूफा	बाबा	बबुआ	भाई	बनाना
pāpā	phūphā	bābā	babuā	bhāī	banānā

य	र	ल	व	**semi-vowels**
ya	**ra**	**la**	**va**	

यार	यकीन	राजा	लाला	लोमड़ी	वन	वायु	आयु
yār	yakīn	rājā	lālā	lomṛī	van	vāyu	āyu

श	ष	स	**sibilants**
śa	**ṣa**	**sa**	

शाम	शान	शिशु	शीश	शुभ	शूर	शोभा
śām	śān	śiśu	śīś	śubh	śūr	śobhā

शौक	शौच	शोक
śauk	śauc	śok

षटकोण	शोष	शोषण	ऋषि	सज	सोना
ṣatkoṇ	śoṣ	śoṣaṇ	ṛṣi	saj	sonā
समझना	सुनना	सुनाना	सोचना	सूखना	सुखाना
samajhnā	sunanā	sunānā	sochnā	sūkhnā	sukhānā

ह	**Glottal**
ha	

हम	है	हो	हैं	हूँ	होना
ham	hai	ho	haiṁ	hūṁ	honā
हमारा	हर	हरि	सहज	सहना	
hamārā	har	hari	sahaj	sahnā	

क्ष	त्र	ज्ञ
kṣa	**tra**	**gya/jña**

क्षमा	कक्षा	शिक्षा	क्षत्रिय		
kṣamā	kakṣā	śikkṣā	kṣatriya		
त्रास	त्रेता	त्रिकोण	पत्र	यात्रा	यात्री
trās	treta	trikoṇ	patra	yātrā	yātrī
ज्ञान	ज्ञाता	विज्ञान	जिज्ञासा		

CONSONANTS

gyān gyātā vigyān ji gyāsā

Ex. G 1.1 Read aloud and transliterate.

☞ **In two letter word, the inherent 'a' sound in the second consonant is silent.**

कल	जल	फल.	हल	नल	बस
सब	फस	जस	नस	रण	रथ
रख	भर	कर	नर	हर	रब
टब	खट	झट	पट	फट	तट
नट	गप	रट	नई	भई	कई

Ex. G 1.2 Read aloud and transliterate.

☞ **If a three letter word ends in a consonant with inherent vowel 'a', it is silent.**

कमल	पवन	हवन	नकल	चमक	भवन
नहर	अजय	तड़प	कलश	अमन	डगर

Ex. G 1.3 Read aloud and transliterate.

☞ **If a three letter word ends in a consonant with some vowel symbol, the inherent 'a' in the middle letter is silent.**

कमला	हमला	बिमला	मटका	चमचा	गमला
तड़का	पकड़ा	झगड़ा	लडकी	मुरगी	ककड़ी

Ex. G 1.4 Read aloud and transliterate.

☞ **In a four letter word, the inherent 'a' if any, of the second letter and the fourth letter is not pronounced.**

EXERCISES

चमचम	खटमल	शलगम	अजगर	जनपथ	अनपढ़
camcam	khaṭmal	śalgam	ajgar	janpath	anpaṛh

Here I would like to introduce you to a couple of things regarding the use of र 'ra' in devanagri script. In devanagri script, the consonant ra is treated somewhat different from other consonants

- **Short or long 'u' (उ, ऊ) symbols (ु or ू) following the consonant र 'ra' are not affixed to it as subscripts, but in the middle as shown below**
  - **र + उ is written as रु and not as रु**

    रुकना, रुपया

    ruknā, rupayā

  - **र + ऊ is written as रू and not as रू**

रूप	शुरू	कुरूप	रूपिका	रूपेण
rūp	śurū	kurūp	rūpikā	rūpeṇ

- **When र 'ra' follows a consonant (without inherent 'a'), it is written as a stroke attached underneath the consonat, moving downward from right to left.**

क्रम	श्रम	प्रेम	प्रीति	प्रेरणा	क्रोध
kram	śram	prem	prīti	prerṇā	krodh

श ś + र ra is written as श्र ।

श्रुति	आश्रम	श्रमिक	श्री	श्रीमान्	श्रीमती
śruti	āśram	śramik	śri	śrimān	śrimatī

☞ It is written as ्र under छ cha, ट ṭa, ड da as ट्र ṭa, ड्र ḍra, छ्र chra.

e.g. ड्रम ḍram, ट्राम ṭrām,

- **When र् 'r' i.e. र without the inherent 'a' precedes a consonant, it is written as a kind of open loop र्‍ (similar to the one on long ई) on top of**

the following consonant, but read before it. If the consonant has any vowel symbol attached to it, it goes on top of this symbol.

अर्थ	गर्मी	नर्मी	शर्म	कीर्ति	वर्षा
arth	garmī	narmī	śarm	kīrti	varṣā

Key G 1.1

kal jal phal hal nal bas
sab phas jas nas raṇ rakh
bhar kar nar har rab ṭab
khaṭ jhaṭ paṭ phaṭ taṭ naṭ
gap raṭ naī bhaī kaī

Key G 1.2

kamal pavan havan nakal camak bhavan
nahar ajay taṛap kalaś aman ḍagar

Key G 1.3

kamlā hamlā bimlā maṭkā camcā gamlā
taṛkā pakṛā jhagṛā laṛkī murgī kakṛī

Key G 1.4

camcam khaṭmal śalgam ajgar janpath anpaṛh

Test yourself:

Test 1: Read aloud and transliterate.

जाओ आओ खाओ बैठो पढ़ो कहो
देखो सुनो बोलो नाचो लाओ करो

जाइए आइए खाइए बैठिए पढ़िए कहिए
देखिए सुनिए नाचिए जागिए कीजिए पीजिए

Test 2:

बाई भाई बालू भालू बोरा भोरा
गोरा घोरा सरक सड़क पड़ना पढ़ना

ढूँढना

Test. 3:

आज्ञा	जिज्ञासा	विज्ञान	ज्ञान	ज्ञानी	
यात्रा	यात्री	त्रास	त्रिकोण	सत्र	सत्रह
शिक्षक	शिक्षा	क्षण	क्षणिक	क्षमा	क्षोभ

Test. 4:

तृष्णा	कृष्णा	वृष्टि	ऋषि	ऋषभ	ऋतु

Key to Test .1

jāo	āo	khāo	baiṭho	paṛho	kaho
dekho	suno	bolo	nāco	lāo	karo
jāie	āie	khāie	baiṭhie	paṛhie	kahie
dekhie	sunie	nācie	jāgie	kījie	pījie

Key to Test 2

bāī	bhāī	bālū	bhālū	borā	bhorā
gorā	ghoṛā	sarak	saṛak	parna	paṛhna
ḍhūṁḍnā					

Key to Test 3:

āgyā	jigyāsā	vigyān	gyān	gyānī	
yātrā	yātrī	trās	trikoṇ	satra	satrah
śikṣak	śikṣā	kṣaṇik	kṣaṇ	kṣamā	kṣobh

Key to Test 4:

tṛiṣṇā	kṛiṣṇā	vṛiṣṭi	ṛṣi	ṛiṣabh	ṛitu

■ CONJUNCT LETTERS

ह्य	ह् + य	hya	हृ	ह् + ऋ	hṛ (hri)
ह्म	ह + म	hma	क्त	क + त	kta
द्र	द् + र	dra	प्र	प् + र	pra
ट्ट	ट् + ट	ṭṭa	ड्ड	ड् + ड	ḍḍa

READING EXERCISES

द्द	द् + द	dda	ड्ढ	ड् + ढ	ḍḍha
द्ध	द् + ध	ddha	स्र	स् + र	sra
स्त्र	स् + त्र	stra	क्क	क् + क	kka
द्य	द्‌य	dya	द्व	द्‌व	dva
श्र	श्‌र	shra			

बाह्य	हृदय	ब्रह्मा	वक्ता	टट्टा	हड्डी
bāhya	hṛdaya	brahmā	vaktā	ṭaṭṭā	haḍḍī
रद्दी	बुड्ढा	बुद्धि	सिद्धि	स्रज	स्रोत
raddī	buḍḍhā	buddhi	siddhi	sraj	srot
चक्की	कुक्की	द्वार	द्वेष	विद्या	विद्यालय
cakkī	kukkī	dvār	dveṣ	vidyā	vidyālaya

■ MODIFIED LETTERS

Spoken language of natives in India is a mixture of Urdu and Hindi. The root s of both these languages are different.. The root of Urdu is Arabic and that of Hindi is Sanskrit. To accomodate the sounds of Urdu tha are alien to Devanagri script, Hindi has modified five letters of the Devanagri script by just affixing a dot underneath. These are क़, ख़, ग़, ज़, फ़ ।

The English sound nearest to क़ is perhaps 'q'; ख़, and ग़, are unfamiliar in English. Bach in german is a good example of ख़, sound. ज़, is like 'z' in 'zoo' in English and फ़ |is like 'f' in 'faith' in English.

■ VISARGA:

Another thing that I would llike you to know at this stage is 'visarga. It looks like colan, written as two dots, one below the other. It is transliterated as an 'h' with a dot underneath. It is pronounced as 'ah'.It occurs mainly in loan words from Sanskrit. For example refer to page 2. क followed by visarga (कः) is pronounced as 'kah'. It is an aspirated sound.

■ HALANT

As I already mentioned to you, the first letter अ is inherent in all the consonants for phonetic ease. A consonant without the vowel अ has a subscript stroke called *halant*, affixed underneath, drawn from left to right downwards. Again for reference, go to page 2. Pronunciation of क् is 'k' and not 'ka'

■ NASALIZATION OF VOWELS AND CONSONANTS

Vowels are nasalized by putting a crescent with a dot (ँ) known as *candra-bindu/anunāsik* above the horizontal bar covering the top of the vowel or vowel symbol that is nasalized. For example, माँ māṁ, हूँ hūṁ,

However if there is already a superscript, only a dot (ं) known as anusvār and not a crescent plus dot *(candra-bindu)* is used. For example, हैं haiṁ., मैं maiṁ.

Anusvār is a nasal consonant. It has no independent existence. It can never come at the beginning of a word. Its use is in the middle. It is written as a dot written above the preceding consonat but read after it. Any of the five nasal consonants when they come before any member of their classification, can be written both in their character form or alternatively, be replaced by *anusvār*.

Examples where both *anusvār* or nasal consonant may be used:

गङ्गा / गंगा gaṅgā, चञ्चू / चंचू cañcū, अण्डा / अंडा aṇḍā,
हिन्दी / हिंदी Hindī चम्पा / चंपा campā

Examples where only *anusvār* only is used:

ङ् *ñ* + ह *ha* ;

न *na* + श *śa* / स *sa* / र *ra*/ ल *la*

Examles:

संहार *saṃhār*, संशय *saṃśay*, संरचना *saṃracnā*, संलग्न *saṃlagna*.

***Anusvār* before conjunct consonants:**

संक्षेप *saṅksep*संज्ञा *sajñā/saṅgyā*

Where both nasal consonant and *anusvār* are used:

संन्यास *sanyās;* संन्यासी *sanyāsī*

***Anusvār* at the end (found inloan words from Sanskrit)**

एवं *evam;* स्वयं *svayam;* अहं *aham*

Where only nasal consonant is used:

- when ङ् *ṅ* is followed by म *ma.* For example: वाङ्मय *vāṅgmaysaj*
- when ण् *ṇ* is followed by ण *ṇa,* म *ma,* य *ya,* व *va.* For example: अक्षुण्ण *akṣuṇṇa* , मृण्मय *mṛṇmay,* पुण्य *puṇyă,* कण्व *kaṇva.*
- when *na* is followed by न 'na', म 'ma', य 'ya', व 'va', ह 'ha'
  अन्न *anna,* अम्ल *amla,* जन्म *janma,* अन्य *anyă,,* अन्वेषण anveṣaṇ, किन्हें *kinheṁ.*
- when म *ma* is followed by न *na,* म *ma,* य *ya,* र *ra,* व *va,* ह *ha*
  निम्न *nimna,* सम्मान *sammān,* साम्य *śāmyă,* ताम्र *tāmra* तुम्हें *tumheṁ,.* ताम्र *tāmra*

Some guidelines to pronunciation:

- **In Hindi, inherent final अ *a* is not pronounced:**
  चल *cal* and not *cala*, कलम *kalam* and not *kalama*, टमटम *tamtam* and *not tamatama*

Exceptions:

- Inherent final अ *a* of monosyllabic words is pronounced:
  e.g. न *na,* व va
- When a word ends in conjunct consonant.
  e.g. नेत्र *netra,* चन्द्र *candra*
- When a word ends in य *ya* preceded by इ *i,* ई *ī,* ऊ *ū* .
  e.g. राजसूय *rājsūya*, इन्द्रिय *indriya,* दर्शनीय *darśanīya*
- When second syllable of a four letter word is a conjunct letter.
  नेत्रहीन *netrahīn.*
- When a four syllabic word has prefix, inherent **अ *a*** of the second syllable is prounced. e.g. आरक्षण *ā-rakṣaṇ,* प्रहसन *pra-hasan*
- When a four syllabic word ends in a long vowel, the inherent **अ *a*** of the third syllable is not prounced. e.g. मचलना *macalnā,* अगरचे *agarce,*

●●●●●

G 2 PRONOUNS

■ PRONOUNS IN THE DIRECT CASE

(when they are the Subject of the sentence)

First Person: maiṁ मैं (I) ham हम (we)

First Person: tū तू , tum तुम , āp आप (you)

☞ Instead of only one form of 'you' in English which can be used regardless of age, rank, intimate, informal or formal nature of relationship with the person addressed, Hindi has three separate forms.

☞ तू 'tū' is grammatically singular form of 'you', and also a very intimate form of addressing the second person.

- तू 'tū' is used between very close friends.
- तू 'tū' is used to address mother as well as gods and goddesses, since the relationship of a child to mother, and that of a devotee to his or her desired deity is very personal and very intimate.
- तू 'tū' is used for the menial class.

☞ तुम 'tum' is grammatically plural form of you. In practice, however, तुम 'tum' is used both as singular and plural address to the second person. This is common among friends, parents addressing the children, new generation of married couples.

The use of तू 'tū' is declining , and in day-to-day usage तुम (tum) is replacing तू 'tū' to a considerable extent.

☞ आप āp is formal, respectful form, used both as singular and plural. This is used to address senior members of the family, new acquaintances where for mality need be observed by way of etiquette.

☞ तुम (tum) and आप (āp) are used both as singular and plural. The Hindi speaking natives add a word लोग (log) to specify that plural is implied. The expressions used as plural are, तुम लोग (tum log) and आप लोग (āp log), both meaning 'you people'.

Caution: As new comer foreigners, with insufficient knowledge of the language, you are advised to avoid the use of तू (tū), the intimate form of 'you', lest you offended the person addressed!

Third Person:	'vah' वह,	'yah' यह	'he', 'she', 'it'
	've' वे	'ye' ये	'they'

- There is no gender discrimination.
- They accord with proximity or non proximity to the speaker.

vah वह corresponds to English 'he, she , it' when these happen to be away from the speaker, and 'yah' यह when these happen to be near the speaker.

've' वे corresponds to English 'they', when they happen to be away from the speaker, and 'ye' ये when they happen to be near the speaker.

☞ आप 'āp' the second person formal, sg. or pl. is also used by the native speakers as third person while introducing somebody to somebody.

For example:

आप श्रीमती कपूर हैं।	āp Srimati Kapoor haim.	She is Mrs Kapoor.
आपसे मिलिए।	āpse milie.	Meet her

* Hindi language meets the cultural requirement of respectful, honorific address for older people, teachers, gurus, formal acquaintances by using the plural forms of the third person pronouns 've' and 'ye' for singular. They take the corresponding plural verb conjugations even when used as singulars. In usage, log is added to वे (ve) or ये (ye) to specify that plural is implied. The expressions used are ये लोग 'ye log', that is 'they' plural and near,... and वे लोग 've log', that is 'they', plural and distant.he, she, it (near) is.

■ SIMPLE POSTPOSITIONS IN HINDI

The nouns or pronouns are said to be in the oblique case when they are used in any case other than as the subject of the sentence. Hindi requires the use of suitable case endings , which for the purpose of teaching Hindi as a foreign language have been given the nomenclature 'postpositions.' Postpositions in Hindi have grammatically the same function as the prepositions in English. As their name suggests they are placed after the noun or pronoun. Hindi has a large number of compound postpositions, which we shall do later. (See pg. 79-80)

The simple postpositions are like this:

Postposition	English equivalent	Case
को (ko)	to	accusative (direct object) dative (indirect object)
से (se)	with, from, time expressions	instrumental, ablative,
में (meṁ)	in	locative
पर (par)	on	locative
का, के, की (kā, ke, kī)	of	genitive*

* **The use of genitive case is a little different. We shall do it separately in chapter 5, 'The Possessessive Case'.**

■ PRONOUNS IN THE OBLIQUE CASE + POSTPOSITIONS को ko, से se, में meṁ, पर par.

{ pp_n = postposition; ⇨ = changes to}

direct		oblique	direct			oblique			
I	⇨	me	maiṁ	मैं ⇨	mujh	मुझ	+	any pp_n
we	⇨	us	ham	हम ⇨	ham	हम	+	any pp_n
you (intimate)	≠		tū	तू ⇨	tujh	तुझ	+	any pp_n
you (informal)	≠		tum	तुम ⇨	tum	तुम	+	any pp_n
you (formal)	≠		āp	आप ⇨	āp	आप	+	any pp_n
he, she, it (far)	⇨	him, her	vah	वह ⇨	us	उस	+	any pp_n
he, she, it (near)	⇨	him her	yah	यह ⇨	is	इस	+	any pp_n

PRONOUNS IN THE OBLIQUE CASE

they (far)	⇨	them	ve	वे ⇨	un	उन +	any pp_n
they(near)	⇨	them	ye	ये ⇨	in	इन +	any pp_n
who (sg.)	⇨	whom	kaun	कौन⇨	kis	किस +	any pp_n
who (pl.)	⇨	whom	kaun	कौन⇨	kin	किन +	any pp_n

☞ **In English the required preposition precedes the oblique form of the noun or pronoun; In Hindi postpositions follow the oblique form .**

COMPREHENSION:

मुझको mujhko to me; मुझसे mujhse from me ;मुझमें mujhmeṁ in me, मुझपर mujhpar on me

हमको hamko to us; हमसे hamse from us ; हममें hammeṁ in us;

हमपर hampar on us

उसको usko to him/ her/ it; उससे usse from him/ her/ it; उसमें usmeṁ in him/ her/ it; उसपर uspar on him/ her/ it;(non-proximate)

इसको isko to him/ her/ it; इससे isse from him/ her/ it; इसमें ismeṁ in him/ her/ it; इसपर ispar on him/ her/ it.(proximate)

उनको unko to them; उनसे unse from them; उनमें unmeṁ in them; उनपर unpar on them (non-proximate)

इनको inko to them; इनसे inse from them; इनमें inmeṁ in them; इनपर inpar on them (proximate)

किसको kisko to whom; किससे kisse from whom; किसमें kismeṁ in whom; किसपर kispar on whom (sg.)

किनको kinko to who all; किनसे kinse from who all; किनमें kinmeṁ in who all; किनपर kinpar on who all (pl.)

☞ **The oblique pronouns take one of the case endings depending upon the case in which the pronoun is being used.**

☞ **In the accusative and dative case, that is, when they are used as direct or indirect object, there are two possibilities:**

- **they take the postposition को 'ko' as shown above.**
- **Alternatively, there is a contracted form in use as shown in the table given below.**

☞ **There is absolutely no difference in meaning. They are just two variations for oblique pronouns when they happen to be direct or indirect object in a sen tence. It is important to learn them both at the same time since the nat-ive speakers keep switching between the two forms all the time.**

to me	mujhe / mujhko	मुझे/मुझको
to us	hameṁ / hamko	हमें/हमको
to you(int.)	tujhe / tujhko	तुझे/तुझको
to you (infor.)	tumheṁ / tumko	तुम्हें/तुमको
to you(form.)	āpko / āpko	आपको/आपको
to him,/her/it (far)	use / usko	उसे/उसको
to him/ her/it (near)	ise / isko	इसे/ इसको
to them (far)	unheṁ / unko	उन्हें / उनको
to them (near)	inheṁ / inko	इन्हें / इनको
to whom (sg.)	kise / kisko	किसे / किसको
to whom (pl.)	kinheṁ / kinko	किन्हें/किनको

Ex. G 2.1 Transliterate and Translate into English.

इसमें; उसमें; उनसे; उनपर; उनको; मुझसे; हमसे; आप लोगों से, किसको, किससे, हमको; इससे; उससे; उनमें, किनमें; किन लोगों में।

Ex. G 2.2 Translate into Hindi.

to them; in it; on that; in me; on that ; on whom (sg.); from them; from her/him; to you(honorific); in them; in us; on us; to you (inf.); to me; to whom (where who is plural)

Key G 2.1 Transliteration:

ismeṁ; usmeṁ; unse; unpar; unko; mujhse; hamse; āp logoṁ se, kisko; kisse;

hamko; isse; usse; unmeṁ; kinmeṁ; kin logoṁ meṁ.

Key G 2.1 Translation:

in it/him/her; in that/him/her; from them; on them; to them; from me; from us; from you people; to whom(wher who is singular); from whom (who sg.) ; to us; from it/him/her; from that/him her; in them; in whom (wherewho is pl.); in who all.

Key G 2.2

उनको; इसमें; उसपर; मुझमें; उसपर; किसपर; उनसे; उससे; आपको; उनमें; हममें; हमपर, तुमको, मुझको, किनको।

unko; ismeṁ; uspar; mujhmeṁ; uspar; kis par; unse; usse; āpko; unmeṁ; hammeṁ; hampar, tumko, mujhko, kinko.

●●●●●

COLORS

रंग	raṅg	safed	गेरुआ	geruā	ochre
सफेद	safed	white	काला	kālā	black
पीला	pīlā	yellow	नीला	nīlā	blue
हरा	harā	green	जामुनी	jāmunī	purple
स्लेटी	sleṭī	grey	गुलाबी	gulābī	pink
भूरा	bhūrā	brown	लाल	lāl	red
संतरा	santrā	orange	भदमैला	bhadmailā	beige
केसरिया	kesariyā	safron			
हल्का नीला	halkā nīlā	light blue	गहरा नीला	gahrā nīlā	dark blue

G 3 NOUNS

Hindi has only masculine and feminine nouns. Even non-living objects are either masculine or feminine. There is no neuter gender.

In Hindi language structures, the verb conjugation agrees with Number and Gender of the Subject or the Object in the appropriate tense. Make it your habit to learn the gender of a noun at the same time as you learn the word meaning. Knowledge of gender is essential for correct verb conjugation in various language structures in the required tense.

Also, nouns in Hindi have two different direct and oblique forms , both in singular and plural. (Nouns are in the direct case when they are used as the subject of the sentence; in their oblique forms when they are in some case other than the subject of the sentence. In the oblique case they are followed by some postposition.)

■ For the purpose of pluralization of the nouns, all masculine nouns can be classified as:

(1) आ (ā)-ending masculine nouns (2) all other masculine nouns

- आ **(ā)-** ending masc. nouns change to ए **(e)**-ending in direct plural and oblique singular case.
- Their oblique plural has ओं **(oṁ)**-ending.

case	masc. singular	masc. plural
direct case	आ **ā**	ए e
oblique case	ए **e**	ओं oṁ

MASCULINE NOUNS

- **All other masculine nouns remain the same in direct singular, direct plural, oblique singular. Their oblique plural has oṁ- or yoṁ ending.**

case	masc. singular	masc.plural
direct case	–	–
oblique case	–	ओं oṁ or यों yoṁ

आ ā -ending masculine nouns:

direct case	laṛkā (boy)	लडका	laṛke(boys)	लड़के
oblique case	laṛke+pp_n	लड़के +pp_n	laṛkoṁ+pp_n	लड़कों+pp_n
direct case	darvāzā (door)	दरवाज़ा	darvāze(doors)	दरवाज़े
oblique case	darvāze+pp_n	दरवाज़े +pp_n	darvāzoṁ +pp_n	दरवाज़ों +pp_n

masculine nouns with all other endings:

direct case	ghar (house)	घर	ghar (houses)	घर
oblique case	ghar+ pp_n	घर +pp_n	ghar oṁ+pp_n	घरों +pp_n
direct case	ādmī(man)	आदमी	ādmī (men)	आदमी
oblique case	ādmī+pp_n	आदमी+pp_n	ādmiyoṁ+pp_n	आदमियों+pp_n
direct case	nīmbū (lemon)	नींबू	nīmbū (lemons)	नींबू
oblique case	nīmbū + pp_n	नींबू +pp_n	nīmbuoṁ+ pp_n	नींबुओं +pp_n
direct case	sādhu(mendicant)	साधु	sādhu (mendicants)	साधु
oblique case	sādhu + pp_n	साधु +pp_n	sādhuoṁ+ pp_n	साधुओं +pp_n

☞ **long ई ī is shortened before adding यों yoṁ- ending in oblique plural cases .**

☞ **long ऊ ū is shortened before adding ओं oṁ ending in the oblique plural cases .**

FEMININE NOUN

For the purpose of pluralisation feminine nouns can be classified as:

(1) इ i , ई ī - ending fem. nouns (2) fem. nouns ending in consonant, आ ā, उ u, ऊ ū.

- **In the direct case all the feminine nouns ending in consonant, आ ā, उ u, ऊ ū- change to eṁ-ending when pluralized. Their oblique plurals have ओं-ending.**

☞ **long ऊ ū is shortened before adding एँ eṁ in the direct plural or ओं oṁ ending in the oblique plural case**

- **In the direct case all the feminine nouns ending in इ i, ई ī, change to याँ yāṁ- ending when pluralized. Their oblique plurals have यों yoṁ-ending.**

☞ **long ई ī is shortened before adding याँ yāṁ in the direct plural or यों yoṁ- ending in oblique plural cases .**

- direct singular and oblique singular is always the same, whatever the noun-endings.
- oblique plurals, like masculine nouns, always have **ओं(oṁ)- or यों (yoṁ)**-ending.

case	fem.singular	fem. plural
direct case	**consonant, आ ā, उ u, ऊ ū-**	**एँ eṁ**
oblique case	–	**ओं oṁ**
direct case	इ i, ई ī,	**याँ yāṁ**
oblique case	–	**यों yoṁ**

FEMININE NOUNS

- **consonant ending fem. nouns:**

direct case aurat (woman) औरत aurteṁ (women) औरतें
obli. case aurat + pp_n औरत +pp_n aurtoṁ + pp_n औरतों +pp_n

direct case kitāb(book) किताब kitābeṁ (books) किताबें
obli. case kitāb+ pp_n किताब +pp_n kitāboṁ + pp_n किताबों +pp_n

- **आ (ā) - ending fem. nouns**

direct case chātrā (student) छात्रा chātrāeṁ (students) छात्राएँ
oblique case chātrā + pp_n छात्रा + pp_n chātrāoṁ + pp_n छात्राओं+pp_n

direct case diśā (direction) दिशा diśāeṁ (directions) दिशाएँ

oblique case diśā+ pp_n दिशा +pp_n diśāoṁ + pp_n दिशाओं+pp_n

- **ऊ ū or उ u -ending fem. nouns.**

(We don't have many feminine nouns ending in long ū or short 'u'.)

direct case vadhū (bride) वधू vadhueṁ(sons'wives)वधुएँ
oblique case vadhū+ pp_n वधू+ pp_n vadhuoṁ + pp_n वधुओं + pp_n

direct case vastu(thing) वस्तु vastueṁ(things) वस्तुएँ
oblique case vastu+ pp_n वस्तु+ pp_n vastuoṁ + pp_n वस्तुओं+ pp_n

- **ī (ई) or i (इ)- ending feminine nouns:**

direct case cūṛī (bangle) चूड़ी cūriyāṁ (bangles) चूड़ियाँ
oblique case cūṛī+ pp_n चूड़ी+ pp_n cūriyoṁ + pp_n चूड़ियों+ pp_n

direct case laṛkī(girl) लड़की larkiyāṁ (girls) लड़कियाँ
oblique case laṛkī+ pp_n लड़की+ pp_n larkiyoṁ + pp_n लड़कियों+ pp_n

direct case tithi (date) तिथि tithiyāṁ (dates) तिथियाँ

oblique case tithi+ pp_n तिथि+ pp_n tithiyoṁ तिथियों+ pp_n

direct case nidhi (treasure) निधि nidhiyāṁ निधियाँ
oblique case nidhi+ pp_n निधि+ pp_n nidhiyoṁ + pp_n निधियों+ pp_n

VERB ' to be' = (honā) होना in the present tense

The present forms of the verb 'to be'—— (honā) होना

The verb 'to be' in English is called (honā) होना in Hindi.In English the verb 'to be' has three present tense forms, 'is', 'are', 'am'.

Instead Hindi has four forms.

The present forms of **honā** are: (hūṁ) हूँ, ho हो, hai है, haiṁ हैं।

- (hūṁ) हूँ corresponds to 'am' in English and is used with मैं (maiṁ) that is 'I' in English.
- (ho) हो is a special form used only with (tum) तुम , the grammatically plural, but in practice used both as singular and plural informal form of 'you'.
- (hai) है corresponds to 'is' in English and is used with second person singular तू (tū) that is intimate you, third person singulars यह (yah), वह (vah) that are he, she, it in English.
- (haiṁ) हैं corresponds to 'are' in English and is used with first person plural (ham) हम that is 'we', second person honorific form आप (āp), third person plural forms वे (ve) , and ये (ye) that are equivalents of 'they' in English.

SENTENCE FORMATION

☞ The w ord order in Hindi is different from the word order in English In English the sentence begins with the Subject, followed by verb and then the object. In Hindi too the sentence begins with Subject, but is followed by object and then comes the verb. **The verb always comes at the end.**

☞ Word order in English	☞ Word order in Hindi
subject + verb + noun object.	**subject + noun object +verb.**

Examples.

I am a woman. ☞ In Hindi the word order would be:

I a woman am. मैं औरत[f.] हूँ। maiṁ aurat[f.] hūṁ.

Similarly:

2. We are women . (We women are.)

   हम औरतें$^{f.pl}$हैं । ham aurteṁ$^{f.pl}$ haiṁ

3. you (intimate) are a shopkeeper. *(You a shopkeeper are.)*

   तू दुकानदार^{m} है । tū dukāndār$^{m.}$ hai.

4. He (far) is a boy. *(He a boy is.)*

   वह लड़का^{m} है । vah laṛkā^{m} hai.

5. They (far) are boys. *(They boys are)*

   वे लड़के$^{m.pl}$ हैं । ve laṛke^{m} haiṁ.

6.. This is (near) a book. (*This a book is.*)

   यह किताब^{f} है । yah kitāb^{f} hai.

7. These (near) are books. (*These books are.*)

   ये किताबें$^{f.pl}$ हैं । ye kitābeṁ$^{f.pl}$ haiṁ.

8. She is a student. (*She a student is.*)

   वह छात्रा^{f} है । vah chātrā^{f} hai.

9. Who are you (informal;sg., pl.) ? *(You (inf.sg/pl; m/f) who are?)*

   तुम$^{m/f}$ कौन हो? tum$^{m/f}$ kaun ho?

10. Who are you (form.m./f, sg, pl.)? *(You (form.m./f, sg, pl.) who are?)*

    आप$^{m/f}$ कौन हैं? āp$^{m/f}$ kaun haiṁ?

- Even if you address one person respectfully as आप (āp), it will take the plural verb form.
- In English language, the interrogatives such as who, when, where etc come at the beginning of the sentence. In Hindi the interrogatives except 'kyā' follow the subject.

☞ 'kyā' is used before the subject when the answer to the question is 'yes' or 'no' Example 12.

☞ 'kyā' follows the subject when the answer to the question is some object. Example. 11.

11. What is this? *This what is?*
यह^m/f. क्या है? yah^m/f kyā hai?

12. Is he a poet?
क्या वह कवि है? kyā vah kavi hai.

Ex. G 3.1 Read aloud and translate into English with the help of word meanings given below:

1.	कमरे में	kamre meṁ	2.	चाकू से	chākū se
3.	कवि को	kavi ko	4.	भाई में	bhāī meṁ
5.	पेड़ से	peṛ se	6.	मेज़ पर	mez par
7.	छत पर	chat par	8.	कक्षा में	kakṣā meṁ
9.	सोमवार को	somvār ko	10.	राम को	Rām ko
11.	कमरों में	kamroṁ meṁ	12.	चाकुओं से	cākuoṁ se
13.	कवियों को	kaviyoṁ ko	14.	भाइयों में	bhāiyoṁ meṁ
15.	पेड़ों से	peṛoṁ se	16.	साधुओं को	sādhuoṁ ko
17.	आलुओं को	āluoṁ ko	18.	कक्षाओं में	kakṣāoṁ meṁ
19.	छतों पर	chatoṁ par	20.	मेज़ों पर	mezoṁ par

कक्षा kakṣā class; छत chat ceiling; चाकू cāku knife; कवि kavi poet; भाई bhāī brother ; पेड़ peṛ tree; आलु ālu potato; सोमवार somvār Monday

Ex. G 3.2 Translate into Hindi.

1. university; universities; in the university; in the universities.

2. student (f.sg.); students (f.pl.); to the student (f.sg.); to the students (f.pl.)

3. language; languages; from the language; in the languages.

4. hospital; hospitals; in the hospital; in the hospitals

Ex. G 3.3 Translate into English.

1. इन छात्रों को; **2.** इस विश्वविद्यालय में; **3.** उन स्कूलों में; **4.**उस छात्र के साथ; **5.** इस कुर्सी पर। **6.** इन मेज़ों के पास; **7.** उन खेतों में; **8.** इस किसान के साथ; **9.** इन कर्मचारियों के लिए; **10.** इस दुकान के अन्दर; **11.** उस सभा में; **12.** उन विद्यार्थियों के बिना; **13.** इस इमारत में;

14. इन घरों में।

1.in chātroṁ ko; 2. is viśvavidyālaya meṁ; 3. un skūloṁ meṁ; 4. us chātra ke sāth. 5. is kursī par; 6. in mezoṁ ke pās; 7. un khetoṁ meṁ; 8. is kisān ke sāth. 9. in karmcāriyoṁ ke lie; 10. is dūkān ke andar; 11. us sabhā meṁ;12. un vidyārthiyoṁ ke binā; 13. is imārat meṁ;14 .in gharoṁ meṁ.

Ex. G 3.4 Translate into English:

1. तस्वीर दीवार पर है। **2.** पिता जी दफ़्तर में हैं। **3.** रानी घर पर है। **4.** किताब मेज़ पर है। **5.** पंखा छत पर है। **6.** छात्र पाठशाला में है। **7.** हम भारतीय हैं। **8.** वह कौन है? **9.** मैं अनिल हूँ। **10.** क्या आप सुधांशु हैं।? **11.** अखबार कहाँ है? **12** यह किताब है। **13.** यहाँ चार कमरे हैं। **14.** एक अलमारी है। **15.** दो दरवाज़े हैं। **16.** तीन खिड़कियाँ हैं। **17.** घर में दो नौकर हैं। **18.** एक बच्चा भी है।

1. tasvīr dīvār par hai. 2. pitā jī daftar meṁ haiṁ. 3. rānī ghar par hai. 4. kitāb mez par hai. 5. paṅkhā chat par hai. 6. chātra pāṭhśālā meṁ hai.7. ham bhārtīy*f* haiṁ. 8. vah kaun hai? 9. maiṁ anil hūṁ. 10. kyā āp sudhānśu haiṁ? 11. akhbār kahāṁ hai? 12. yah kitāb hai. 13. yahāṁ cār kamre haiṁ. 14. ek almārī hai. 15. do darvāze haiṁ. 16. tin khiṛkiyāṁ haiṁ. 17. ghar meṁ do naukar haiṁ. 18. ek baccā bhī hai.

तस्वीर$^{f.}$ tasvīr picture; दफ़्तर daftar office; मेज़$^{f.}$ mez table; पंखा paṅkhā fan; छत$^{f.}$ chat roof/ceiling. पाठशाला pāṭhśālā$^{f.}$ school; भारतीय bhārtīyă Indian; दुकान$^{f.}$ dukān shop; कुर्सी$^{f.}$ kursī chair; छात्रा$^{f.}$ chātrā student; छात्र$^{m.}$ chātra student; अख़बार$^{m.}$ akhbār newspaper. अलमारी almārī cupboard; खिड़की$^{f.}$ khiṛki window; अध्यापक$^{m.}$ adhyāpak teacher; कक्षा$^{f.}$ kakṣā class; नौकर$^{m.}$ naukar servant.

Ex. G 3.5 Reading comprehnsion. गंगा नदी Gaṅgā Nadī

गंगा भारत में एक बहुत प्रसिद्ध नदी है। यह बहुत लंबी है। यह हिमालय से निकलती है। इस नदी के किनारे अनेक प्रसिद्ध नगर स्थित हैं, उदाहरण के लिए कानपुर, इलाहाबाद

(प्रयाग), वाराणसी, पटना, कोलकाता आदि। इन प्रसिद्ध नगरों में प्रयाग और वाराणसी बहुत बड़े तीर्थस्थान हैं।

Gaṅgā bhārat meṁ ek bahut prasiddh nadī hai. yah bahut lambī hai. yah himālay se nikaltī hai. is nadī ke kināre anek prasiddh nagar sthit haiṁ, udāharaṇ ke lie Kānpur, AIlāhābād (Prayāg), Vārāṇasī, Patna, Kolkātā ādi. in prasiddh nagroṁ meṁ Prayāg aur Vārāṇasī bahut baṛe tīrthsthān haiṁ.

प्रसिद्ध[adj.] prasiddh famous; नदी nadī river; लंबी lambī long; निकलना[v.i.] nikalnā to emerge; किनारा[m] kinārā coast; नगर[m] nagar city; स्थित sthit situated; उदाहरण[m] udāharan example; तीर्थस्थान[m] tīrthsthān pilgrimage place; के लिए ke lie for; आदि ādi etc

Key G 3.1

1. in the room;2. with the knife; 3. to the poet; 4. in brother; 5. from the tree; 6. on the table; 7.on the roof; 8. in class 9. on Monday 10. to Ram 11. in the rooms;12. with knives; 13. to the poets; 14. among brothers; 15. from the trees;16. to the mendicants 17. to potatoes; 18. in classes 19. on the roofs; 20. on the tables

Key G 3.2

1. विश्वविद्यालय; विश्वविद्यालय; विश्वविद्यालय में; विश्वविद्यालयों में।

2. छात्रा; छात्राएँ; छात्रा को; छात्राओं को।

3. भाषा; भाषाएँ; भाषा से; भाषाओं में।

4. अस्पताल; अस्पताल; अस्पताल में; अस्पतालों में।

1. viśvavidyālay, viśvavidyālay, viśvavidyālay meṁ, viśvavidyālayoṁ meṁ.
2. chātrā; chātrāeṁ; chātrā ko; chātrāoṁ ko.
3. bhāśā; bhāśāeṁ; bhāśā se ; bhāśāoṁ meṁ.
4. aspatāl; aspatāl; aspatāl meṁ; aspatāloṁ meṁ

Key G 3.3

1. to these students 2. in this university 3. in those schools 4. with that student 5. on this chair 6. near these tables 7. in those fields 8. with this farmer 9. for these workers 10. in this shop 11. in that assembly.12. without those students 13. in this building 14. in these houses.

NOUNS: EXERCISES

Key G 3.4

1.The picture is on the wall. 2. Father is in the office. 3. Rani is at home. 4. Book is on the table. 5. Fan is on the ceiling. 6. Student is in school. 7. We are Indians. 8. Who is he/she? 9. I am Anil. 10. Are you Sudhanshu. 11. Where is the newpaper. 12. This is a book. 13. Here are four rooms. 14. This is a cupboard. 15. There are two doors. 16. There are three windows. 17. There are two servants in the house. 18. There is also one child.

Key G 3. 5

Ganges is a famous river in India. It is very long. It comes out of the Himalayas. On the banks of this river, many famous cities are situated, for instance, Kanpur, Allahabad, Varanasi, Patna, Kolkata etc. Among these famous cities, Prayag and Varanasi are big pilgrimage places.

●●●●●●

G 4 ADJECTIVES

■ In Hindi adjectives are classified into two groups.

- आ (ā)- ending adjectives such as महँगा mahaṁgā = expensive, अच्छा acchā = good, बूढ़ा būṛhā = old, पुराना purānā = old etc.

☞ **बूढ़ा (būṛhā) is equivalent of 'old' in English , used for person, but not for 'old' thing. Equivalent of 'old' as used with things, in Hindi is** पुराना purānā.

- all other adjectives, that is adjectives other than those that end in आ (ā) such as javān जवान = **'young'**, rocak रोचक = **interesting,** hośiyār होशियार = **clever,** bahādur बहादुर = **brave'**, bhārī भारी = **heavy,** dayālu दयालु = **kind' etc**

☞ आ (ā)- ending adjectives are declined to accord with the number and gender of the noun or pronoun they qualify. This is different from English. In English, the adjective remains the same regardless of the gender, number or the case of the noun it qualifies. For instance one would say:

m.sg	**m.pl**	**case**
a good man	good men	**direct case**
to a good man	to good men	**oblique case**

Similarly a good woman, good women, to a good woman, or to good women. We have seen, whatever the number, gender or the case of the noun, the adjective 'good' remains the same.

In Hindi it is not always the same.

- The आ (ā)- ending adjectives retain their base आ (ā)- form when qualifying mas. singular nouns of any ending in the direct case.
- They change to ए (e)-form when qualifying a masculine noun of any ending in direct plural, oblique singular and oblique plural form. For instance:

ADJECTIVES

good boy	**good boys**	
acchā laṛkā	acche laṛke	direct case
अच्छा लड़का	अच्छे लड़के	
to good boy	**to good boys**	
acche laṛke ko	acche laṛkoṁ ko	oblique case
अच्छे लड़के को	अच्छे लड़कों को	

- They change to ई (ī)-ending when qualifying feminine nouns in their singular or plural form., direct as well as oblique case.

For instance:

good girl	**good girls**	
acchī laṛkī	acchī laṛkiyāṁ	direct case
अच्छी लड़की	अच्छी लड़कियाँ	
to good girl	**to good girls**	
acchī laṛkī ko	acchī laṛkiyoṁ ko	oblique case
अच्छी लड़की को	अच्छी लड़कियों को	

Similarly all the ā- ending adjectives have three forms. such as :

m.sg.	**m.pl.**	**f.sg.,pl.**
būṛhā	būṛhe	būṛhī
बूढ़ा	बूढ़े	बूढ़ी
purānā	purāne	purānī
पुराना	पुराने	पुरानी
mahaṁgā	mahaṁge	mahaṁgī
महँगा	महँगे	महँगी

- **All other adjectives with any other ending always remain the same regardless of the number, gender and the case of the noun they qualify. For example using the adjective** javān जवान **with laṛkā** लड़का **(m.) boy** ,laṛkī लड़की **(f.) girl , we have:**

young boy javān laṛkā जवान लड़का	**young boys** javān laṛke जवान लड़के	**direct case**
to young boy javān laṛke ko जवान लड़के को	**to young boys** javān laṛkoṁ ko जवान लड़कों को	**oblique case**
young girl javān laṛkī जवान लड़की	**young girls** javānlaṛkiyāṁ जवान लड़कियाँ	**direct case**
to young girl javān laṛkī ko जवान लड़की को	**to young girls** javān laṛkiyoṁ ko जवान लड़कियों को	**oblique case**

☞ As you have seen, the ā-ending masc.noun laṛkā changes to laṛke in direct plural and oblique singular case, and to laṛkoṁ in the oblique plural case; also the feminine singular noun laṛkī changes to laṛkiyāṁ in the direct plural and laṛkiyoṁ in the oblique plural case. However the non ā-ending adjective always retains its base form and remains unchanged.

■ SENTENCE FORMATION USING ADJECTIVES

WORD ORDER IN ENGLISH	WORD ORDER IN HINDI
subj. + verb + adj. +noun object.	subj. + adj. + noun object +verb.
1, I am an old woman.	maiṁ būṛhī aurat[f] hūṁ. मैं बूढ़ी औरत[f] हूँ ।
2. We are old women.	ham[f.] būṛhī aurteṁ[f.pl] haiṁ हम[f.] बूढ़ी औरतें[f.pl] हैं।
3. You (m.intimate) are a good shopkeeper.	tū[m.sg] acchā dukāndār[m] hai. तू अच्छा दुकानदार है।
4. You (m.inform;sg./ pl.) are tall.	tum[m] lambe (sg. and pl.) ho. तुम[m] लम्बे हो।

* **Even if ' tum' is used as informal singular, since grammatically it is plural**

'you', the adjective लम्बा (lambā) meaning 'tall' changes to लम्बे (lambe).

5. You (formal;hon.;sg. /pl.)are a kind man.	āp dayālu ādmī[m] haiṁ. आप दयालु आदमी[m] हैं।
6. He (far) is a young boy.	vah javān laṛkā[m] hai. वह जवान लड़का[m] है।
7. She(far) is a clever student.	vah hośiyār chātrā[f] hai. वह होशियार छात्रा[f] है।
9. They (far) are brave boys.	ve bahādur laṛke[m.pl] haiṁ. वे बहादुर लड़के[m.pl] हैं।
10.These are interesting books.	ye rocak kitābeṁ [f.pl] haiṁ. ये रोचक किताबें[f.pl] हैं।

Ex. G 4.1 Translate into English:

1. पुराना मकान[m.sg.] 2. पुराने मकान[m.pl.] 3. सरल भाषा[f.sg.] 4. सरल भाषाएँ[f.pl.] 5/6. विदेशी छात्र[m.sg./pl.]7. अच्छी किताब[f.sg.] 8. अच्छी किताबें[f.pl.] 9. सुन्दर लड़की[f.sg.] 10. सुन्दर फूल[m.sg.] 11. सुन्दर लड़का[m.sg.] 12. बड़ा देश [m.sg]13. नई इमारत[f.sg.] 14. लम्बी नदी[f.sg.] 15. ग़रीब आदमी[m.sg/pl.] 16. ग़रीब औरत[f.sg.] 17. मेहनती छात्र, 18. बूढ़ी औरत, 19. बूढ़ी औरतें[m.pl.] ।

1. purānā makān 2. purāne makān 3. saral bhāṣā 4. saral bhāṣāeṁ 5 / 6. videśī chātra (sg./pl. same) 7. acchī kitāb 8.. acchī kitābeṁ 9. sundar laṛkī 10 . sundar phūl 11. sundar laṛkā 12. baṛā deś 13. naī imārat 14. lambī nadī 15. garīb ādmī 16. garīb aurat 17. mehantī chātra 18. būṛhī aurat 19. būṛhī aurteṁ.

Ex. G 4.2 Translate into Hindi:

1. big room 2. big rooms 3. big table 4. big tables 5. in big room 6. in big rooms 7. on big table 8. on big tables 9. kind man 10. kind men11.to kind man 12.to kind men 13. kind woman 14. kind women 15. to kind woman 16. to kind women 17. beautiful house 18. beautiful houses 19. beautiful hut 20. beautiful huts 21. in beautiful house 22. in beautiful houses 23. in beautiful hut 24. in beautiful huts 25. stale 'samosa' 26. stale 'samosas' 27. stale 'roṭi' 28. stale 'roṭies' 29. to stale 'samosa' 30. to stale 'samosas' 31. to stale 'roṭi' 32. to stale

'roṭies'.

Ex. G 4.3 Translate into English:

1. कमला खुश नहीं है। 2. मैं बहुत निराश हूँ। 3. माँ कुछ चिन्तित हैं। 4. हम बहुत चकित हैं। 5. औरत$^{f.sg.}$ सुन्दर है। 6. घर$^{m.}$ नया है। 7. सेब$^{m.pl.}$ महँगे हैं। 8. युवक$^{m.sg.}$ काफ़ी लम्बा है। 9. युवती$^{f.sg.}$ लम्बी नहीं है। 10. सड़क$^{f.sg.}$ सँकड़ी नहीं है। 11. रास्ता$^{m.sg.}$ सँकड़ा है। 12. सड़क$^{f.}$ बहुत चौड़ी है।

1. Kamlā khuś nahīṁ hai. 2. maiṁ bahut nirāś hūṁ. 3. māṁ kuch cintit haiṁ. 4. ham bahut cakit haiṁ. 5. aurat sundar hai. 6. ghar nayā hai. 7. seb mahaṁge haiṁ. 8. yuvak kāfī lambā hai. 9. yuvtī lambī nahīṁ hai. 10. saṛak saṁkṛī nahīṁ hai. 11. rāstā saṁkṛā hai. 12. saṛak bahut cauṛī hai.

Ex. G 4.4 Translate into Hindi:

1.Yogurt$^{m.sg.}$ is sour. 2. Food$^{m.sg.}$ is stale. 3.The teacher$^{f.sg.}$ is kind. 4.The student$^{m.sg.}$ is intelligent. 5.The child$^{m.sg.}$ is naughty.6.This man is honest. 7.You$^{m.inf.}$ are very cruel. 8.She is a little annoyed. 9.The sky$^{m.}$ is blue. 10.The floor$^{m.}$ is clean. 11.The ceiling$^{f.}$ is low.12. The window$^{f.sg.}$ is small.

Key G 4.1

an old house 2.old houses 3. easy language; 4. easy languages 5. foreign student 6. foreign students 7. a good book 8. good books 9. beautiful girl 10.beautiful flower 11. beautiful boy 12. a big country. 13. new building 14. long river 15. poor man 16. poor woman 17. hardwoking student(s) 18. old woman 19.old women;

Key G 4.2

1. बड़ा कमरा$^{m.sg.dir.}$ 2. बड़े कमरे$^{m.pl.dir.}$ 3. बड़ी मेज$^{f.sg.dir.}$ 4. बड़ी मेज़ें $^{f.pl.dir.}$ 5. बड़े कमरे में$^{m.sg.obl.}$ 6. बड़े कमरों$^{m.pl.obl.}$ में 7. बड़ी मेज़ पर$^{f.sg.obl.}$ 8. बड़ी मेज़ों पर$^{f.pl.obl.}$ 9/10. दयालु आदमी$^{m.sg./pl.dir.}$ 11. दयालु आदमी$^{m.sg.obl.}$ को 12. दयालु आदमियों$^{m.pl.obl.}$ को 13. दयालु औरत $^{f.sg.dir.}$ 14. दयालु औरतें$^{f.pl.dir.}$ 15. दयालु औरत$^{f.sg.obl.}$को 16. दयालु औरतों$^{f.pl .obl.}$को 17/18. सुन्दर घर$^{m.sg./pldir.}$ 19. सुन्दर झोंपड़ी$^{f.sg.dir.}$ 20. सुन्दर झोपड़ियाँ$^{f.pl.dir.}$ 21. सुन्दर घर में$^{m.sg.obl.}$ 22. सुन्दर घरों में$^{m.pl.obl.}$ 23. सुन्दर झोंपड़ी में$^{f.sg.obl.}$ 24. सुन्दर झोंपड़ियों में$^{f.pl.obl.}$ 25. बासी समोसा$^{m.sg.dir.}$ 26. बासी समोसे$^{m.pl.dir.}$ 27. बासी रोटी$^{f.sg.dir.}$ 28. बासी रोटियाँ$^{f.sg.dir.}$ 29. बासी समोसे को$^{m.sg.obl.}$ 30. बासी

समोसों को$^{m.pl.obl.}$31. बासी रोटी को$^{f.sg.obl.}$ 32. बासी रोटियों$^{f.pl.obl.}$ को

1. baṛā kamrā 2. baṛe kamre 3. baṛī mez 4. baṛī mezeṁ 5. baṛe kamre meṁ 6. baṛe kamroṁ meṁ 7. baṛī mez par 8. baṛī mezoṁ par; 9. / 10 dayālu ādmī 11. dayālu ādmī se 12. dayālu ādmiyoṁ se 13.dayālu aurat 14. dayālu aurteṁ 15. dayālu aurat se 16. dayālu aurtoṁ se 17. /18. sundar ghar 19. sundar jhoṁpṛī 20. sundar jhoṁpriyāṁ 21. sundar ghar meṁ 22. sundar gharoṁ meṁ 23. sundar jhoṁpṛī meṁ 24. sundar jhoṁpṛīyoṁ meṁ 25. bāsī samosā 26 . bāsī samose 27. bāsī roṭī 28. bāsī roṭīyāṁ 29. bāsī samoṣe ko 30. bāsī samosoṁ ko 31. bāsī roṭī ko 32. bāsī roṭīyoṁ ko

Key G 4.3

Kamla is not happy. 2. I am very disappointed. 3. Mother is a little worried. 4. We are very astonished. 5. The woman is beautiful. 6. The house is new. 7. Apples are expensive. 8. The young man is quite tall. 9. The young woman is not tall. 10. The road is not narrow. 11. The path is narrow. 12. The road is very wide.

Key G 4.4

1. दही$^{m.}$ खट्टा है। 2. खाना$^{m.}$ बासी है। 3. शिक्षिका$^{f.sg.}$ दयालु है। 4. छात्र$^{m.sg.}$ बुद्धिमान है। 5. बच्चा$^{m.sg.}$ शैतान हैं। 6. यह आदमी$^{m.}$ ईमानदार है। 7. तुम बहुत क्रूर हो। 8. वह कुछ नाराज़ है। 9. आसमान$^{m.}$ नीला है। 10. फ़र्श$^{m.}$ साफ़ है। 11. छत$^{f.sg.}$ नीची है। 12. खिड़की$^{f.sg.}$ छोटी है।

1. dahī khaṭṭā hai.2. khānā bāsī hai. 3. śikṣikā dayālu hai. 4. chātra buddhimān hai. 5. baccā śaitān hai. 6. yah ādmī īmāndār hai. 7. tum bahut krūr ho. 8. vah kuch nārāz hai. 9. āsmān nīlā hai. 10. farś sāf hai.11. chat nīcī hai. 12. khiṛkī choṭī hai.

ADJECTIVES: COMPARATIVES AND SUPERLATIVES :

comparative = x + से + base form of adjective

Examples :

X से अच्छा	X se acchā	better than X
X से महँगा	X se mahaṁgā	more expensive than X
X से छोटा	X se choṭā	smaller than X
X से सुन्दर	X se sundar	more beautiful than X

X से दयालु X se dayālu — kinder than X

1. कमला रानी से होशियार है।
Kamlā Rāni se hośiyār hai.
Kamla is cleverer than Rani.

2. आज कल से कम गर्म है।
āj kal se kam garm hai.
Today is less hot than yesterday.

3. अब मौसम$^{m.sg}$ पहले से अच्छा है।
ab mausam$^{m.sg}$ pahle se acchā hai.
Now weather is better than before.

4. यह उससे सस्ता है।
yah usse sastā hai.
This is cheaper than that.

5. दिल्ली मुम्बई से महँगा शहर$^{m.sg}$ है।
dillī mumbaī se mahaṁgā śahar hai.
Delhi is more expensive city than Mumbai.

6. राम अपने भाई$^{m.sg}$ से लम्बा है।
rām apne bhāī se lambā hai.
Ram is taller than his brother.

7. सीता अपनी सहेली$^{f.sg}$ से अच्छा गाती है।
sitā apnī sahelī se acchā gātī hai.
Sita sings better than her friend.

8. मेरा कुत्ता$^{m.sg}$ तुम्हारे कुत्ते से ज़्यादा खूंखार हैं।
merā kuttā tumhāre kutte se zyādā khūṁkhār hai.
My dog is more ferocious than your dog.

9. यह भोजन$^{m.sg}$ उससे स्वादिष्ट है।
yah bhojan usse swādiṣṭ hai.
This food is tastier than that.

Superlative = सब + से + base form of the verb.

सबसे अच्छा sab se acchā	the best
सबसे महँगा sab se mahaṁgā	the most expensive
सबसे छोटा sab se choṭā	the smallest
सबसे सुन्दर sab se sundar	the most beautiful

ADJECTIVES: SUPERLATIVES

सबसे दयालु sab se dayālu	the kindest
1. यह सबसे अच्छा है। yah sab se acchā hai.	This is the best.
2. वह कक्षा में सबसे छोटा है। vah kakṣā meṁ sab se choṭā hai.	He is the smallest in class.
3. यह साड़ी सबसे सुन्दर है। yah sāṛī sab se sundar hai.	This is the most beautiful sari.

WORD POWER:

dictionary	śabdkoś	शब्दकोश
sunset	sūryāst	सूर्यास्त
smoking	dhūmrapān	धूम्रपान
hatred	nafrat	नफ़रत
harmful	hānikārak	हानिकारक
important	mahattvapūrṇ	महत्त्वपूर्ण
modern	ādhunik	आधुनिक
plesant	suhāvnā	सुहावना
interesting	rocak	रोचक
family	parivār	परिवार
mutual	āpsī	आपसी

Ex. G 4.5 Translate into Hindi:

1. This is the best dictionary. 2. This book is most interesting. 3. This city is most modern. 4. This soap is most expensive. 5. She is the most intelligent woman. 6. The weather today was most pleasant. 7. Mutual hatred is the worst thing. 8. The sunset of Kanyakumari is the most beautiful one. 9. Smoking is the most harmful thing for health. 10. This is the most important thing for me.

Key G 4.5

1. यह सब से अच्छा शब्दकोश (m.sg,) है। 2. यह किताब (f.sg,) सब से रोचक है। 3. यह शहर (m.sg,) सब से आधुनिक है। 4. यह साबुन (m.sg.) सब से महँगा है। 5. वह सब से बुद्विमान औरत है। 6. आज मौसम (m.sg.) सब से सुहावना था। 7. आपसी नफ़रत (f.sg.) सब से ख़राब चीज़ है। 8. कन्याकुमारी का सूर्यास्त (m.sg.) सब से सुन्दर होता है। 9. धूम्रपान (m.sg.) स्वास्थ्य के लिए सब से हानिकारक चीज़ है। 10. यह मेरे लिए सब से महत्त्वपूर्ण बात (m.sg.) है।

1. yah sab se acchā śabd koś hai. 2. yah kitāb sab se rocak hai. 3. yah śahar sab se ādhunik hai. 4. yah sābun sab se mahaṁgā hai. 5.vah sab se buddhimān aurat hai. 6. āj mausam sab se suhāvnā thā. 7. āpsī nafrat sab se kharāb cīz hai. 8. kanyākumārī kā sūryāst sab se sundar hotā hai. 9. dhūmrapān svāsthyă ke lie sab se hānikārak cīz hai. 10 yah mere lie sab se mahattvapūrṇ bāt hai.

■ **Use of the adjectival expressions कितना kitnā (m.sg.), कितने kitne (m.pl.), कितनी kitnī (f.sg./pl.) meaning how much, how many. They agree with the number and gender of the noun they qualify.**

1. कितनी चाय	kitnī cāy (f.)	how much tea
2. कितना दूध	kitnā dūdh (m.)	how much milk
3. कितने छात्र	kitne chātra (m.pl.)	how many students
4. कितनी छात्राएँ	kitnī chātrāeṁ (f.pl.)	how many students

These are also sometimes used to qualify adjectives to mean 'How!'

कितना सुन्दर! How beautiful! ; कितना स्वादिष्ट! How delicious!

■ **कौन-सा kaun-sā (m.sg.), ; कौन-से kaun-se (m.pl.); कौन-सी kaun-sī (f.sg/pl.) These are adjectival expressions meaning which one or which ones. They accord with the number and gender of the noun they qualify.**

1. कौन–सा मकान	kaun-sā makān (m.sg.)	which house
2. कौन–से मकान	kaun-se makān (m.pl.)	which houses
3. कौन–सा लड़का	kaun-sa laṛkā (m.sg.)	which boy
4. कौन–से लड़के	kaun-se laṛke (m.pl.)	which boys

5. कौन–से बच्चे	kaun-se bacce (m.pl.)	which children
7. कौन–सी इमारत	kaun-sī imārat (f.sg.)	which building
8. कौन–सी लड़की	kaun-sī laṛkī (f.sg.)	which girl
9. कौन–सी इमारतें	kaun-sī imārteṁ (f.pl.)	which buildings
10.कौन–सी लड़कियाँ	kaun-sī laṛkiyāṁ (f.pl.)	which girls

■ **Use of : कैसा kaisā (m.sg.), कैसे kaise (m.pl.), कैसी kaisī (f.sg./pl.) — these have both adjectival and adverbial use meaning (1) How? or (2) What kind of..? They agree with the noun or pronoun they qualify.**

1. मकान[m.sg] कैसा है? makān kaisā hai? — How is the house?
2. आपका कमरा[m.sg] कैसा है? āpkā kamrā kaisā hai? — How is your room?[m.sg]
3. आपका शहर[m.sg] कैसा है? āpkā śahar kaisā hai? — How is you city?
4. तू कैसा/कैसी है? tū kaisā/ kaisī hai? — How are you? (intimate you)
5. तुम कैसे/कैसी हो? tum[m.pl.] kaise/ kaisī ho? — How are you? (informal you)

Ex. G 4.6 Translate into Hindi:

1. How many eggs?2. How many girls? 3. How much yogurt? 4. How much fish? 5. Which flower? 6. Which river? 7. Which pilgrimage place? 8. How are you? (formal/honorific you) 9.. How are those bananas? 10. What kind of a city is Banaras? 11. What kind of a country is India? 12. How is the weather today? 13. How is life? 14. How is your family?

Ex. G 4.7 Translate into English:

1. फ़्लैट[m.sg] कैसा है? 2. पड़ोसी[m.pl] कैसे हैं? 3. फ़्लैट में कितने कमरे[m.pl] हैं? 4. कमरे में कितनी अलमारियाँ[f.pl] हैं? 5. दीवार[f.sg] कितनी ऊँची है? 6. कमरे में कितनी खिड़कियाँ[f.pl] हैं? 7. कमरे में कितने दरवाज़े[m.pl] हैं? 8. कमरा[m.sg] कितना लम्बा और कितना चौडा है? 9. किरायेदार[m.sg]

कैसा है? 10. किराया[m.sg] कितना है?

1. flaiṭ kaisā hai? 2. paṛosī kaise haiṁ? 3. flaiṭ meṁ kitne kamre haiṁ? 4. kamre meṁ kitnī almāriyāṁ haiṁ? 5. dīvār kitnī ūṁcī hai? 6. kamre meṁ kitnī khiṛkiyāṁ haiṁ? 7. kamre meṁ kitne darvāze haiṁ? 8. kamrā kitnā lambā aur kitnā cauṛā hai? 9. kirayedār kaisā hai? 10. kirayā kitnā hai?

Key G 4.6

1. कितने अण्डे? 2. कितनी लड़कियाँ? 3. कितना दही? 4. कितनी मछली? 5. कौन–सा फूल? 6. कौन–सी नदी? 7. कौन–सा तीर्थस्थान? 8. आप[m.pl.] कैसे/कैसी हैं? 9. यह किताब[f.sg.] कैसी है? 10. वे केले[m.pl.] कैसे हैं? 11. बनारस कैसा शहर[m.sg] है? 12. भारत कैसा देश[m.sg] है? 13. आज मौसम[m.sg] कैसा है? 14. जीवन कैसा है? 15. आपका परिवार कैसा है?

1. kitne aṇḍe? 2. kitnī laṛkiyāṁ? 3. kitnā dahī? 4. kitnī machlī? 5. kaun-sā phūl? 6. kaun sī nadī ? 7. kaun-sā tīrthsthān? 8. āp kaise/kaisī haiṁ? 9. yah kitāb kaisī hai? 10. ve kele (m.pl.) kaise haiṁ? 11. banāras kaisā śahar hai? 12. bhārat kaisā deś hai? 13. āj mausam kaisā hai?14. jīvan kaisā hai? 15. āpkā parivār kaisā hai?

Key G 4.7

1. How is the flat? 2. How are neighbors? 3. How many rooms are their in the flat? 4. How many cupboards are there in the room? 5. How high is the wall? 6. How many windows are there in the room? 7. How many doors are there in the room? 8. How long and how wide is the room? 9. How is the tenant? 10. How much is the rent?

●●●●●

G 5 THE POSSESSIVE CASE

■ The genitive case endings are **का 'kā' के 'ke' की 'kī'**. Their English equivalent is 'of' or alternatively the use of apostrophe. **का 'kā' के 'ke' की 'kī'** accords with the N and G of the object possessed and not that of the possesser.

In the direct case:

son of Kamla	is	Kamla kā beṭā m.sg.	कमला का बेटा m.sg.
sons of Kamla	is	Kamla ke beṭe m.pl	कमला के बेटे m.pl.
daughter of Kamla	is	Kamla kī beṭī f.sg.	कमला की बेटी f.sg.
daughters of Kamla	is	Kamla kī beṭiyāṁ f.pl.	कमला की बेटियाँ f.pl

☞ **In the oblique case:* का kā changes to के ke when a mas. sg. noun representing the object possessed is followed by any postposition. Even if it is a non ā-ending masculine noun, which does not need to change in the oblique case, the preceding 'kā' will change to 'ke'. However के 'ke' preceding mas.pl. noun, and ' की 'kī' preceding fem. sg. or plural noun remains the same even when these nouns are followed by some postposition.**

For Instance:

to Kamla's son	Kamla ke beṭe ko	कमला के बेटे को
to Kamla's sons	Kamla ke beṭoṁ ko	कमला के बेटों को
similarly		
in Kamla's house	Kamla ke ghar meṁ	कमला के घर में
in Kamla's houses	Kamla ke gharoṁ meṁ	कमला के घरों में

PRONOUNS IN POSSESSIVE CASE

THE POSSESSIVE PRONOUNS :

m.sg	m.pl	f.sg./pl.	
merā मेरा	mere मेरे	merī मेरी	my, mine
hamārā हमारा	hamāre हमारे	hamārī हमारी	our, ours
terā तेरा	tere तेरे	terī तेरी	your, yours
tumhārā तुम्हारा	tumhāre तुम्हारे	tumhārī तुम्हारी	your, yours
āpkā आपका	āpke आपके	āpkī आपकी	your, yours
uskā उसका	uske उसके	uskī उसकी	his/her/hers
iskā इसका	iske इसके	iskī इसकी	his/her,hers
unkā उनका	unke उनके	unkī उनकी	their/theirs
inkā इनका	inke इनके	inkī इनकी	their/theirs
kiskā किसका	kiske किसके	kiskī किसकी	whose sg.
kinkā किनका	kinke किनके	kinkī किनकी	whose pl.

COMPREHENSION

1. This is my house. — yah merā ghar m.sg. hai.
यह मेरा घर m.sg. है।

2. This is their house.	yah unkā ghar m.sg. hai. यह उनका घर m.sg. है।
3 .Those are their dogs.	ve unke kutte m.pl. haiṁ. वे उनके कुत्ते m.pl. हैं।
4. This is his/her car.	yah uskī kār fsg. hai. यह उसकी 'कार' f.sg. है।
5. This is not your(inf.) umbreḷla.	yah tumhārā chātā m.sg. nahīṁ hai. यह तुम्हारा छाता m.sg. नहीं है।
6. Whose (sg.) office is this?	yah kiskā daftar m.sg. hai? यह किसका दफ़्तर m.sg. है?
7 .Whose(sg.) book is this?	yah kiskī pustak f.sg. hai? यह किसकी पुस्तक f.sg. है?

☞ **'kis' is used for 'whose' when the 'possessor' is singular.**

8. Whose (pl.) children are they?	ye kinke bacce m.pl. haiṁ. ये किनके बच्चे m.pl. हैं?

☞ **'kin' is used for 'whose' when the 'possessor' is plural)**

9. My brother is in Delhi.	merā bhāī dillī meṁ hai. मेरा भाई दिल्ली में है।
10.My daughters are in America.	merī beṭiyāṁ amrīkā meṁ haiṁ. मेरी बेटियाँ अमरीका में हैं।

☞ **Remember: The आ ā- or का kā-ending possessive determiners change to ए e -ending when qualifying masc.sg. noun followed by any post-position.**

For Example:

मेरा घर	merā ghar	my house
but		
मेरे घर में	mere ghar meṁ	in my house

similarly:

उसका बेटा	uskā beṭā	my house
but		
मेरे घर में	uske beṭe ko	in my house

WORD POWER

पुस्तकालय^m.sg pustakālay library; खेत^m.sg khet field; सभा^f.sg sabhā assembly; ऐतिहासिक ^adj. aitihāsik historical ; संग्राहलय^m.sg saṅgrāhlay museum; कारखाना^m.sg kārkhānā factory; राष्ट्रभाषा^f.sg rāṣṭra-bhāṣā national language; मातृभाषा^f.sg matṛbhāṣā mother tongue; मकबरा^m.sg makbarā tomb; मीनार^f.sg mīnār tower. बुद्धिमानी^f.sg buddhimānī wisdom; साहस ^m.sg sāhas courage; कठिनाई^f.sg kaṭhīnāī difficulty; धैर्य^m.sg dhairyă patience; परिश्रम ^m.sg pariśram diligence; ईमानदारी^f.sg īmāndārī honesty; चिन्ता^f.sg cintā worry.

Ex. G 5.1 Write in Hindi:

1.my house
2. my sister
3. her/his daughter
4. her husband
5. their cat
6. Hindi newspaper
7. child's toy
8. children's toys
9. boys' school
10. my brother
11. their son
12. her book
13. their dog
14. your servant
15. English Newspaper
16. bird's nest
17. birds' nests
18. girls' school

Ex. G 5.2 Translate into Hindi:

1. my son's education 2. address of our house 3.my mother's book 4. name of their city 5. .his/her country's culture 6. house of my brother 7. my sister's son 8. his brother's daughter 9. their wisdom 10. her /his courage 11.her/ his difficulty 12. their patience 13. your diligence 14. her/his honesty 15. mother's worry

Ex. 5.3 Translate into English:

1. मेरे बड़े भाई के साथ; 2. उसके बड़े कमरे में, 3. उनकी छोटी बहनों के लिए 4. हमारे नए पुस्तकालय में, 5. इनकी नई किताबों में, 6. उस स्कूल के मेहनती छात्रों से, 7.तुम्हारी बड़ी बहन के यहाँ। 8.उनके बड़े खेतों में। 9. उनकी बड़ी सभा में। 10. इनकी किताबों से। 11.

भारत की ऐतिहासिक इमारतों में। 12.जयपुर के पुराने संग्रहालय में। 13. उसके घर में। 14. उसके लड़के को। 16. उनके बड़े कारख़ानों में।

1.mere baṛe bhāī ke sāth; 2.uske baṛe kamre meṁ; 3. unkī choṭī bahnoṁ ke lie; 4. hamāre nae pustakālay meṁ; 5. inkī naī kitāboṁ meṁ 6. us skūl ke mehantī chātroṁ se; 7. tumhārī baṛī bahan ke yahāṁ; 8. unke baṛe khetoṁ meṁ ; 9. unkī baṛī sabhā meṁ; 10. inkī kitāboṁ se; 11. bhārat kī aitihāsik imārtoṁ meṁ; 12. jaipur ke purāne saṅgrahālay meṁ; 13. uske ghar meṁ; 14. uske laṛke ko; 15. unke baṛe kārkhānoṁ meṁ,

Ex. G 5.4 Translate into English:

1. आपका नाम क्या है? 2. आपकी जन्म तिथि क्या है? 3. आपके जन्म का समय क्या है? 4. आपके जन्म के स्थान का नाम क्या है? 5. आपके कितने भाई हैं? 6. मेरे दो भाई हैं। 7. आपकी कितनी बहनें हैं? 8. मेरी एक बहन है। 9. आपकी बहन का नाम क्या है? 10. मेरी बहन का नाम सरिता है। 11. क्या ये आपके जूते हैं? 12. यह मेरी समस्या है। 13. ये किनके बच्चे हैं?14. यह किसका छाता है? 15. ये किसकी पुस्तकें हैं?

1. āpkā nām kyā hai? 2. āpkī janm tithi kyā hai? 3. āpke janm kā samay kyā hai? 4. āpke janm ke sthān kā nām kyā hai? 5. āpke kitne bhāī haiṁ? 6. mere do bhāī haiṁ. 7. āpkī kitnī bahneṁ haiṁ. 8. merī ek bahan hai. 9. āpkī bahan kā nām kyā hai? 10. merī bahan kā nām saritā hai. 11. kyā ye āpke jūte haiṁ? 12. yah merī samasyā hai? 13. ye kinke bacce haiṁ? 14. yah kiskā chātā hai? 15. ye kiskī pustakeṁ haiṁ?

Ex. G 5.5 Translate into Hindi:

1. This book is mine. 2. This house is theirs. 3. Those dogs are ours. 4. Is this bag yours? 5. Is this her bicycle? 6. This is his/her umbrella. 7. This is my fiance. 8. That is our office. 9. Hindi is my mother tongue.10. She is my friend. 11. Is that your dog? 12. No, this is my neighbor's dog. 13. Whose (sg.) idea is this? 14. Whose (pl) problem is this?15. This is not our problem.

Ex. G 5.6 Translate into English:

हम भारतीय हैं। भारत हमारा देश है। हिन्दी भारत की राष्ट्रभाषा है। गंगा और यमुना भारत में बड़ी नदियाँ हैं। उत्तर प्रदेश, महाराष्ट्र, राजस्थान भारत में प्रान्त हैं। हमारे दल में बारह

लड़कियाँ और तीन लड़के हैं। दिल्ली में बहुत ऐतिहासिक इमारतें हैं, उदाहरण के लिए, लाल किला, हमायूँ का मकबरा, कुतुब मीनार आदि।

ham bhāratīya haiṁ. bhārat hamārā deś hai. Hindī bhārat kī rāṣṭra-bhāṣā hai. gaṅgā aur yamunā bhārat meṁ baṛī nadiyāṁ haiṁ. uttar pradeś, mahārāṣṭra, rājasthān bhārat meṁ prānt haiṁ. hamāre dal meṁ bārah laṛkiyāṁ aur tīn laṛke haiṁ. dillī meṁ bahut aitihāsik imārteṁ haiṁ , udāharaṇ ke lie, lālkilā, humā-yūṁ kā makbarā, kutub mīnār ādi.

Key G 5.1

1. मेरा घर$^{\text{m.sg}}$ **2.** मेरी बहन$^{\text{f.sg}}$ **3.** उसकी बेटी$^{\text{f.sg}}$ **4.** उसका पति$^{\text{m.sg}}$ **5.** उनकी बिल्ली$^{\text{f.sg}}$ **6.** हिन्दी का अख़बार$^{\text{m.sg}}$ **7.** बच्चे का खिलौना$^{\text{m.sg}}$ **8.** बच्चों के खिलौने$^{\text{m.pl.}}$ **9.** लड़कों का स्कूल$^{\text{m.sg}}$ **10.** मेरा भाई$^{\text{m.sg}}$ **11.** उनका बेटा$^{\text{m.sg}}$ **12.** उसकी किताब$^{\text{f.sg}}$ **13.** उनका कुत्ता$^{\text{m.sg}}$ **14.** तुम्हारा / आपका नौकर$^{\text{m.sg}}$ **15.** अंग्रेज़ी का अख़बार$^{\text{m.sg}}$ **16.** चिड़िया का घोंसला$^{\text{m.sg}}$ **17.** चिड़ियाओं के घोंसले$^{\text{m..pl}}$ **18.** लड़कियों का स्कूल$^{\text{m.sg}}$

1.merā ghar 2. merī bahan 3.uskī beṭī 4.uskā pati 5. unkī billī 6. hindī kā akhbār 7. bacce kā khilaunā 8. baccoṁ ke khilaune 9. laṛkoṁ kā skūl 10. merā bhāī 11 unkā beṭā. 12. uskī kitāb 13. unkā kuttā 14.āpkā naukar 15. angrezi kā akhbār 16. ciṛiyā kā ghoṁslā 17. ciṛiyāoṁ ke ghoṁsle 18. laṛkiyoṁ kā skūl.

Key G 5.2

मेरे बेटे की शिक्षा **2.** हमारे घर का पता **3.** मेरी माता जी की किताब$^{\text{f.sg}}$ **4.** उनके शहर का नाम **5.** उसके देश की संस्कृति **6.** मेरे भाई का घर$^{\text{m.sg}}$ **7.** मेरी बहन का बेटा$^{\text{m.sg}}$ **8.** उसके भाई की बेटी$^{\text{f.sg}}$ **9.** उनकी बुद्धिमानी$^{\text{f.sg}}$ **10.** उसका साहस$^{\text{m.sg}}$ **11.** उसकी कठिनाई$^{\text{f.sg}}$ **12.** उनका धैर्य$^{\text{m.sg}}$ **13.** तुम्हारा परिश्रम$^{\text{m.sg}}$ **14.** उसकी ईमानदारी$^{\text{f.sg}}$ **15.** माता जी की चिन्ता$^{\text{f.sg}}$

1. mere beṭe kī śikṣā$^{\text{f.sg}}$ 2. hamāre ghar$^{\text{m.sg}}$ kā patā$^{\text{m.sg}}$ 3. merī mātā jī kī kitāb$^{\text{f.sg}}$ 4. unke śahar$^{\text{m.sg}}$ kā nām$^{\text{m.sg}}$ 5.uske deś$^{\text{m.sg}}$ kī saṁskṛti$^{\text{f.sg}}$ 6. mere bhāī kā ghar 7. merī bahan kā beṭā 8. uske bhāī kī beṭī$^{\text{f.sg}}$ 9. unkī buddhimānī$^{\text{f.sg}}$ 10. uskā sāhas$^{\text{m.sg}}$ 11. uskī kaṭhināī$^{\text{f.sg}}$ 12. unkā dhairyă$^{\text{m.sg}}$ 13 tumhārā priśram$^{\text{m.sg}}$ 14. uskī imāndārī$^{\text{f.sg}}$ 15. mātā jī kī cintā$^{\text{f.sg}}$.

Key G 5.3

1.with my older brother 2. in his big room 3. for their younger sisters 4. in our new library. 5. in their new books 6. from diligent students of that school 7. at your elder sister's place 8. in their big fields 9. in their big assembly 10. from their books 11. in India's historical monuments 12. in the old museum of Jaipur 13. in his / her house 14. to his son 15. in their big factories

Key G 5. 4

1. What is your name? 2. What is your birth date? 3. What is the time of your birth. 4. What is the name of your birth place? 5. How many brothers do you have? 6. I have two brothers. 7. How many sisters do you have? 8 . I have one sister. 9. What is your sister's name? 10. My sister's name is Sarita. 11. Are these your shoes? 12. This is my problem? 13. Whose children are they?14. Whose umbrella is this? 15. Whose books are these?

Key G 5. 5

1.यह किताब मेरी है। 2.यह घर उनका है। 3. वे कुत्ते हमारे हैं। 4. क्या यह बैग तुम्हारा है? 5. क्या यह उसकी साइकिल है? 6 .यह उसका छाता है। 7. यह मेरा मंगेतर है। 8. वह हमारा दफ्तर है। 9. हिन्दी मेरी मातृभाषा है।10. वह मेरी दोस्त है। 11. क्या वह आपका कुत्ता है? 12. नहीं, वह मेरे पड़ोसी का कुत्ता है? 13. यह किसका विचार है? 14. यह किनकी समस्या है? 15. यह हमारी समस्या नहीं है?

1.yah kitāb merī hai. 2.yah ghar unkā hai. 3.ve kutte hamāre haiṁ. 4. kyā yah baig tumhārā / āpkā hai? 5. kyā yah uskī sāikil hai? 6. yah uskā chātā hai. 7. yah merā maṅgetar hai. 8. vah hamārā daftar hai. 9. hindī merī matṛbhāṣā hai. 10. vah merī dost hai.11.kyā vah āpkā kuttā hai? 12. nahīṁ, vah mere paṛosī kā kuttā hai.13. yah kiskā vicār hai? 14. yah kinkī samasyā hai? 15. yah hamārī samasyā nahīṁ hai.

Key G 5.6

We are Indian. India is our country. Hindi is the national language of India. Ganges and Yamunā are big rivers in India. Uttar Pradesh, Mahārāṣṭra, Rājasthān are states in India. In our group, there are twelve girls and three boys. In Delhi there are many historical monuments, for example, the Red Fort, the Hamāyūṁ's

●●●●●

6 VOCABULARY

1 ADJECTIVES

Adjectives in Hindi can be classified into(1) आ ā-ending adjectives, and (2) all others.

आ ā- ending ajectives in their base form qualify masculine singular nouns. They change to ए e-ending when qualifying masculine plural nouns, and ई ī- ending when qualifying feminine singular or plural nouns.

All other adjectives with any ending other than 'आ ā' remain the same, regardless of the number, gender or case of the noun they qualify.

airy	havādār	हवादार
angry	krodhit	क्रोधित
bad	kharāb	ख़राब
big	baṛā	बड़ा
bitter	kaṛvā	कड़वा
bland	phīkā	फीका
boring	ubāū	उबाऊ
brackish	khārā	खारा
brave	bahādur	बहादुर
carefree	niścint	निश्चिन्त
clever	hośiyār	होशियार
cold	ṭhaṇḍā	ठण्डा
contrary	pratikūl	प्रतिकूल
conventional	paramparāgat	परमपरागत
cruel	krūr	क्रूर
cunning	cālāk	चालाक
deep	gahrā	गहरा
delicious	svādiṣṭ	स्वादिष्ट

ADJECTIVES

depressed	khinn	खिन्न
diligent	mehantī	मेहनती
disappointed	nirāś	निराश
dishonest	beīmān	बेईमान
distressed	hairān	हैरान
dry	sūkhā	सूखा
eccentric	sankī	सनकी
entertaining	manorañjak	मनोरंजक
evidently	pratyakṣa	प्रत्यक्ष
excellent	baṛhiyā	बढ़िया
excited	uttejit	उत्तेजित
exciting	uttejak	उत्तेजक
expensive	mahaṁgā	महँगा
faithful	vafādār	वफ़ादार
fake	naklī	नकली
famous	maśhūr	मशहूर
fat	moṭā	मोटा
foreign	videśī	विदेशी
formal	aupcārik	औपचारिक
fresh	tāzā	ताज़ा
frivolous (matter)	tucch	तुच्छ
frivolous (person)	chichorā	छिछोरा
frustrated	kuṇṭhit	कुण्ठित
generous	udār	उदार
genuine	aslī	असली
glittering	camkīla	चमकीला
good	acchā	अच्छा
grateful	kṛtagyă	कृतज्ञ
greasy	ciknā	चिकना

happy	khuś	खुश
healthy	svasth	स्वस्थ
heavy	bhārī	भारी
high	ūṁcā	ऊँचा
holy	pavitra	पवित्र
honest	īmāndār	ईमानदार
hot	garam	गरम
ight(color)	halkā	हल्का
impressed	prabhāvit	प्रभावित
impure	aśudh	अशुद्ध
inexpensive	sastā	सस्ता
infamous	badnām	बदनाम
inferior	ghaṭiā	घटिया
informal	an-aupcārik	अनौपचारिक
innocent	bholā	भोला
insolent	ḍhīṭh	ढीठ
intelligent	buddhimān	बुद्धिमान
interesting	rocak	रोचक
kind	dayālu	दयालु
lazy	ālsī	आलसी
light(weight)	halkā	हल्का
low	nīcā	नीचा
lukewarm	gungunā	गुनगुना
miserly	kañjūs	कंजूस
modern	ādhunik	आधुनिक
mundane	sāmsārik	सांसारिक
natural	svabhāvik	स्वभाविक
new	nayā	नया
nutritious	pauṣṭik	पौष्टिक

ADJECTIVES

old	būṛhā	बूढ़ा
old	purānā	पुराना
peaceful	śānt	शान्त
poor	garīb	ग़रीब
pungent	tītā	तीता
pure	śudh	शुद्ध
reliable	viśvasnīyă	विश्वस्नीय
religeous	dhārmik	धार्मिक
reticent	mitḃhāṣī	मितभाषी
rich	amīr	अमीर
rough	khurdurā	खुरदुरा
round	gol	गोल
sad	udās	उदास
safe	surakṣit	सुरक्षित
salty	namkīn	नमकीन
secular	dharm-nirpeksa	धर्मनिर्पेक्ष
sensible	samajhdār	समझदार
sensitive(person)	bhāvuk	भावुक
serious (matter)	sanjīdā	संजीदा
serious (person)	gambhīr	गम्भीर
sick	bīmār	बीमार
slippery	phislahā	फिसलहा
small	choṭā	छोटा
soft	mulāyam	मुलायम
sour	khaṭṭā	खट्टा
spicy	masāledār	मसालेदार
spiritual	adhyātmik	आध्यात्मिक
square	cakor	चकोर

stale	bāsī	बासी
sticky	cipcipā	चिपचिपा
strong	balvān	बलवान
stupid	mūrkh	मूर्ख
surprised	cakit	चकित
sweet	mīṭhā	मीठा
talented	pratibhāśālī	प्रतिभाशाली
talkative	bātūnī	बातूनी
tall	lambā	लम्बा
thin	patlā	पतला
timid	ḍarpok	डरपोक
triangular	tikon	तिकोन
unfaithful	bevafā	बेवफ़ा
ungrateful	akṛtagyă	अकृतज्ञ
unhappy	dukhī	दुखी
unhealthy	a-svasth	अस्वस्थ
unholy	apavitra	अपवित्र
unkind	niṣṭhur	निष्ठुर
unnatural	a-svabhāvik	अस्वभाविक
unsafe	a-surakṣit	असुरक्षित
upset	pareśān	परेशान
violent	hiṃsak	हिंसक
weak	kamzor	कमज़ोर
wet	gīlā	गीला
wide	cauṛā	चौड़ा
worried	cintit	चिंतित
wise	budhimān	बुद्धिमान
young	javān	जवान

ADJECTIVES

AGGREGATES

दोनों	donoṁ	both	तीनों	tīnoṁ	all three
चारों	cāroṁ	all four	पाँचों	pāṁcoṁ	all five
बीसों	bīsoṁ	scores of	हज़ारों	hazāroṁ	thousands of
लाखों	lākhoṁ	millions of	करोड़ों	karoṛoṁ	millions of

MULTIPLICATIVES

double	dugunā	दुगुना
thrice	tigunā	तिगुना
four times	caugunā	चौगुना
five times	pañcgunā	पंचगुना
six times	chahgunā	छहगुना/छगुना
seven times	satgunā	सतगुना
eight times	aṭhgunā	अठगुना
nine times	naugunā	नौगुना
ten times	dasgunā	दसगुना
a hundred times	saugunā	सौगुना
a thousand time	hazārgunā	हज़ारगुना
a million times	lākhgunā	लाखगुना

FRACTIONS

a quarter	ek- cauthāī	एक चौथाई
half	ādhā	आधा
three fourth	paun	पौन
one and three fourth	paune do	पौने दो
one-onefourth	savā	सवा
one and a half	ḍeṛh	डेढ़
two and a half	ḍhāī	ढाई
three and a half	sāṛhe tīn	साढे तीन

NUMBERS

CARDINALS

zero	śūnya	शून्य
one	ek	एक
two	do	दो
three	tīn	तीन
four	cār	चार
five	pāṁc	पाँच
six	chah	छः
seven	sāt	सात
eight	āṭh	आठ
nine	nau	नौ
ten	das	दस
eleven	gyārah	ग्यारह
twelve	bārah	बारह
thirteen	terah	तेरह
fourteen	caudah	चौदह
fifteen	pandrah	पन्द्रह
sixteen	solah	सोलह
seventeen	sattrah	सत्रह
eighteen	aṭhārah	अट्ठारह
nineteen	unnīs	उन्नीस
twenty	bīs	बीस
twenty-one	ikkīs	इक्कीस
twenty-two	bāīs	बाईस
twenty-three	teīs	तेईस
twenty-four	caubīs	चौबीस
twenty-five	paccīs	पच्चीस
twenty-six	chabbīs	छब्बीस
twenty-seven	sattāīs	सत्ताईस

NUMBERS

twenty-eight	aṭhāīs	अठाईस
twenty-nine	untīs	उनतीस
thirty	tīs	तीस
thirty-one	iktīs	इकतीस
thirty-two	battīs	बत्तीस
thirty-three	taiṁtīs	तैंतीस
thirty-four	cauṁtīs	चौंतीस
thirty-five	paiṁtīs	पैंतीस
thirty-six	chattīs	छत्तीस
thirty-seven	saiṁtīs	सैंतीस
thirty-eight	aṛtīś	अड़तीस
thirty-nine	untālīs	उन्तालीस
forty	cālīs	चालीस
forty-one	iktālīs	इकतालीस
forty-two	bayālīs	बयालीस
forty-three	taiṁtālīs	तैंतालीस
forty -four	cauvālīs	चौवालीस
forty-five	paiṁtālīs	पैंतालीस
forty-six	chiyālīs	छियालीस
forty-seven	saiṁtālīs	सैंतालीस
forty-eight	aṛtālīs	अडतालीस
forty-nine	uncās	उन्चास
fifty	pacās	पचास
fifty-one	ikyāvan	इक्यावन
fifty-two	bāvan	बावन
fifty-three	trepan	तिरपन
fifty-four	cauvan	चौवन
fifty-five	pacpan	पचपन
fifty-six	chappan	छप्पन
fifty-seven	sattāvan	सत्तावन
fifty-eight	aṭṭāvan	अट्ठावन
fift-nine	unsaṭh	उनसठ

sixty	sāṭh	साठ
sixty-one	iksaṭh	इकसठ
sixty-two	bāsaṭh	बासठ
sixty-three	tirsaṭh	तिरसठ
sixty-four	causaṭh	चौसठ
sixty-five	paiṁsaṭh	पैसठ
sixty-six	chiyāsaṭh	छियासठ
sixty-seven	saṛsaṭh	सड़सठ
sixty-eight	aṛsaṭh	अड़सठ
sixty-nine	unhattar	उनहत्तर
seventy	sattar	सत्तर
seventy-one	ik'hattar	इकहत्तर
seventy-two	bahattar	बहत्तर
seventy-three	tihattar	तिहत्तर
seventy-four	cauhattar	चौहत्तर
seventy-five	pac'hattar	पचहत्तर
seventy-six	chi'hattar	छिहत्तर
seventy-seven	satattar	सतत्तर
seventy-eight	aṭh'hattar	अठहत्तर
seventy-nine	unnāsī	उन्नासी
eighty	assī	अस्सी
eighty-one	ikyāsī	इक्यासी
eighty-two	bayāsī	बयासी
eighty-three	tirāsī	तिरासी
eighty-four	caurāsī	चौरासी
eighty-five	pacāsī	पचासी
eighty-six	chiyāsī	छियासी
eighty-seven	sattāsī	सत्तासी
eighty-eight	aṭṭhāsī	अट्ठासी
eighty-nine	navāsī	नवासी
ninety	navve/nabbe	नव्वे/नब्बे
ninety-one	ikānve	इकानवे

CARDINAL NUMBERS

ninety-two	bānve	बानबे
ninety-three	tirānve	तिरानवे
ninety-four	caurānve	चौरानवे
ninety-five	pacānve	पचानवे
ninety-six	chiyānve	छियानवे
ninety-seven	sattānve	सत्तानवे
ninety-eight	aṭhānve	अट्ठानवे
ninety-nine	ninyānve	निन्यानवे
hundred	sau	सौ
thousand	hazār	हज़ार
a hundred thousand	lākh	लाख
a thousand thousand	karoṛ pahlā	करोड़

ORDINALS

first	pahlā	पहला
second	dūsrā	दूसरा
third	tīsrā	तीसरा
fourth	cauthā	चौथा
fifth	pāṁcvāṁ	पाँचवा
sixth	chaṭhā	छठा
seventh	sātvāṁ	सातवाँ
eighth	āṭhvāṁ	आठवाँ
ninth	nauvāṁ	नौवाँ
tenth	dasvāṁ	दसवाँ
eleventh	gyārahvāṁ	ग्यारहवाँ
twelfth	bārahvāṁ	बारहवाँ
twentieth	bīsvāṁ	बीसवाँ
thirtieth	tīsvāṁ	तीसवाँ
fiftieth	pacāsvāṁ	पचासवाँ
hundredth	sauvāṁ	सौवाँ
hundred and first	ek sau ekvāṁ	एक सौ एकवाँ
thousandth	hazārvāṁ	हज़ारवाँ

2. ADVERBS

today	āj	आज
yesterday	kal	कल
tomorrow	kal	कल
day after tomorrow	parsoṁ	परसों
day before yesterday	parsoṁ	परसों
in the morning	subah	सुबह
in the evening	śām ko	शाम को
at noon	dopahar ko	दोपहर को
at night	rāt ko	रात को
all night	rāt bhar	रात भर
all day	din bhar	दिन भर
now	ab	अब
then	tab	तब
when	kab	कब
always	hameśā	हमेशा
	sadaiv	सदैव
sometime	kabhī	कभी
sometimes	kabhī-kabhī	कभी–कभी
never	kabhī-nahīṁ	कभी–नहीं
often	aksar	अक्सर
occasionally	prāyaḥ	प्रायः
seldom	yadā-kadā	यदा–कदा
formerly	pahle	पहले
once	ek bār	एक बार
twice	do bār	दो बार
thrice	tin bār	तीन बार

Hindi uses the same words for yesterday and tomorrow.**(see Introduction pg.ii)**

ADVERBS

repeatedly	bār bār	बार बार
one by one	ek ek karke	एक एक करके
here	yahāṁ	यहाँ
there	vahāṁ	वहाँ
where	kahāṁ	कहाँ
over here	idhar	इधर
over there	udhar	उधर
under	nīce	नीचे
above	ūpar	ऊपर
in front	sāmne	सामने
behind	pīche	पीछे
why	kyoṁ	क्यों
how	kaise	कैसे
somehow	jaise-taise	जैसे तैसे
as (gradually)	jaise-jaise	जैसे जैसे
actually	vāstav meṁ	वास्तव में
aloud	zor se	ज़ोर से
alternatively	vikalp se	विकल्प से
boldly	bekhaṭke	बेखटके
carefully	sāvdhānī se	सावधानी से
carelessly	lāparvāhī se	लापरवाही से
certainly	nissandeh	निस्सन्देह
cleverly	caturāī se	चतुराई से
courageously	himmat se	हिम्मत से
deliberately	jānbūjhkar	जानबूझकर
diligently	mehnat se	मेहनत से
comfortably	ārām se	आराम से

completely	pūrṇtayā	पूर्णतया
consequently	phalataḥ	फलतः
easily	āsānī se	आसानी से
emphatically	zor dekar	ज़ोर देकर
forcibly	balāt	बलात्
fortunately	bhāgyă se	भाग्य से
frankly	sāf sāf	साफ़ साफ़
	spaṣṭtayā	स्पष्टतया
frequently	bahudhā	बहुधा
honestly	īmāndārī se	ईमानदारी से
humbly	vinamratā se	विनम्रता से
inadvertantly	anjāne meṁ	अनजाने में
intentionaly	jān-būjhkar	जानबूझकर
kindly	kṛipā karke	कृपा करके
legitimately	aucityăpūrvak	औचित्यपूर्वक
literally	akṣraśaḥ	अक्षरशः
later	bād meṁ	बाद में
lazily	sustī se	सुस्ती से
loudly	zor se	ज़ोर से
luckily	bhāgyă se	भाग्य से
normally	sādhāraṇtayā	साधारणतया
optimistically	āśāvāditā se	आशावादिता से
ordinarily	sāmānyatā	सामान्यता
patiently	dhairyapūrvak	धैर्यपूर्वक
peacefully	śānti se	शान्ति से
perhaps	śāyad	शायद
preferably	acchā ho ki	अच्छा हो कि
probably	sambhavtā	सम्भवता

ADVERBS

promptly	tatpartā se	तत्परता से
quietly	cupcāp	चुपचाप
quickly	jaldī	जल्दी
rarely	virle hī	विरले ही
rationally	samajhdārī se	समझदारी से
relatively	dūsroṁ kī tulnā meṁ	दूसरों की तुलना में
shortly	jaldī hī	जल्दी ही
shrewdly	cālākī se	चालाकी से
shyly	saṅkoc se	संकोच से
sincerely	lagan se	लगन से
silently	cupcāp	चुपचाप
slowly	dhīre	धीरे
subsequently	tadnantar	तदनन्तर;
	bād meṁ	बाद में
suddenly	anāyās	अनायास
	acānak	अचानक
thoroughly	acchī tarah se	अच्छी तरह से
truly	asal meṁ	असल में
	vastutaḥ	वस्तुतः
unanimously	ek āvāz se	एक आवाज़ से
unfortunately	durbhāgyă se	दुर्भाग्य से
visibly	pratyakṣtaḥ	प्रत्यक्षतः
violently	zabardastī se	ज़बरदस्ती से
wisely	buddhimānī se	बुद्धिमानी से

VERBS

Now I shall give some verbs in day to day use. Hindi has several sentence structures where it is important to know whether the verb is transitive or intransitive. Remember: Transitive verbs have a direct object. There is always an answer to the question,'What?' Intransitive verbs have no direct object. . For instance, if you say, ' I eat.', there can be a legitimate question, ' What do you eat?', the answer to which would be some object....X, Y, Z. But if you say, 'I go.', there can be questions with 'when', 'where', 'how', but never with 'what'. Eat is verb transitive, 'go' is verb intransitive.

ask	pūchnā	पूछना
ask (for something)	māṁgnā	माँगना
bake	tandūr meṁ seknā	तंदूर में सेकना
be	honā	होना
boil	ubālnā	उबालना
bring	lānā	लाना
buy	<u>kh</u>arīdnā	ख़रीदना
call	bulānā	बुलाना
cough	khāṁsnā	खाँसना
cry $^{v.t.}$(cause someone to ...)	rulānā	रुलाना
come	ānā	आना
cook	pakānā	पकाना
cover	ḍhaknā	ढकना
cry $^{v.i.}$	ronā	रोना
cut	kāṭnā	काटना
do	karnā	करना
drink (oneself)	pīnā	पीना
drink (offer to others)	pilānā	पिलाना
dust	jhāṛnā	झाड़ना
dry $^{v.i.}$	sūkhnā	सूखना

VERBS

dry$^{v.t.}$	sukhānā	सुखाना
eat	khānā	खाना
feed (solid)	khilānā	खिलाना
feed(liquid)	pilānā	पिलाना
fry	talnā	तलना
garnish	sajānā	सजाना
get up	uṭhnā	उठना
give	denā	देना
go	jānā	जाना
grate	retnā	रेतना
grill	āṁc par bhūnanā	आँच पर भूनना
grind	pīsnā	पीसना
hear	sunanā	सुनना
keep	rakhnā	रखना
laugh$^{v.i.}$(to ..oneself)	haṁsnā	हँसना
laugh$^{v.t.}$ (to make others…)	haṁsānā	हँसाना
listen	sunanā	सुनना
live	rahnā	रहना
look / see/ watch	dekhnā	देखना
make	banānā	बनाना
narrate	sunānā	सुनाना
peel	chīlnā	छीलना
play(instrument)	bajānā	बजाना
play(a game)	khelnā	खेलना
roast	bhūnanā	भूनना
run	dauṛnā	दौड़ना
	bhāgnā	भागना
say	kahnā	कहना
see	dekhnā	देखना

sell	becnā	बेचना
send	bhejnā	भेजना
shake	hilānā	हिलाना
show	dikhānā	दिखाना
sing	gānā	गाना
sit down	baiṭhnā	बैठना
sleep	sonā	सोना
sneeze	chīṁkā	छींकना
smear	chupaṛna	चुपड़ना
smell	sūṁghnā	सूँघना
soak	bhigonā	भिगोना
speak	bolnā	बोलना
spoil	bigāṛnā	बिगाड़ना
sprinkle	chiṛaknā	छिड़कना
stay	ṭhaharnā	ठहरना
steal	curānā	चुराना
stop v.i. (one self)	ruknā	रुकना
stop v.t. (someone/something)	roknā	रोकना
study	paṛhnā	पढ़ना
swallow	līlnā, niglnā	लीलना, निगलना
take	lenā	लेना
taste	cakhnā	चखना
teach	paṛhānā	पढ़ाना
tear	phāṛnā	फाड़ना
touch	chūnā	छूना
wake(up oneself)	jāgnā	जागना
wake(someone else up)	jagānā	जगाना
wash	dhonā	धोना
wear	pahananā	पहनना
win	jītnā	जीतना

NOUNS

acquaintance	vākfīat	वाकफ़ीयत[f.]
afternoon	aprāhn	अपराह्न[m]
anger	krodh	क्रोध[m.sg]
arrogance	ghamaṇḍ	घमण्ड[m.sg]
article	lekh	लेख[m.sg]
bed	palaṅg	पलंग[m.sg]
bedding	bistar	बिस्तर[m.sg.]
	(matress,sheet, pillow etc. all combined)	
bitterness	kaṛvāhaṭ	कड़वाहट[f.sg]
blanket	kambal	कम्बल[m.sg.]
book	kitāb	किताब [f.sg]
book	pustak	पुस्तक[f.sg]
boredom	ūb	ऊब[f.sg]
boy	laṛkā	लड़का[m.sg]
boyhood	laṛakpan	लड़कपन[m.sg]
brackishness	khārāpan	खारापन[m.sg]
breakfast	nāśtā	नाश्ता[m.sg]
brother	bhāī	भाई[m.sg]
chair	kursī	कुर्सी [f.sg.]
child	baccā	बच्चा[m.sg]
childhood	bacpan	बचपन[m.sg]
church	girjāghar	गिरजाघर[m.sg]
cleverness	caturāī	चतुराई[f.sg]
cloud	bādal	बादल[m.sg]
courage	himmat	हिम्मत[f.sg]

Date ....

Max 09648565641

jenningsp@gmail.com

Paul Jennings

Sophie Hoff.

Kieran Gray

Perry Lavin the 3rd esquire,
prince of yo' mama

Date

cunningness	cālākī	चालाकी$^{f.sg}$
cupboard	almārī,	अलमारी,$^{f.sg}$
day	din	दिन^{m}
defect	kharābī	ख़राबी$^{f.sg}$
delicacies	pakvān	पकवान$^{m.sg}$
depth	gahrāī	गहराई$^{f.sg}$
dew	os	ओस$^{f.sg}$
diligence	mehant	मेहनत$^{f.sg}$
dinner	rāt kā khānā	रात का खाना^{m}
disappointment	nirāśā	निराशा$^{f.sg}$
dishonesty	beīmānī	बेईमानी$^{f.sg}$
door	darvāzā	दरवाज़ा^{m}
drizzle	būṁdā-bāṁdī	बूँदा–बाँदी$^{f.sg}$
dust	dhūl	धूल$^{f.sg}$
earth	dhartī	धरती$^{f.sg}$
editor	sampādak	सम्पादक$^{m.sg}$
education	śikṣā	शिक्षा$^{f.sg}$
eloquence	vākpaṭutā	वाकपटुता$^{f.sg}$
emotion	bhāvnā	भावना$^{f.sg}$
entertainment	manorañjan	मनोरंजन^{m}
essay	nibandh	निबन्ध$^{m.sg}$
evening	śām	शाम$^{f.sg}$
excitement	uttejnā	उत्तेजना$^{f.sg}$
fall	patjhaṛ	पतझड़$^{f.sg}$
family	parivār	परिवार$^{m.sg}$
father	pitā	पिता

NOUNS

fiance	maṅgetar	मंगेतर
floor	farś	फर्श ^{m}
food	khānā	खाना$^{m.sg}$
forenoon	pūrvāhn	पूर्वाह्न^{m}
formality	aupcāriktā	औपचारिकता$^{f.sg}$
frustration	kunṭhā	कुण्ठा$^{f.sg}$
goodness	acchāī	अच्छाई$^{f.sg}$
greatness	baṛāppan	बड़प्पन$^{m.sg}$
hail	ole	ओले$^{m.sg}$
happiness	khuśī	खुशी$^{f.sg}$
health	swāsthyă	स्वास्थ्य$^{m.sg}$
heaviness	bhārīpan	भारीपन$^{m.sg}$
height	uṁcāī	उंचाई$^{f.sg}$
honesty	īmāndārī	ईमानदारी$^{f.sg}$
hope	āśā	आशा$^{f.sg}$
	ummīd	उम्मीद$^{f.sg}$
house	makān	मकान m.sg.
ceiling	chat	छत $^{f.sg.}$
habit	ādat	आदत $^{f.sg.}$
humidity	umas	उमस$^{f.sg}$
humility	vinamratā	विनम्रता$^{f.sg}$
hurricane	tūfān	तूफ़ान$^{m.sg}$
husband	pati	पति
inflation	mahṁgāī	महँगाई$^{f.sg}$
insipidity	phīkāpan	फीकापन$^{m.sg}$
injustice	anyāy	अन्याय$^{m.sg}$
insolence	dhithāī	ढिठाई $^{f.sg}$

intelligence	hośiyārī	होशियारी$^{f.sg}$
interest	ruci	रुचि$^{f.sg}$
journalist	samvāddātā	संवाददाता$^{m.sg}$
justice	nyāy	न्याय$^{m.sg}$
largeness	baṛāī	बड़ाई$^{f.sg}$
laziness	ālas	आलस$^{m.sg}$
length	lambāī	लम्बाई$^{f.sg}$
lightening	bijlī	बिजली$^{m.sg}$
lightness	halkāpan	हल्कापन$^{m.sg}$
lunch	din kā khānā	दिन का खाना^{m}
man	ādmī	आदमी$^{m.sg}$
manhood	ādmiat	आदमियत$^{f.sg}$
matress	gaddā	गद्दा$^{m.sg}$
mist	dhundh	धुंध$^{f.sg}$
moherhood	mātṛtva	मातृत्व$^{m.sg}$
morning	subah	सुबह^{f}
mosque	masjid	मस्जिद$^{m.sg}$
mother	mātā	माता
nervousness	ghabrāhaṭ	घबराहट^{f}
news	khabar	ख़बर$^{f.sg}$
	samācār	समाचार$^{m.sg}$
newspaper	samācārpatra	समाचारपत्र$^{m.sg}$
	akhbār	अख़बार$^{m.sg}$
night	rāt	रात^{f}
noon	dopahar	दोपहर^{f}
novel	upanyās	उपन्यास$^{m.sg}$

NOUNS

obstruction	rukāvaṭ	रुकावट^{f}
ocean	samudra	समुद्र$^{m.sg}$
old age	buṛhāpā	बुढ़ापा^{m}
optimism	āśāvād	आशावाद$^{m.sg}$
pessimism	nirāśāvād	निराशावाद$^{m.sg}$
pillow	palaṅgpoś	सिरहाना^{m}
praise	praśansā	प्रशंसा$^{f.sg}$
pungency	tītāpan	तीतापन^{m}
quilt	razāī	रज़ाई$^{f.sg}$
rain	bāriś	बारिश$^{f.sg}$
religeon	dharm	धर्म$^{m.sg}$
rich	dhanī	धनी$^{m.sg/adj.}$
river	nadī	नदी$^{f.sg}$
mountain	pahāṛ	पहाड़$^{m.sg}$
rock	caṭṭān	चट्टान$^{f.sg}$
room	kamrā	कमरा$^{m.sg.}$
roundness	golāī	गोलाई$^{f.}$
sadness	udāsī	उदासी$^{f.sg}$
sale	bikrī	बिक्री$^{f.sg}$
sand	ret	रेत$^{f.sg}$
season	ṛitu	ऋतु$^{f.sg}$
sheet	cādar	चादर$^{f.sg}$
shopping	kharīdārī	ख़रीदारी$^{f.sg}$
sickness	bīmārī	बीमारी$^{f.sg}$
sister	bahan	बहन$^{f.sg}$
sky	āsmā n	आकाश ।$^{m.sg}$
smallness	choṭāpan	छोटापन^{m}

snow	barf	बर्फ़ f.sg
soil	miṭṭī	मिट्टी f.sg
sorrow	dukh	दुख m.
sourness	khaṭās	खटास f.sg
spring	basant	बसंत f.sg
stone	patthar	पत्थर m.sg
storm	āṁdhī	आँधी m.sg
story	kahānī	कहानी f.sg
student	chātra	छात्र m.sg
stupidity	mūrkhtā	मूर्खता f.sg
summer	garmī	गर्मी f.sg
surprise	hairānī	हैरानी f.sg
sweet	miṭhās	मिठास f.sg
table	mez	मेज़ f.sg.
tablecloth	mezpoś	मेज़पोश f.sg.
talk	bāt	बात f.sg
teacher	śikṣak	शिक्षक m.sg
temple(Hindu-)	mandir	मंदिर m.sg
temple(Sikh-)	gurudvārā	गुरुद्वारा m.sg
tension	tanāv	तनाव m.sg
train	gāṛī	गाड़ी f.sg.
trench	khāī	खाई f.sg
trouble	pareśānī	परेशानी f.sg
unhappiness	dukh	दुख m.sg
wall	dīvār	दीवार m
weather	mausam	मौसम m.sg

width	cauṛāī	चौड़ाई f.sg
wife	patnī	पत्नी
wind	havā	हवा f.sg
window	khiṛkī	खिड़की f.sg
winter	sardī	सर्दी f.sg
wisdom	buddhimānī	बुद्धिमानी f.sg
woman	aurat/ nārī	औरत/नारी f.sg
womanhood	auratpan	औरतपन m.sg
	nārītva	नारीत्व
youth	javānī	जवानी f.sg

KINSHIP

AUNTS:

wife of younger brother of father	cācī	चाची
wife of older brother of father	tāī	ताई
wife of mother's brother	māmī	मामी
mother's sister	mausī	मौसी
father's sister	phūphī, buā	फूफी, बुआ

SIBLINGS:

brother	bhāī	भाई
brother's wife	bhābhī	भाभी
sister	bahan	बहन

sister's husband	jījā	जीजा

COUSINS

son of mother's sister	mauserā bhāī	मौसेरा भाई
daughter of mother's sister	mauserī bahan	मौसेरी बहन
mother's brother's son	mamerā bhāī	ममेरा भाई
mother's brother's daughter	mamerī bahan	ममेरी बहन
son of father's brother	cacerā bhāī	चचेरा भाई
daughter of father's brother	cacerī bahan	चचेरी बहन
son of father's sister	phupherā bhāī	फुफेरा भाई
daughter of father's sister	phupherī bahan	फुफेरी बहन

GRANDPARENTS

father's father	dādā	दादा
mother'ss father	nānā	नाना
father's mother	dādī	दादी
mother's mother	nānī	नानी

PARENTS:

father	pitā jī	पिता जी
mother	mātā jī	माता जी

UNCLES:

younger brother of father	cācā	चाचा
older brother of father	tāyā	ताया
brother of mother	māmā	मामा
husband of mother's sister	mausa	मौसा
husband of father's sister	phūphā	फूफा

CONJUNCTIONS

and	aur	और
	va	व
	ataḥ	अतः
	evam	एवम्
although	yadyapi	यद्यपि
as if	māno	मानो
as though	jaise ki	जैसे कि (relative conjunct)
because	kyoṁki	क्योंकि
but	lekin	लेकिन
	parantu	परन्तु
	magar	मगर
	par	पर
either..X.. or...Y..	ya X.......ya..... Y	या X.... या Y.....
if	yadi	यदि
in that case	to	तो

(तो has several uses. It functions as a conjunct at the beginning of a clause)

nevertheless	tathāpi	तथापि
neither..X.. nor...Y..	na X.......na..... Y	न X....न Y.....
on the contrary	balki	बल्कि
or	yā /athvā	या /अथवा
or else	nahīṁ to /varnā	नहीं तो/वरना
so that	tāki	ताकि

that	ki	कि
therefore	islie	इसलिए
that is	yānī	यानी
the one who, which	jo ki	जो कि (relative conjunct)
neither..X.. nor.Y...	na X. .....na..... Y	न X...... न Y.....

COMPOUND POSTPOSITIONS

के बारे में	ke bāre meṁ	about
के अनुसार	ke anusār	according to
के बाद	ke bād	after
के आगे	ke āge	ahead of
के कारण	ke kāraṇ	because of
की वजह से	kī vajah se	because of
के पहले	ke pahle	before
के पीछे	ke pīche	behind
के अतिरिक्त	ke atirikt	besides
के लिए	ke lie	for
के सामने	ke sāmne	in front of
की तरह/भांति	kī tarah/bhāṁti	like
के पास *	ke pā s *	near
की ओर/तरफ़	kī or/taraf	towards
के ऊपर	ke ūpar	upon
के नीचे	ke nī ce	under
के साथ	ke sāth	with
के बिना	ke binā	without

POSTPOSITIONS

1. नमक के बिना 2. राम के साथ 3. उसके लिए 4. दो बजे के बाद 5. घर के अन्दर 6. घर के बाहर 7. मेरे पीछे 8. मेरे आगे 9. मेज़ के ऊपर 10. मेज़ के नीचे। 11. उस के बारे में। 12. आप के कारण।

1. namak ke binā 2. rām ke sāth 3. uske lie 4. do baje ke bād, 5. ghar ke andar 6. ghar ke bāhar 7. mere pīche 8. mere āge, 9. mez ke ūpar 10. mez ke nīce. 11. us ke bāre meṁ 12. āp ke kāraṇ

1. without salt 2. with Ram 3. for him/ her 4. after 2 o'clock 5. in the house 6. out of the house 7. behind me 8. ahead of me 9. on the table 10. under the table. 11 . about him/her 12. because of you.

☞ **के पास** *** ke pās has two uses. (1) to express proximity, and (2) to express possession .Examples:**

1. मेरे पास दो किताबें हैं। mere pās do kitābeṁ haiṁ.	I have two books.
2.उसके पास बहुत धन है। uske pās bahut dhan hai.	She has much money.
3. क्या आपके पास कलम है? kyā āpke pās kalam hai?	Do you have a pen?
4.उसके पास छाता है। uske pās chātā hai.	He/She has an umbrella.

☞ *** के पास ke pās in the sense of possession is not used for relatives, or body limbs, for which the possessive pronouns such as मेरा merā, मेरे mere, मेरी merī etc. are used. Example:**

मेरे दो हाथ हैं।	mere do hāṭh haiṁ.	I have two hands
उसकी दो माताएँ हैं।	uskī do mātāeṁ haiṁ.	He/ She has two mothers.

Weather Related Vocabulary

cloud	megh/ bādal	मेघ/ बादल (m.)
cloudy	meghāchādit	मेघाच्छादित (adj.)
cold	ṭhaṇḍ / śīt	ठण्ड/ शीत (f.)
drizzle	būṁdā-bāṁdī	बूँदा–बाँदी (f.)
good weather	acchā mausam	अच्छा मौसम
hail	ole	ओले (m.pl.
heat	garmī	गर्मी (f.)
humid	umas	उमस (f.)
lightning	bijlī	बिजली (f.)
mild/pleasant weather	suhāvnā mausam	सुहावना मौसम (m.)
mist	dhuṁdh/kuhrā	धुंध (f.) /कुहरा (m.)
nasty weather	<u>kh</u>arāb mausam	खराब मौसम
overcast	meghāchann	मेघाच्छन्न (adj.)
rain	bāriś	बारिश (f.)
showers	bauchār	बौछार (f.)
storm	tūfān	तूफ़ान (m.)
stormy	tūfānī	तूफ़ानी (adj.)
strong wind	tez havā	तेज़ हवा
thunder	garaj	गरज
thunder	garajnā (vi.)	गरजना
to be misty	dhuṁdh honā	धुंध होना
to drizzle	būṁdā-bāṁdī honā	बूँदा–बाँदी होना
to hail	ole paṛnā	ओले पड़ना (v.i..)
to pour	muslādhār bāriś honā	मूसलादार बारिश होना
to rain	bāriś hona	बारिश होना
wind	havā (f.)	हवा
windstorm/gale	āṁdhī(f.)	आँधी
windy day	tūfānī din	तूफ़ानी दिन

●●●

G 7 PAST FORMS OF 'honā' होना

The past forms of the verb होना honā are:

thā	था	m.sg.;	the	थे	m.pl.
thī,	थी	f.sg.;	thīṁ	थीं	f.pl.

subject	masc.	fem.
maiṁ, tū, vah. yah, kyā, kaun (sg) मैं, तू, वह, यह, क्या, कौन (sg)	thā था	thī थी
ham, tum, āp, ve, ye (pl.) हम, तुम, आप, वे, ये (pl.)	the थे	thīṁ थीं

COMPREHENSION

1. कल शनिवार^{m} था।
   kal śanivār thā.
   Yesterday was Saturday.

2. परसों शुक्रवार^{m} था।
   parsoṁ śukravār thā.
   Day before yesterday was Friday.

- **In Hindi, the days of the week are masculine. (see pg. 412)**

3. कल आप^{m} *कहाँ थे?
   kal āp (m.) kahāṁ the?
   Where were you (masc.hon.) yesterday?

4. कल आप^{f} *कहाँ थीं?
   kal āp (f.) kahāṁ thīṁ?
   Where were you(fem.hon) yesterday?

5. मैं^{m} जयपुर में था।
   maiṁ ^{m} Jaipur meṁ thā.
   I was in Jaipur

6. वह^{f} बीमार थी।
vah^{f} bīmār thī.
She was sick.

7. उनका लड़का^{m} दयालु था।
unkā larkā^{m} dayālu thā.
Their boy was kind.

8. वे$^{m.pl}$ दुखी थे।
ve$^{m.pl}$ dukhī the.
They (m; far) were unhappy.

9. *मेरी माता जी खुश थीं।
merī mātā jī khuś thīṁ.
My mother was happy.

10. *पिता जी परेशान थे।
pitā jī pareśān the.
Father was upset.

11. उसका भाई होशियार था।
uskā bhāī hośiyār thā.
His/Her brother was clever.

• माता जी and पिता जी are honorific expressions for mother and father respectively, hence though singulars, take थीं (thīṁ), थे (the), which are the plural forms of the verb होना (honā) in the past tense.

Ex. G 7.1 Give the meaning of:

bīmār$^{adj.}$ बीमार; dayālu$^{adj.}$ दयालु ; dukhī$^{adj.}$ दुखी ; khuś$^{adj.}$ खुश ; pareśān $^{adj.}$परेशान ; svasth$^{adj.}$ स्वस्थ; nirāś$^{adj.}$ निराश ; śanivār शनिवार$^{m.}$; śukravār शुक्रवार nārāz$^{adj.}$ नाराज़; krodhit$^{adj.}$ क्रोधित; śānt$^{adj.}$ शान्त; aśānt$^{adj.}$ अशान्त।

Ex. G 7.2 Translate into English.

1. किताब$^{f.}$ अच्छी थी। 2. दही$^{m.}$ खट्टा था। 3. आम$^{m.}$ मीठा था।4. लड़का$^{m.}$ बीमार था। 5. यात्री$^{m.}$ दयालु था। 6. वह$^{m.}$ कैसे था? 7. वहाँ कौन$^{m.}$ था? 8. हम$^{m.pl}$ परेशान थे। 9. माँ दुखी थीं। 10. कल सोमवार$^{m.}$ था। 11. मैं व्यस्त था/थी। 12. वे उत्तेजित थे/थीं। 13. दाम बहुत ज़्यादा था। 14. दृश्य सुन्दर था।

1. kitāb$^{f.}$ acchī thī. 2. dahī$^{m.}$ khaṭṭā thā. 3. ām$^{m.}$ mīṭhā thā.4. laṛkā$^{m.}$ bīmār thā. 5. yātrī$^{m.}$ dayālu thā. 6. vah$^{m.}$ kaise thā? 7. vahāṁ kaun$^{m.}$ thā? 8. ham$^{m.pl.}$ pareśān the. 9. māṁ dukhī thīṁ. 10. kal somvār$^{m.}$ thā. 11.maiṁ vyast thā/ thī. 12. ve uttejit the/ thīṁ. 13. dām bahut zyāda thā. 14. dṛśyă sundar thā.

PAST FORM OF THE VERB 'honā'

Ex. G 7 3 Translate into Hindi.

1. Who was he? 2. Milk$^{m.}$ was expensive. 3. Food$^{m.}$ was delicious. 4. Robert was ill. 5. Film$^{f.}$ was interesting. 6. Bread$^{f.}$ was stale. 7. Fruit $^{m.}$was fresh. 8. Grapes $^{m.}$pl.were sour. 9. I$^{f.}$ was not here. 10. Mother was depressed. 11. Water was cold. 12. He was confused.

Key G 7.1

sick; kind; unhappy; happy; upset; healthy; disappointed; Saturday; Friday; annoyed; angry; peaceful; restless.

Key G 7.2

1. The book was good. 2. Yogurt was sour. 3. Mango was sweet. 4. The boy was sick. 5. Traveler was kind. 6. How was he? 7. Who was there? 8. We were upset. 9. Mother was unhappy.10.Yesterday was Monday. 11. I was busy. 12. He/ She was excited. 13. The price was too high. 14. The view was beautiful.

Key G 7.3

1. वह कौन था? 2. दूध$^{m.}$ महँगा था। 3. खाना$^{m.}$ स्वादिष्ट था? 4. राबर्ट बीमार था? 5. फ़िल्म$^{f.}$ रोचक थी। 6. डबलरोटी$^{f.}$ बासी थी। 7. फल$^{m.}$ ताज़ा था। 8. अंगूर$^{m.pl.}$ खट्टे थे। 9. मैं$^{f.}$ यहाँ नहीं थी। 10. माँ खिन्न थीं। 11. पानी ठण्डा था। 12. वह व्याकुल था।

1. vah kaun thā. 2.dūdh mahaṁgā thā. 3. khānā svādiṣṭ thā. 4. raubarṭ bīmār thā. 5. film rocak thī. 6. dabalroṭī bāsī thī.7. phal tāzā thā. 8. angūr khaṭṭe the. 9. maiṁ yahāṁ nahīṁ thī.10. māṁ khinn thīṁ. 11. pānī ṭhaṇḍā thā.12. vah vyākul thā.

●●●●●

VEGETATION

लता/बेल	latā, bel	creeper	जड़ी बूटी	jaṛī būṭī	herb
झाड़ी	jhāṛī	shrub	पौधा	paudhā	plant
पेड़	peṛ	tree	घास	ghās	grass
फूल	phūl	flower			
अंगूर की बेल		angūr kī bel	vine		

G 8 FUTURE FORM OF 'honā' होना

subject	verb 'honā' होना	
	masc.	**fem.**
maiṁ मैं	hoūṁgā/ hūṁgā होऊँगा/हूँगा	hoūṁgī/ hūṁgī होऊँगी/हूँगी
tum तुम	hoge होगे	hogī होगी
tū, yah, vah तू, वह, यह	hogā होगा	hogī होगी
ham, āp, ve, ye हम, आप, वे, ये	hoṁge होंगे	hoṁgī होंगी

COMPREHENSION

1. कल शनिवार[m] होगा। kal śanivār hogā. — It will be Saturday tomorrow.
2. परसों रविवार[m] होगा। parsoṁ ravivār hogā. — It will be Sunday, the day after tomorrow
3. नरसों सोमवार[m] होगा। narsoṁ somvār hogā. — Two days after tomorrow, it will be Monday
4. कल यहाँ संगीत गोष्ठी[f] होगी। kal yahāṁ saṅgīt goṣṭhī hogī. — Tomorrow, there will be a music concert here.

☞ Hindi has no translation for 'it is', 'there is', 'it was', 'there was', 'it will be', 'there will'etc. Hindi speakers come straight to the subject.

WORD POWER

saṅgīt संगीत[m] **music;** goṣṭhī गोष्ठी[f] **concert;** saṅgīt goṣṭhī संगीत गोष्ठी[f] This is a compound noun meaning music concert.

FUTURE FORM OF THE VERB 'honā'

Ex. G 8.1 Translate into English:

1. वह खुश होगा। 2. कल धूप^{f} होगी। 3. माता जी परेशान होंगी।4. अध्यापक नाराज़ होंगे। 5. बहन^{f} उदास होगी।6. फ़सल^{f} अच्छी होगी। 7. पुस्तक मेला^{m} कब होगा? 8. कल तापमान ज़्यादा^{m} होगा। 9. अगले हफ़्ते आसमान^{m} साफ़ होगा। 10. तुम^{m} बीमार होगे।

1. vah khuś hogā. 2.kal dhūp$^{f.}$ hogī.3. mātā jī pareśān hoṁgī. 4. adhyāpak nārāz hoṁge.5. bahan udās hogī. 6. fasal acchī hogī. 7. pustak melā^{m} kab hogā? 8. kal tāpmān zyādā hogā. 9. agle hafte āsmān^{m} sāf hogā. 10. tum$^{m.}$ bīmār hoge.

Ex. G 8.2 Translate into Hindi:

1. Film will be good. 2. It will rain today. 3. There will be fog tomorrow. 4. Mother will be upset. 5. Sister will be disappointed. 6. Robert will be happy. 7. Where will you (m.informal) be tomorrow at this time? 8. Tomorrow at this time , I (m.) will be here. 9. There will a book fair next week. 10. You will be astonished.

Key G 8.1

1. He will be happy. 2. It will be sunny tomorrow. 3. Mother will be upset. 4. Teacher will be displeased. 5. Sister will be sad. 6. Crop will be good. 7. When will book fare be. 8. Temperature will be higher tomorrow. 9. Sky will be clear next week. 10. you will be sick.

Key G 8.2

1. फ़िल्म$^{f.}$ अच्छी होगी। 2. आज बारिश^{f} होगी। 3. कल धुंध^{f} होगी।4. माता जी परेशान होंगी। 5. बहन^{f} निराश होगी।6. रॉबर्ट खुश होगा। 7. कल इस समय तुम^{m} कहाँ होगे? 8. कल इस समय मैं^{m} यहाँ होऊँगा। 9. अगले हफ़्ते पुस्तक मेला^{m} होगा। 10. तुम^{m} चकित होगे।

1. film$^{f.}$ acchī hogī. 2. āj bāriś$^{f.}$ hogī. 3. kal dhundh$^{f.}$ hogī. 4. mātā jī pareśān hoṁgī. 5. bahan nirāś hogī. 6. raubarṭ khuś hogā. 7. kal is samay tum^{m}kahāṁ hoge? 8. kal is samay maiṁ^{m} yahāṁ hoūṁgā. 9. agle hafte pustak melā^{m} hogā. 10. tum$^{m.}$ cakit hoge.

●●●●●

G 9 IMPERATIVE

Hindi has two imperative forms. The present and the future imperative.

Present Imperative		
tū (sg.)	तू	verb root
tum (sg. and plural)	तुम	verb root + o
āp (sg. and plural)	आप	verb root +i + e or ye

Examples:

subject	**verbs**				
	go	**come**	**eat**	**sit**	**get up**
	jānā जाना	ānā आना	khānā खाना	baiṭhnā बैठना	uṭhnā उठना
tū तू	jā जा	ā आ	khā खा	baiṭh बैठ	uṭh उठ
tum तुम	jāo जाओ	āo आओ	khāo खाओ	baiṭho बैठो	uṭho उठो
āp आप	jāie जाइए	āie आइए	khāie खाइए	baiṭhie बैठिए	uṭhie उठिए

☞ **To make negative sentences, put मत 'mat' before the verb with तू 'tū' and तुम 'tum' forms, and न 'na' before the verb in आप 'āp' form.**

For example:

1. तू मत खा।	tū mat khā.	Do not eat!
2. तुम मत खाओ।	tum mat khāo	Do not eat!
3. आप न खाइए।	āp na khāie.	Please, do not eat!

IMPERATIVE

COMPREHENSION

1. किताब[f..sg] पढ़िए। — Please read a book.

   kitāb paṛhie.

2. खाना[m.sg] पकाओ। — Cook food.

   khānā pakāo.

3. बच्चे[m.sg.obl.] को उठाओ। — Pick up the baby.

   bacce ko uṭhāo

4. लड़के[m.sg.obl] को बुलाओ। — Call the boy.

   laṛke ko bulāo.

5. मरीज़[m.sg] को दवाई[f..sg] दो। — Give medicine to the patient.

   marīz ko davāī do.

6. गाहक[m.sg] को सामान[m.sg] बेचो। — Sell goods to the customer.

   gāhak ko sāmān beco.

7. पिता जी को पत्र लिखिए। — Write a letter to father.

   pitā jī ko patra likhie.

8. बच्चे को मुझको दो। — Give the child to me.

   bacce ko mujh ko do.

At this point, I would like to dwell on the use of the postposition को 'ko' in the sentences avove.

Grammatically the postposition को 'ko' can be used both with direct and indirect, living as well as non-living object.

In practice:

☞ **Use of को 'ko' with direct non-living object is not obligatory. Ref. sentences 1, 2 above.**

☞ **Use of को 'ko' with direct living object is obligatory. Ref. sentences 3, 4 above.**

☞ **In a sentence which has both direct as well as indirect object, use of को 'ko' with indirect living object is obligatory, while it is usually dropped with direct non-living object. Ref. sentences 5, 6, 7 above.**

☞ **If a sentence has two objects, and both the direct and the indirect objects are living, use of the postposition 'ko' को after both the objects is obligatory. Ref. sentence 8 above.**

Here, both direct object बच्चा baccā 'child' and the indirect object मुझको 'mujhko' are living; hence the postposition 'को' follows both.

Some verbs have irregular imperative form such as —

		tū	**tum**	**āp**
		तू	तुम	आप
karnā (to do)	करना	कर kar	करो karo	कीजिए kījie
pinā (to drink)	पीना	पी pī	पिओ pio	पीजिए pījie
lenā (to take)	लेना	ले le	लो lo	लीजिए lījie
denā (to give)	देना	दे de	दो do	दीजिए dījie

IMPERATIVE: EXERCISES

Ex. G 9.1 Give the appropriate forms of the below given verbs in the present imperative.

			tū	**tum**	**āp**
			तू	तुम	आप
चखना	cakhnā	(to taste)			
बनाना	banānā	(to make)			
बेचना	becnā	(to sell)			
ख़रीदना	kharīdnā	(to buy)			
हँसना	haṁsnā	(to laugh)			
जागना	jāgnā	(to wake up)			

Ex G 9.2 Translate into English:

1. आप यहाँ बैठिए। 2. तुम वहाँ बैठो। 3. आप बाज़ार जाइए। 4. तुम यहाँ आओ। 5. तुम इधर लेटो। 6. कृपया बाहर जाइए। 7. नल खोलो। 8. नल बन्द करो। 9. बत्ती बुझाओ। 10.बत्ती जलाओ। 11. सामने देखो। 12.दाँये मुड़ो।

1. āp yahāṁ baiṭhie. 2. tum vahāṁ baiṭho. 3. āp bāzār jāie.4. tum yahāṁ āo. 5. tum īdhar leṭo. 6. kṛpayā bāhar jāie. 7. nal kholo. 8. nal band karo. 9. battī bujhāo. 10. battī jalāo. 11. sāmne dekho. 12. dāṁye muṛo.

Ex. G 9.3 Translate into Hindi:

1. Call the child. 2. Please give to me! 3. Buy the book. 4. Write to father. 5. Sell to the customer. 6. Buy from the shopkeeper. 7. Sit near me. 8. Keep on the table. 9. Please tell us. 10. Look at them. 11. Read from my book. 12. Please stay in our house.

Key G 9. 2

1. Please be seated here! 2. You sit there. 3. Please go to market. 4. You come here. 5. You lie down over here. 6. Please go out. 7. Turn the tap on! 8. Turn the tap off. 9. Turn the light off. 10. Turn the light on. 11. Look ahead! 12. Turn right.

Key G 9.3

1. बच्चे को बुलाओ/बुलाइए। 2. कृपया मुझे दीजिए। 3. किताब ख़रीदो। 4. पिता जी को लिखो। 5. गाहक को बेचो। 6. दुकानदार से ख़रीदो। 7. मेरे पास बैठो। 8. मेज़ पर रखो। 9. कृपया हमें बताइए। 10. उनको देखो। 11. मेरी किताब से पढ़ो। 12. कृपया हमारे घर

में रहिए।

1. bacce ko bulāo/bulāie. 2. kṛpayā mujhe dījie. 3. kitāb kharīdo. 4. pitā jī ko likho. 5. gāhak ko beco. 6. dukāndār se kharīdo 7. mere pas baiṭho. 8. mez par rakho. 9. kṛpayā hameṁ batāie 10. unko dekho. 11. merī kitāb se paṛho. 12. kṛpayā hamāre ghar meṁ rahie.

Future Imperative

Unlike English, Hindi has a future imperative form too, which is used when the command or request is not expected to be executed instantly, but some time later in the near or distant future.

- **Both with तू tū (sg.), the intimate 'you' and तुम tum (sg. and pl.) the informal form of 'you', the verb in its infinitive form is used.**
- **With आप āp (sg. and pl.), verb root +i + e or ye+ gā is used.**

☞ **Regardless of the number and gender of the the person addressed as आप āp, the 'ga'-ending is affixed.**

subject	verbs				
	go **jānā** **जाना**	**come** **ānā** **आना**	**eat** **khānā** **खाना**	**sit** **baiṭhnā** **बैठना**	**get up** **uṭhnā** **उठना**
tū तू / tum तुम	jānā जाना	ānā आना	khānā खाना	baiṭhnā बैठना	uṭhnā उठना
āp आप	jāiegā जाइएगा	āiegā आइएगा	khāiegā खाइएगा	baiṭhiegā बैठिएगा	uṭhiegā उठिएगा

☞ **To make negative sentences, put मत 'mat' before the verb with तू 'tū' and तुम 'tum', and न 'na' before the verb with आप 'āp'.**

FUTURE IMPERATIVE

Examples:

1. तू / तुम मत खाना।	tū / tum mat khānā.	Don't eat !
2. तू /तुम कुछ मत कहना।	tū /tum kuch mat kahnā.	You don't say anything!
3. आप न खाइएगा।	āp na khāiegā.	Please don't eat!
4. आप बाहर न जाइएगा।	āp bāhar na jāiegā.	Please don't go out.

Future Imperative: Irregular Verbs

verbs	tu / tum तू / तुम		āp आप	
करना karnā (to do)	करना	karnā	कीजिएगा	kījiega
पीना pīnā (to drink)	पीना	pīnā	पीजिएगा	pījiegā
लेना lenā (to take)	लेना	lenā	लीजिएगा	lījiegā
देना denā (to give)	देना	denā	दीजिएगा	dījiegā

Ex. G 9.4 Write the appropriate imperative future forms of the verbs given below.

		tū / tum तू / तुम	āp आप
चखना	cakhnā (to taste)		
बनाना	banānā (to make)		
बेचना	becnā (to sell)		
ख़रीदना	kharīdnā (to buy)		
हँसना	haṁsnā (to laugh)		
जागना	jāgnā (to wake up)		

Ex. G 9.5 Translate the sentences given below into English:

1.पत्र लिखिएगा। 2. जल्दी लौटिएगा। 3. सबको मेरा प्रणाम कहिएगा। 4.आप कल शाम को हमारे घर आइएगा । 5. लड़कियों को अच्छी शिक्षा दीजिएगा। 6. आप भारत में हिन्दी बोलिएगा। 7. आप गंगा में स्नान अवश्य कीजिएगा। 8. मेरे लिए उपहार लाइएगा। 9. धूम्रपान न कीजिएगा। 10. इस साल दीपावली हमारे साथ मनाइएगा।

1. patra likhiegā. 2. jaldī lauṭiegā. 3. sabko merā praṇām kahiegā. 4. āp kal sām ko hamāre ghar āiegā . 5. laṛkiyoṁ ko acchī śikṣā dījiegā. 6. āp bhārat meṁ hindī boliegā. 7. āp gaṅgā meṁ snān avaśyă kījiegā. 8. mere lie uphār lāiegā. 9. dhūmrapān na kījiegā. 10. is sāl dīpāvlī hamāre sāth manāiegā.

Ex. G 9.6 Translate the sentences given below into Hindi using the polite future imperative:

1. Please give me these books. 2. Please translate these words. 3. Please give correct answer. 4. Please listen carefully . 5. Please open the door. 6. Please don't shut the window. 7. Please speak quickly/slowly/loudly . 8. Please be attentive. 9. Please ask Mr .../Mrs... Kapoor. 10. Please take care of your health.

Key G 9.5

Please write letter. 2. Please return soon. 3. Please convey my respectful greetings to every body. 4 Please come to our house tomorrow evening. 5. Please give good education to girls . 6. Please speak Hindi in India. 7.Please certainly bathe in the Ganges.. 8. Please bring gift for me. 9. Please don't smoke. 10. Please celebrate Deepavli with us this year.

Key G 9.6 .

1.मुझे ये किताबें दीजिएगा। 2. इन शब्दों का अनुवाद कीजिएगा। 3. ठीक उत्तर दीजिएगा। 4. ध्यान से सुनिएगा । 5. दरवाज़ा खोलिएगा। 6. खिड़की बंद न कीजिएगा। 7. कृपया शीघ्र /धीरे/ज़ोर से बोलिएगा। 8. ध्यान दीजिएगा 9. श्री......./. श्रीमती. कपूर.. से पूछिएगा। 10. सेहत का ध्यान रखिएगा।

1. mujhe ye kitābeṁ dījiegā. 2. in śabdoṁ kā anuvād kījiegā. 3. ṭhīk uttar dījiegā. 4. dhyān se suniegā. 5. darvāzā kholiegā. 6. khiṛkī band na kījiegā. 7. kṛpayā śīghra / dhīre /zor se boliegā. 8. dhyān dījiegā. 9. śrī. Kapoor.../ śrimatī. Kapoor...... se pūchiegā. 10. sehat kā dhyān rakhiegā.

SUBJUNCTIVE IMPERATIVE

Subjunctive Imperative

Hindi has one more very polite form of the present imperative, that is (v.r.+ एँ eṁ). This is used only with आप āp, the formal 'you' and not with तू tū or तुम tum , the intimate and the informal you respectively.

For example:

1. आप यहाँ बैठें।	āp yahāṁ baitheṁ	Please be seated here.
2. खाना खाएँ।	khānā khāeṁ.	Please eat food.
3. चाय पिएँ।	cāy pieṁ.	Please have tea.

Ex. G 9.7 Translate into English using the subjunctive imperative:

1. तनिक आराम करें। 2. धूम्रपान न करें। 3. घास पर न चलें। 4. पौष्टिक भोजन खाएँ। 5. ध्यान से पढ़ें। 6. हिन्दी में बात करें। 7. रोज़ व्यायाम करें। 8. स्वास्थ्य का ध्यान रखें। 9. ग़रीबों की मदद करें। 10. दूरदर्शन पर ख़बरें देखें। 11. दवाई समय पर लें। 12. व्यर्थ समय न गँवाएँ।

1. tanik ārām kareṁ. 2. dhūmrapān na kareṁ. 3. ghās par na caleṁ. 4. pauṣṭik bhojan khāeṁ. 5. dhyān se paṛheṁ. 6. hindī meṁ bāt kareṁ. 7. roz vyāyām kareṁ. 8. svāsthyă kā dhyān rakheṁ. 9. garīboṁ kī madad kareṁ. 10. dūrdarśan par khabreṁ dekheṁ. 11. davāī samay par leṁ. 12. vyarth samay na gaṁvāeṁ.

Key G 9.7

1. Please rest a short while. 2. Please don't smoke. 3.Please don't walk on the grass. 4. Please eat nutritious food. 5. please read carefully. 6. please talk in Hindi. 7. please exercise daily. 8. Please take care of health. 9. please help the poor. 10 Please watch news on TV. 11. Please take the medicine on time. 12. Please don't waste time in vain.

●●●●●

G10 PRESENT INDEFINITE

subj. +	obj. +	v.r. +	tā ता[m.sg] / te ते[m.pl.] / tī ती[f.sg/pl]	+	hūṁ, ho, hai, haiṁ / हूँ, हो, है, हैं
		written together			agree with theNumber and Gender of the subject

	subject	main verb masc.	aux.verb fem.	
I go.	maiṁ मैं	jātā जाता	jātī जाती	hūṁ हूँ
we go.	ham हम	jāte जाते	jātī जाती	haiṁ हैं
you (intimate) go.	tū तू	jātā जाता	jātī जाती	hai है
you (informal) go.	tum तुम	jāte जाते	jātī जाती	ho हो
you (form.,hon.)go.	āp आप	jāte जाते	jātī जाती	haiṁ हैं
he, she, it (far) goes.	vah वह	jātā जाता	jātī जाती	hai. है
he, she, it (near) goes.	yah यह	jātā जाता	jātī जाती	hai है
they (far) go.	ve वे	jāte जाते	jātī जाती	haiṁ हैं
they (near) go.	ye ये	jāte जाते	jātī जाती	haiṁ हैं

PRESENT INDEFINITE EXERCISES

who	goes?	kaun	jātā	jātī	hai?
		कौन	जाता	जाती	है ?
what	goes?.	kyā	jātā hai?		
		क्या	जाता है ?		

COMPREHENSION

1. मैं^f हिन्दी पढ़ाती हूँ।	I (f) teach Hindi.
maiṁ hindi paṛhātī hūṁ.	(paṛhānā पढ़ाना = to teach)
2. तुम^m विज्ञान पढ़ते हो।	You (m.inf.) study science.
tum^m vijñān^m paṛhte ho.	(paṛhnā पढ़ना = to study)
3. वे^f मछली^f खाती हैं।	They(f. far) eat fish.
ve^f 'machlī^f khātī haiṁ.	(khānā खाना = to eat)
4 .वे^m खेलते हैं।	They (m.+f., far) play.
ve^m khelte haiṁ.	(khelnā खेलना= to play)
5. हम^m टी.वी. देखते हैं।	We(m) watch TV.
ham^m ṭī.vī. dekhte haiṁ.	(dekhnā देखना = to look)

Ex.G 10.1 Translate into Hindi.

1. दूधवाला दूध लाता है। 2. अख़बारवाला अख़वार बाँटता है। 3. धोबी कपड़े धोता है। 4. सब्ज़ीवाला सब्ज़ी बेचता है। 5.फलवाला फल बेचता है। 6. व्यापारी व्यापार करता है। 7. मोची जूते बनाता है। 8. नाई बाल काटता है। 9. बच्चे स्कूल में वर्दी पहनते हैं। 10. सूर्य सुबह छह बजे निकलता है।

1. dūdhvālā dūdh lātā hai. 2. akhbārvālā akhbār bāṁṭtā hai. 3. dhobī kapṛe dhotā hai. 4. sabzīvālā sabzī bectā hai. 5. phalvālā phal bectā hai. 6. vyāpārī vyāpār kartā hai. 7. mocī jūte banātā hai. 8. nāī bāl kāṭtā hai. 9. bacce skūl meṁ vardī pahnte haiṁ. 10. sūryă subah chaḥ baje nikaltā hai.

लाना lānā to bring; बाँटना bāṁṭnā to deliver; धोना dhonā to wash; करना karnā to do; बनाना banānā to make; पहनना pahnanā to wear; निकलना nikalnā to come out, **here:**to rise.

व्यापारी vyāpārī businessman; व्यापार vyāpār business; मोची mocī cobler
नाई nāī barbar; बाल bāl hair; वर्दी vardī uniform ; सूर्य sūryă sun;
सुबह subah in the morning; छह बजे chaḥ baje six o'clock.

Ex. G 10.2 Translate into Hindi.

1. ये^{m} यहाँ रहते हैं। 2. क्या तुम^{m} भी यहाँ रहते हो? 3. दुकानदार^{m} गाहक को क्या बेचता है? 4. दुकानदार^{m} गाहक^{m} को सामान बेचता है। 5. गाहक^{m} दुकानदार से क्या ख़रीदता है? 6. गाहक^{m} दुकानदार से सामान ख़रीदता है? 7. शिक्षक^{m} बोलता है। 8. छात्र^{m} सुनते हैं। 9. माँ किसको खिलाती है? 10. माँ बच्चे को खिलाती है। 11. डाक्टर मरीज़$^{m.sg}$ को कितनी बार दवाई देता है। 12. डाक्टर मरीज़$^{m.sg}$ को चार बार दवाई देता है। 13. आप^{m} कहाँ काम करते हैं? 14. मै दूरसंचार में काम करता हूँ 15. आप की पत्नी कहाँ काम करती है?16. मेरी पत्नी पर्यटन–विभाग में काम करती है।

1.ye^{m} yahāṁ rahte haiṁ. 2. kyā tum^{m} bhī yahāṁ rahte ho? 3. dukāndār^{m} gāhak ko kyā bectā hai? 4. dukāndār^{m} gāhak^{m} ko sāmān bectā hai. 5. gāhak^{m} dukāndār se kyā <u>kh</u>arīdtā hai? 6. gāhak^{m} dukāndār se sāman <u>kh</u>arīdtā hai. 7. śikṣak^{m} boltā hai. 8. chātra$^{m.pl.}$ sunte haiṁ. 9. māṁ kisko khilātī hai? 10. māṁ bacce ko khilātī hai.11. doctor^{m} marīz^{m} ko kitnī bār davāī detā hai. 12. doctor^{m} marīz^{m} ko cār bār davāī detā hai. 13. āp kahāṁ kām karte haiṁ? 14. maiṁ dūrsancār meṁ kām kartā hūṁ. 15. āpkī patnī kahāṁ kām kartī hai? 16. merī patnī paryaṭan vibhāg mem kām kartī hai.

खिलाना khilānā to feed; दूरसंचार dūrsancār telecommunications;
पर्यटन–विभाग paryaṭan vibhāg tourism department

Ex. G 10.3 Translate into Hindi.

Q. What time do you get up in the morning?

A. I get up at five o'clock.

Q. What do you do after that?

A. I have a bath. I brush my teeth. I prepare breakfast. I eat break fast at 7 o'clock. I read the newspaper. I go to Sanskrit class at 10 o'clock.

Q. Do you go to the Sanskrit class daily?

A. Yes, I go to the Sanskrit class daily.

PRESENT INDEFINITE: EXERCISES

Q. At what time do you have lunch/ dinner?
A. I have lunch at 1 o'clock./dinner at 8 o'clock
Q. Do you eat at home?
A. No, I don't eat at home. Usually I eat out.
Q. Do you sometimes go to the temple?
A. No, I never go the temple. I go to church every Sunday/ to mosque every Friday.

WORD POWER

brush teeth	dāṁt sāf karnā	दाँत साफ करना v.t.
prepare	taiyār karnā	तैयार करना v.t.
breakfast	nāśtā	नाश्ता m
newspaper	a<u>kh</u>bār	अख़बार m
daily	roz	रोज़ adv.
two times a week	hafte meṁ do bār	हफ़्ते में दो बार adv.;
once a month	mahīne meṁ ek bār	महीने में एक बार adv.
every Sunday	har ravivar ko	हर रविवार को
Church	girjāghar	गिरजाघर m
Mosque	masjid	मस्जिद f
usually	prāyaḥ	प्रायः adv.
sometimes	kabhī kabhī	कभी–कभी
temple	mandir	मंदिर, m
never	kabhī nahīṁ	कभी नहीं
lunch	din kā khānā	दिन का खाना m
dinner	rāt kā khānā	रात का खाना m
often	aksar	अक्सर adv.

Key G 10.1

1.Milkman brings milk. 2. Newspaperman delivers newpaper. 3. Washerman washes clothes. 4. Greengrocer sells vegetables. 5. Fruitseller sells fruit. 6. Businessman does business. 7. Cobbler makes shoes. 8. Barbar cuts the hair. 9. Children wear uniform in school. 10. The sun rses at six o'clock in the morning.

Key G 10.2

1. They(m. near) live here. 2. Do you also (m.informal) live here? 3. What does the shopkeeper(m.)sell to the customer? 4. Shopkeeper sells goods to the customer. 5. What does the customer[m] buy from the shopkeeper? 6.The customer[m] buys goods from the shopkeeper. 7. The teacher[m.pl.] talks. 8. The students[m.pl.] listen. 9. Whom does the mother pick up? 10.Mother picks up the baby.11.How many times does the doctor give medicine to the patient. 12 The doctor gives medicine to the patient four times. 13. Where do you work? 14. I work for the tele-communications. 15. Where does your wife work? 16. My wife works for the tourism department.

Key G 10.3

Q. आप सुबह कितने बजे उठते/उठती हैं?

A. मैं सुबह पाँच बजे उठता/उठती हूँ।

Q. उसके बाद आप क्या करते/करती हैं?

A. मैं नहाता/नहाती हूँ। मैं दाँत साफ़ करता/करती हूँ।
मैं नाश्ता बनाता/बनाती हूँ।
मैं सुबह सात बजे नाश्ता करता/ करती हूँ।
मैं अख़बार पढ़ता/पढ़ती हूँ।
मैं दस बजे संस्कृत की कक्षा में जाता/जाती हूँ।

Q. क्या आप संस्कृत की कक्षा में रोज़ जाते/जाती हैं?

A. जी, मैं संस्कृत की कक्षा में रोज़ जाता/जाती हूँ।

Q. आप दिन का खाना/ रात का खाना कितने बजे खाते/खाती हैं?

A. मैं दिन का खाना एक बजे खाता/खाती हूँ।
मैं रात का खाना आठ बजे खाता/खाती हूँ।

Q. क्या आप घर पर खाते/खाती हैं?

A. जी नहीं, मैं घर पर नहीं खाता/खाती।
मैं प्रायः बाहर खाता/खाती हूँ।

Q. क्या आप कभी मंदिर जाते/जाती हैं?

A. मैं मन्दिर कभी नहीं जाता /जाती । मैं हर इतवार को गिरजाघर

PRESENT INDEFINITE: EXERCISES

जाता/जाती हूँ। मैं हर शुक्रवार को मस्जिद जाता/जाती हूँ।

Q. āp subah kitne baje uṭhte / uṭhtī haiṁ?
A. maim subah pāṁc baje uṭhtā / uṭhtī hūṁ.
Q. uske bād āp kyā karte / kartī haiṁ?
A. maiṁ nahātā /nahātī hūṁ. maiṁ dāṁt sāf kartā / kartī hūṁ.
maiṁ nāśtā banātā /banātī hūṁ.
maiṁ subah sāt baje nāśtā kartā /kartī hūṁ.
maiṁ akhbār paṛhtā /paṛhtī hūṁ.
maiṁ das baje saṁskṛt kī kakṣā meṁ jātā/jātī hūṁ.
Q. kyā āp saṁskṛt kī kakṣā meṁ roz jāte /jātī haiṁ?
A. jī, maiṁ saṁskṛt kī kakṣā meṁ roz jātā/jātī hūṁ.
Q. āp din kā khānā/ rāt kā khānā kitne baje khāte/ khātī haiṁ?
A. maiṁ din kā khānā ek baje khātā / khātī hūṁ.
maiṁ rāt kā khānā āṭh baje khātā/ khātī hūṁ.
Q. kyā āp ghar par khāte/ khātī haiṁ?
A. jī nahīṁ, maiṁ ghar par nahīṁ khātā / khātī .
maiṁ prāyaḥ bāhar khātā / khātī hūṁ.
Q. kyā āp kabhī mandir jāte/ jātī haiṁ?
A. maiṁ mandir kabhī nahīṁ jātā / jātī.
maiṁ har ravivār ko girjāghar jātā / jātī hūṁ.
maiṁ har śukravār ko masjid jātā / jātī hūṁ.

Read :

1. **डाकिया dakia Postman pg. 239**

2. **मिशायल और एमि भारत में Michael and Amy in India pg. 254**
miśāyal aur emī bhārat meṁ

●●●●●

G 11 PAST HABITUAL

The past habitual tense is used to talk about activities that we did in the past but don't do anymore. It is exactly like the present simple tense , except that the past form of the verb होना 'honā' (i.e. to be) follows the verb root + tā ता, te ते, tī ती।

subj. + obj. + verbroot +	tā **ता** (m.sg.) +	thā, the, thī, thīṁ	
	te **ते** (m.pl.)	**था, थे, थी, थीं**	
	tī **ती** (f. sg. and pl.)		
	written together	agree with the Number and Gender of the subject	

	subject	**main + verb** **masc.**	**auxiliary verb** **fem.**
I used to go.	maiṁ मैं	jātā thā. जाता था	jātī thī जाती थी
We used to go.	ham हम	jāte the. जाते थे	jātī thīṁ जाती थीं
You (int.) used to go.	tū तू	jātā thā. जाता था	jātī thī. जाती थी
You (inf.) used to go.	tum तुम	jāte the. जाते थे	jātī thīṁ जाती थीं
You (form;hon.) used to go.	āp आप	jāte the. जाते थे	jātī thīṁ जाती थीं
He, She, It (far) used	vah	jātā thā.	jātī thī

to go.	वह	जाता था	जाती थी
He, She, It (near) used to go.	yah यह	jātā thā. जाता था	jātī thī जाती थी
They used to (far) go.	ve वे	jāte the. जाते थे	jātī thīṁ जाती थीं
They (near) used to go.	ye ये	jāte the. जाते थे	jātī thīṁ जाती थीं
Who used to go?	kaun कौन	jātā thā? जाता था?	jātī thī? जाती थी?
What used to go?.	kyā क्या	jātā thā? जाता था?	

COMPREHENSION

1. नौकर^m खाना पकाता था। — The servant (m) used to
naukar ^m khānā pakātā thā. — cook food. (पकाना pakānā)

2 .बच्चे^m.pl फल^m खाते थे। — Children used to eat fruit.
bacce^m.pl phal khāte the. — (खाना khānā)

3. वे^f कहानियाँ लिखती थीं। — She(honorific) used to write
ve^f kahāniyāṁ likhtī thīṁ. — stories. (लिखना likhnā)

('ve' is plural'they'; here it is used for singular 'she' as respectful expression.)

4. वे^m क्रिकेट खेलते थे। — They (m.) used to play.
ve^m kriketạ khelte the. — cricket . (खेलना khelnā)

5. हम^m.pl. टी.वी. देखते थे। — We(m) used to watch TV.
ham ^m.pl. ṭī.vī.dekhte the. — (देखना dekhnā)

Ex. G 11.1 Translate into English

1. वे^m.pl. यहाँ रहते थे। 2. क्या तुम^m यहाँ रहते थे? 3. दुकानदार^m गाहकों को कपड़े^m.pl. बेचता था। 4. गाहक^m. दुकानदार से कपड़े^m.pl. ख़रीदता था।5. शिक्षक^m छात्रों^m.pl.obl. को पाठ पढ़ाता

था। 6. छात्र$^{m.pl.}$ शिक्षक^{m} को सुनते थे। 7. मैं$^{f.}$ विदेशी पोशाकें पहनती थी। 8. हम$^{m/m+f}$ अक्सर संगीत गोष्ठी में जाते थे। 9.मेरी बहन$^{f.}$ मुझे बहुत प्यार करती थी। 10. माता जी बहुत स्वादिष्ट भोजन बनाती थीं।

1.ve^{m} yahāṁ rahte the. 2. kyā tum yahāṁ rahte the? 3. dukānd.ār ^{m} gāhkoṁ ko kapṛe bectā thā. 4. gāhak^{m} dukānd.ār se kapṛe $^{m.pl.}$ kharīdtā thā. 5. śikṣak$^{m.}$ chātroṁ ko pāṭh paṛhātā thā. 6. chātra^{m} śikṣak^{m} ko sunte the. 7 . maiṁ videśī pośākeṁ pahntī thī. 8. ham aksar saṅgīt goṣṭhī meṁ jāte the. 9. merī bahan mujhe bahut pyār kartī thī. 10. mātā jī bahut svādiṣt bhojan banātī thīṁ.

Ex. G 11.2 Translate into Hindi:

1. I$^{f.}$ used to go to school on foot. 2. We$^{m/m+f}$ used to live in a small house. 3. He^{m} used to teach us Hindi. 4. Father used to give us gifts. 5. We^{m} used to swim in the Ganges. 6. I$^{f.}$ used to take part in drama. 7. They^{m} used to climb up the mountains. 8. The teacher^{m} (m.) used to take us to the zoo. 9. We$^{m/m+f}$ used to do all work manually. 10. Children^{m} used to climb up the tamarind tree, and eat tamarind.

Ex. G 11. 3 Reading Comprehension:

जब मेरी बेटी छोटी थी, वह आलसी नहीं थी। वह बहुत मेहनती थी। वह रोज़ कम से कम बारह घण्टे काम करती थी। वह अब भी बहुत मेहनती है, परन्तु उतना काम नहीं करती, जितना पहले करती थी। आजकल वह रोज़ नौ घण्टे काम करती है।

jab merī beṭī choṭī thī, vah ālsī nahīṁ thī. vah bahut mehantī thī. vah roz kam-se-kam bārah ghaṇṭe kām kartī thī. vah ab bhī bahut mehantī hai, parantu utnā kām nahīṁ kartī jitnā pahle kartī thī. ājkal vah roz nau ghaṇṭe kām kartī hai.

Key G 11.1

1. They used to live here 2. Did you (m.informal) use to live here? 3. Shopkeeper used to sell clothes to the customers. 4. Customer used to buy clothes from the shopkeeper. 5. The teacher used to teach the lesson to the students.6. The students used to listen to the teacher. 7. I used to wear foreign dresses. 8. Often we used to go to music concert. 9. My sister used to love me much. 10. Mother used to make very delicious food.

Key G 11.2

1.मैं$^{f.}$ स्कूल पैदल जाती थी। 2.हम$^{m/m+f}$ छोटे घर में रहते थे।3. वह^{m} हमे हिन्दी पढ़ाता था। 4. पिता जी हमें उपहार देते थे।5. हम^{m} गंगा मे तैरते थे। 6. मैं^{f} नाटक में भाग लेती थी।

7. वे[m.pl] पहाड़ों पर चढ़ते थे। 8 शिक्षक[m] हमें चिड़ियाघर में ले जाते थे। 9. हम[m/m+f] सब काम हाथ से करते थे। 10. बच्चे[m.pl.] इमली के पेड़ पर चढ़ते थे, और इमली खाते थे।

1. maiṁ skūl paidal jātī thī. 2. ham choṭe ghar meṁ rahte the. 3. vah hameṁ hindī paṛhātā thā. 4. pitā jī hameṁ uphār dete the. 5. ham gangā meṁ tairte the. 6. maiṁ nāṭak meṁ bhāg letī thī. 7. ve pahāṛoṁ par chaṛhte the. 8. śikṣak hameṁ ciṛiyāghar meṁ le jāte the. 9. ham sab kām hāth se karte the. 10. bacce imlī ke peṛ par caṛhte the, aur imlī khāte the.

Key G 11.3

When my daughter was younger, she was not lazy. She was very diligent. She used to work at least twelve hours every day. She is still very hardworking, but she does not work as much as she used to work before. These days she works nine hours every day.

●●●●●

USE OF INFINITIVE AS NOUN

हिन्दी सीखना आसान है।	It is easy to learn Hindi.
Hindī sīkhnā āsān hai.	
सैर करना सेहत के लिए अच्छा होता है।	Leisure walking is good for health.

sair karnā sehat ke lie acchā hotā hai.

☞ **ना nā- ending changes to ne when followed by any post - postion , implied or expressed.**

मैं रोज़ हिन्दी सीखने जाती हूँ। I go to learn Hindi everyday.
maiṁ roz hindī sīkhne jātī hūṁ.
हम रोज़ सैर करने जाएँगे। We will go for a walk everyday.
ham roz sair karne jāeṁge.

G 12 FUTURE INDEFINITE

subj. + obj. + verbroot + ūṁgā, ūṁgī (with maiṁ)
ऊँगा^{m}, ऊँगी^{f} (with मैं)
oge, ogī (with tum),
ओगे^{m}, ओगी^{f} (with तुम)
egā, egī (with tū, vah, yah),
एगा^{m}, एगी^{f} (with तू, वह, यह)
eṁge, eṁgī (with ham, āp, ve, ye)
एँगे^{m} एँगी^{f} (with हम, आप, वे, ये)

written together
agree with the N and G of the subject

	subject	main verb masc.	main verb fem.
I will go.	maiṁ मैं	jāūṁgā जाऊँगा	jāūṁgī जाऊँगी
We will go.	ham हम	jāeṁge जाएँगे	jāeṁgī जाएँगी
You (intimate)will go.	tū तू	jāegā जाएगा	jāegī जाएगी
You (informal)will go.	tum तुम	jāoge जाओगे	jāogī जाओगी
You (formal;hon.) will go.	āp आप	jāeṁge जाएँगे	jāeṁgī जाएँगी
He/ She/ It (far)will go.	vah वह	jāegā जाएगा	jāegī जाएगी
He, she, it (near) will go.	yah यह	jāegā जाएगा	jāegī जाएगी

They (far) will go.	ve वे	jāeṁge जाएँगे	jāeṁgī जाएँगी
They (near) will go.	ye ये	jāeṁge जाएँगे	jāeṁgī जाएँगी
Who will go?	kaun कौन	jāegā जाएगा	jāegī ? जाएगी?
What will go?.	kyā क्या	jāegā ? जाएगा?	

COMPREHENSION

1. मैं[f] हिन्दी पढ़ाऊँगी।
   maiṁ Hindi paṛhāūṁgī.
   I[f..] will teach Hindi.
   (paṛhānā = to teach)
2. तुम[f] पढोगी।
   tum paṛhogī .
   You [f..inf.] will study.
   (paṛhnā = to study)
3. वे[f.pl] हिन्दी नहीं पढेंगी।
   ve [f.pl.] Hindi nahīṁ paṛheṁgī
   They[f..] (far) will not study Hindi.
4. वे[f.pl] तैरेंगी।
   ve[f.pl] taireṁgī.
   They[f.] (far) will swim.
   (tairnā = to swim)
5. आज हम[m/m+f] बैंक जाएँगे।
   āj ham baink jāeṁge.
   We[m/m+f] will go to bank today.
6. हम[m/m+f] बैंक से पैसा निकालेंगे ।
   ham baink se paisā nikāleṁge.
   We[m/m+f] will withdraw money from the bank.
7. मैं[f] बैंक में 'चैक' जमा कराऊँगी।
   maiṁ 'baink' mem jamā 'chaik' jamā karāūṁgī.
   I[f..] will teach Hindi.
   (karānā = to get done; jamā karānā = to deposit)

Ex. G 12.1 Read and translate into English:

1. मैं[m] अगले महीने ६० (साठ) वर्ष का हूँगा/होऊँगा। 2. इस साल बारिशें [f..pl]जल्दी होंगी। 3. मैं[m] रॉबर्ट को शाम को मिलूँगा। 4. आज से दुकानें[f..pl.] आठ बजे बन्द होंगी। 5. इस बार दीवाली[f.] किस महीने में होगी? 6. मैं[m] बड़ा होकर विदेश भ्रमण करूँगा। 7. हम[m.pl] अनाथों

के लिए एक स्कूल खोलेंगे। 8. आज हम सब$^{m/m.+f.}$ रेस्टोरेंट में खाएँगे। 9. आज मैं^{m} जल्दी सोऊँगा। 10. हम^{m} सारा कर्ज़ अगले साल लौटाएँगे। 11. तुम^{m} धूम्रपान करना कब छोड़ोगे?12. शायद वह^{m} अगले साल शादी करेगा। 13. क्या आप^{m} चाय लेंगे? 14. आप^{m} रोटी लेंगे या चावल? 15. वह^{m} आपको उधार देगा या नहीं? 16. मैं$^{f.}$ आपको सच्चाई बताऊँगी। 17. हम^{m} आपको डाक से सूचना भेजेंगे।18. मेरी अगली कार$^{f.sg.}$ लाल होगी। 19. इस दुकान पर सब कुछ मिलेगा। 20. हम$^{m.pl}$ कल वृन्दावन जाएँगे।

1. maiṁ^{m} agle mahīne sāṭh varṣ kā hūṁgā/hoūṁgā . 2. is sāl bāriśeṁ$^{f.pl}$ jaldī hoṁgī 3. maiṁ^{m} raubarṭ ko śām ko milūṁgā. 4. āj se dukāneṁ$^{f.pl}$ āṭh baje band hoṁgī 5. is bār dīvālī kis mahīne meṁ hogī? 6. maiṁ^{m} baṛā hokar videś bhramaṇ karūṁgā. 7. ham^{m} anāthoṁ ke lie ek skūl kholeṁge. 8.āj ham sab raisṭoraiṁṭ meṁ khāeṁge. 9. āj maiṁ^{m} jaldī soūṁgā. 10. ham$^{m/m+f}$ sārā karz agle sāl lauṭāeṁge. 11. tum^{m} dhūmrapān karnā kab choṛoge? 12. śāyad vah^{m} agle sāl śādī karegā. 13. kyā āp^{m} cāy leṁge? 14. āp^{m} roṭī leṁge yā cāval ? 15. vah^{m} āpko udhār degā yā nahīṁ? 16. maiṁ$^{f.}$ āpko saccāī batāūṁgī. 17. ham^{m} āpko ḍak se sūcnā bhejeṁge. 18. merī aglī kār^{f} lāl hogī. 19. apko is dukān par sab kuch milegā. 20. ham^{m} kal vṛndāvan jāeṁge.

WORD POWER

अगले महीने	agle mahīne	next month
वर्ष	varṣ	year
इस साल	is sāl	this year
बारिशें $^{f..pl}$	bāriśeṁ$^{f.pl}$	rains
जल्दी	jaldī	soon
मिलना	milnā	to meet
आठ बजे	āṭh baje	at 8o'clock
बन्द होना	band honā	to close
किस महीने में	kis mahīne meṁ	in which month

बड़ा होकर	baṛā hokar	here: when I grow up
विदेश	videś	foreign country
भ्रमण करना	bhramaṇ karnā	travel
अनाथ	anāth	orphan
मेरा ख़्याल है	merā khyāl hai	in my opinion
सारा	sārā	entire
कर्ज़	karz	loan
लौटाना	lauṭānā	to return
धूम्रपान करना	dhūmrapān karnā	to smoke
छोड़ना	choṛnā	here: to stop
शायद	śāyad	perhaps
शादी	śādī	marriage
उधार	udhār	loan
सच्चाई बताना	saccāī batānā	to tell the truth
डाक से	ḍak se	by mail
सूचना भेजना	sūcnā bhejnā	to send information
अगली कार$^{f.sg.}$	aglī kār^{f}	next car

Ex. G 12.2 Translate into Hindi

1. I^{m} will come tomorrow. 2. They$^{m/m+f}$ will help you. 3. Where will you$^{m.formal}$ go in summer? 4. My brother ^{m}will wait for me. 5. I$^{f.}$ will cook all day tomorrow. 6. I^{m} will exercise every day. 7. She will study in America next year. 8. She will live in the students hostel. 9. She will work hard. 10. She will become a doctor. 11. Father will watch television in the evening. 12. She will decide tomorrow. 13. I^{m} will never smoke. 14. In India, we $^{m/m+f}$ will speak Hindi only. 15. She will invite you.

Key G 12.1

1. I will be 60 next month. 2. Rains will begin early this year. 3. I will meet Robert in the evening. 4. From today shops will close at eight o'clock. 5. In which month will Diwali be this year? 6. When I grow up, I will travel abroad. 7. We will open a school for orphans. 8. Today we will all eat in the restaurant. 9. I think I will sleep early today.10. We will return all the debts next year. 11. When will you stop smoking.?12 Perhaps he will marry next year. 13. Will you have tea? 14. Will you have roti or rice? 15. Will he give you loan or not? 16. I will tell you the truth. 17. We will send you information by mail. 18. My next car will be red. 19. You will get everything at this shop. 20. Tomorrow, we will go to Vrindavan.

Key G 12.2

1.मैं कल आऊँगा। 2. वे आपकी मदद करेंगे। 3. आप गर्मी में कहाँ जाएँगे । 4. मेरा भाई मेरा इन्तज़ार करेगा। 5. आज मैं सारा दिन खाना बनाऊँगी। 6. मैं रोज़ व्यायाम करूँगा। 7. वह अगले साल अमरीका में पढ़ेगी। 8.वह छात्रावास में रहेगी। 9. वह मेहनत करेगी। 10. वह डाक्टर बनेगी।11. पिता जी शाम को दूरदर्शन देखेंगे। 12. वह कल फ़ैसला करेगी। 13. मैं धूम्रपान कभी नहीं करूँगा। 14.भारत में हम सिर्फ़ हिन्दी बोलेंगे। 15. वह आपको निमन्त्रण देगी।

1. maiṁ kal āūṁgā. 2. ve āpkī madad kareṁge. 3. āp garmī meṁ kahāṁ jāeṁge. 4. merā bhāī merā intzār daregā. 5. āj maiṁ sārā din khānā banāūṁgī.6. maiṁ roz vyāyām karūṁgā. 7. vah agle sāl amrīkā meṁ paṛhegī 8. vah chātrāvās meṁ rahegī. 9. vah mehnat karegī. 10. vah dauktạr banegī. 11. pitā jī śām ko dūrdarśan dekheṁge. 12. vah kal faislā karegī. 13. maiṁ dūmrapān kabhī nahīṁ karūṁgā. 14. bhārat meṁ ham sirf hindī meṁ boleṁge. 15. vah āp ko nimantraṇ degī.

●●●●●

G 13 PRESENT PROGRESSIVE

subj. + obj. + v.r. + rahā रहा (m.sg.) + hūṁ, ho, hai, haiṁ
rahe रहे (m.pl.) हूँ, हो, है, हैं
rahī रही (f. sg. and pl.)
written separately
agree with the N &G of the subj.

		main verb	auxiliary	
	subject	**masc.**	**fem.**	**verb**
I am going.	maiṁ मैं	jā rahā जा रहा	jā rahī जा रही	hūṁ. हूँ।
We are going.	ham हम	jā rahe जा रहे	jā rahī जा रही	haiṁ. हैं
You (int.) are going.	tū तू	jā rahā जा रहा	jā rahī जा रही	hai. है
You (infor.) are going.	tum तुम	jā rahe जा रहे	jā rahī जा रही	ho. हो
You (formal) are going.	āp आप	jā rahe जा रहे	jā rahī जा रही	haiṁ. हैं
He/ She/It (far) is going.	vah वह	jā rahā जा रहा	jā rahī जा रही	hai. है
He/She/It (near) is going.	yah यह	jā rahā जा रहा	jā rahī जा रही	hai. है
They(far) are going.	ve वे	jā rahe जा रहे	jā rahī जा रही	haiṁ. हैं
They (near) are going.	ye ये	jā rahe जा रहे	jā rahī जा रही	haiṁ. हैं

Who is going?	kaun कौन	jā rahā जा रहा	jā rahī जा रही	hai? है ?
What is going?.	kyā क्या	jā rahā जा रहा	hai? है ?	

COMPREHENSION

1. मैं^{m} नहा रहा हूँ। maiṁ nahā rahā hūṁ.	I(m.) am having a, bath
2. हम$^{f.}$ पढ़ रही हैं। ham paṛh rahī haiṁ	We(f.) are reading.
4. तुम^{m} कहाँ जा रहे हो? tum kahāṁ jā rahe ho?	Where are you (m.informal) going?
5. आप$^{f.}$ पढ़ा रही हैं। āp paṛhā rahī haiṁ.	You (f. formal)are teaching.
6. लड़का^{m} हँस रहा है। laṛkā haṁs rahā hai.	The boy is laughing.
8. वे$^{m.pl.}$ मंदिर जा रहे हैं। ve$^{m.pl.}$ mandir jā rahe haiṁ	They(m.far) are going to the temple .
9. लड़कियाँ$^{f.pl.}$ गा रही हैं। laṛkiyāṁ$^{f.pl.}$ gā rahī haiṁ.	The girls are singing.
10. कौन चिल्ला रहा है ? kaun cillā rahā hai?	Who is shouting?

Ex. G 13. 1 Translate into English:

1. आप^{m} कहाँ जा रहे हैं? 2. लड़क$^{m.pl.}$ खेल रहे हैं। 3. हम$^{f.pl.}$ पढ़ रही हैं। 4. माता जी खाना पका रही हैं। 5. औरतें$^{f.pl.}$ गा रही हैं। 6. सब्ज़ीवाला$^{m.}$ सब्ज़ी बेच रहा है। 7. माली$^{m.}$ फूल लगा रहा है। 8. कुत्ता$^{m.}$ भौंक रहा है। 9. वे$^{m.pl.}$ बात कर रहे हैं। 10. हम$^{m.pl.}$ टी.वी. देख रहे हैं। 11. पक्षी$^{m.pl.}$ उड़ रहे हैं। 12. आप$^{m.hon.}$ क्या सोच रहे हैं ?13. वह$^{m.}$ कुछ खोज रहा है। 14. एमी कहीं जा रही है। 15. सुबह से बर्फ़ पड़ रही है। 16. मैं$^{f.}$ समाचार पत्र पढ़ रही हूँ 17. धोबी^{m} कपड़े धो रहा है। 18. लड़के शोर मचा रहे हैं। 19. दर्ज़ी कपड़े सी रहा है। 20. नाई बाल काट रहा है।

PRESENT PROGRESSIVE: EXERCISES

1. āp kahāṁ jā rahe haiṁ.2.laṛke khel rahe haiṁ.3. ham paṛh rahī haiṁ. 4. mātā jī khānā pakā rahī haiṁ. 5. aurteṁ gā rahī haiṁ. 6. sabzīvālā sabzī bec rahā hai. 7.mālī phūl lagā rahā hai. 8. kuttā bhauṁk rahā hai. 9. ve bāt kar rahe haiṁ. 10. ham ṭ ī. vī. dekh rahe haiṁ. 11. pakṣī uṛ rahe haiṁ. 12. āp kyā soc rahe haiṁ? 13. vah kuch khoj rahā hai. 14. emī kahīṁ jā rahī hai. 15. subah se barf paṛ rahī hai. 16. maiṁ samācār patra paṛh rahī hūṁ. 17. dhobhī kapṛe dho rahā hai. 18. laṛke śor macā rahe haiṁ. 19. darzī kapṛe sī rahā hai. 20. nāī bāl kāṭ rahā hai.

Ex. G 13.2 Translate into Hindi:

1. Train[f.] is coming from Agra. 2 Travelers[m] are waiting for the train. 3. They[m] are bargaining with the porters. 4 Some people are getting on the train. 5 Some people are getting off the train. 6 . The train is departing. 7. The train is going to Delhi. 8. Some travelers are talking among themselves. 9. Some are peeping out of the window. 10. Some are buying magazine. 11. Some people are going into the post office. 12. Some are coming out of the post office. 13. One man is buying some postage stamps. 14. A woman is buying envelopes. 15. The posman is talking to the boss.

Ex. G 13. 3 Translate into Hindi:

1. They[m] eat rice. 2. They[m] are eating rice. 3. Father reads newpaper every day. 4. Father is reading newpaper at this time. 5. Usually I[f] drink coffee. 6. I[f] am drinking coffee now. 7. It rains here every year in June. 8. At this time it is raining here. 9. we[m] watch news on TV every day. 10. At this time, we[m] are watching news on TV. 11. The woman (far) is sleeping. 12. What is happening? 13. Mother is cooking. 14. Servant is cleaning the house. 15. Children are playing.

Key G 13.1

1. Where are you going? 2. The boys are playing. 3. We are studying. 4. Mother is cooking food. 5. Women are singing. 6.The greengrocer is selling vegetables. 7. Gardner is planting flowers. 8. Dog is barking. 9.They are talking.10. We are watching T.V. 11. The birds are flying. 12. What are you thinking? 13. He is looking for something. 14. Amy is going somewhere. 15. It has been snowing since morning. 16. I am reading the newspaper. 17. Washerman is washing clothes. 18. Boys are making noise. 19. Tailor is stiching clothes. 20. The barbar is cutting the hair.

Key G 13.2

1. गाड़ी^f. आगरा से आ रही है। 2. यात्री^m.pl गाड़ी का इंतज़ार कर रहे हैं। 3. वे^m.pl कुलियों से मोलभाव कर रहे हैं। 4. कुछ लोग गाड़ी में चढ़ रहे हैं। 5. कुछ लोग गाड़ी से उतर रहे हैं। 6. गाड़ी^f.sg. छूट रही है। 7. गाड़ी दिल्ली जा रही है। 8. कुछ यात्री^m.pl आपस में बात कर रहे हैं। 9. कुछ खिड़की से बाहर झाँक रहे हैं। 10. कुछ पत्रिका ख़रीद रहे हैं। 11. कुछ लोग डाक घर के अन्दर जा रहे हैं। 12. कुछ डाक घर से बाहर निकल रहे हैं। 13. एक आदमी डाक टिकट ख़रीद रहा है। 14. एक औरत लिफ़ाफ़े ख़रीद रही है। 15. डाकिया अधिकारी से बात कर रहा है।

1. gāṛi āgrā se ā rahī hai. 2. yātrī gāṛī kā intzār kar rahe haiṁ. 3. ve kuliyoṁ ke sāth molbhāv kar rahe haiṁ. 4. kuch log gārī par caṛh rahe haiṁ. 5. kuch log gāṛī se utar rahe haiṁ. 6. gārī chūṭ rahī hai. 7. gāṛī dillī jā rahī hai. 8. kuch yātrī āpas meṁ bāteṁ kar rahe haiṁ. 9. kuch khiṛkī se bāhar jhāṁk rahe haiṁ. 10. kuch patrikā <u>kh</u>arīd rahe haiṁ. 11. kuch log ḍāk ghar ke andar jā rahe haiṁ. 12. kuch log ḍāk ghar se bāhar nikal rahe haiṁ.13. ek ādmī ḍāk ṭikaṭ kharīd rahā hai. 14. ek aurat lifāfe kharīd rahī hai. 5. ḍākiyā adhikārī se bāt kar rahā hai.

Key G 13.3

1. वे^m.pl. चावल खाते हैं। 2. वे^m.pl.. चावल खा रहे हैं। 3. पिता जी रोज़ अख़बार पढ़ते हैं। 4. पिता जी इस समय़ अख़बार पढ़ रहे हैं। 5. मैं^f. प्रायः काफ़ी पीती हूँ। 6. मैं^f. इस समय काफ़ी पी रही हूँ। 7. यहाँ प्रति वर्ष जून में बारिश^f. होती है। 8. यहाँ इस समय बारिश^f. हो रही है। 9. हम^m.pl. प्रतिदिन दूरदर्शन पर समाचार देखते हैं। 10..हम^m.pl. इस समय दूरदर्शन पर समाचार देख रहे है। 11. औरत^f.सो रही है। 12. क्या हो रहा है ? 13. माँ पका रही है। 14. नौकर^m घर^m साफ़ कर रहा है। 15. बच्चे^m.pl खेल रहे हैं।

1. ve cāval khāte haiṁ. 2. ve cāval khā rahe haiṁ. 3. pitā jī roz a<u>kh</u>bār paṛhte haiṁ. 4. pitā jī is samay a<u>kh</u>bār paṛh rahe haiṁ. 5. maiṁ prāyaḥ kaufī pītī hūṁ. 6. maiṁ is samay kaufī pī rahī hūṁ. 7. yahāṁ prati varṣ jūn meṁ bāriś hotī hai. 8. yahāṁ is samay bāriś ho rahī hai. 9. ham prati din dūrdarśan par samācār dekhte haiṁ. 10. ham is samay dūrdarśan par samācār dekh rahe haiṁ. 11. aurat^f. so rahī hai. 12.kyā ho rahā hai? 13. māṁ pakā rahī hai. 14. naukar ghar sāf kar rahā hai. 15. bacche khel rahe haiṁ.

●●●●●

G 14 PAST PROGRESSIVE

subj. + obj. + v.r. + rahā रहा (m.sg.) + thā, the, thī, thīṁ
rahe रहे (m.pl.) था, थे, थी, थीं
rahī रही (f. sg. and pl.)
written separately
agree with the N and G of the subject

		main verb + auxiliary verb	
	subject	**masc.**	**fem.**
I was going.	maiṁ मैं	jā rahā thā जा रहा था	jā rahī thī जा रही थी
We were going.	ham हम	jā rahe the जा रहे थे	jā rahī thīṁ जा रही थीं
You (int.) were going.	tū तू	jā rahā thā जा रहा था	jā rahī thī. जा रही थी
You (infor.)were going.	tum तुम	jā rahe the जा रहे थे	jā rahī thīṁ जा रही थीं
You (formal) were going.	āp आप	jā rahe the जा रहे थे	jā rahī thīṁ जा रही थीं
He/ She/ It (far) was going.	vah वह	jā rahā thā जा रहा था	jā rahī thī जा रही थी
He/ She/ It (near) was going.	yah यह	jā rahā thā जा रहा था	jā rahī thī जा रही थी
They(far) were going.	ve वे	jā rahe the जा रहे थे	jā rahī thīṁ जा रही थीं।

They (near) were going.	ye ये	jā rahe the जा रहे थे	jā rahī thīṁ जा रही थीं।
Who was going?	kaun कौन	jā rahā thā? जा रहा था ?	jā rahī thī? जा रही थी ?
What was going?.	kyā क्या	jā rahā thā ? जा रहा था ?	

COMPREHENSION

1. मैं[m] खा रहा था ।
maiṁ khā rahā thā.
I was eating.
2. हम[f.pl] पढ़ रही थीं ।
ham paṛh rahī thīṁ
We were reading.
3. तू[m] क्या कर रहा था ?
tū kyā kar rahā thā?
What were you doing?
4. तुम[m] कहाँ जा रहे थे ?
tum kahāṁ jā rahe the?
Where were you going?
5. आप[f.hon.] पढ़ा रही थीं ।
āp paṛhā rahī thīṁ.
You were teaching.
6. वह[m.] हँस रहा था ।
vah haṁs rahā thā.
He (far) was laughing.
7. वह[f.] सो रही थी ।
vah so rahī thī.
She (far) was sleeping.
8. आदमी[m.pl] मंदिर जा रहे थे ।
ādmī mandir jā rahe the.
Men were going to the temple .
9. औरतें[f.pl.] गा रही थीं।
aurteṁ gā rahī thīṁ.
Women were singing.
10. कौन[m] चिल्ला रहा था ?
kaun cillā rahā thā.?
Who was shouting?
11. क्या हो रहा था ?
kyā ho rahā thā.?
What was happening?

PAST PROGRESSIVE: EXERCISES

Ex. G 14.1 Translate into English:

1. डाकियाm डाक बाँट रहा था। 2. अख़बारवालाm अख़बार बेच रहा था। 3. लड़कियाँf.pl. नाच रही थीं। 4. लड़केm.pl. गा रहे थे। 5. गाहकm सामान ख़रीद रहे थे। 6. दुकानदारm सामान बेच रहे थे। 7. डाक्टरm मरीज़ की जाँच कर रहा था। 8. मरीज़m.sg. दर्द से कराह रहा था। 9. माँ डाँट रही थीं। 10. बच्चाm. सुन रहा था। 11. क्याm. हो रहा था ? 12. बच्चेm.pl. खेल रहे थे। 13. माँ खाना पका रही थीं। 14. दादा जी बच्चों को कहानीf सुना रहे थे। 15. नौकरm घर साफ़ कर रहा था। 16. हमm टी.वी. देख रहे थे । 17. धोबीm कपड़े धो रहा था। 18. धोबिनf कपड़े सुखा रही थी।

1. ḍākiyām. ḍāk bāṁṭ rahā thā. 2 .akhbārvālā m akhbār bec rahā thā. 3. laṛkiyāṁ nāc rahī thiṁ. 4. laṛkem.pl. gā rahe the. 5. gāhakm sāmān kharīd rahe the. 6. dukāndār sāmān bec rahā thā. 7. ḍaukṭarm marīz kī jāṁch kar rahā thā. 8. marīzm dard se karāh rahā thā. 9. māṁ dāṁṭ rahī thī. 10. baccām sun rahā thā. 11. kyā m ho rahā thā.? 12. baccem.pl. khel rahe the. 13. māṁ khānā pakā rahī thīṁ. 14. dādā jī baccoṁ ko kahānī sunā rahe the. 15. naukarm ghar sāf kar rahā thā. 16. hamm T.V. dekh rahe the.17. dhobīm kapṛe dho rahā thā. 18. dhobinf. kapṛe sukhā rahī thī.

Ex. G 14.2 Translate into Hindi

1. The teacher was teaching. 2. The students were learning. 3. The teacher was asking. 4. The students were answering. 5. The teacher was explaining. 6. The students were understanding. 7. The birds were chirping. 8. The bell was ringing. 9. An old woman was crossing the road. 10. Someone was knocking at the door.11.Beggar was begging. 12. Boys were shouting.

Ex. G 14.3 Translate into Hindi

1.He used to teach. 2. He was teaching. 3. He used to play the sitar. 4. He was playing the sitar. 5. She used to learn English. 6.She was learning English. 7. What used to happen there? 8. What was happening there. 9. Children used to play. 10. Children were playing.11. Mother used to cook. 12. Mother was cooking. 13. Grandfather used to narrate stories. 14. Grandfather was narrating a story. 15. Th watchman used to guard the house.. 16. Servant was guarding the house.

Key G 14.1

1. Postman was delivering the mail. 2. The newspaperman was selling newspaper. 3. The girls were dancing. 4. The boys were singing. 5. Customers were buying

goods. 6. Shopkeepers were selling goods. 7. The patient was groaning in pain. 8. The doctor was examining the patient. 9. Mother was scolding. 10.Child was listening. 11. What was happening? 12. Children were playing . 13. Grandfather was narrating a story to the children. 14. Mother was cooking food. 15. Servant was cleaning the house. 16. We were watching TV. 17. Washerman was washing clothes. 18. The washerwoman was drying clothes.

Key G 14.2

1. शिक्षक सिखा रहा था। 2. छात्र सीख रहे थे 3. शिक्षक पूछ रहा था। 4. छात्र उत्तर दे रहे थे। 5. शिक्षक समझा रहा था। 6. छात्र समझ रहे थे। 7. चिड़ियाएँ चहक रही थीं। 8. घण्टी बज रही थी। 9. एक बूढ़ी औरत सड़क पार कर रही थी। 10. कोई दरवाज़ा खटखटा रहा था। 11. भिखारी भीख माँग रहा था। 12. लड़के चिल्ला रहे थे।

1. śikṣak^{m} sikhā rahā thā. 2. chātra$^{m.pl.}$ sīkh rahe the. 3. śikṣak pūch rahā thā. 4. chātra uttar de rahe the. 5. śikṣak samjhā rahā thā. 6. chātra samajh rahe the. 7.ciṛiyāeṁ$^{f.pl.}$ cahak rahī thīṁ. 8. ghaṇṭī$^{f.}$ baj rahī thī. 9. ek būṛhī aurat$^{f.}$ saṛak pār kar rahī thī. 10. koī^{m} darvāzā khaṭkhaṭā rahā thā. 11. bhikhārī^{m} bhīkh māṁg rahā thā. 12. laṛke$^{m.pl.}$ chillā rahe the.

Key G 14.3

1. वह पढ़ाता था। 2. वह पढ़ा रहा था। 3. वह सितार बजाता था। 4. वह सितार बजा रहा था। 5. वह अंग्रेज़ी सीखती थी। 6. वह अंग्रेज़ी सीख रही थी। 7. वहाँ क्या होता था? 8. वहाँ क्या हो रहा था? 9. बच्चे खेलते थे। 10. बच्चे खेल रहे थे। 11. माँ खाना पकाती थीं। 12. माँ खाना पका रही थीं। 13.दादा जी कहानी सुनाते थे। 14. दादा जी कहानी सुना रहे थे। 15. चौकीदार घर की रखवाली करता था 16. चौकीदार घर की रखवाली कर रहा था।

1. vah^{m} paṛhātā thā. 2. vah^{m} paṛhā rahā thā. 3. vah^{m} sitār bajātā thā. 4. vah^{m} sitār bajā rahā thā. 5. vah$^{f.}$ aṅgrezī sīkhtī thī. 6. vah$^{f.}$ aṅgrezī sīkh rahī thī. 7. vahāṁ kyā hotā thā. 8. vahāṁ kyā ho rahā thā. 9. bacce$^{m.pl.}$ khelte the. 10. bacce khel rahe the. 11. māṁ khānā pakātī thīṁ. 12. māṁ khānā pakā rahī thīṁ. 13. dādā jī kahānī sunāte the. 14. dādā jī kahānī sunā rahe the. 15. caukīdār$^{m.}$ ghar kī rakhvālī kartā thā. 16. caukīdār ghar kī rakhvālī kar rahā thā.

●●●●●

G 15 PAST SIMPLE TENSE

So far we have done language structures in the Present Simple Tense, Past Habitual Tense, Present and Past Progressive Tenses, as well as the Future Simple Tense. In all these structures, the verb conjugation is in agreement with the subject.

Before doing past simple tense, I would like you to know a couple of more things about Hindi.

Remember that in Hindi:

- Subject of a sentence is not always in the nominative case. In several language structures, the Subject is in the oblique case followed by postpositions 'ko', 'ne', 'se' etc.
- In all such cases where the Subject is followed by some postposition, the verb conjugation is not in agreement with the Number and Gender of the subject.
- It is only a noun or a pronoun clause which is not followed by any postposition that can control the verb conjugation. In case the subject is followed by any postposition, the verb is conjugated in agreement with the N and G of the object.
- If the Subject as well as the Object are followed by some postposition, both lose the power to control the verb conjugation. In all such cases, the verb is free of both the Subject and the Object and only masculine singular third person form is used.

☞ In the past simple tense, and present or past perfect tenses, we have two language structures each; one for intransitive activities where the verb conjugation is in agreement with the subject, and another one for transitive activities where the verb conjugation is in agreement either with the object, or in masculine singular third person.

PAST SIMPLE TENSE: VERB INTRANSITIVE

Past Simple Tense : Intransitive Activity

subject + verb root + ā / yā $^{m.sg}$, e $^{m.pl.}$, ī $^{f.sg}$, īṁ $^{f.pl}$.
आ / या $^{m.sg}$, ए $^{m.pl}$, ई $^{f.sg}$, ईं $^{f.pl}$

to agree with N & G of the subject

Some example of intransitive verbs:

Infinitive	**m.sg.**	**m.pl.**	**f.sg.**	**f.pl.**
baiṭhnā	baiṭhā	baiṭhe	baiṭhī	baiṭhīṁ
बैठना	बैठा	बैठे	बैठी	बैठीं
(to sit)				
uṭhnā	uṭhā	uṭhe	uṭhī	uṭhīṁ
उठना	उठा	उठे	उठी	उठीं
(to get up)				
dauṛnā	dauṛā	dauṛe	dauṛī	dauṛīṁ
दौड़ना	दौड़ा	दौड़े	दौड़ी	दौड़ीं
(to run)				
ronā	royā	roe	roī	roīṁ
रोना	रोया	रोए	रोई	रोईं
(to cry)				
ānā	āyā	āe	āī	āīṁ
आना	आया	आए	आई	आईं
(to come)				

☞ **The verbs जाना 'jānā' to go and , होना 'honā' to be, are irregular.**

जाना 'jānā' to go changes to:

gayā	gae	gaī	gaīṁ
गया	गए	गई	गईं

होना 'honā' to be changes to:

huā	hue	huī	huīṁ
हुआ	हुए	हुई	हुईं

PAST SIMPLE TENSE: VERB INTRANSITIVE

COMPREHENSION:

1. मैं[f.] बाज़ार गई। maiṁ bāzār gaī.	I went to bazar.
2. वह[m.sg] कब आया? vah kab āyā.	When did he come?
3. मेरी बहन[f.sg] कल आई। merī bahan kal āī	My sister came yesterday.
4. गाड़ी[f.sg.] अभी–अभी पहुँची। gāṛī abhī - abhī pahuṁcī.	The train arrived just now.
5. बच्चा[m.sg] क्यों रोया? baccā kyoṁ royā.	Why did the child cry?
6. पिता जी अमरीका से क्या लाए? pitā jī amrīkā se kyā lāe.	What did father bring from America?

☞ लाना **'lana' is an exceptional verb; though by nature transitive, is used intransitively. Subject in the past tense too is in the nominative case.**

7. तुम[m.inf.] कहाँ गए? tum kahāṁ gae?	Where did you (m. informal) go?
8. तुम[m.inf.] कब आए? tum kab āe?	When did you(m. informal) come?
9. तुम[m.inf.] कैसे आए? tum kaise āe?	How did you(m. informal) come?
10. आप[m.formal] कितने बजे उठे? āp kitne baje uṭhe?	What time did you(m.formal) get up?
11.. बच्चा कितने बजे सोया? baccā kitne baje soyā?	What time did the child sleep?
12. चोर किधर भागा? cor kidhar bhāgā?	Which way did the thief run?

Past Simple Tense : Transitive Verb

(subj. + ने 'ne') + obj. + (v.r. + ā / yā $^{m.sg}$, e $^{m.pl.}$, ī $^{f.sg}$, īṁ$^{f.pl}$.)
आ/या $^{m.sg}$, ए $^{m.pl.}$, ई $^{f.sg}$, ईं $^{f.pl}$

to agree with N & G of the object*

* If object is either not given (sentence 7, 8) or has a postposition after it (sentences 9, 10) use only masculine singular form of the verb, that is (v.r. + आ ā /या yā).

☞ Rules of combining the the subject with ने 'ne':

- Common nouns followed by ने 'ne' follow the same rules as any noun in the oblique case. In writing , ने 'ne' is written separately from the noun.
- Pronouns followed by ने 'ne' slightly vary from the oblique forms which they take when followed by other postpositions such as को ko, से se, में meṁ, पर par etc.

  (pronoun + ने 'ne') are written together .

मैंने	maiṁne	हमने	hamne
तूने	tūne	तुमने	tumne
		तुम लोगोंने	tum logoṁne
आपने	āpne	आपलोगोंने	āp logoṁne
उसने	usne	उन्होंने	unhoṁne isne
इसने	isne	इन्होंने	inhoṁne
किसने	kisne	किन्होंने	kinhoṁne

Examples of transitive verbs:

khānā	khāyā	khāe	khāī	khāīṁ
खाना	खाया	खाए	खाई	खाईं
(to eat)				

PAST SIMPLE TENSE: VERB TRANSITIVE

pakānā पकाना (to cook)	pakāyā पकाया	pakāe पकाए	pakāī पकाई	pakāīṁ पकाईं
becnā बेचना (to sell)	becā बेचा	bece बेचे	becī बेची	becīṁ बेचीं
kharīdnā खरीदना (to buy)	kharīdā खरीदा	kharīde खरीदे	kharīdī खरीदी	kharīdīṁ खरीदीं
paṛhnā पढ़ना (to study)	paṛhā पढ़ा	paṛhe पढ़े	paṛhī पढ़ी	paṛhīṁ पढ़ीं
socnā सोचना (to think)	socā सोचा	soche सोचे	socī सोची	socīṁ सोचीं

☞ **The verbs करना karnā (to do), लेना lenā (to take), देना denā (to give) are irregular.**

करना (karnā) **'to do' changes to**

	kiyā किया	kie किए	kī की	kīṁ कीं

लेना (lenā) **'to take' changes to**

	liyā लिया	lie लिए	lī ली	līṁ लीं

देना (denā) **to give** **changes to**

	diyā दिया	die दिए	dī दी	dīṁ दीं

COMPREHENSION

1. मैंने चावल[m.sg.] खाया। — I ate rice.
   maiṁne cāval khāyā.

2. मैंने केले m.pl. खरीदे। maiṁne kele kharīde.	I bought bananas.
3. उसने रोटी f.sg. खाई। usne roṭī khāī.	He/She ate roti.
4. उसने साड़ियाँ f.pl. खरीदीं। usne sāṛiyāṁ kharīdīṁ.	He / She bought saris.
5. कविता ने पाठ m.sg. पढाया। Kavita ne pā ṭh paṛhāyā	Kavita taught the lesson.
6. नौकर ने घर m.sg. साफ़ किया। naukar ne ghar sāf kiyā.	The servant cleaned the house.

Transitive verb, but object not explicitly stated:

7. मैंने सोचा। maiṁne socā.	I thought.
8. हमने देखा। hamne dekhā	We saw.

सोचना socnā (to think) , देखना dekhnā (to look), are transitive verbs. However, the object of thought or vision is not given, hence the gender of these is not known. In such cases verb ending is m.sg., such as सोचा socā , देखा dekhā in the sentences 7, 8 given above.

Transitive verb, but object is followed by postposition.

9. अध्यापक ने छात्रों को बुलाया। adhyāpak ne chātroṁ ko bulāyā.	The teacher called the students.

☞ छात्रों chātroṁ is m.pl. noun. The verb ending should be बुलाए bulāye **.**

Because of ko को after it, verb ending is mas. sg., that is bulāyā बुलाया।

10. मैंने इस किताब को पढ़ा। maiṁne is kitāb ko paṛhā.	I read this book.

☞ किताब kitāb is fem.sg. noun. The verb ending should be पढ़ी paṛhī

Because of को ko after it, verb ending is mas. sg., that is पढ़ा paṛhā.

Exceptions:

☞ Some transitive verbs such as बोलना bolnā (to speak), समझना samajhnā(to understand), भूलना bhūlnā (to forget), लाना lānā (to bring), are used intransitively. The subject is not followed by 'ne', and the verb agrees with the subject in the past simple, present and past perfect tenses.

For example:

He forgot.	vah $^{m.sg.}$ bhūlā	वह $^{m.sg.}$ भूला।
I(m.) spoke.	maiṁ $^{m.sg.}$ bolā	मैं $^{m.sg.}$ बोला।

☞ Also some intransitive verbs such as खाँसना khaṁsnā (to cough), छींकना chīṁknā (to sneeze), are used transitively. The subject is followed by ने 'ne' in the past simple, present and past perfect tenses, and the verb is always in the m. sg. third person.

He sneezed.	usne chīṁkā.	उसने छींका।
I coughed.	maine khāṁsā.	मैंने खाँसा।

Ex. G 15.1 Translate into English:

1. उसने मुझको दिया। 2. मैंने उससे लिया। 3. मैंने उसको बुलाया। 4. हमने उनसे पूछा। 5. उन्होंने हमको बताया। 6. मैंने उसको कहा। 7. मैंने बहुत सीखा। 8. आपने क्या देखा? 9. क्या आपने सुना? 10. उन्होंने क्या सोचा?

1. usne mujhko diyā. 2. maiṁne usse liyā. 3. maiṁne usko bulāyā. 4. hamne unse pūchā. 5. unhoṁne hamko batāyā. 6. maiṁne usko kahā. 7. maiṁne bahut sīkhā. 8. apne kyā dekhā. 9. kyā āpne sunā? 10. unhoṁne kyā socā.

Ex. G 15.2 Translate into Hindi:

1. I fed the dog. 2. He/ She apologized to everybody. 3. Everybody forgave him/ her. 4. Mother gave the gift 5. The child took the gift and said thanks. 6. The dog bit the boy. 7. I saw nothing. 8. He/ She heard everything. 9. He/ She did not reply. 10. Did you find out?

Ex. G 15.3 Say in Hindi ,what all you did yesterday?

Q. What time did you get up in the morning?

A. I got up in the morning at 5 o'clock.

Q. What did you do after that?

A. I had a bath. I brushed my teeth. I had breakfast at 7 o'clock in the morning. I read the newpaper. I went to Sanskrit class at 10 o'clock.

Q. What time did you have lunch/dinner?

A. I had lunch at one o'clock.
I had dinner at 8 o'clock.

Q. Did you eat at home?

A. No, I did not eat at home. I ate out.

Q. What else did you do?

A. I went to the bank. I withdrew money from the bank. Then after I went to the market and bought some things. I went to the post office too. There I bought some postage stamps and some aerograms. I returned home at about 8 o'clock. Italked for a while with my children. I watched television and ate with them. We went to bed at about 10 o'clock.

WORD POWER

to withdraw money	paise nikālnā	पैसे निकालना
post office	ḍāk ghar	डाकघर
postage stamps	ḍāk ṭikaṭ	डाक टिकट
aerograms	havāī patra	हवाई पत्र
to return	lauṭnā	लौटना
a short while	thoṛī der	थोड़ी देर
to talk	bāt karrnā	बात करना

Key G 15.1

1.He/ She gave me. 2. I took from him/her. 3.I called him. 4. We asked them. 5. They told us. 6. I said to him/her. 7. I learnt a lot. 8. What did you see? 9. Did you hear? 10. What did they think?

Key G 15.2

1. मैंने कुत्ते को खिलाया। 2. उसने सबसे माफ़ी[f.sg] माँगी। 3. सबने उसको माफ़ किया। 4. माँ ने उपहार[m.sg] दिया। 5. बच्चे ने उपहार[m.sg] लिया और धन्यवाद[m.sg] कहा। 6. कुत्ते ने लड़के को काटा। 7. मैंने कुछ नहीं देखा।8. उसने सब सुना। 9. उसने

उत्तर$^{m.sg}$ नहीं दिया। 10. आपने पता$^{m.sg}$ लगाया?

1. miaṁne kutte ko khilāyā. 2. usne sabse māfī$^{f.sg}$ māṁgī. 3. sabne usko māf kiyā. 4. māṁ ne uphār$^{m.sg}$ diyā. 5. bacce ne uphār$^{m.sg}$ liyā aur dhanyavād$^{m.sg}$ kahā. 6. kutte ne larke ko kāṭā. 7. maiṁne kuch nahīṁ dekhā. 8. usne sab sunā. 9. usne uttar$^{m.sg}$ nahīṁ diyā. 10. āpne patā $^{m.sg}$ lagāyā.

Key G 15.3

Q. आप सुबह कितने बजे उठे/उठीं ?
A. मैं सुबह पाँच बजे उठा/उठी ।
Q. उसके बाद आपने क्या किया ?
A. मैं नहाया / नहाई।
मैंने दाँत साफ़ किए।
मैंने सुबह सात बजे नाश्ता किया।
मैंने अख़बार पढा।
मैं दस बजे संस्कृत की कक्षा में गया/गई।
Q. आपने दिन का खाना/ रात का खाना कितने बजे खाया ?
A. मैनें दिन का खाना एक बजे खाया।
मैंने रात का खाना आठ बजे खाया।
Q. क्या आपने घर पर खाया?
A. जी नहीं, मैंने घर पर नहीं खाया।
मैंने बाहर खाया।
Q. आपने और क्या–क्या किया?
A. आपने और क्या–क्या किया?
मैं बैंक गया/गई। मैंने बैंक से पैसे निकाले। उसके बाद मैंने बाज़ार जाकर कुछ सामान ख़रीदा। मैं डाकघर भी गया/गई। वहा मैंने कुछ डाक टिकट और कुछ हवाई पत्र ख़रीदे।
मैं शाम को लगभग आठ बजे घर लौटा/लौटी। मैंने थोड़ी देर अपने बच्चों से बात की। मैंने उनके साथ दूरदर्शन देखा और खाना खाया। लगभग दस बजे हम सो गए।

Q. āp subah kitne baje uṭhe / uṭhīṁ?

A. maim subah pāṁc baje uṭhā / uṭhī.

Q. uske bād āpne kyā kiyā?

A. maiṁ nahāyā /nahāī . maiṁne dāṁt sāf kie.
maiṁne subah sāt baje nāśtā kiyā . maiṁne akhbār paṛhā.
maiṁ das baje saṁskṛt kī kakṣā meṁ gayā/ gaī

Q. āpne din kā khānā/ rāt kā khānā kitne baje khāyā.?

A. maiṁne din kā khānā ek baje khāyā.
maiṁne rāt kā khānā āṭh baje khāyā.

Q. kyā āpne ghar par khāyā?

A. jī nahīṁ, maiṁne ghar par nahīṁ khāyā.
maiṁne bāhar khāyā .

Q. āpne aur kyā-kyā kiyā?

A. maiṁ bank gayā/gaī . maiṁne bank se paise nikāle. uske bād maiṁne bāzār jākar kuch sāmān kharīdā. maiṁ ḍāk ghar bhī gayā/gaī. vahāṁ maiṁne kuch ḍāk ṭikaṭ aur kuch havāī patra kharīde.
maiṁ śām ko āṭh baje ghar lauṭā/ lauṭī. maiṁne thoṛī der apne baccoṁ se bāt kī. maiṁne unke sāth dūrdarśan dekhā aur khānā khāyā. lagbhag das baje ham so gae.

Read: एक कौवा ek kauva pg. 259

●●●●●

G 16 PRESENT AND PAST PERFECT

Present Perfect Tense in Hindi is exactly like the Past Simple Tense we did in the previous lesson except that at the end you are required to put suitable present form of 'honā' to agree with subject or object depending upon whether it is an intransitive or transitive activity.

Present Perfect Tense : Intransitive Verb

subj. + v.r. + ā / yā $^{m.sg}$, e $^{m.pl.}$, ī $^{f.sg/pl}$, + hūṁ, ho, hai, haiṁ

आ/या $^{m.sg}$, ए $^{m.pl}$, ई $^{f.sg/pl}$, + हूँ, हो, है, हैं.

to agree with N & G of the subj.

COMPREHENSION

1. बच्चा $^{m.sg.}$ क्यों रोया है?
   baccā kyoṁ royā hai.
   Why has the child cried?
2. डाकिया $^{m.sg.}$ आया है ।
   ḍākiyā āyā hai.
   The postman has come.
3. पिता जी अमरीका से क्या लाए हैं?
   pitā jī amrīkā se kyā lāe haiṁ.
   What has father brought from America?
4. तुम कैसे आए हो?
   tum kaise āe ho?
   How have you come?
5. छात्र क्यों हँसे हैं?
   chātra kyoṁ haṁse haiṁ.
   Why have the students laughed?
6. चोर किस ओर भागा है।
   cor kis or bhāgā hai?
   In which direction has the thief run away?

Present Perfect Tense : Transitive Activity

subj. + obj. + v.r. + ā / yā m.sg, e m.pl., ī f.sg/pl, + hai, haiṁ
+ ने आ/या m.sg, ए m.pl, ई f.sg/pl, + है, हैं
to agree with N & G of the object

COMPREHENSION:

1. उसने रोटी f.sg. खाई है। usne roṭī khāī hai.	He/She has eaten roti.
2. उसने साड़ियाँ f.pl. खरीदी हैं। usne sāṛiyāṁ kharīdīṁ haiṁ.	He / She has bought saris.
3. डालिया ने खाना m.sg पकाया है। Daliyah ne khānā pakāyā hai.	Daliah has cooked food.
4. कविता ने पाठ m.sg पढाया है। Kavita ne pāṭh paṛhāyā hai.	Kavita has taught the lesson.
5. नौकर ने घर m.sg. साफ़ किया है। naukar ne ghar sāf kiyā hai.	The sevant has cleaned the house.
6. छात्र ने किताब f.sg. पढ़ी है। chātra ne kitāb paṛhī hai.	The student has read the book.

☞ **Transitive verb, but object not explicitly stated:**

7. मैंने सोचा है। maiṁne socā hai.	I have thought.
8. हमने देखा है। hamne dekhā hai.	We have seen.

सोचना sochnā , देखना dekhnā are transitive verbs. However, the object of thought or vision is not given, hence their gender is unknown. In such cases verb ending is m.sg., that is सोचा sochā, देखा dekhā followed by है hai.

PAST PERFECT: VERB INTRANSITIVE

☞ **Transitive verb, but object is followed by postposition.**

9. अध्यापक ने छात्रों को बुलाया है। adhyāpak ne chātroṁ ko bulāyā hai.	The teacher has called the students.

chātroṁ छात्रों is m.pl. noun followed by the postposition ko को। Hence the verb ending is mas. sg., that is bulāyā बुलाया followed by hai है।

- Past Perfect Tense is exactly like the Present Perfect Tense but for the use of past form of होना 'hona' as helping verb at the end.

Past Perfect Tense : Intransitive Activity

subj. + v.r.+ ā / yā $^{m.sg.}$, e $^{m.pl.}$, ī $^{f.sg/pl}$ + thā, the, thī, thīṁ
आ/या $^{m.sg}$, ए $^{m.pl}$, ई $^{f.sg/pl}$, + था, थे, थी, थीं
to agree with N & G of the subj.

COMPREHENSION:

1. बच्चा $^{m.sg.}$ क्यों रोया था? baccā kyoṁ royā thā?	Why had the child cried?
2. डाकिया $^{m.sg.}$ आया था। dākiyā āyā thā.	The postman had come.
3. पिता जी अमरीका से क्या लाए थे? pitā jī amrīkā se kyā lāe the.	What had father brought from America?
4. तुम $^{m.inf.}$ कैसे आए थे? tum kaise āe the?	How had you (m. informal) come?
5. छात्र क्यों हँसे थे? chātra kyoṁ haṁse the.	Why had the students laughed?

6. चोर किस ओर भागा था?
cor kis or bhāgā thā?

In which direction had the thief run?

Past Perfect Tense : Transitive Activity

subj. + obj. + v.r. + ā / yā m.sg, e m.pl., ī f.sg./pl, + thā, the, thī, thīṁ
+ ने आ/या m.sg., ए m.pl., ई f.sg./pl, + था, थे, थी, थीं

to agree with N & G of the object

COMPREHENSION

1. उसने रोटी f.sg खाई थी।
usne roṭī khāī thī.

He/She had eaten roti.

2. उसने साड़ियाँ f.pl. खरीदी थीं।
usne sāṛiyāṁ kharīdī thīṁ.

He / She had bought saris.

3. डालिया ने खाना m.sg पकाया था।
Daliyah ne khānā pakāyā thā.

Daliah had cooked food.

4. धोबी ने कपड़े m.sg धोए थे।
dhobī ne kapṛe dhoe the.

The washerman had washed the clothes.

5. छात्र ने किताब f.sg पढ़ी थी।
chātra ne kitāb paṛhī thī.

The student had read the book.

☞ **Transitive verb, but object not explicitly stated:**

6. मैने सोचा था।
maiṁne socā thā.

I had thought.

7. हमने देखा था।
hamne dekhā thā.

We had seen.

सोचना sochnā (to think) , देखना dekhnā (to see) are transitive verbs. However, the object of thought or vision is not given, hence the gender of these unknown. In such cases verb ending is m.sg., that is सोचा sochā , देखा dekhā followed by था thā.

PRESENT AND PAST PERFECT:EXERCISES

☞ **Transitive verb, but object is followed by postposition.**

8. अध्यापक ने छात्रों को बुलाया था।
adhyāpak ne chātroṁ ko bulāyā thā.
The teacher had called the students.

छात्रों chātroṁ (students) is m.pl. noun followed by the postposition को ko ; hence the verb ending is mas. sg., that is बुलाया bulāyā followed by था thā.

Ex. G 16. Translate into English:

(1)

- आप कभी भारत गए हैं?
- जी, मैं उन्नीस सौ नव्वे में भारत गया था।
- क्या आप एथन्स , लन्दन और पैरिस भी गए हैं?
- जी, मैं एथन्स नहीं गया, परन्तु लन्दन और पैरिस गया हूँ।
- आप वहाँ कब–कब गए थे?
- मैं लन्दन सन् उन्नीस सौ अट्ठासी, माह मई में गया था, और पैरिस में उन्नीस सौ नवासी, माह जुलाई में गया था।
- आपको कौन–सा शहर ज़्यादा पसन्द आया?
- मुझे दोनों स्थान अच्छे लगे।
नमस्ते। फिर मिलेंगे।

(2)

- लगता है, मैं अपनी* बरसाती अन्दर छोड़ आई हूँ।
- तुम्हें पक्का पता है कि जब तुम अन्दर गई थीं, तुम्हारे पास बरसाती थी?
- बिलकुल पक्का। बरसाती कुछ गीली थी, इस लिए मैंने उसे सीट के नीचे रखा था।
- चलो, वापस चलें और जल्दी से ढूँढ लें।

*** See page 135 for अपना, अपने, अपनी**

(1)

- āp kabhī bhārat gae haiṁ.
- jī, maiṁ unnīs sau navve meiṁ gayā thā.
- kyā āp ethens, landan aur pairis bhī gae haiṁ?
- jī, maiṁ ethens nahīṁ gayā, parantu landan aur pairis gayā hūṁ.
- āp vahāṁ kab-kab gae the?
- maiṁ landan san unnīs sau aṭṭhāsī, māh maī meṁ gayā thā, aur pairis meṁ unnīs sau navāsī, māh julāī meṁ gayā thā.
- ākpo inmeṁ kaun sā śahar zyādā acchā lagā.
- mujhe donoṁ sthān acche lage.
- namaste. phir mileṁ

(2)

- lagtā hai maiṁ apnī* barsātī andar choṛ āī hūṁ.
- tumheṁ pakkā patā hai ki jab tum andar gaī thīṁ, tumhāre pās barsātī thī.
- bilkul pakkā.
- barsatī kuch gīlī thī, is lie maiṁne use sīṭ ke nīce rakhā thā.
- calo vāpas caleṁ, aur jaldī se dhūṁdh leṁ.

Glossary:

उन्नीस सौ नव्वे unnīs sau navve 1990; उन्नीस सौ अट्ठासी unnīs sau aṭṭhāsī1988; उन्नीस सौ नवासी unnīs sau navāsī 1979; कौन–सा kaun- sā which one?; शहर śahar city; दोनों donoṁ both; स्थान sthān place; लगता है lagtā hai it seems; पक्का पता होना paccā patā honā to know for sure; बिलकुल पक्का bilkul paccā absolutely sure; बरसाती barsatī raincoat; जल्दी से jaldī se quickly; ढूँढना to ḍhūṁḍhnā look for; पिछले हफ़्ते pichle hafte last week.

Key G 16.

(1)

- Have you ever been to India?
- Yes, I went to India in 1990.
- Have you been to Athens, London and Paris too?
- Well, I have not been to Athens, but I have been to London

and Paris.

- When did you go there?
- I went to London in 1988 in May, and to Paris in 1989 July.
- Which city you liked more?
- I liked them both.
- Namaste. See you again.

(2)

- It seems I left my raincoat inside.
- Are you sure that when you went in, you had the raincoat.
- Absolutely sure. The raincoat was a little wet, therefore I had put it underneath the seat.
- Come, let's go back and look for it quickly

●●●●●

Use of दिखाई देना dikhāī denā (to be visible)
सुनाई देना sunāī denā (to be audible)

(subj.+ को ko) + obj. + dikhāī denā/ sunāī denā
दिखाई देना/सुनाई देना
to agree with N and G of the obj.

मुझको एक मोर$^{m.}$ दिखाई दे रहा है। mujhko ek mor$^{m.}$ dikhāī de rahā hai.	I can see a peacock.
मुझको कुछ आवाज़ें$^{f.pl.}$ सुनाई दे रही हैं। mujhko kuch āvāzeṁ$^{f.pl.}$ sunāī de rahī haiṁ.	I can hear some sounds.

G 17 apnā, apne, apnī ' one's own' (अपना अपने अपनी)

Use of apnā, apne, apnī (अपना अपने अपनी) corresponds to English 'one's own'. It is used adjectively and agrees with the Number and Gender of the noun it modifies. The object in the sentence or a clause belongs to the subject.

COMPREHENSION

1. यह मेरी अपनी कहानी[f.sg.] है। yaha merī apnī kahānī hai.	This is my own story.
2. पिता जी ने अपने पैसे[m.pl.] अपनी अलमारी[f.sg.] में रखे। pitā jī ne apne paise apnī almārī meṁ rakhe.	Father kept his money in his cupboard.
3. कमला ने मुझे अपना पता[m..sg.] दिया; kamlā ne mujhe apnā patā diyā.	Kamla gave me her address.
4. मैंने उसको अपना पता[m..sg.] दिया। maiṁne use apnā patā diyā.	I gave her my address.

☞ New learners are often confused about when to use possessive pronouns and when to use reflexive pronouns. Let me explain this with the help of a couple of examples. In sentence 5, the subject is expected to tell someone else's father (in this case the speaker's father). Hence the possessive pronoun is used. But in sentence 6, the subject is being asked to tell his own father. Hence the reflexive 'apne' has been used.

5. तुम मेरे पिता जी को बताओ। tum mere pitā jī ko batāo.	You tell my father.
6. तुम अपने पिता जी को बताओ। tum apne pitā jī ko batāo.	You tell your father.

7. वह मेरे घर आया। — He came to my house.
vah mere ghar āyā.

8. वह अपने घर गया। — He went to his (own) house.
vah apne ghar gayā.

9. मुझे आपकी भाषा पसन्द है। — I like your language.
mujhe apkī bhāṣā pasand hai.

10. मुझे अपनी भाषा पसन्द है। — I like my (own) language.
mujhe apnī bhāṣā pasand hai.

Reduplicative use of अपना-अपना, अपने-अपने, अपनी-अपनी

11. अपना–अपना नाम बताओ। — Tell your (respective) names.
apnā-apnā nām batāo.

12. अपनी–अपनी पत्रिका पढ़ो। — Read your (respective) magazines.
apnī-apnī patrikā paṛho.

13. अपने–अपने कपड़े तहाओ। — Fold your (respective) clothes.
apne-apne kapṛe tahāo.

14. हम अपने–अपने पिता जी को बताएँगे। — We(m.) will tell our (respective) fathers.
ham apne-apne pitā jī ko bataeṁge.

Ex. G 17. Translate into Hindi.

1. I will go to my (own) house. 2. He will go to my house.3. She is reading her/ his book. 4. She is reading her (own) book. 5. Tell me her name. 6. Tell me your name. 7. He likes my country. 8. I like my country. 9. Open your (respective) books. 10. Go to your (respective) homes.

Key G 17.

1. मैं अपने घर जाऊँगी। 2. वह मेरे घर जाएगा। 3. वह उसकी किताब पढ़ रही है। 4. वह अपनी किताब पढ़ रही है। 5. मुझको उसका नाम बताओ।6. मुझको अपना नाम बताओ। 7. वह मेरा देश पसन्द करता है। 8. मैं अपना देश पसन्द करता हूँ। 9. अपनी–अपनी किताब खोलिए। 10. अपने–अपने घर जाइए।

1.maiṁ apne ghar jāūṁgī. 2.vah mere ghar jāegā. 3. vah uskī kitāb paṛh rahī hai. 4. vah apnī kitāb paṛh rahī hai. 5. mujhko uskā nām batāo.6. mujhko apnā nām batāo. 7. vah merā deś pasand kartā hai. 8. maiṁ apnā deś pasand kartā hūṁ. 9. apnī-apnī kitāb kholie. 10. apne-apne ghar jāie.

Reading: Deevali pg. 288

●●●●●

Commonly used expressions by native speakers when somebody dies are:

मर जाना, की मृत्यु होना mar jānā , kī mṛtyu honā

to die (these expressions are less used)

Preferred expressions showing respect for the departed soul are:

का स्वर्गवास होना kā svargvās honā

(one’s going to heavenly abode)

का देहान्त होना kā dehānt honā

(one’s body coming to an end. The soul is believed to be eternal)

G18 Uses of the verb लगना lagnā

The verb लगना **lagnā** in Hindi has several uses.

1. लगना **lagnā** can be used to express feelings of hunger, thirst, cold, heat etc.
2. लगना **lagnā** can be used as sense verb such as 'to look', 'to feel', 'to seem','to sound', 'to taste' etc.
3. लगना **lagnā** is used in the sense of fixtures, collection, assembly etc of some living or nonliving object on , in, or at a certain place.
4. लगना **lagnā** is used in combination with the inflected infinitive to express the beginning of some action.

■ Use of लगना **lagnā to express feeling of hunger, thirst, cold etc.**

☞ In Hindi, this use of ' लगना **lagnā** ' requires the subject in the oblique case followed by the postposition **को** 'ko' such as '**मुझको** mujhko, **हमको** hamko, **तुमको** tumko etc. The feeling is expressed by using the relevant abstract noun followed by the verb लगना **lagnā** in the required tense to agree with the gender of the abstract noun used. The corresponding English sentence has the subject in the nominative case and the feeling is expressed in adjectival form.

1. मुझको सुबह–सुबह भूख$^{f.sg}$ लगती है। mujhko subah-subah bhūkh lagtī hai.	I feel hungry in the early morning. (bhūkh lagnā = to feel hungry)
2. उसको रोज़ रात को प्यास$^{f.sg}$ लगती थी। usko roz rāt ko pyās lagtī thī.	He/She used to feel thirsty at night every day. (pyās lagnā = to feel thirsty)
3. उसको ठण्ड$^{f.sg}$ लग रही है। usko ṭhaṇḍ lag rahī hai.	He/She is feeling cold. (ṭhaṇḍ lagnā = to feel cold)
4. उनको गर्मी$^{f.sg}$ लग रही थी।	They were feeling hot.

unko garmī lag rahī thī.	(garmī lagnā to feel hot)
5. हमको वहाँ बहुत उमस[f.sg] लगी। hamko vahāṁ bahut umas lagī.	We felt very humid there. (umas lagnā to feel muggy)
6. आपको यहाँ घुटन[f.sg] लगेगी। āpko yahāṁ ghuṭan lagegī.	You will feel suffocated here. (ghuṭan lagnā to feel suffocated)

■ लगना lagnā as sense verb

In Hindi just this one verb लगना lagnā can be used for all sense verbs such as to look, to seem, to tase, to sound, to feel etc.

sentence structure requires: subject + adjective + lagnā

☞ **लगना lagnā agrees with the number and gender of the subject, in the required tense.**

1. यह मेज[f.sg] चिपचिपी[adj.] लगती है। yah mez[f.] cipcipī lagtī hai.	This table feels sticky.
2. यह कपड़ा[m.sg] खुरदुरा[adj.] लग रहा है। yah kapṛā khurdurā lag rahā hai.	This cloth feels rough.
3. ये सेब[m.] ताज़े[adj.] नहीं लगे। ye seb tāze nahīṁ lage .	These apples did not taste fresh.
4. यह खाना[msg.] मुझको बासी[adj.] लगा। yah khānā mujhko bāsī lagā.	This food tasted stale to me.
5. यह मकान[m.sg] काफ़ी महँगा[adj.] लगता है। yah makān kāfī mahaṁgā lagtā hai.	This building looks quite expensive.
6. वह[m.sg] ईमानदार[adj.] लगता है। vah imāndār lagtā hai.	He sounds honest.

VERB lagnā: EXERCISES

■ **लगना lagnā in the sense of fixure, collection or assembly of living or nonliving objects at a certain place. It agrees with the number and gender of the object that is fixed , or collected at , on or in a certain place.**

1. घड़ी[f.sg] दीवार पर लगी है। gharī dīvār par lagī hai.	The clock is on the wall.
2. इस कमरे में ए .सी[m.] लगा है। is kamre meṁ e.cī lagā hai.	There is an A.C in this room.
3. ज़मीन पर कपड़ों का ढेर[m.] लगा है। zamīn par kapṛoṁ kā ḍher lagā hai.	There is a pile of clothes on the floor.
4. यहाँ भीड़ क्यों लगी है? yahāṁ bhīṛ kyoṁ lagī hai?	Why has the crowd collected here?

■ **लगना lagnā preceded by inflected infinitive (v.r. + ने 'ne') is used to express the beginning of some activity. In this sentence structure, the subject is always in the nominative case and the verb लगना agrees with number and gender of the subject.**

1. बच्चा[m..sg.] हँसने लगता है। baccā haṁsne lagtā hai.	The child begins to laugh.
2. खिलाड़ी[m.] खेलने लगते हैं। khilāṛī khelne lagte haiṁ.	The atheletes begin to play.
3. वह[m.] रोज़ सुबह–सुबह संगीत–अभ्यास करने लगता था। vah roz subah-subah saṅgīt-abhyās karne lagtā thā.	He used to begin to practice music early morning every day.
4. यात्री[m.] भजन गाने लगे। yātrī bhajan gāne lage.	Travelers began to sing hymns.

5. अध्यापक^m. पढ़ाने लगे हैं। — Teachers have begun to teach.
adhyāpak paṛhāne lage haiṁ.

6. लड़कियाँ^f.pl. नाचने लगी थीं। — The girls had begun to dance.
laṛkiyāṁ nācne lagī thīṁ.

7. जल्दी बारिश^f.sg होने लगेगी। — Soon it will begin to rain.
jaldī bāriś hone lagegī.

8. माँ पूजा करने लगेंगी। — Mother will begin to do puja.
māṁ pūjā karne lagemgī.

Ex. G 18.1: Read aloud and translate into English:

(1)

- आपकी साड़ी बहुत सुन्दर लग रही है।
- सच! धन्यवाद!
- लगता है आपने अभी–अभी ख़रीदी है।
- यह नई नहीं है।
- लगती तो नई है! यह बहुत महँगी भी लगती है। यह कितने की है?
- पता नहीं। यह मेरी माता जी से उपहार था।

(2)

- आज सुबह मैं गुसलख़ाने में गई।
  वहाँ बहुत फिसलन लग रही थी। मैं गिरते–गिरते बची।
  अब मैं अपने पढ़ने के कमरे में हूँ । पढ़ने की मेज़ भी चिपचिपी लग रही है।
  क्या किसीने इसपर कुछ गिराया है?

(3)

- इस अगरबत्ती की महक बहुत बढ़िया लग रही है। क्या यह भारतीय है? आपने कहाँ से ख़रीदी?
- यह भारतीय नहीं है। मेरे पति इसे जापान से लाए थे।

(4)

- यह मिठाई बहुत स्वादिष्ट लग रही है। आपने कौन–सी दुकान से

ख़रीदी?

- माता जी ने घर पर बनाई है।
- विश्वास नही होता ! ऐसे लगता है जैसे किसी मिठाई बनानेवाले ने बनाई हो ।
  और ये समोसे? क्या ये भी माता जी ने बनाए हैं?
- जी नहीं। ये हमारी नौकरानी ने बनाए हैं।
- कमाल है ! आपके घर में सभी इतने अच्छे पकवान बनाते हैं!

(5)

- मैंने हाल में एक तबला ख़रीदा है। मुझे इसकी आवाज़ ठीक नहीं लगती।
- ज़रा बजाइए। मुझे तो इसकी आवाज़ बिल्कुल ठीक लग रही है।
  वास्तव में, मैंने अभी तक जितने तबले सुने हैं, मुझे इसकी आवाज़ सब से अच्छी लगी है।

- āpkī sārī bahut sundar lag rahī hai.
- sac! dhanyăvād!
- lagtā hai āpne abhī-abhī kharīdī hai.
- yah naī nahīṁ hai.
- lagtī to naī hai! yah bahut mahaṁgī bhī lagtī hai. yah kitne kī hai?
- patā nahīṁ, yah merī mātā jī se uphār thā.

(2)

- āj subah maiṁ gusal<u>kh</u>āne meṁ gaī.
  vahāṁ bahut phislan lag rahī thī. maiṁ girte-girte bacī.
  ab maiṁ apne paṛhne ke kamre meṁ hūṁ.
  paṛhne kī mez bhī cipcipī lag rahī hai.
  kyā kisī ne ispar kuch girāyā hai?

(3)

- is agarbattī kī mahak bahut baṛhiyā lag rahī hai.
- kyā yah bhārtīyă hai ? āpne kahāṁse <u>kh</u>arīdī.

- yah bhārtīyă nahīṁ hai. mere pati ise jāpān se lāe the.

(4)

- yah miṭhāī bahut svādiṣṭ lag rahī hai. āpne kaun-sī dukān se kharīdī?
- mātā jī ne ghar par banāī hai.
- viśvās nahīṁ hotā! aise lagtā hai jaise kisī miṭhāī banānevāle ne banāī ho.
- aur ye samose? kyā ye bhī mātājī ne banāe haiṁ?
- jī nahīṁ. ye hamārī naukrānī ne banāe haiṁ.
- kamāl hai! āpke ghar meṁ sabhī itne acche pakvān banāte haiṁ!

(5)

- maiṁne hāl meṁ ek tablā kharīdā hai. mujhe iskī āvāz ṭhīk nahīṁ lagtī.
- zarā bajāie. mujhe to iskī āvāz bilkul ṭhīk lag rahī hai. vāstav meṁ, maiṁne abhī tak jitne table sune haiṁ, mujhe iskī āvāz sabse acchī lagī hai.

Key G 18.1

(1)

- Your saree looks very beautiful!
- Really! Thanks.
- It seems you just bought it.
- It is not new.
- It looks new. It looks expensive too. How much was this?
- I don't know. It was a gift from my mother.

(2)

- This morning I went into the bathroom. It felt very slippery there.
  I almost fell.
  Now I am in my study room. The study table feels sticky too.
  Did anyone drop something on it?

(3)

- This incense smells terrific! Is this Indian? Where did you buy it?
- This is not Indian. My husband brought it from Japan.

(4)

- This sweet tastes delicious. Which shop did you buy it at?

VERB lagnā: EXERCISES

- Mother has prepared it at home.
- Incredible! It tastes as if prepared by some confectioner. And these samosas'? Has mother made them too.
- No, our maid servant has prepared them.
- Vow! In your house, everybody prepares such nice delicacies!

(5)

- Recently I bought a 'tabla'. It doesn't sound good to me.
- Just play it! It sounds perfect to me. In fact, of all the 'tablas' that I have listened to so far, this sounds the best to me.

To be used to doing something

- **subj. + obj. + का kā , के ke, की kī * + आदी ādī + होना honā**
  (noun / v.r.+ ne)

  * kā, ke, kī and honā agree with the N & G of the subject.

  * ādī is invariable.

1. मैं[f.sg.] चाय की आदी हूँ । — I am used to tea.
   maiṁ cāy kā ādī hūṁ.
1. मैं[m.sg] जल्दी सोने की आदी हूँ । — I am used to drinking tea.
   maiṁ jaldī sone kī ādī hūṁ

- **(subj. + को ko) + obj. + की kī * + आदत ādat + होना honā**

1. मुझको चाय की आदत है । — I am used to tea.
   mujhko cāy kā ādat hai.
2. मुझको जल्दी सोने की आदत है । — I am used to drinking tea.
   mujhko jaldī sone kī ādat hai

   * kī is invariable regardless of the N & G of the subject.

G19 Use of the verb 'jānanā' जानना
to know

The verb जानना jānanā 'to know' has several uses:

■ **The use of जानना jānanā in the sense of knowing a person.**

1.	मैं[f] कविता को जानती हूँ। maiṁ Kavita ko jāntī hūṁ.	I know Kavita.
2.	हम अपने नए पड़ोसी को नहीं जानते। ham apne nae paṛosī ko nahīṁ. jānte.	We don't know our new neighbor.

■ **The use of जानना jānanā in the sense of knowing a fact, or having some information.**

3.	मैं[f] जानती हूँ कि कविता हिन्दी पढ़ाती है। maiṁ jāntī hūṁ. ki Kavita Hindī paṛhātī hai.	I know that Kavita teaches Hindi.
4.	हम जानते हैं कि आज बारिश होगी। ham jānte haiṁ ki āj bāriś hogī.	We know that it will rain today.

■ **The use of जानना jānanā in the sense of knowing how to do something:**

5.	वह[m] अंग्रेज़ी जानता है। vah angrezī jāntā hai.	He knows English.

5. वह^f खाना **बनाना** जानती है । — She knows how to cook food.
vah khānā banānā jāntī hai.

6. क्या **आप^f तैरना** जानती हैं? — Do you know how to swim?
kyā āp tairnā jāntī haiṁ?

■ **Corresponding to the use of जानना jānanā in the sense of knowing a fact, or having some information , the native speakers alternatively use two other expressions, that are मालूम होना 'malūm honā', or पता होना 'patā honā.**

☞ **The point to remember is that jāṇanā agrees with the subject in the nominative case, where as these two expressions मालूम होना 'malūm honā', or पता होना 'patā honā are used with the subject followed by the postposition को 'ko.**

क्या आप^m जानते हैं? — Do you know? (= Do you have the information?)
kyā āp jānte haiṁ?

=

क्या आपको पता है?
kyā āpko patā hai?

=

क्या आपको मालूम है?
kyā āpko mālūm hai?

जी, मैं^m जानता हूँ। — Yes, I know. (Yes, I have the information.)
Jī, maiṁ jāntā hūṁ.

=

जी, मुझको पता है।
Jī, mujhko patā hai?

=

जी, मुझको मालूम है।

Jī, mujhko mālūm hai?

जी नहीं, मैं^m नहीं जानता।	No, I don't know.
Jī nahīṁ, maiṁ nahīṁ jāntā.	(No, I don't have the information.)

=

जी नहीं, मुझको पता नहीं।
Jī nahīṁ, mujhko patā nahīṁ.

=

जी नहीं, मुझको मालूम नहीं।
Jī nahīṁ, mujhko mālūm nahīṁ.

■ **Corresponding to the use of the verb जानना jānanā in the sense of ' to know how to do some thing', the native speakers alternatively use the verb आना ānā (to come).**

☞ **Remember that the verb आना ānā in the sense of 'to come' agrees always with the subject in the nominative case.**

☞ **However, आना ānā in the sense of 'how to do something' agrees with the N and G of the object, and subject is in the oblique case followed by the postposition को 'ko'.**

Examples.

1. मैं^m अंग्रेज़ी जानता हूँ।	I know English.
maiṁ aṅgrezī jāntā hūṁ.	
1a. मुझको अंग्रेज़ी आती है।	
mujhko aṅgrezī ātī hai.	
2. वह^f तैरना जानती है ।	I know how to cook food.
vah tairnā jāntī hūṁ.	
2a. उसको तैरना आता है।	
usko tairnā ātā hai.	

VERB jānanā: EXERCISES

Ex. G 19.1 Rewrite the sentences given below using the verb जानना jānanā instead of पता होना patā honā or मालूम होना mālūm honā. Also translate them into English.

1. मुझे पता है माता जी इस समय कहाँ हैं। 2. मुझे मालूम है यह दूध ताज़ा है। 3. आपको पता है कल रेलगाड़ियों की हड़ताल होगी। 4. आपको मालूम है कि बनारस भगवान शिव की नगरी है। 5. आपको मालूम है कि फ़रवरी में भारत काफ़ी गरम होता है। 6. आपको मालूम है न्यूयॉर्क की जनसंख्या कितनी है। 7. मुझे मालूम है तुम अगले हफ़्ते विदेश जा रही हो। 8. उसको पता है कि मैं आजकल भारत में हूँ। 9. उसको कुछ मालूम नहीं था। 10. सिर्फ़ मुझे मालूम था।

1. mujhe patā hai mātā jī is samay kahāṁ haiṁ. 2. mujhe mālūm hai yah dūdh tāzā hai. 3. āpko patā hai kal relgāṛiyoṁ kī haṛtāl hogī. 4 āpko mālūm hai ki banāras bhagvān shiva kī nagrī hai. 5. āpko mālūm hai ki farvarī meṁ bhārat kāfī garam hotā hai. 6. āpko mālūm hai nyuyaurk kī jansaṅkhyā kitnī hai. 7. mujhe mālūm hai tum agle hafte videś jā rahī ho. 8. usko patā hai ki ājkal maiṁ bhārat meṁ hūṁ. 9. usko kuch mālūm nahīṁ thā. 10 sirf muje mālūm thā.

Ex. G 19.2 Translate into Hindi using the verb आना ānā in the sense of knowing or having the ability to do something.

1. I know how to play the tabla. 2. She can sing classical music. 3. He cannot cook. 4. I know English but I don't know Spanish. 5. My sister knows both these languages. 6. I don't know how to drive a car. 7. Do you know how to row a boat. 8. Can you swim? 9. I know how to bargain. 10. He doen't know how to teach properly.

Key G 19.1

1. मैं जानता/जानती हूँ माता जी इस समय कहाँ पर हैं। 2. मैं जानता/जानती हूँ यह दूध ताज़ा है। 3. आप जानते/जानती हैं कल रेलगाड़ियों की हड़ताल होगी। 4. आप जानते/जानती हैं कि बनारस भगवान शिव की नगरी है। 5. आप जानते/जानती हैं कि फ़रवरी में भारत काफ़ी गरम होता है। 6. आप जानते/जानती हैं न्यूयॉर्क की जनसंख्या कितनी है। 7. मैं जानता/जानती हूँ तुम अगले हफ़्ते विदेश जा रही हो। 8. वह जानता/जानती है कि

मैं आजकल भारत में हूँ । 9. वह कुछ नहीं जानता था ।/जानती थी। 10. सिर्फ़ मैं जानता था ।/जानती थी।

1. maiṁ jāntā/jāntī hūṁ mātā jī is samay kahāṁ par haiṁ. 2.maiṁ jāntā/jāntī hūṁ yah dūdh tāzā hai. 3. āp jānte/jāntī haiṁ kal relgāṛyoṁ kī haṛtāl hogī. 4 āp jānte/ jāntī haiṁ kī banāras bhagvān shiva kī nagrī hai. 5. āp jānte/jāntī haiṁ ki farvarī meṁ bhārat kāfī garam hotā hai. 6. āp jānte/jāntī haiṁ nyuyaurk kī jansaṅkhyā kitnī hai. 7. maiṁ jāntā/jāntī hūṁ tum agle hafte videś jā rahī ho. 8. vah jāntā/jāntī hai ki ājkal maiṁ bhārat meṁ hūṁ. 9. vah kuch nahīṁ jāntā thā. /jāntī thī. 10 sirf maiṁ jāntā thā. /jāntī thī

Translation:

1. I know where mother is at this time. 2. I know this milk is fresh. 3. Do you know that tomorrow there is railway strike. 4. Do you know that Banaras is the city of Lord Shiva. 5. Do you know India is quite hot in February. 6. Do you know what the population of New York is. 7. I know you are going abroad next week. 8. He/ She knows that I am in India these days. 9. He knew nothing. 10. Only I knew.

Key G 19.2

1. मुझको तबला^m बजाना आता है। 2. उसको शास्त्रीय संगीत^m आता है। 3. उसको खाना बनाना नहीं आता। 4. मुझको अंग्रेज़ी आती है परंतु स्पैनिश नहीं आती। 5. मेरी बहन को दोनों भाषाएँ^f.pl. आती हैं। 6. मुझको कार^f चलानी नहीं आती । 7. तुमको नाव^f खेनी आती है। 8. तुमको तैरना आता है। 9. मुझको मोलभाव^m करना आता है। 10. उसको ठीक से पढ़ाना नहीं आता।

1. mujhko tablā bajānā ātā hai. 2. usko śāstriyā saṅgīt ātā hai. 3. usko khānā banānā nahīṁ ātā. 4. mujhko aṅgrezī ātī hai parantu spainiś nahīṁ ātī. 5. merī bahan ko donoṁ bhāṣāeṁ ātī haiṁ. 6. mujhko kār^f. calānī nahīṁ ātī. 7. tumko nāv^f. khenī ātī hai. 8. tumko tairnā ātā hai. 9. mujhko molbhāv karna ātā hai.

10. usko ṭhīk se paṛhānā nahīṁ ātā.

●●●●●

G 20 Use of the verb चाहना cāhnā (to want)

subject + object *+ चाहना + होना

agree with N and G of the subject in the appropriate tense

* object of desire may be some noun or activity. If object is some activity, infinitive form of the verb is used.

■ **when object wanted is activity:**

Present simple tense

1. मैं[f] अंग्रेज़ी सीखना चाहती हूँ। — I want to learn English.
   maiṁ aṅgrezī sīkhnā cāhtī hūṁ.

2. अब मैं[f] आराम[m] करना चाहती हूँ। — Now I want to rest.
   ab maiṁ ārām karnā cāhtī hūṁ.

Past habitual tense

3. हम[m] अमरीका जाना चाहते थे। — We wanted to go to America.
   ham amrīkā jānā cāhte the.

4. माता जी पूजा करना चाहती थीं। — Mother wanted to do 'pooja'.
   mātā ji pūjā karnā cāhtī thīṁ.

Future simple tense

5. पिता जी अख़बार पढ़ना चाहेंगे। — Father would want to read the newpaper
   pitā jī akhbār paṛhnā cāheṁge.

6. दादा जी बागीचे में टहलना चाहेंगे। — Grandfather would want to walk in the garden.
   dādā jī bāgīce meṁ ṭahlnā cāheṁge.

THE VERB cāhnā ' to want'

■ **when object wanted is a noun:**

Present Simple Tense

1. आप[m] क्या चाहते हैं? āp kyā cāhte haiṁ?	What do you want ?
2. मैं[m] दो कमरे का मकान चाहता हूँ। maiṁ do kamre kā makān cāhtā hūṁ.	I want a two room house.

Past habitual

3. आप[m] क्या चाहते थे ? āp kyā cāhte the?	What did you want?
6. मैं[m] दो कमरे का मकान चाहता था। maiṁ do kamre kā makān cāhtā thā.	I wanted a two room house.

Future simple

5. आप[m] क्या चाहेंगे? āp kyā cāheṁge?	What would you want?
6. मैं[m] दो कमरे का मकान चाहूँगा। maiṁ do kamre kā makān cāhūṁgā.	I would like to have a two room house.

Ex. G 20.1 Translate into English:

1. मैं आपसे मिलना चाहता हूँ। 2. आप इस होटल में रहना चाहते हैं? 3. वे यहाँ एक दिन/ एक हफ़्ता रहना चाहते हैं। 4. क्या आप दिल्ली में नहीं रहना चाहते? 5. मेरी बहन जर्मन भाषा सीखना चाहती थी। 6. मैं काफ़ी/ चाय/ दूध/ पानी पीना चाहती थी। 7. हम अपने कपड़े धोना चाहते थे। 8. तुम अपने जूते साफ़ करना चाहोगे? 9. वे (m. hon.) आज पत्र नहीं लिखना चाहेंगे। 10. वह नए शब्द सीखना चाहेगा। 11.मेरी माता जी मुझको डाक्टर

बनाना चाहती थीं। 12.मेरे माता–पिता मुझको इन्जीनियर बनाना चाहते थे। 13. कोई यह नहीं जानना चाहता था कि मैं^{m} क्या करना चाहता था। 14. मैं^{m} हर वक्त केवल खेलना चाहता था। 15. अब मेरे माता–पिता चाहते हैं कि मैं उनकी सेवा करूँ। 16. मेरी पत्नी^{f} चाहती है कि मैं बहुत धन कमाऊँ। 17. मेरे बच्चे चाहते हैं कि मैं उनके साथ खेलूँ। 18. अब भी कोई यह नहीं जानना चाहता कि मैं क्या चाहता हूँ। 19. मैं सब कुछ त्यागकर एकान्त में रहना चाहता हूँ। 20. आप क्या चाहते हैं?

1. maiṁ āp se milnā cāhtā hūṁ.2. āp is hoṭal meṁ rahnā cāhte haiṁ? 3. ve yahāṁ ek din / haftā rahnā cāhte haiṁ. 4. kyā āp dillī meṁ nahīṁ rahnā cāhte? 5. merī bahan jarman bhāṣā sīkhnā cāhtī thī .6. maiṁ kaufi / cāy / dūdh/ pānī pīnā cāhtī thī. 7. ham apne kapṛe dhonā cāhte the. 8. tum apne jūte sāf karnā cāhoge? 9. ve āj patra nahīṁ likhnā cāheṁge. 10. vah nae śabd sīkhnā cāhegā. 11. merī mātā jī mujhko daukṭar banānā cāhtī thīṁ. 12. mere mātā-pitā mujhko injīniyar banānā cāhte the. 13. koī yah nahīṁ jananā cāhtā thā ki maiṁ kyā karnā cāhtā thā. 14. maiṁ har vakt keval khelnā cāhtā thā. 15. ab mere mātā-pitā cāhte haiṁ ki maiṁ unkī sevā karūṁ. 16. merī patnī cāhtī hai ki maiṁ bahut dhan kamāūṁ. 17. mere bacce cāhte haiṁ ki maiṁ unke sāth khelūṁ. 18. ab bhī koī yah nahīṁ jānanā cāhtā ki maiṁ kyā cāhtā hūṁ. 19. maiṁ sab kuch tyāg kar ekānt meṁ rahnā cāhtā hūṁ. 20. āp kyā cāhte haiṁ?

Ex. G 20.2 Translate into Hindi:

1. I^{m} want to talk to you. 2. He wants to change jobs. 3. She wants to buy a new flat. 4. He wants to sell his car. 5. What do you$^{m.form.}$ want to do this evening? 6. Where did they^{m} want to go last week? 7. We^{m} wanted to live longer in Varanasi. 8. They^{m} wanted to go for a walk. 9. I^{m} want to listen to news. 10. I want to go boating. 11. Today we want to eat out somewhere. 12. My daughter wants to learn sewing. 13. My father wanted to establish a research institute. 14. My mother wanted to open an orphanage.

Key G 20.1

1. I want to meet you? 2. Do you want to stay in this hotel? 3. They want to stay here for a day/a week. 4. Don't you want to stay in Delhi? 5. My sister wanted to learn German language. 6. I wanted to have coffee/tea/milk/water. 7. We wanted to wash our clothes. 8. Would you like to clean your shoes? 9. He would not like to write a letter today. 10. He would like to learn new words. 11. My mother wanted to make me a doctor. 12. My parents wanted to make me an engineer. 13.

No one wanted to know what I wanted to do. 14. I wanted to play all the time. 15. Now my parents want that I serve them. 16. My wife wants that I earn much money. 17. My children want that I play with them. 18. Even now no one wants to know what I want. 19. I want to renounce everything and live in solitude. 20. What do you want?

Key G 20. 2

1. मैं आपसे बात करना चाहता हूँ। 2. वह काम बदलना चाहता है। 3. वह [f] नया फ्लैट ख़रीदना चाहती है। 4. वह [m] अपनी कार बेचना चाहता है। 5. आज शाम को आप क्या करना चाहते हैं? 6. वे पिछले हफ्ते कहाँ जाना चाहते थे? 7. हम बनारस में और रहना चाहते थे। 8. वे सैर करने जाना चाहते थे।। 9. मैं ख़बरें सुनना चाहता हूँ। 10. मैं नौका विहार करना चाहता हूँ। 11. आज हम कहीं बाहर खाना चाहते हैं। 12. मेरी बेटी सिलाई सीखना चाहती है। 13. हमारे पिता जी शोध संस्थान स्थापित करना चाहते थे। 14. मेरी माता जी एक अनाथालय खोलना चाहती थीं।

1. maiṁ āpse bāt karnā cāhtā hūṁ. 2. vah kām badalnā cāhtā hai. 3. vah nayā flaiṭ <u>kh</u>arīdnā cāhtī hai. 4. vah apnī kār becnā cāhtā hai. 5. āj śām ko āp kyā karnā cāhte haiṁ? 6. ve pichle hafte kahāṁ jānā cāhte the? 7. ham banāras meṁ aur rahnā cāhte the. 8. ve sair karne jānā cāhte the. 9. maiṁ khabreṁ sunanā cāhtā hūṁ. 10. maiṁ naukā vihār karnā cāhtā hūṁ. 11. āj ham kahīṁ bāhar khānā cāhte hūṁ. 12. merī beṭī silāī sīkhnā cāhtī hai.13. ham- āre pitā jī śodh saṃsthān sthāpit karnā cāhte the.14. hamārī mātā jī ek anāthālay kholnā cāhtī thīṁ.

●●●●●

G 21 The verb saknā सकना/ pānā पाना

(can or be able to do something)

subj. + obj. + v.r. + सकना saknā / पाना pānā + होना honā
in the required tense
to agree with N and G of subject

☞ **Remember: The natives use पाना pānā instead of सकना saknā when one is able to manage to do something by putting in some extra effort or alternatively unable to do something despite extra effort.**

COMPREHENSION

1. मैं[f] हिन्दी पढ़ सकती हूँ। maiṁ[f] hindī paṛh saktī hūṁ	I can read Hindi. (present simple tense)
2. वे[f] हिन्दी नहीं पढ़ सकतीं। ve[f] hindī nahīṁ paṛh saktīṁ.	They cannot read Hindi. (present simple tense)
3. वह[m.] मिठाई बना सकता था। vah [m] miṭhāī banā saktā thā.	He used to be able to make sweets. (past habitual tense)
4. रवि[m] कार नहीं चला सका। Ravi [m] kār nahīṁ calā sakā.	Ravi could not drive a car. (past simple tense)
5. हम[f] पेड़ पर नहीं चढ़ सकीं। ham [f] peṛ par nahīṁ caṛh sakīṁ.	We couldnot climb up the tree. (past simple tense)
6. मैं मसालेदार भोजन नहीं पचा पाती। maiṁ masāledār bhojan nahīṁ pacā pātī.	I [f] am not able to digest spicy food. (present simple tense)

7. बच्चा रात भर सो नहीं पाया। baccā rāt bhar so nahīṁ pāyā.	The child could not sleep all night. (past simple tense)
8. हम आपके घर नहीं आ पाएँगे। ham āpke ghar nahīṁ ā pāeṁge.	We will not be able to come to your house. (future simple tense)

Ex. G 21.1 Translate into English:

1. क्या मैं (f.) अंदर आ सकती हूँ? **2.** क्या वह (m.) यह शब्दकोश ले सकता है? **3.** क्या वह (m.) यहाँ बैठ सकता है? **4.** क्या आप (m.) हिंदी का समाचारपत्र पढ़ सकते हैं? **5.** क्या आप (m.) मुझे बता सकते हैं कि वे कहाँ हैं? **6.** क्या आप (f.) आज शाम को छह बजे मुझे मिल सकेंगी? **7.** क्या हमें इस फ़िल्म के लिए टिकट मिल सकते हैं? 8. हम (m.) इतने छोटे घर में नहीं रह पाएँगे। **9.** मैं (m.) आपकी मदद नहीं कर पाऊँगा।। **10.** वह (f.) कोई उपहार नहीं ख़रीद पाई। **11.** क्या पुलिस (f.) अपराधी को पकड़ पाई है? **12.** हम लोग (m.) वहाँ कैसे जा सकते हैं?

1. kyā maiṁ andar ā saktī hūṁ? 2. kyā vah yah śabdkoś le saktā hai? 3. kyā vah yahāṁ baiṭh saktā hai. 4. kyā āp Hindī kā samācār-patra paṛh sakte haiṁ? 5. kyā āp mujhe batā sakte haiṁ ki ve kahāṁ haiṁ? 6. kyā āp āj śām ko chah baje mujhe mil sakeṁgī? 7. kyā hameṁ is film ke lie ṭikaṭ mil sakte haiṁ? 8. ham itne choṭe ghar meṁ nahīṁ rah pāeṁge. 9. maiṁ āpkī madad nahīṁ kar pāūṁgā.? 10 vah koī uphār nahīṁ kharīd pāī . 11. kyā pulis aprādhī ko pakaṛ pāī hai? 12. ham log vahāṁ kaise jā sakte haiṁ?

Ex. G 21.2 Translate into Hindi:

1.We$^{m/m+f}$ can speak, read and write Hindi. 2. I (f.) cannot come with you. 3. He never used to be able to travel by car. 4. Could you not go there by yourself . 5. We$^{m/m+f}$ will not be able to reach on time today. 6. Everybody will not be able to go to Agra. 7. I (f.) couldnot understand them at all. 8. They$^{m.pl}$ will not be able to tolerate injustice. 9. She will not be able to tell a lie. 10. You$^{f.formal}$ will not be able to listen to the truth.

Ex G 21. 3 Read and translate into English:

- क्या मैं अंदर आ सकता हूँ?
- अवश्य, अंदर आइए! आप क्या चाहते हैं? मैं आपकी क्या सहायता

कर सकता हूँ?

- मैं प्रोफ़ेसर शर्मा से मिलना चाहता हूँ। क्या आप मेरी सहायता कर सकते हैं?
- अवश्य, बैठिए, ज़रा इंतज़ार कीजिए। आपका नाम क्या है?
- मेरा नाम प्रकाश है।
- राजू, प्रोफ़ेसर शर्मा से कहो कि श्री प्रकाश उनसे मिलना चाहते हैं।
- जी साहब।
- प्रोफ़ेसर शर्मा केवल हिंदी ही बोलते हैं। क्या आप हिंदी बोल सकते हैं?
- जी, थोड़ी–सी। मैं एक साल से हिंदी सीख़ रहा हूँ।

  अच्छा राजू, ज़रा श्रीमती कपूर को बुलाओ। वे अंग्रेज़ी और हिंदी दोनों भाषाएँ जानती हैं। वे अंग्रेज़ी से हिंदी में अनुवाद कर सकेंगी।
- बहुत बहुत धन्यवाद। आप बहुत कृपालु हैं।

- kyā maiṁ andar ā saktā hūṁ?
- avaśyă, andar āie! āp kyā cāhte haiṁ? maiṁ āpkī kyā sahāyatā kar saktā hūṁ?
- maiṁ profaissar śarmā se milnā cāhtā hūṁ. kyā āp merī sahāyatā kar sakte haiṁ?
- avaśyă, baiṭhie, zarā intzār kījie. āpkā nām kyā hai?
- merā nām prakāś hai.
- rājū, profaissar śarmā se kaho ki śrī prakāś unse milnā cāhte haiṁ.
- jī sāhab.
- profaissar śarmā keval Hindī hī bolte haiṁ. kyā āp Hindī bol sakte haiṁ ?
- jī, ṭhoṛī-sī. maiṁ ek sāl se Hindī sīkh rahā hūṁ.
- acchā rājū! zarā śrīmatī Kapoor ko bulāo. ve aṅgrezī aur hindī, donoṁ bhāṣāeṁ jāntī haiṁ. ve aṅgrezī se hindī meṁ anvād kar sakeṁgī .
- bahut bahut dhanyăvād. āpkī bahut kṛpālu haiṁ.

Key G 21.1

1. May I come in? 2. Can he take this dictionary? 3. Can he sit here? 4. Can you read Hindi newspaper? 5. Could you tell me where they are? 6. Will you be able

to meet me at six o'clock in the evening today. 7.Can we get the tickets for this film? 8.We will not be able to live in such a small house. 9. I won't be able to help you. 10. She could not buy any gift. 11. Has the police been able to arrest the criminal? 12. How can we go there?

Key G 21. 2

1. हम हिन्दी बोल, पढ़ और लिख सकते हैं। 2. मैं आपके साथ नहीं आ सकती। 3. वह कार से यात्रा कभी नहीं कर सकता था। 4. क्या तुम वहाँ अपने से नहीं जा सकते थे? 5. आज हम समय पर नही पहुँच सकेंगे। 6. सब आगरा नहीं जा सकेंगे। 7. मैं उनको बिल्कुल नहीं समझ सका 8. वे अन्याय नहीं सह पाएँगे। 9. वह झूठ नहीं बोल पाएगी। 10. आप सच नहीं सुन पाएँगी।

1. ham hindī bol, paṛh aur likh sakte haiṁ . 2. maiṁ āpke sāth nahīṁ ā saktī. 3. vah kār se yātrā kabhī nahīṁ kar saktā thā. 4. kyā tum vahāṁ apne se nahīṁ jā sakte the. 5. āj ham samay se nahīṁ pahuṁc sakeṁge. 6. sab āgrā nahīṁ jā sakeṁge. 7. maiṁ unko bilkul nahīṁ samajh sakā 8. ve anyāy nahīṁ sah pāeṁge. 9. vah jhūṭh nahīṁ bol pāegī. 10. āp sac nahīṁ sun pāeṁgī.

Key G 21.3

- May I come in?
- Certainly. Come in. What do you want? How may I help you?
- I want to meet Prof. Sharma. Could you help me please?
- Certainly. Please be seated; wait a moment. What is your name, please?
- My name is Mr. Prakash.
- Raju, tell Prof, Sharma that Mr. Prakash wants to meet him.
- Yes Sir!
- Prof. Sharma speaks only Hindi. Can you speak Hindi?
- Yes. a little. I have been learning Hindi for one year.
- Alright Raju, just call Mrs Kapoor. She knows both the languages, English and Hindi. She will be able to translate English into Hindi.
- Many thanks. You have been very kind.

●●●●●

G 22 The verb चाहिए (cāhie)

(need, should/ ought to)

चाहिए (cāhie)is used in two ways. (1) to express need for some thing. (2) in the sense of 'ought to' or 'should' do some thing.

■ Sentence structure for the use of चाहिए to express need:

subject + को	noun object +	चाहिए +	honā in required tense (if necessary) to agree with the N and G of the obj.

COMPREHENSION:

1.	मुझको एक प्याला गरम चाय^f. चाहिए। mujhko ek pyālā garam cāy^f. cāhie.	I need a cup of hot tea. (Need in the Present)
1a.	मुझको एक प्याला गरम चाय चाहिए थी। mujhko ek pyālā garam cāy cāhie thī.	I needed a cup of hot tea. (Need in the Past)
1b.	मुझको एक प्याला गरम चाय^f. चाहिए होगी। mujhko ek pyālā garam cāy cāhie hogī.	I will need a cup of hot tea. (Need in the Future)
2.	उनको एक मकान^m चाहिए। unko ek makān^m cāhie.	They need a house. (Need in the Present)
2a.	उनको एक मकान^m. चाहिए था। unko ek makān cāhie thā.	They needed a house. (Need in the Past)
2b.	उनको एक मकान^m. चाहिए होगा। unko ek makān cāhie hogā.	They will need a house. (Need in the Future)

3. आपको क्या चाहिए? āpko kyā cāhie.	What do you need? (Need in the Present)
3a. आपको क्या चाहिए था? āpko kyā cāhie thā.	What did you need? (Need in the Past)
3b. आपको क्या चाहिए होगा? āpko kyā cāhie hogā.	What will you need? (Need in the Future)
4. माता को कुछ नहीं चाहिए। mātā ko kuch nahīṁ cāhie.	Mother does not need anything. (Need in the Present)
4a. माता को कुछ नहीं चाहिए था। mātā ko kuch nahim cāhie thā.	Mother did not need anything. (Need in the Past)
4b. माता को कुछ नहीं चाहिए होगा। mātā ko kuch nahīṁ cāhie hogā.	Mother will not need anything. (Need in the Future)
5. उसको नए गहने[m.pl.] चाहिए। usko nae gahne cāhie.	He/She needs new ornaments. (Need in thePast)
5a. उसको नए गहने[m.pl.] चाहिए थे। usko nae gahne cāhie the.	He/She needed new ornaments. (Need in thePast)
5b. उसको नए गहने चाहिए होंगे। usko nae gahne cāhie hoṁge.	He/She will need new ornaments (Need in the Future)

■ **Use of चाहिए in the sense of should/ought to do something i.e. to express moral obligation**:

subj. + activity* as obj. + चाहिए + honā in required tense (if necessary)
+ को **to agree with the N and G of the obj.**
☞ ***If it is intransitive activity, use the verb infinitive**

1. अब आपको जाना चाहिए। ab āpko jānā cāhie.	You ought to go now.
1a. आपको जाना चाहिए था।	You ought to have gone.

āpko jānā cāhie thā.

☞ *** Even in the case of transitive activities, if object is not clearly stated, use the infinitive (i.e.the verb ending in ना nā).**

2. मरीज़ को क्या खाना चाहिए? — What should the patient eat ?
   marīz ko kyā khānā cāhie.

2a. मरीज़ को क्या खाना चाहिए था? — What should the patient have eaten ?
   marīz ko kyā khānā cāhie thā.

☞ ***In the case of transitive activities, if the object is explicitly stated, use (v.r. + ना nā, ने, ne नी nī) to agree with the N and G of the object.**

3. उसको नए गहने[m.pl.] पहनने चाहिए। — She should wear new ornaments.
   usko nae gahne pahnane cāhie.

3a. उसको नए गहने[m.pl] पहनने चाहिए थे। — She should have worn new ornaments.
   usko nae gahne pahnane cāhie the.

4. माता को आराम[msg.] करना चाहिए। — Mother should rest.
   mātā ko ārām karnā cāhie.

4a. माता को आराम[m.sg] करना चाहिए था। — Mother should have rested.
   mātā ko ārām karnā cāhie thā.

5. उसको यह किताब[f] खरीदनी चाहिए। — She should buy this book.
   usko yah kitāb kharīdnī cāhie.

5a. उसको यह किताब[f] खरीदनी चाहिए थी। — She should have bought this book.
   usko yah kitāb kharīdnī cāhie thī.

Ex. G 22.1 Translate into Hindi:

1. What do you need? 2. He/She needs much money. 3. I want peace. 4. You need a good job. 5. My sister needs a new watch. 6. Rani needs a cycle. 7. I need a new dress. 8. She needs some rest. 9. We need some chairs. 10. They need a four-room house. 11. Children need a play-ground. 12 Students need a good library.

Ex. 22.2: Translate into English:

1. आप बहुत ज़्यादा धूम्रपान करते हैं।	आपको इतना धूम्रपान नहीं करना चाहिए।
2. वह बहुत ज़्यादा पढ़ता है।	मेरे विचार में उसे इतना ज़्यादा नहीं पढ़ना चाहिए।
3. वे बहुत ज़्यादा सोती हैं।	उन्हें इतना नहीं सोना चाहिए।
4. आप बहुत ज़्यादा खाते हैं।	आपको इतना नहीं खाना चाहिए।
5. वह बहुत ज़्यादा शराब पीता है।	उसे इतनी शराब नहीं पीनी चाहिए।
1. āp bahut zyādā dhūmrapān karte haiṁ.	āpko itnā dhūmrapān nahīṁ karnā cāhie.
2. vah bahut zyādā paṛhtā hai.	mere vicār meṁ use itnā zyādā nahīṁ paṛhnā cāhie.
3. ve bahut zyādā sotī haiṁ.	unheṁ itnā nahīṁ sonā cāhie.
4. āp bahut zyādā khāte haiṁ.	āpko itnā nahīṁ khānā cāhie.
5. vah bahut zyādā śarāb[f.] pītā hai.	use itnī śarāb[f] nahīṁ pīnī cāhie.

Ex. G 22.3 Translate into Hindi :

1. You ought to live peacefully.	1a. You ought to have lived peacefully.
2. You should rest.	2a. You should have rested.
3. You ought to be careful.	3a. You ought to have been careful.
4. Patients should take medicine on time.	4a. Patients should have taken medicine on time.
5. Kamla should buy a new car.	5a. Kamla should have bought a new car.

Key G 22. 1

1. आपको क्या चाहिए? 2. उसे बहुत धन चाहिए। 3. मुझे शान्ति चाहिए। 4. तुम्हें/आपको

अच्छी नौकरी चाहिए। 5.मेरी बहन को एक नई घड़ी चाहिए। 6. रानी को एक साइकिल चाहिए। 7. मुझे नई पोशाक चाहिए। 8. उसे कुछ आराम चाहिए। 9. हमें कुछ कुर्सियाँ चाहिए। 10. उन्हें एक चार कमरों का मकान चाहिए। 11. बच्चों को खेल का मैदान चाहिए। 12. छात्रों को अच्छा पुस्तकालय चाहिए।

1. āpko kyā cāhie. 2. use bahut dhan cāhie. 3. mujhe śānti cāhie. 4. tumheṁ /āpko acchī naukrī cāhie. 5. merī bahan ko ek naī ghaṛī cāhie. 6. Rani ko ek naī sāikil cāhie. 7. mujhe naī pośāk çāhie. 8. use kuch ārām cāhie. 9. hameṁ kuch kursiyāṁ cāhie. 10. unheṁ ek cār kamroṁ kā makān cāhie. 11. baccoṁ ko khel kā maidān cāhie. 12. chātroṁ ko acchā pustakālay cāhie.

Key G 22. 2

1. You[m] smoke too much.	1a. You ought not to smoke so much.
2. He studies too much.	2a. I think he ought not to study so much.
3. She sleeps too much.	3a. She should not sleep so much.
4. You[m] eat too much.	4a. You[m] should not eat so much.
5. He drinks too much alcohol.	5a. He should not drink so much alcohol.

Key G 22. 3

1. आपको शान्ति से रहना चाहिए।	1a. आपको शान्ति से रहना चाहिए था।
2. आपको आराम करना चाहिए।	2a. आपको आराम करना चाहिए था।
3. आपको सावधान रहना चाहिए।	3a. आपको सावधान रहना चाहिए था।
4. मरीज़ों को समय पर दवाई खानी चाहिए।	4a. मरीज़ों को समय पर दवाई खानी चाहिए थी।
5. कमला को नई कार ख़रीदनी चाहिए।	6a. कमला को नई कार ख़रीदनी चाहिए थी।
1. āpko śānti se rahnā cāhie .	1a. āpko śānti se rahnā cāhie thā.
2. āpko ārām karnā cāhie .	2a. āpko ārām karnā cāhie thā.

3. āpko sāvdhān rahnā cāhie .

3a. āpko sāvdhān rahnā cāhie thā.

4. marīzoṁ ko davāī khānī cāhie

4a. marīzoṁ ko davāī khānī cāhie thī.

5. kamla ko naī kār kharīdnī cāhie .

5a. kamla ko naī kār kharīdnī cāhie thī.

•••••

SHAPES

1. सर्पिल	sarpil	spiral
2. गोला	golā	sphere
3. घनाकार	ghanākār	cube
4. सूची स्तम्भ	sūcī stambh	pyramid
5. बेलन	belan	cylinder

G 23 है, होता है, रहता है
hai, hotā hai, rahtā hai

■ है **'hai' is used to speak about the being / non being, or state of living or non-living object at a certain time.**

1.	मेरी माता जी शिक्षिका हैं। merī mātā jī śikṣikā haiṁ.	My mother is a teacher.
2.	मेरे पिता जी घर में नहीं हैं। mere pitā jī ghar meṁ nahīṁ haiṁ.	My father is not at home.
3.	वह अकेला नहीं है। vah akelā nahīṁ hai.	He is not alone .
4.	आज गर्मी है। āj garmī hai.	It is hot today.

■ **होता है 'hotā hai' is used for:**

- **all time truths:**

1.	सोना पीला होता है। sonā pilā hotā hai.	Gold is yellow.
2.	सत्य की सदैव जीत होती है। satyă kī sadaiv jīt hotī hai.	Truth always wins.
3.	दो और दो चार होते हैं। do aur do cār hote haiṁ.	Two and two is four.

- **To talk about happenings following a regular time pattern.**

1.	मंगलवार को हमारा पाठ सुबह नौ बजे शुरू होता है।	On Tuesday our lesson start at 9 O'clock.

maṅgalvār ko hamārā pāṭh subah nau baje śurū hotā hai.

2. यहाँ जून से अक्तूबर तक वर्षा होती है। — It rains here from June to October.
yahāṁ jūn se aktūbar tak varṣā hotī hai.

- **It is also used in commentaries on activities in progress e.g. cricket match, seminar, concerts etc.**

1. लोग खड़े होते हैं। — People stand.
log khaṛe hote haiṁ.

2. अब खेल खत्म होता है। — Now the game finishes.
ab khel khatm hotā hai.

■ **रहता है 'rahtā hai' is used for extended continuity of a certain state over a span of time:**

1. वह हमेशा उदास रहती है। — She always remains sad.
vah hameśā udās rahtī hai.

2. यहाँ हमेशा उमस रहती है। — It always remains humid here.
yahāṁ hameśā umas rahtī hai.

Ex. G 23.1 Translate into Hindi:

1. He is sick today. 2. He often remains sick. 3. What day is it today? 4. How many days are there in a week? 5. It rains here a lot in the rainy season. 6. In India it is neither hot nor cold during January and February. 7. Our lesson begins at nine o' clock. 8. My father is much disappointed. 9 Here there is a music concert today. 10.Often music concert takes place here. 11. Why is there so much crowd today? 12. This place is usually crowded. 13. What was there yesterday evening? 14. What all used to take place there usually in the evening.

Ex. G 23.2 Translate into English:

भारतीय मरुस्थल में मार्च से अक्तूबर तक तेज़ गर्मी होती है। जून का महीना असहनीय गर्म होता है। नवंबर और दिसम्बर में सहनीय गर्मी होती है। जनवरी और फ़रवरी के महीने, वास्तव

में, काफ़ी ठण्डे होते हैं। मरुस्थल की रातें हमेशा ठंडी और सुहावनी होती हैं। कभी–कभी तो दिन और रात के तापमान में २० डिगरी सेन्टीग्रेड तक का अन्तर होता है।

bhārtīyă marusthal meṁ mārc se aktūbar tak tez garmī hotī hai. jūn kā mahīnā asahnīyă garm hotā hai. navambar aur disambar meṁ sahnīyă garmī hotī hai. janvarī aur farvarī ke mahīne, vāstav meṁ, kāfī ṭhaṇḍe hote haiṁ. marusthal kī rāteṁ hameśā ṭhaṇḍī aur suhāvnī hotī haiṁ. kabhī-kabhī to din aur rāt meṁ ke tāpmān bīs digrī tak kā antar hotā hai.

Key G 23.1

1. आज वह बीमार है। 2. वह अक्सर बीमार रहता है। 3. आज कौन–सा दिन है? 4. एक हफ़्ते में कितने दिन होते हैं? 5. यहाँ वर्षा–ऋतु में खूब वर्षा होती है। 6. जनवरी और फरवरी में भारत में न गर्मी होती है, न सर्दी। 7. हमारा पाठ नौ बजे शुरू होता है। 8. मेरे पिता जी बहुत निराश हैं। 9. यहाँ आज संगीत गोष्ठी है। 10. यहाँ अक्सर संगीत गोष्ठी होती है। 11. आज यहाँ पर इतनी भीड़ क्यों है? 12. यहाँ आम तौर पर भीड़ होती है। 13. वहाँ कल शाम को क्या था? 14. वहाँ प्रायः शाम को क्या–क्या होता था?

1. aj vah bīmār hai. 2. vah aksar bīmār rahtā hai. 3. āj kaun-sā din hai?? 4. ek hafte meṁ kitne din hote haiṁ? 5. yahāṁ varṣā ṛtu meṁ khūb varṣā hotī hai. 6. janvarī aur farvarī meṁ bhārat meṁ na garmī hotī hai na sardī.7. hamārā pāṭh nau baje śurū hotā hai. 8. mere pitā jī bahut niraś haiṁ. 9. yahāṁ āj saṅgīt goṣṭhī hai. 10. yahāṁ aksar saṅgīt goṣṭhī hotī hai. 11. āj yahāṁ par itnī bhīṛ kyoṁ hai? 12. yahāṁ ām taur par bhīṛ hotī hai. 13. vahāṁ kal śām ko kyā thā? 14. vahāṁ prāyaḥ śām ko kyā-kyā hotā thā?

Key G 23.2

Indian deserts are very hot from March to October. The month of June is intolerably hot. Heat in November and December is tolerable. The months of January and February are, truly, quite cold. Nights in the desert are always cool and pleasant. Sometimes there is a difference of twenty degrees between day and night.

Read: Weather Talk pg. 409

●●●●●

G 24 The Suffix vālā वाला

vālā वाला is a much used suffix in Hindi. Depending upon the base word to which it is affixed, it conveys varied meanings such as (1) the doer of a certain activity, (2) as highlighter of a certain dimension, form, color, price etc; (3) as demonstrative adjective pointing to a certain object, this one, that one etc. (4) about to do a certain activity.

Remember:

☞ **When this suffix is used as adjective, the base form of the suffix vālā वाला is used to qualify mas. sg. noun. However, like any other ā-ending adjective, it changes to vāle वाले when qualifying m.pl. noun, and vālī वाली when qualifying fem. sg. or plural noun.**

☞ **When these are used as noun, they change like any other noun, depending upon the number, gender and case of the noun they are taking place of.**

Let us understand it with the help of some examples.

■ **noun followed by vālā वाला, vāle वाले, vālī वाली**

दूधवाला$^{m.sg.}$	dūdhvālā	milkman;
दूधवाले$^{m.pl.}$	dūdhvāle	milkmen
दूधवाली$^{f.sg.}$	dūdhvālī	milkwoman
दूधवालियाँ$^{f.pl.}$	dūdhvālīyāṁ	milkwomen
अख़बारवाला$^{m.sg.}$	akhbārvālā	newspaperman
अख़बारवाले$^{m.pl.}$	akhhbārvāle	newpapermen
अख़बारवाली$^{f.sg.}$	akhbārvālī	newpaperwoman
अख़बारवालियाँ$^{f.pl.}$	akhbārvāliyāṁ	newpaperwomen

■ **adjective followed by vālā वाला, vāle वाले, vālī वाली**

कालावाला$^{m.sg}$	kālāvālā	the black one
कालवाले$^{m.pl}$	kāle vāle	the black ones

SUFFIX vālā , vāle vālī

कालीवाली f.sg.	kālīvālī	the black one
नयावाला m.sg	nayāvālā	the new one
गोलवाला m.sg	golvālā	the round one
बड़ावाला m.sg	baṛāvālā	the big one
पचास पैसेवाला m.sg	pacās paisevālā	the one priced fifty paisa.
संगमरमरवाला m.sg	saṅgmarmarvālā	the one made of marble

■ **adverb followed by vālā वाला, vāle वाले, vālī वाली**

नीचेवाला m.sg	nīcevālā	the one below
नीचेवाले m.pl.	nīcevāle	the ones below
नीचेवाली f.sg.	nīcevālī	the one below
सामनेवाला m.sg	sāmnevālā	the one in front
सामनेवाले m.pl.	sāmnevāle	the ones in front
सामनेवाली f.sg.	sāmnevālī	the one in front

☞ **In this manner you could affix vālā to most adverbs such as:**

पासवाला m.sg	pāsvālā	the one near
दूरवाला m.sg	dūrvālā	the one away
ऊपरवाला m.sg	ūparvālā	the one above
पीछेवाला m.sg	pīchevālā	the one behind

and so on

■ **pronoun followed by vālā वाला, vāle वाले, vālī वाली**

यहवाला m.sg	yahvālā	this one(near)
येवाले m.pl	yevāle	these ones(near)
यहवाली f.sg.	yahvālī	this one (f. near)
येवाली f.pl.	yevālī	these ones (near).
वहवाला m.sg	vahvālā	that one (far)

वेवाले m.pl.	vevāle	those ones (far)
वहवाली f.sg.	vahvālī	that one(f.sg. far)
वेवाली f.pl.	vevālī	those ones(far)
कौन–सा वाला m.sg	kaun-sā vālā	which one
कौन–से वाले m.pl.	kaun-se vāle	which one(s)
कौन–सी वाली f.pl.	kaun-sī vālī	which one

कैसावाला m.sg kaisāvālā, कैसेवाले m.pl. kaisevāle, कैसीवाली f.pl. kaisīvālī all three meaning 'what kind of'

☞ **Remember: adjectives, adverbs or pronous followed by the suffix vālā वाला, vāle वाले, vālī वाली may be used as adjective or noun itself.**

COMPREHENSION

1. सामनेवाले बागीचे में खेलो। sāmnevāle bāgīce meṁ khelo.	Play in the park in front.
2. बाहरवाले कमरे में बैठिए। bāharvāle kamre meṁ baiṭhie.	Be seated in the room out side.
3. कपड़े धोनेवाले को हिन्दी में क्या कहते हैं? kapṛe dhonevāle ko Hindi meṁ kyā kahte haiṁ?	What is the one who washes clothes called in Hindi?
4. कपड़े धोनेवाले को हिन्दी में धोबी कहते है। kapṛe dhonevāle ko Hindī meṁ dhobī kahte haiṁ.	The one who washed clothes is called 'dhobī' in Hindi.
5. हमारा दूधवाला m.sg. सुबह दस बजे आता था । hamārā dūdhvālā subah das baje ātā thā.	Our milkman used to come in the morning at 10 o'clock.
6. मैं इसवाले स्कूल में पढ़ती थी। maiṁ isvāle skūl meṁ paṛhtī thī.	I used to study in this school.

7. आप[f.hon.] कौन–सी वाली पोशाक पहनेंगी?
ap kaun-sī vālī pośāk pahneṁgī? — Which dress will you wear?

8. मैं[f.] कालीवाली पहनूँगी।
maiṁ kālīvālī pahnūṁgī. — I will wear the black one.

■ **(verbroot + ने ne) followed by vālā वाला, vāle वाले, vālī वाली has two uses.**

1. doer of an activity

गानेवाला[m.sg]	gānevālā	गानेवाले[m.pl]	gānevāle
गानेवाली[f..sg.]	gānevālī	गानेवालियाँ	gānevāliyāṁ
	singer		singer(s)
पढ़ानेवाला[m.sg]।	paṛhānevālā	पढ़ानेवाले[m.pl.]	paṛhānevāle
पढ़ानेवाली[f..sg.]	paṛhānevālī	पढ़ानेवालियाँ[f..pl]	paṛhānevāliyāṁ
	teacher		teacher(s)
नाचनेवाला[m.sg]	nācnevālā;	नाचनेवाले[m.pl.]	nācnevāle
नाचनेवाली[f..sg.]	nācnevālī	नाचनेवालियाँ[f..pl]	nācnevāliyāṁ
	dancer		dancers

2. about to do something

1. गाड़ी[f..sg] आनेवाली है।
gāṛī ānevālī hai. — The train is about to come.

2. भाषण[m.sg] शुरू होनेवाला है।
bhāṣaṇ śurū honevāla hai. — The speech is about to begin.

3. श्रुति विदेश[m..sg.] जानेवाली थी, परन्तु गई नहीं।
śruti videś jānevālī thī, parantu gaī nahīṁ. — Shruti was (about) to go abroad but did not go.

4. बच्चे^m..sg. स्कूल से लौटनेवाले होंगे। bacce skūl se lauṭnevāle hoṁge. — Children must be about to return from school.

5. वे सोनेवाले होंगे। ve sonevāle hoṁge. — They must be about to sleep.

Ex. G 24.1 Translate into English:

1. सब्ज़ीवाला 2. पैसेवाला 3. अख़बारवाला 4. दूधवाला 5. चायवाला 6. सुननेवाला 7. देखनेवाला 8. रहनेवाला 9.ऊपरवाला 10. नीचेवाला 11. मिठाईवाला 12. दिल्ली का रहनेवाला 13.अमरीका का रहनेवाला 14.वहवाला 15.यहवाला 16. अच्छावाला 17.लालवाला 18. सस्तावाला।

1. sabzīvālā 2. paisevālā 3. akhbārvālā 4. dūdhvālā 5. cāyvālā 6. sunanevālā 7. dekhnevālā 8. rahnevālā 9. ūparvālā 10 nīcevālā 11. miṭhāīvālā 12. dillī kā rahnevālā 13. amrīkā kā rahnevālā 14. vahvālā 15. yahvālā. 16. acchāvālā 17. lālvālā 18. sastāvālā.

Ex. G 24.2 Translate into English:

1. कालेकोटवाला^m..sg. आदमी 2. ऊपरवाली^f..sg. किताब 3. पीछे आनेवाली बस 4. देर से आनेवाला छात्र^m..sg. 5. आगरा जानेवाला जहाज़^m..sg. 6. समय पर आनेवाले लड़के^m..sg. 7. यहाँ पढ़नेवाले विदेशी छात्र^m..pl. 8. इस घर में रहनेवाले लोग^m..pl. 9. पासवाली ईमारत^f..sg.। 10. पिछले हफ़्तेवाली पत्रिका^f..sg.।

1. kālekoṭvālā ādmī 2. ūparvālī kitāb 3. pīche ānevālī bas 4. der se ānevālā chātra 5. āgrā jānevālā jahāz 6. samay par ānevāle laṛke 7. yahāṁ paṛhnevāle videśī chātra 8. is ghar meṁ rahnevāle log 9. pāsvālī īmārat. 10. pichle haftevālī patrikā

Ex. G 24.3 Translate into Hindi using the suffix 'vālā':

1. the one (m.&f.) who washes clothes 2. the one (m.) who cuts the hair 3. the one(m.) who makes ornaments 4. the one (m.) who sells eggs 5. the one(m. and f.) who teaches 6. the house owner (m. and f.) 7. the one who cooks (m. and f.) 8. the ones(m.&f.) who works in an office 9. the one(m) who makes shoes. 10 the ones(m.pl. &f.pl.) who clean the house

Ex. G 24.4 Translate into Hindi using the suffix 'vālā':

1. to these ones(f.) 2. on those ones(m.) 3. from the teachers 4. with the learners.5.

near the ones (m.) in the back 6. away from the ones (f.) in front 7. without the one that is below 8. except this one.(f). 9. like which one (m.) 10. towards that one (m.).

Ex. G 24.5: Translate into Hindi:

1. The child is about to sleep. 2. Storm is about to come. 3. Film is about to start. 4. The minister is about to arrive. 5. The train is about to depart. 6. I like this one.7.I am going to my **front door neighbors**.(=neighbors across from the house) 8. Let these ones (m./m+f) go. 9. Please send those ones in. 10. The wedding of my next door neighbor took place yesterday. 11. My brother lives on the storey(level) below. 12. This locality is good for residence. 13. Robert will stay in the house next to ours. 14. Mother is about to go to Bombay. 15. The book is about to fall off the table.16. The child is about to fall off the tree. 17. It is about to rain. 18. It is about to snow.

Key G 24.1

1. vegetable seller 2. a man with much money (rich man) 3. newspaper man 4. milkman 5. tea seller 6. listener 7. viewer 8. resident 9. the one above 10. the one below 11. the sweets seller 12. the resident of Delhi 13. resident of America 14. that one 15. this one 16. the good one 17. the red one 18. the inexpensive one.

Key G 24.2

1. the man with the black coat 2. the book that is on the top 3. the bus that is following 4. the student who comes late 5. the airplane going to Agra 6. the boys who come on time 7. the foreign students who study here 8. the people who live in this house, 9. the building that is nearby. 10. last week's magazine

Key G 24.3

1. कपड़े धोनेवाला^{m} or कपड़े धोनेवाली$^{f.}$ 2. बाल काटनेवाला^{m} 3. आभूषण बनानेवाला^{m} 4. अण्डे बेचनेवाला^{m} 5. पढ़ानेवाला^{m}/पढ़ोनवाली$^{f.}$ 6. मकानवाला^{m}/मकानवाली$^{f.}$ 7. पकानेवाला^{m}/पकानेवाली^{f} 8. दफ़्तर में काम करनेवाला^{m}/दफ़्तऱ में काम करनेवाली$^{f.}$ 9. जूते बनानेवाला^{m} 10. सफ़ाई करनेवाले$^{m.pl}$/सफ़ाई करनेवालियाँ$^{f.pl}$

1. kapṛedhonevālā / kapṛedhonevālī 2. bāl kāṭnevālā 3. ābhūṣaṇ banānevālā 4. aṇḍe becnevālā 5. paṛhānevālā /paṛhānevālī 6. makānvālā / makānvālī 7. pakānevālā /pakānevālī 8. daftar meṁ kām karnevālā/daftar meṁ kām karnevālī

9. jūte banānevālā 10. safāī karnevāle /safāī karnevāliyāṁ

Key G 24.4

1. इनवालियों को 2. उनवालों के ऊपर 3. पढ़ानेवालों से 4. पढ़नेवालों के साथ 5. पीछेवालों के पास 6. सामनेवालियों से दूर 7. नीचेवाले के बिना 8. इसवाली के अलावा 9. किसवाले की तरह 10. उसवाले की ओर

1. invāliyoṁ ko 2. unvāloṁ ke ūpar 3. paṛhānevāloṁ se 4.paṛhnevāloṁ ke sāth 5. pīchevāloṁ ke pās 6. sāmnevāliyoṁ se dūr 7. nīcevāloṁ ke binā 8. isvālī ke alāvā 9. kisvāle kī tarah 10. usvāle kī or

Key G 24.5

1. बच्चा^{m} सोनेवाला है। 2. आँधी^{f} आनेवाली हैं। 3. फ़िल्म$^{f.}$ शुरू होनेवाली है। 4. मँत्री$^{m.hon.}$ जी पहुँचनेवाले हैं। 5. गाड़ी^{f} छूटनेवाली है। 7.मुझको यहवाली$^{f.}$ पसन्द है। 7. मैं अपने सामनेवालों$^{m.pl.obl.}$ के यहाँ जा रही हूँ। 8.कृपया इनवालों को जाने दीजिए। 9. कृपया उनवालों$^{m.pl.obl.}$ को अन्दर भेजिए। 10. मेरे बगलवाले$^{m.sg..obl.}$ की शादी$^{f.}$ कल हुई। 11. मेरा भाई नीचेवाली मंज़िल$^{f.sg}$ पर रहता है। 12. यहवाला इलाका$^{m.sg.}$ रहने के लिए अच्छा है। 13. रौबर्ट हमारे बग़लवाले मकान में रहेगा। 14. माता जी मुम्बई जानेवाली हैं। 15. पुस्तक$^{f..sg.}$ मेज़ से गिरनेवाली है। 16. बच्चा$^{m..sg.}$ पेड$^{m..sg.}$ से गिरनेवाला है। 17. वर्षा$^{f..sg.}$ होनेवाली है। 18. बर्फ़$^{f..sg.}$ पड़नेवाली है।

1. baccā sonevālā hai. 2. āṁdhī ānevālī hai. 3. film śurū honevālī hai. 4. mantrī jī pahuṁcnevāle haiṁ. 5. gāṛī chūṭnevālī hai. 6. mujhko yahvālī pasand hai. 7. maiṁ apne sāmnevāloṁ ke yahāṁ jā rahī hūṁ. 8. kṛpayā invāloṁ ko jāne dījie. 9. kṛpayā unvāloṁ ko andar bhejie. 10. mere bagalvāle kī śādī kal huī. 11. merā bhāī nīcevālī manjil par rahtā hai. 12. yahavālā ilākā rahne ke lie acchā hai. 13. raubar ṭ hamāre bagalvāle makān meṁ rahegā. 14. mātā jī mumbaī jānevālī haiṁ. 15. pustak mez se girnevālī hai. 16. baccā peṛ se girnevālā hai 17. varṣā honevālī hai. 18. barf paṛnevālī hai.

●●●●●

G 25 कर (kar)- conjunct

When the same subject does several activities one following the other, instead of making several sentences with repeated use of the same subject and verb conjugations, Hindi has a device called कर (kar)-conjunct to join the sentences.

☞ Use the subject only once at the beginning of the compound sentence.

☞ Use only the verb root followed by कर 'kar' for all preceding activi**ties.**

☞ If the verb root is कर 'kar', only के 'ke' follows it.

☞ Verb of the final activity is conjugated to agree with the subject or object, as per requirement of the tense and language structure in question.

☞ In case of past simple, present perfect or past perfect tense, if the finalactivity is transitive, the subject at the beginning of the sentence will have the postposition ने (ne) after it and the verb agrees with the object.

Examples:

- सोचो। बोलो। — Think. Speak.
  soco. bolo.
  =
  सोचकर बोलो। — Think **and** speak.
  soc **kar** bolo.

- हाथ धोइए। खाना खाइए। — Wash hands! Eat food!
  hāth dhoie! khānā khāie!
  =
  हाथ धोकर खाना खाइए। — Wash hands **and** eat food.
  hāth **dhokar** khānā khāie.

• मैं स्नान करती हूँ। maiṁ snān kartī hūṁ.	I take a bath.
+	
मैं पूजा करती हूँ। maiṁ pūjā kartī hūṁ.	I do puja.
=	
मैं स्नान करके पूजा करती हूँ। maiṁ snān karke pūjā kartī hūṁ.	I take a bath **and** do puja
• बच्चे स्कूल से आते हैं। bacce skūl se āte haiṁ.	The children come from school.
+	
बच्चे बागीचे में खेलते हैं bacce bāgīce meṁ khelte haiṁ.	The children play in the park.
=	
बच्चे स्कूल से आकर बागीचे में खेलते हैं। bacce skūl se ākar bāgīce meṁ khelte haiṁ.	The children come from school and play in the park.
• मैं सुबह उठती थी। maiṁ subah uṭhtī thī.	I used to get up in the morning.
+	
मैं नाशता बनाती थी। maiṁ nāśtā banātī thī.	I used to prepare breakfast.
+	
मैं काम पर जाती थी। maiṁ kām par jātī thī.	I used to go to work.
=	
मैं सुबह उठकर, नाशता बनाकर काम पर जाती थी।	I used to get up in the morning, prepare breakfast and go to

maiṁ subah **uṭhkar,** nāśtā **banākar** kām par jātī thī.	to work.
• मैंने किताब ख़रीदी। maiṁne kitāb kharīdī.	I bought a book.
+	
मैं घर गई। maiṁ ghar gaī.	I went home.
=	
मैं किताब ख़रीदकर घर गई। maiṁ kitāb kharīdkar ghar gaī.	I bought a book **and** went home.
• मैं बैंक गई। maiṁ baink gaī.	I went to the bank.
+	
मैंने पैसे निकाले। maiṁne paise nikāle.	I withdrew money.
+	
मैंने कपड़े ख़रीदे। maiṁne kapṛe kharīde.	I bought clothes.
=	
मैंने बैंक जाकर, पैसे निकालकर कपड़े ख़रीदे। maiṁne baiṅk jākar, paise nikāl kar kapṛe kharīde.	I went to the bank, withdrew money and bought clothes.
• मैं भारत जाऊँगी। maiṁ bhārat jāūṁgī.	I will go to India.
+	
मैं हिन्दी सीखूँगी। maiṁ Hindī sīkhūṁgī.	I will learn Hindi.
=	
मैं भारत जाकर हिन्दी सीखूँगी। maiṁ bhārat jākar Hindī sīkhūṁgī.	I will go to India and learn Hindi.

Ex. G 25.1 Translate into English:

1. जूते उतारकर अन्दर आओ। 2. हम घाट पर जाकर गंगा में स्नान करते हैं। 3. वह उठकर बोली। 4. वह खबर सुनकर रोई। 5. मैं मंदिर जाकर पूजा करूँगा। 6. आप बाज़ार जाकर फल लाइए। 7. मैं उनसे मिलकर बहुत खुश होऊँगा। 8. मैं भारत आकर हिन्दी सीखूँगा। 9. हम कहानी सुनकर सोएँगे। 10. हम पहले खाना खाकर दूरदर्शन देखेंगे।

1. jūte utārkar andar āo. 2. ham ghāṭ par jākar gaṅgā meṁ snān karte haiṁ. 3. vah uṭhkar bolī. 4. vah khabar sunkar roī. 5. maiṁ mandir jākar pūjā karūṁgā. 6. āp bāzār jākar phal lāie. 7. maiṁ unse milkar bahut khuś hoūṁgā. 8. maiṁ bhārat ākar hindī sīkhūṁgā. 9. ham kahānī sunkar soeṁge. 10. ham pahle khānā khākar dūrdarśan dekheṁge.

Ex. G 25.2 Join the sentences given below with the help of 'kar'- conjunct.

1. मैं बैंक से पैसा उधार लूँगा। मैं व्यापार करूँगा।
2. चोर खिड़की से कूदा। चोर भाग गया।
3. उसने दरवाज़ा बन्द किया था। वह सोने जा रहा था।
4. वह अमरीका गई। उसने चिकित्सा विज्ञान पढ़ा।
5. आप कपड़े धोइए। आप कपड़े सुखाइए। आप कपड़े तहाइए। आप कपड़े अलमारी में रखिए।

1. maiṁ baink se paisā udhār lūṁgā. maiṁ vyāpār karūṁgā
2. cor khiṛkī se kūdā. cor bhāg gayā.
3. usne darvāzā band kiyā thā. vah sone jā rahā thā.
4. vah amrīkā gaī. usne cikitsā vigyān paṛhā.
5. āp kapṛe dhoie. āp kapṛe sukhāie. āp kapṛe tahāie. āp kapṛe almārī meṁ rakhie.

Key G 25.1

1. Remove your shoes and come in. 2. We go on the ghat and have a bath in the Ganges. 3. She got up and spoke. 4. She heard the new and cried. 5. I will go to the temple and worship. 6. You go to market and bring fruit.7 I will be very

pleased to meet them. 8. I will go to India and learn Hindi. 9. We will listen to the story and go to sleep. 10. We will first eat and then watch T.V.

Key G 25.2

1. मैं बैंक से पैसा उधार लेकर व्यापार करूँगा।

2. चोर खिड़की से कूदकर भाग गया।

3. वह दरवाज़ा बन्द करके सोने जा रहा था।

4. उसने अमरीका जाकर चिकित्सा विज्ञान पढ़ा।

5. आप कपड़े धोकर, सुखाकर, तहाकर अलमारी में रखिए ।

1. maiṁ baink se paisā udhār lekar vyāpār karūṁgā
2. cor khiṛkī se kūdkar bhāg gayā.
3. vah darvāzā band karke sone jā rahā thā.
4. usne amrīkā jākar cikitsā vigyān paṛhā.
5. āp kapṛe dhokar, sukhākar, tahākar almārī meṁ rakhie.

●●●●●

G 26 SIMULTANEOUS ACTIVITIES

Use of (v.r + te + hī) corresponding to 'as soon as' clause in English.

When two activities happen or are done almost simultaneously by the same person or by two different persons, corresponding to the English 'as soon as' clause, Hindi uses ke + (v.r. + te + hī) or only (v.r. + te + hī).

☞ Regardless of the tense in question, the 'as soon as' clause is invariable, and always has (v.r. + te + hī). Conjugated verb-clause of the following activity is the key to the tense.

■ ke + (v.r. + te + h ī) when the subject of two sentences is different and living, and the subject of the as soon as clause happens to be a noun.

1. माता जाती है। बच्चा रोता है । mātā jātī hai. baccā rotā hai.	Mother goes. The child cries.
1a. माता के जाते ही बच्चा रोता है। mātā ke jāte hī baccā rotā hai .	As soon as mother goes, the child cries.
2. माता गई। बच्चा रोया। mātā gaī . baccā royā .	Mother went. The child cried.
2a. माता के जाते ही बच्चा रोया। mātā ke jāte hī baccā royā.	As soon as mother went, the child cried.
3. माता जाएगी। बच्चा रोएगा। mātā jāegī. baccā roegā .	Mother will go. The child will cry.
3a. माता के जाते ही बच्चा रोएगा। mātā ke jāte hī baccā roegā	As soon as mother goes, the child will cry.

☞ **When the subject of two sentences is different, living , but the subject of the 'as soon as' clause happens to be one of the pronouns such as मैं maiṁ, हम ham, तू tu, तुम tum , then their ए e- ending possessive**

pronoun form i.e. मेरे mere, हमारे hamāre, तेरे tere, तुम्हारे tumhāre, + {v.r. +ते + ही} is used:

मेरे सोते ही टेलीफ़ोन बजने लगा। mere sote hī ṭailīfon bajne lagā.	As soon as I slept, telephone began to ring.
हमारे घर से निकलते ही बारिश होने लगी। hamāre ghar se nikalte hī bāriś hone lagī.	As soon as we got out of the house, it began to rain.

■ **(v.r. + te + hī) is used when the subject of 'as soon as' clause is non-living.**

6. बारिश हुई। हम अन्दर आए। bāriś huī. ham andar āe.	It rained. We came in.
6a. बारिश होते ही हम अन्दर आए। bāriś hote hī ham andar āe.	As soon as it rained we came in.

☞ **The subject of the 'as soon as-clause' bāriś is non living. Hence only v.r. + ते te + ही hī (होते ही hote hī) is used.**

■ **When the subject of both the sentences is living and the same, only (v.r. + ते te + ही hī) is used. Also subject is used usually only once at the beginning of the as soon as clause, however it could be used at the beginning of the second clause as shown below. Examples 4, 4a given below.**

☞ **In case this common subject happens to be in different cases, then the subject- form of the following activity is used once at the beginning of the 'as soon as' clause . Examples: 5, 5a , 6, 6a given below.**

4. माता घर आती है। माता सोती है। mātā ghar ātī hai. mātā sotī hai.	Mother comes home. Mother sleeps.

4a. माता घर आते ही सोती है। — As soon as mother comes home, she sleeps.

mātā ghar āte hī sotī hai.

or

घर आते ही माता सोती है।

ghar āte hī mātā sotī hai.

☞ **In the past tense, if the final activity is transitive verb, the subject at the beginning of the sentence is followed by ने 'ne'. Example 5, 5a.**

5. माता घर आई। माता ने खाना पकाया। — Mother came home. Mother cooked food.

mātā ghar āī . mātā ne khānā pakāyā.

5a. माता ने घर आते ही खाना पकाया। — As soon as mother came home, she cooked food.

mātā ne ghar āte hī khānā pakāyā.

6. मैं दफ़्तर पहुँची। मुझको दाँत में दर्द होने लगा। — I reached office. I began to have tooth-ache.

maiṁ daftar pahuṁcī. mujhko dāṁt meṁ dard hone lagā.

6a. मुझको दफ़्तर पहुँचते ही दाँत में दर्द होने लगा। — As soon as I reached office, I began to have tooth ache.

mujhko daftar pahuṁcte hī dāṁt meṁ dard hone lagā.

Ex. G 26.1 Translate into English:

1. उसने पत्र पढ़ते ही फाड़ दिया। 2. उसने विज्ञापन देखते ही आवेदन पत्र भेज दिया। 3. मैं (f.) हिन्दी सीखते ही भारत जाऊँगी। 4. परीक्षा में उत्तीर्ण होते ही उसे नौकरी मिल गई। 5. बच्चे घर लौटते ही कुछ खाने को मांगते हैं। 6. वे घर बेचते ही देहात में चले गए।

7. चोर पुलिस को देखते ही भाग गया। 8. मकानमालिक के कहते ही हमने घर खाली कर दिया। 9. सन्ध्या होते ही हम दरवाज़े और खिड़कियाँ बन्द कर लेते हैं। 10. कपड़े सूखते ही तहा कर रख देना।

1. usne patra paṛhte hī phāṛ diyā. 2. usne vigyāpan dekhte hī āvedan patra bhej diyā. 3. maiṁ (f.)Hindī sīkhte hī bhārat jāūṁgī. 4. parīkṣā meṁ uttīrṇ hote hī use naukrī mil gaī. 5. bacce ghar lauṭte hī kuch khāne ko māṁgte haiṁ. 6. ve ghar becte hī dehāt meṁ cale gae. 7. cor pulis ko dekhte hī bhāg gayā. 8. makānmālik ke kahte hī hamne ghar khālī kar diyā. 9. sandhyā hote hī ham darvāze aur khiṛkiyāṁ band kar lete haiṁ. 10. kapṛe sūkhte hī tahā kar rakh denā.

Ex. G 26.2 Translate into Hindi:

1. As soon as it is morning mother begins to do Puja. 2. As soon as it is 4 o'clock temple bells begin to ring. 3. As soon as Robert came to India, he started speaking Hindi. 4. As soon as food is laid on the table, everybody sit down to eat. 5. As soon as the teacher comes to the class,the students will become quiet. 6.As soon as father enters the house, he begins to shout at everybody. 7. As soon as you[inf.] are ready, we[m.pl] will set out. 8. As soon as we buy a new house, we will invite you. 9. As soon as you decide please inform us. 10. As soon as it is evening, the birds fly back to their nests.

Key G 26.1

1. As soon as she/he read the letter, she/he tore it. 2. As soon as she/he saw the advertisement, she/he sent in the application. 3. As soon as I[f.] learn Hindi, I will go to India. 4. As soon as he/she passed the exam, he/she got a job. 5. As soon as children return home, they ask for something to eat. 6. As soon as they[m.pl.] sold the house, they went to the countryside. 7 As soon as the thief saw the police, he ran away. 8. As soon as the landlord said we vacated the house. 9. As soon as it is evening, we shut the doors and the windows. 10.As soon as the clothes dry, fold and keep them.

Key G 26.2

1. सुबह होते ही माता जी पूजा करने लगती हैं। 2. चार बजते ही मंदिर में घण्टियाँ बजने लगती हैं। 3. रॉबर्ट भारत आते ही हिन्दी बोलने लगा। 4. खाना मेज़ पर लगते ही आप सब खाने बैठ जाइए। 5. अध्यापक के कक्षा में आते ही, छात्र चुप हो जाएँगे। 6. पिता जी घर में घुसते ही सब पर चिल्लाने लगेंगे। 7. तुम्हारे तैयार होते ही हम चल पड़ेंगे। 8. हम नया

घर ख़रीदते ही आपको निमंत्रण देंगे। 9. आप निर्णय लेते ही हमें सूचित कीजिएगा।

10. सन्ध्या होते ही पक्षी अपने घोसलों को लौटने लगते हैं

1. subah hote hī mātā jī pūjā karne lagtī haiṁ. 2. cār bajte hī mandir meṁ ghaṇṭiyāṁ bajne lagtī haiṁ. 3. Robert bhārat āte hī hindī bolne lagā. 4. khānā mez par lagte hī sab khāne baiṭh jāie. 5. adhyāpak ke kakṣā meṁ āte hī chātra cup ho jāeṁge. 6. pitā jī ghar meṁ ghuste hī sab par cillāne lageṁge. 7. tumhāre taiyār hote hi ham cal paṛeṁge. 8. ham nayā ghar kharīdte hī āpko nimantraṇ deṁge. 9. āp nirṇay lete hī hameṁ sūcit kījiegā. 10. sandhyā hote hī pakṣī apne ghoṁsloṁ ko lauṭne lagte haiṁ.

☞ **Often new learners confuse between kar- conjunct and simultaneous activity.**

- **kar- conjunct is used only when it is the same subject doing several activities, one following the other, not necessarily immediately.**
- **v.r. + te + hī is used when the activities immediately follow each other, they are almost simultaneous, regardless whether the subject of the two activities is same or different.**

●●●●●

G 27 'to like' something or somebody

■ पसन्द करना pasand karnā

subject in the Nom. case	+	object	+	pasand karnā पसन्द करना	+	honā होना in the required tense to agree with the subject

COMPREHENSION – पसन्द करना pasand karnā

1. मैं m.sg तैरना पसन्द करता हूँ। maiṁ tairnā pasand kartā hūṁ.	I like to swim.
2. वह msg. क्रिकेट खेलना पसन्द करता था । vah kriket khelnā pasand kartā thā.	He used to like to play cricket.
3. तुम m.inf. क्या करना पसन्द करोगे? tum kyā karnā pasand karoge?	What would you like to do?

■ पसन्द होना pasand honā / अच्छा लगना acchā lagnā

(subj.+ को ko)	+	obj.	+	पसन्द pasand / अच्छा लगता m.sg acchā lagtā / अच्छे लगते m.pl. acche lagte / अच्छी लगती f.sg./pl. acchā lagtī	+	होना honā in the required tense to agree with the object

THE VERB - 'pasand karnā/honā/ānā

COMPREHENSION – पसन्द होना pasand honā / अच्छा लगना acchā lagnā

1. मुझको तैरना पसन्द है। mujhko tairnā pasand hai.	I like to swim.
1a. मुझको तैरना अच्छा लगता है। mujhko tairnā acchā lagtā hai	Swimming pleases me.
2. उसको क्रिकेट खेलना पसन्द था । usko kriketॖ khelnā pasand thā.	He/She used to like to play cricket.
2a. उसको क्रिकेट खेलना अच्छा लगता था । usko kriketॖ khelnā acchā lagtā thā.	Playing criket used to please him/her.
3. उसको हिन्दी बोलना पसन्द होगा । usko Hindi bolnā pasand hogā.	She would like to speak Hindi.
3a. उसको हिन्दी बोलना अच्छा लगेगा । usko Hindi bolnā acchā lagegā.	Speaking Hindi would please her.

■ **पसन्द आना pasand ānā (This is used to express liking or disliking for something after actually experiencing the object, a noun or activity.)**

(subject+ **को** ko) + object + पसन्द आना pasand ānā + होना honā

in the required tense
to agree with the object

COMPREHENSION – पसन्द आना pasand ānā

1. मुझको डरावनी फ़िल्में हमेशा पसन्द आती है। mujhko ḍrāvnī filmeṁ hameśā pasand ātī haiṁ.	I always like horror films.

2. क्या आपको नया घर पसन्द आया। kyā āpko nayā ghar pasand āyā. — Did you like the new house?

3. मुझे उसका स्वभाव बहुत पसन्द आया। mujhe uskā svabhāv bahut pasand āyā. — I liked his nature very much.

4. आपको भारत ज़रूर पसन्द आएगा। āpko bhārat zarūr pasand āegā. — You will certainly like India.

Ex. G 27. Translate into English:

1. हम m.pl. दूरदर्शन देखना पसन्द करते हैं । 2. वे m.pl. भारतीय खाना पसन्द करते थे । 3. वह f.sg. हिन्दी बोलना पसन्द करेगी। 4. हमें दूरदर्शन देखना पसन्द है / हमें दूरदर्शन देखना अच्छा लगता है। 5. उनको भारतीय खाना पसन्द था। / उनको भारतीय खाना अच्छा लगता था। 6. तुम्हें क्या करना पसन्द होगा ?/ तुम्हें क्या करना अच्छा लगेगा? 7. मुझे उसका व्यवहार पसन्द नहीं आया। 8. मुझे उनका रहन–सहन बहुत पसन्द आया। 9. क्या आपको उस भोजनालय का खाना पसन्द आया?10. हमें यह पत्रिका कोई ख़ास पसन्द नहीं आई।

1. ham dūrdarśan dekhnā pasand karte haiṁ. 2. ve bhārtīyă khānā pasand karte the. 3. vah hindī bolnā pasand karegī. 4. hameṁ dūrdarśan dekhnā pasand hai. / hameṁ dūrdarśan dekhnā acchā lagtā hai. 5. unko bhārtīyă khānā pasand thā./ unko bhārtīyă khānā acchā lagtā thā. 6. tumheṁ kyā karnā pasand hogā?/ tumheṁ kyā karnā acchā lagegā? 7. mujhe uskā vyavhār pasand nahīṁ āyā. 8. mujhe unkā rahan-sahan bahut pasand āyā. 9. kyā āpko us bhojanālay kā khānā pasand āyā. 10. hameṁ yah patrikā koī khās pasand nahīṁ āī.

Key 27.

1. We like to watch TV. 2. They used to like Indian food. 3. She would like to speak Hindi. 4. We like to watch TV. 5. They used to like Indian food. 6. What would you like to do? 7. I did not like his/ her behavior. 8. I liked their life-style very much. 9. Did you like food in that restaurant. 10. We did not quite like this magazine.

●●●●●

G 28 COMPOUND VERBS

root of the main verb + some other verb + honā होना when necessary

Compound verbs in Hindi are much used syntactic device by the native speakers. It is used in all tenses, but more so in the past simple, present as well as past perfect tense.

- meaning is given by the root of the main verb.
- the compounded verb, which is actually conjugated in agreement with the subject or object as per grammatical requirement does not lend its meaning at all. This contributes by way of ' emphasis' and 'nuance'.
- The compound verbs can be used both in interrogative and affirmative sentences.
- They are not used in negative sentences.

Several verbs that are used to make compound verbs.

Three such verbs are jānā, जाना, lenā लेना, and denā. देना।

■ **jānā जाना is used in compound verbs to highlight the completion of action, change of state. It is used only with intransitive activities.**

1. तुम अब सो जाओ। tum ab so jāo.	Now you go to sleep (imperative)
2. बच्चा आठ बजे तक सो जाता है। baccā āṭh baje tak so jātā hai.	The child goes to sleep by eight o'clock. (present simple tense)
3. बच्चा सो गया है। baccā so gayā hai.	The child has fallen asleep. (present perfect tense)

4. बच्चा आठ बजे तक सो गया था।
baccā āṭh baje tak so gayā thā.
The child had fallen asleep by 8 o'clock. (past perfect tense)

In the sentences given above the compound verb used consists of the verb root of सोना sonā followed by जाना jānā and होना honā conjugated in agreement with the N and G of the Subject in the required tense. As you see, the meaning has been lent by the main verb सोना sonā of which only the root has been used. The verb जाना jānā only conveys the sense of completion of action and change from awake to sleeping state.

More examples:

1. महमान आ गए हैं।
mahmān ā gae haiṁ.
The guests have already come.

2. मौसम बदल गया है।
mausam badal gayā hai.
The weather has changed.

3. दूध फट गया है।
dūdh phaṭ gayā hai.
Milk has curdled.

4. कपड़े सूख गए हैं।
kapṛe sūkh gae haiṁ.
The clothes have dried.

5. डाक आ गई है।
ḍāk ā gaī hai.
The mail has already come.

6. बच्चा गिर गया था।
baccā gir gayā thā.
The child had fallen.

7. बरिश रुक गई थी।
bāriś ruk gaī thī.
The rain had stopped.

8. गाड़ी छूट गई थी।
gāṛī chūṭ gaī thī.
The train had departed.

■ लेना **lenā and** देना **denā are used with transitive verbs to convey the sense of completion of an activity.**

☞ लेना **lenā is used when the activity is to the favor of the doer.**

1. दवाई खा लीजिए। davāī khā lījie.	Please take the medicine. (imperative)
2. मैंने दवाई f.sg. खा ली है। maiṁne davāī khā lī hai.	I have already taken the medicine. (pres.perf.)
3. पिता जी ने अखबार m.sg. पढ़ लिया है। pitā jī ne akhbār paṛh liyā hai.	Father has already read the newspaper. (pres. perf.)

☞ देना **denā is used when the activity benefits someone other than the doer.**

1. नौकर ने घर m.sg. साफ़ कर दिया है। naukar ne ghar m.sg. sāf kar diyā hai.	The servant has cleaned the house. (pres. perf.)
2. धोबी ने कपड़े m.spl. धो दिए हैं। dhobī ne kapṛe m.sg..pl. dho die haiṁ.	The washerman has washed the clothes. (pres. perf.)
3. मैंने किताबें f.pl. लौटा दी थीं। maiṁne kitābeṁ f.pl. lauṭā dī thīṁ.	I had returned the books. (past. perf)

■ चुकना cuknā is another much used verb in compound verb constructions to denote the completion of the activity. Where as जाना jānā is used for intran sitive activities and always agrees with the N and G of the Subject, and लेना lenā or देना denā are used for transitive activities, which in the past tense agree with the N and G of the Object.

☞ The verb चुकना cuknā can be used with transitive as well as intransitive activities in compound verbs. It agrees with the N and G of the Subject in all tenses. See examples given below.

1. महमान आ गए हैं। mahmān ā gae haiṁ. — The guests have already come.

=

महमान आ चुके हैं।

mahmān ā cuke haiṁ.

2. मैंने दवाई[f.sg.] खा ली है। — I have already taken the medicine.
mait̆ne davāī khā lī hai.

=

मैं दवाई[f.sg.] खा चुका / चुकी हूँ ।
maiṁne davāī khā cukā /cukī hūṁ.

3. पिता जी ने अखबार[m.sg.] पढ़ लिया है। — Father has already read the newspaper.
pitā jī ne akhbār paṛh liyā hai.

=

पिता जी अखबार[m.sg.] पढ़ चुके हैं।
pitā jī akhbār paṛh cuke haiṁ.

4. नौकर ने घर[m.sg.] साफ़ कर दिया है। — The servant has cleaned the house.
naukar ne ghar[m.sg.] sāf kar diyā hai.

=

नौकर घर[m.sg.] साफ़ कर चुका है।

naukar ghar[m.sg.] sāf kar cukā hai.

5. धोबी ने कपड़े[m.spl.] धो दिए हैं। — The washerman has washed the clothes.
dhobī ne kapṛe[m.sg..pl.] dho die haiṁ.

=

धोबी कपड़े[m.spl.] धो चुका है।

dhobī kapṛe[m.sg..pl.] dho cukā hai .

■ Use of the verbs पड़ना paṛnā, उठना uṭhnā for sudden, rash and impulsive actions

1. चोर दीवार से कूद पड़ा। — The thief jumped off the wall.

cor dīvār se kūd paṛā.

2. लड़का पेड़ से गिर पड़ा। larka per se gir parā.	The boy fell off the tree.
3. वह दर्द से कराह उठा। vah dard se karāh uthā.	He cried out of pain.
4. छात्र बीच में बोल उठे। chātra bīc meṁ bol uthe.	The student spoke in between. (The students cut in.)

■ **Use of डालना ḍālnā, बैठना baiṭhnā, for rash, impulsive action:**

1. बच्चे ने कागज़ फाड़ डाला। bacce ne kāgaz phāṛ ḍāla.	The child tore the paper.
2. उसने दरवाज़ा तोड़ डाला। usne darvāzā toṛ ḍāla.	He smashed the door down.
3. वह मालिक बन बैठा है। vah mālik ban baiṭhā hai.	He has become the owner.
4. कुत्ता मालिक के पैरों में जा बैठा। kuttā mālik ke pairoṁ meṁ jā baiṭhā.	The dog went and sat down at the feet of his owner.

■ **Inability expression (verb root + पाना) imply ability with some special effort or inability despite effort.**

1. मैं कल तक काम ख़त्म नहीं कर पाऊँगा। maiṁ kal tak kām khatma nahīṁ, kar pāuṁgā.	I will not be able to finish the work by tomorrow evening.
2. आज हम बाहर नहीं जा पाए। āj ham bāhar nahīṁ jā pāe.	We could not go out today.

●●●●●

CONJUNCT VERBS

■ **को + noun/adjective+ verb**

X को पसन्द$^{f.}$ करना	X ko pasand karnā	to like X
X को शुरू$^{m.}$ करना	X ko śurū karnā	to start X
X को ख़त्म$^{adj.}$ करना	X ko khatm karnā	to finish
X को भंग$^{adj.}$ करना	X ko bhaṅg karnā	to dissolve X
X को महसूस करना	X ko mahsūs karnā	to feel X
X को याद$^{f.}$ करना	X ko yād karnā	to remember X
X को सावधान करना	X ko sāvdhān karnā	to caution X
X को प्रेम$^{m.}$ करना	X ko prem karnā	to love X
X को क्षमा$^{f.}$ करना	X ko kṣamā karnā	to forgive X
X को दुखी करना	X ko dukhī karnā	to hurt 'X'
X को खुश करना	X ko khuś karnā	to please X
X को दिखाई देना	X ko dikhāī denā	to be visible to X
X को सुनाई देना	X ko sunāī denā	to be audible to X
X को सलाह$^{f.}$ देना	X ko salāh denā	to advice X
X को चेतावनी$^{f.}$ देना	X ko cetāvnī denā	to warn X
X को सज़ा$^{f.}$/दण्ड$^{m.}$ देना	X ko sazā / daṇḍ denā	to punish X
X को आज्ञा^{f}/इजाज़त देना	X ko agyā / ijāzat denā	to permit X
X को उत्तर$^{m.}$/जवाब$^{m.}$ देना	X ko uttar /javāb denā	to answer X
X को वचन$^{m.}$ देना	X ko vacan denā	to promise X
X को होश$^{f.}$ आना	X ko hoś ānā	to regain conciousness
X को क्रोध$^{m.}$ आना	X ko krodh ānā	for X to become angry
X को पसन्द$^{f.}$ आना	X ko pasand ānā	for X to like something
X को महक$^{f.}$ आना	X ko mahak ānā	for X to smell
X को नींद$^{f.}$ आना	X ko nīṁd ānā	for X to feel sleepy
X को बुखार$^{m.}$ आना	X ko bukhār ānā	for X to get fever
X को गुस्सा$^{m.}$ आना	X ko gussā ānā	for X to get angry

X को मज़ा[m.] आना/	X ko mazā ānā/	for X to enjoy
आनन्द[m.] आना	ānand ānā	" "
X को Y (activity) आना	X koY(activity) ānā	for X to know how to do Y
X को नज़र[f.] आना	X ko nazar ānā	to be visible to X
X को भूख[f.] लगना	X ko bhūkh lagnā	for X to feel hungry
X को प्यास[f.] लगना	X ko pyās lagnā	for X to feel thirsty
X को गर्मी[f.] लगना	X ko garmī lagnā	for X to feel hot
X को ठण्ड[f.] लगना	X ko ṭhaṇḍ lagnā	for X to feel cold
X को चोट[f.] लगना	X ko coṭ lagnā	for X to be injured
X को अच्छा लगना	X ko acchā lagnā	for X to like something
X को ख़राब लगना	X ko kharāb lagnā	for X to dislike something
X को महँगा लगना	X ko mahṁgā lagnā	for X to find s.th. expen sive
X को बासी लगना	X ko bāsi lagnā	for X to find s.th. stale
X को ताज़ा लगना	X ko tāzā lagnā	for X to find s.th. fresh
X को चिपचिपा लगना	X ko cipcipā lagnā	for X to find s.th. sticky
X को फिसलना लगना	X ko phisalnā lagnā	for X to find s.th. slippery
X को Y की आदत[f.] होना	X koY kī ādat honā	for X to be used to Y
X को नुकसान[m.] पहुँचाना	ko nuksān pahuṁcānā	to cause harm to X
X को मार[f.] पड़ना	X ko mār paṛnā	for X to be beaten
X को बेवकूफ बनाना	X ko bevkūf banānā	to befool X

■ **की + noun (f.)+ verb**

X की बात[f.] मानना	X kī bāt mānanā	to listen to X
X की हानि[f.] करना	X kī hāni karnā	to cause loss to X
X की मरम्मत[f.] करना	X kī marammat karnā	to repair X
X की हँसी[f.] उड़ाना	X kī haṁsī uṛānā	to jeer at X
X की तलाश[f.]/खोज[f.] करना	X kī talāś / khoj karnā	to search X
X की देखभाल[f.] करना	X kī dekhbhāl karnā	to look after X

X की सहायता[f.] करना	X kī sahāyatā	to help X
X की मदद[m.] करना	X kī madad karnā	to help X
X की प्रशंसा[f.] करना	X kī praśaṁsā karnā	to praise X
X की प्रतीक्षा[f.] करना	X kī pratīkṣā karnā	to wait X
X की सलाह[f.] मानना	X kī salāh mānanā	to listen to X's advice
X की आज्ञा[f.] मानना	X kī āgyā mānanā	to obey X

■ **का + noun + verb**

X का आयोजन[m.] करना	X kā āyojan karnā	to organise X
X का इन्तज़ार[m.] करना	X kā intzār karnā	to wait X
X का इलाज[m.] करना	X kā ilāj karnā	to treat X
X का निश्चय[m.] करना	X kā niścay karnnā	to resolve to do X
X का संकल्प[m.] करना	X kā saṅkalp karnā	to vow to do X
X का ध्यान[m.] रखना	X kā dhyān rakhnā	to take care of X
X का अनुमान[m.] लगाना	X kā anumān lagānā	to guess about X

■ **से + noun /adj.+ verb**

X से बदला लेना	X se badlā lenā	to revenge oneself on X
X से मन मिलना	X se man milnā	to find X congenial with one's temperament
X से डर लगना	X se ḍar lagnā	to be afraid of X
X से संतुष्ट होना	X se santuṣṭ honā	to be content with X

■ **पर + noun + verb**

X पर विश्वास करना	X par viśvās karnnā	to have faith in X
X पर सन्देह करना	X par sandeh karnnā	to suspect X
X पर दया करना	X par dayā karnnā	to have mercy on X

●●●●●

CAUSATIVE VERBS

Hindi discriminates between causative 1 and causative 2.

Causative 1 verbs are used were X causes Y to do something.

Causative 2 verbs are used where 'X' uses some agent to cause 'Y' to do something.

Examples - Causative 1

☞ **All the (-a) sentences given below are intransitive or transitive verbs; the subject is doing the activity himself.**

☞ **All the (-b) sentences given below are causative 1; the subject is causing someone else to do the activity.**

1a.	माता जी ने मिठाई **खाई**। mātā jī ne miṭhāī khāī.	Mother **ate** sweets.
1b.	माता जी ने हमको मिठाई **खिलाई**। mātā jī ne hamko miṭhāī khilāī.	Mother **offered** us sweets **to eat.**
2a.	हमने लस्सी **पी**। hamne lassī pī.	We **drank** 'lassi'.
2b.	हमने उनको लस्सी **पिलाई**। hamne unko lassī pilāī	We **offered** them 'Lassi' **to drink.**
3a.	विद्यार्थी ने पाठ **पढ़ा**। vidyārthī ne pāṭh paṛhā.	The student **learnt** the lesson.
3b.	अध्यापक ने पाठ **पढ़ाया**। adhyāpak ne pāṭh paṛhāyā.	The teacher **taught** the lesson.
4a.	मैं गंगा में **नहाई**। maiṁ gaṅgā meṁ nahāī.	I **bathed** in the Ganges.

4b. मैंने बच्चे को **नहलाया।** maiṁne bacce ko nahlāyā.	I **bathed** the child.
5a. नौकरानी **सोई।** naukrānī soī.	The maidservant **slept**.
5b. नौकरानी ने बच्चे को **सुलाया।** naukrānī ne bacce ko sulāyā.	The maidservant **put** the child **to sleep**.

Causative 2

Initiator subject + mediary agent + obj. followed by 'से' + causative verb + होना in the required tense

COMPREHENSION

1. मेरा सामान गाड़ी में रखवा दीजिए। merā sāmān gāṛī meṁ rakhvā dījie.	Have my things loaded on the train.
2. हम अपना घर नौकर से साफ़ करवाते है। ham apnā ghar naukar se sāf karvāte haiṁ.	We have our house cleaned by the servant.
3. मैं महीने में एक बार अपने बाल कटवाती हूँ। maiṁ mahīne meṁ ek bār apne bāl kaṭvātī hūṁ.	I get my hair cut once a month.
4. आप अपने कपड़े किससे सिलवाती हैं? āp apne kapṛe kisse silvātī haiṁ.	By whom do you get your clothes stitched?
5. माता जी ने यह साड़ी बनारस से मंगवाई। mātā jī ne yah sāṛī banāras se maṁgvāī.	Mother had the sari brought from Banaras.

Ex. G 28 Translate into English:

1. माता जी पाँच बजे **उठीं।** 2. माता जी ने मुझको पाँच बजे **उठाया।** 3. हमने कहानी **सुनी।** 4. दादी जी ने हमको कहानी **सुनाई।** 5. उसने अपनी घड़ी ठीक करवाई। 6. शाहजहाँ ने ताजमहल कब बनवाया था? 7. हमने यह मकान पिछले साल बनवाया। 8. हम अगले सोमवार को अपने घर में रुद्र अभिषेक करवाएँगे। 9. मैं अपने बागीचे में पीला गुलाब लगवाऊँगी। 10. उसने ये कपड़े धोबी से धुलवाए है। 11. इस पत्र पर अधिकारी के हस्ताक्षर करवाइए । 12. उसके बाद, इस पर मोहर लगवाइए।

1. mātā jī pāṁc baje uṭhīṁ. 2. mātā jī ne mujhko pāṁc baje uṭhāyā. 3. hamne kahānī sunī. 4. dādī jī ne hamko kahānī sunāī. 5. usne apnī ghaṛī ṭhīk karvāī

6. śhahjahāṁ ne Tājmahal kab banvāyā thā? 7. hamne yah makān pichle sāl banvāyā. 8. ham apne ghar meṁ agle somvār ko rudra abhiṣek karvāeṁge. 9. maiṁ apne bāgīce meṁ pīlā gulāb lagvāūṁgī. 10. usne ye kapṛe dhobhī se dhulvāe haiṁ. 11. āp is patra par adhikārī ke hastākṣar karvāie. 12. uske bād, is par mohar lagvāie.

Key G 28

1. Mother got up at 5 o'clock.2. Mother woke me up at 5 o'clock. 3. We listened to the story. 4. Grandmother narrated to us a story. 5. She had her watch repaired. 6. When did Shahjahan get the Tajmahal built? 7. We had this house built last year. 8. Next Monday, we will have Rudra-Abhishek done in our house . 9. I will have yellow rose planted in my garden. 10. She has had these clothes washed by the washerman. 11. Have this letter signed by the chief. 12. After that, have it stamped.

●●●●●

G 29 CONTINUATIVE COMPOUND

(' keep on/go on verb+ing')

Hindi differentiates between ongoing activities and on going states.

- For ongoing activities, Hindi uses (verb root + tā / te / tī) + the verb 'rahnā' in the required tense to agree with the N and G of the Subject .

subject + object + (v.r.+ tā / te / tī) + रहना rahnā + होना honā in the required tense to agree with the N and G of the subject

COMPREHENSION

1. बच्चा[m.sg] रोता रहता है। baccā rotā rahtā hai.	The child keeps crying. (present simple tense)
2. बच्चा[m.sg] रोता रहता था। baccā rotā rahtā thā.	The child used to keep crying. (past habitual tense)
3. बच्चा[m.sg] रोता रहा। baccā rotā rahā.	The child kept crying. (past simple tense)
4. बच्चा[m.sg] रोता रहेगा। baccā rotā rahegā.	The child will keep crying. (future simple tense)

- **For ongoing states, Hindi uses (verb root + ā / e / ī) + the verb 'rahnā' in the required tense to agree with the N and G of the subject.**

For Example:

1. बच्चा[m.sg] सोया रहता है। baccā soyā rahtā hai.	The child keeps sleeping. (present simple tense)
2. बच्चा[m.sg] सोया रहता था।	The child used to keep sleep

	baccā soyā rahtā thā.	ing. (past habitual tense)
3.	बच्चा^m.sg सोया रहा। baccā soyā rahā.	The child kept sleeping. (past simple tense)
4.	बच्चा^m.sg सोया रहेगा। baccā soyā rahegā.	The child will keep sleeping. (future simple tense)

Ex. G 29 Translate into Hindi.

1.छात्र हँसते रहते थे। 2. वह खाता रहता है। 3. तुम क्यों धूम्रपान करते रहते हो? 4. बोलते रहिए। 5. आप अभ्यास करते रहिएगा। 6. वह हर समय कुछ सोचती रहती है। 7. आप बिना वजह चिन्ता करती रहती हैं। 8. आजकल मेरे पेट में हल्का–हल्का दर्द होता रहता है। 9. मैं कोशिश करता रहूँगा।10.पिता जी रात भर खाँसते रहे। 11. मैं दिन भर लेटी रही। 12. ये किताबें सदैव इसी अलमारी में रखी रहती हैं।

1. chātra haṁste rahte the. 2. vah khātā rahtā thā. 3. tum kyoṁ dhūmrapān karte rahte ho? 4. bolte rahie. 5. āp abhyās karte rahiegā. 6. vah har samay kuch soctī rahtī hai. 7. āp binā vajah cintā kartī rahtī haiṁ. 8. ājkal mere peṭ meṁ halkā-halkā dard hotā rahtā hai. 9. maiṁ kośiś kartā rahūṁgā. 10. pitā jī rāt bhar khāṁste rahe.11. maiṁ din bhar leṭī rahī. 12. ye kitābeṁ sadaiv isī almārī meṁ rakhī rahtī haiṁ.

Key G 29

1. The students used to keep laughing. 2. He keeps eating. 3. Why do you keep smoking all the time.? 4. Keep talking. 5. Keep practicing. 6. She keeps thinking about something all the time. 7. You keep worrying for no reason.8. These days, I keep getting faint stomach aches. 9. I will keep trying. 10 . Father kept coughing all night. 11. I kept lying all day. 12. These books are always kept in this cupboard.

●●●●●

G 30 TELLING TIME

nh = number of the hour ; nm = number of minutes

■ Talking about complete hour : nh + bajā hai/baje haiṁ:

कितने बजे हैं?	kitne baje haiṁ	What time is it?
एक बजा है।	ek bajā hai.	It is one o'clock.
दो बजे हैं।	do baje haiṁ	It is two o'clock.
तीन बजे हैं।	tīn baje haiṁ	It is three o'clock.

■ a quarter past — savā + nh + bajā hai[sg.]/baje haiṁ:

सवा (एक) बजा है।	savā (ek) bajā hai.	It is a quarter past one.
सवा दो बजे हैं।	savā do baje haiṁ	It is a quarter past two.
सवा तीन बजे हैं।	savā tīn baje haiṁ	It is a quarter past three.

■ a quarter to —- paun/paune + nh + bajā hai/baje haiṁ

पौन बजा है।	paun bajā hai.	It is a quarter to one.
पौने दो बजे हैं।	paune do baje haiṁ	It is a quarter to two.
पौने तीन बजे हैं।	paune tīn baje haiṁ	It is a quarter to three.

■ half past the hour

डेढ़ बजा है।	deṛh bajā hai.	It is half past one.
ढ़ाई बजे हैं।	dhāi baje haiṁ	It is half past two.
साढ़े तीन बजे हैं।	sāṛhe tīn baje haiṁ	It is half past three.

■ minutes past the hour = nh + bajkar + nm

दो बजकर पाँच मिनट	do bajkar pāṁc minaṭ	five past two
दस बजकर बीस मिनट	das bajkar bīs minaṭ	ten past twenty

■ **minutes before the hour = nh + bajne meṁ + nm**

दो बजने में पाँच मिनट	do bajne meṁ pāṁc minaṭ	five to two
दस बजने में बीस मिनट	das bajne meṁ bīs minaṭ	twenty to ten

Ex. G 30.1 Say in Hindi.

1. 2:30; 2. 1:50; 3. 7:30; 4. 10:55; 5. 8:15; 6. 12:45; 7. 1:15; 8. 1:30; 9. 5.08

Ex. G 30.2: Translate into Hindi.

1. He comes to my house daily at 2:10. 2. We watch news at ten to two. (1:50). 3. The school bell rings daily at a quarter to two (1:45). 4. We eat lunch at 12:30. 5. Mother gets up at 4: 45 in the morning. 6. We sleep at 11 o'clock at night. 7. He came at 8:20 in the morning. 8. We will go out at a quarter to seven in the evening. 9. The postman will come at about 2.30.

Key G 30.1

1. ढाई; 2. दो बजने में दस मिनट; 3. साढ़े सात; 4. ग्यारह बजने में पाँच मिनट; 5. सवा आठ; 6. पौना: एक; 7. सवा एक; 8. डेढ़; 9. पाँच बजकर आठ मिनट।

1. ḍhāī; 2..do bajne meṁ das minaṭ; 3. sāṛhe sāt; 4. gyārah bajne meṁ pāṁc minaṭ; 5. savā āṭh; 6. paunā ek; 7. savā ek; 8. ḍeṛh; 9. pāṁc bajkar āṭh minaṭ.

Key G 30.2

1. वह रोज़ मेरे घर दो बजकर दस मिनट पर आता है। 2. हम दो बजने में दस मिनट पर समाचार देखते हैं। 3. स्कूल की घंटी रोज़ पौने दो बजे बजती है। 4. हम साढ़े बारह बजे दिन का खाना खाते है। 5. माँ सुबह पौने पाँच बजे उठती है। 6. हम रात को ग्यारह बजे सोते है। 7. वह सुबह आठ बजकर बीस मिनट पर आया। 8. हम शाम को पौने सात बजे बाहर जाएँगे। 9. डाकिया लगभग ढाई बजे आएगा।

1. vah roz mere ghar do bajkar das minaṭ par ātā hai. 2. ham do bajne meṁ das minaṭ par samācār dekhte haiṁ 3. skūl kī ghaṇṭī roz paune do baje bajtī hai. 4. ham sāṛhe bārah baje din kā khānā khāte haiṁ. 5. māṁ subah paune paṁc baje uṭhtī haiṁ. 6. ham rāt ko gyārah baje sote haiṁ. 7. vah subah āṭh bajkar bīs minaṭ par āyā. 8. ham śām ko paune sāt baje bāhar jāeṁge. 9. ḍākiyā lagbhag ḍhāi baje āegā.

●●●●●

G 31 PRESUMPTION

■ Present Presumptive

- **Use the future form of होना honā to agree with the subject when presuming the probability of 'being' or 'non being' of something.**

1.	श्रीमती शर्मा यहीं कहीं होंगी। srīmatī śarmā yahīṁ kahīṁ hoṁgī.	Mrs. Sharma must be somewhere here.
2.	उसकी आयु लगभग पचास वर्ष होगी। uskī āyu lagbhag pachās varṣ hogī.	He/She must be about fifty years old.

- **Use (v.r. + ता,ते,ती) + future form of होना honā, both to agree with the subject when presuming the probability of a habitual activity.**

1.	वह जानती होगी। vah jāntī hogī.	She must be knowing.
2	वे चावल खाते होंगे। ve cāval khāte hoṁge.	They must be eating rice.

☞ **Imperfect participle of आना ānā + future form of होना honā is an execeptional use meaning the subject is expected to arrive any moment.**

3.	आपकी बहन आती होगी। āpkī bahan ātī hogī.	Your sister must be coming.

■ Progressive Presumptive

- **Use (v.r. + रहा, रहे, रही) + future form of होना to agree with the subject when presuming the probability of some action in progress at a certain time.**

1.	अध्यापिका पढ़ा रही होंगी। adhyāpikā paṛhā rahī hoṁgī.	The teacher must be teaching.
2.	मेरे ख्याल में बच्चे खेल रहे होंगे।	I think children must be playing.

mere khayāl mem bacce khel
rahe homge.

Past Presumptive

- **Use past participle (i.e. v.r. + आ ā ,ए e, ई ī) + future form of होना honā**

(a) to agree with the subject when verb transitive. (example 1)
(b) to agree with the object when v.t. (example 2)
(b) when it is transitive verb without mentioning the object, use only masculine singular third person i.e. -आ-form.. (example 3)

1. वह यहाँ आया होगा। — He must have come here.
   vah yahāṁ āyā hogā.
2. किसीने उसे ख़बर दी होगी। — Someone must have informed her/him.
   kisīne use khabar dī hogī.
3. कल सभा में क्या हुआ होगा? — What could have happened in the meeting yesterday?
   kal sabhā meṁ kyā huā hogā?

Alternatively use of (v.r.+ चुकना cuknā) + future form of होना honā in present or past presumptive.:

☞ **चुकना cuknā and होना honā always agree with the subject.**

1. वे **(m.pl.)** सुबह सात बजे तक नाश्ता कर चुकते होंगे। — They must be finished with their breakfast by 7 a.m. **(habitual presumptive)**
   ve subah sāt baje tak nāśta kar cukte hoṁge.
2. वह **(m.sg.)** आ चुका होगा। — He must have already come. **(past presumtive)**
   vah ā cukā hogā.
3. वे **(m.pl.)** खा चुके होंगे। — They must have already eaten.
   ve khā cuke hoṁge.
4. औरतें **(f.pl.)**पानी भर चुकी होंगी। — Women must have already filled water.
   aurteṁ pānī bhar cukī hoṁgī.

●●●●●

G 32 INTERJECTION

■ Joy — हर्षबोधक

वाह! Vāh — Splendid!, Wonderful!

वाह वाह! Vāh vāh! — expression of applaud and praise

आहा! Āhā! — Vow! (to express pleasant surprise)

■ Praise, acknowledgement, inspirational
प्रशंसार्थक, स्वीकृति बोधक, विनय बोधक

शाबाश Śābāś! — Bravo!; बस! Bas! — Thats all!

ठीक! Ṭhīk !— Correct! ; अच्छा! Acchā! — Okay

■ Surprise — आश्चर्यबोधक अव्यय

क्या! Kkyā! — what ; ऐं! Aiṁ! — astonishment

हैं! Haiṁ! — "" "" """

■ Anger, Regret, Worry — शोकबोधक

आह! (āh) — Oh! — grief हाय! Hāy! — Oh!

बाप रे! — Bāp re! —surprise अफ़सोस! Aphsos) —Sad! (sorrow)

राम राम! Rām Rām — Oh God!

■ Fear — भयबोधक अव्यय

त्राहि! Trāhi! — Help; दुहाई! Duhāī!— Cry for help

राम राम! Rām Rām! — God forbid!

Irritation, comtempt, scorn, disgust

छी छी! Chī Chī! — ugh! shame! चुप! Chup — quite
हट! Haṭ!—Out of the way! दुर! दुर दुर! dur! dur !dur! — be ff! clear out!

थू थू! Thū thū — Shame!
धिक्कार! (dhikkār) — fie! Be cursed!

Common Greetings Among Hindus

राम राम! Rām Rām; जय श्रीकृष्ण! Jay śrī Kṛṣṇa
नमस्ते Namaste); नमस्कार Namaskār
पालागी Pālāgī; प्रणाम Praṇām

Among muslims:

सलाम salām; तसलीमात taslīmāt
बंदगी bandagī;

Some other polite expression

कृपया kṛpayā; मेहरबानी करके meharbānī karke Please!
धन्यवाद dhanyăvād; शुक्रिया Sśukriyā Thanks!

●●●●●

G 33 RELATIVE PRONOUN

जो is used in the direct case.

जिस sg. / जिन pl. followed by suitable postposition are used in the oblique case.

In Hindi use of को is not obligatory when the object is non living. In this case जो can be used in the oblique case.

Examples :

1. जो किताब खोई है, उसको ढूँढ़िए। — Look for the book that is lost.
   jo kitāb khoī hai, usko ḍhūṁḍhie.
2. जो ज़्यादा सोता है, वह बहुत खोता है। — The one who sleeps more, he loses a lot.
   jo zyādā sotā hai, vah bahut khotā hai.
3. मैं उस शहर में कभी नहीं गई जिसमे मेरा जनम हुआ था। — I have never been to the city in which I was born.
   maiṁ us śahar meṁ kabhī nahīṁ gaī jismeṁ merā janam huā thā.
4. तुम पहले आदमी हो जिसने सब काम ठीक से किया है। — You are the first man who has done everything properly.
   tum pahle ādmī ho jisne sab kām ṭhīk se kiyā hai.
5. यही वह लड़की है, जिससे सब मिलना चाहते हैं। — This is that girl whom everyone wants to meet.
   yahī vah laṛkī hai, jisse sab milnā cāhte haiṁ.
6. यही अध्यापिका है जिसको — This is the teacher whom all

सब छात्र बहुत प्यार करते हैं। yahī adhyāpikā hai jisko sab chātra bahut pyār karte haiṁ.	students love much.
9. जिस जगह पर राम बैठा है, वहाँ पहले मैं बैठा था। jis jagah par rām baiṭhā hai, vahāṁ pahle meṁ baiṭhā thā.	The place at which Ram is sitting, formerly I was sitting there.

CORELATIVES

Time related corelatives

जब .... तब	jab..............tab	when....then
जबसे ....तबसे	jab se.............tab se	since....since then
जबभी...........तभी	jab bhī.............tabhī	whenever....just then
ज्यों ही..........त्यों ही	jyoṁ hī....... .tyoṁ hī	as soon as......just then
जैसे ही............ वैस ही	jaise hī............vaise hī	as.soon as.......just then

1. **जब** तुम बुलाओगे, **तब** मैं आऊँगा।
   jab tum bulāoge, tab maiṁ āūṁgā.
   When you call me, I will come.

2 **जबसे** मै यहाँ आई हूँ, **तबसे** वह यहाँ नहीं है।
   jabse maiṁ yahāṁ āī hūṁ, tab se vah yahāṁ nahīṁ haiṁ.
   She/ He has not been here since I came here.

3. **जब भी** मैं उन्हें याद करती हूँ, **तभी** वे आ जाते हैं।
   jab bhī maiṁ unheṁ yād kartī hūṁ, tabhī ve ā jāte haiṁ.
   Whenever I remember them, (just then) they come over.

4. **जैसे ही** वे पहुँचे, **वैसे ही** बिजली चली गई।
   jaise hī ve pahuṁce, vaise hī bijlī calī gaī.
   As soon as they arrived, the electricity went off.

RELATIVE PRONOUNS

Place related corelatives

जहाँ ....वहाँ	jahāṁ...........vahāṁ	where........there

1. जहाँ उमस होती है, वहाँ मच्छर होते है।
   jahāṁ umas hotī hai, vahāṁ macchar hote haiṁ.
   Where there is humidity, (there) there are mosquitoes.

2 .जहाँ वह रहता है, वहाँ बहुत गर्मी होती है।
   jahāṁ vah rahtā hai, vahāṁ bahut garmī hotī hai.
   Where he lives (there) it is very hot.

Manner Related Corelatives

जैसे ....वैसे	jaise ....vaise......	as ......so..........

1. **जैसे** वह पढ़ाती है, **वैसे** कोई नहीं पढ़ाता।
   jaise vah paṛhātī hai, vaise koī nahīṁ paṛhātā.
   The way she teaches, (like that) no one teaches.
2. **जैसे** आप चाहेंगे, **वैसे** ही होगा।
   jaise āp cāheṁge, vaise hī hogā.
   As you wish, so will happen.

Adjectival Corelatives

जितनी .... **उतनी**	jitnī.....utnī	as much .....that much

1. **जितनी** मेहनत आप करते हैं, **उतनी** मैं नहीं कर सकता।
   jitnī mehnat āp karte haiṁ. utnī maiṁ nahīṁ kar saktā.
   As much hard work you do, that much I cannot do.

2 .**जितना** धन उसके पास है, **उतना** बहुत कम लोगों के पास है।
   jitnā dhan uske pās hai, utnā bahut kam logoṁ ke pās hai.
   As much wealth he has, that much very few people have.

Ex. G 33. 1: Translate in Hindi:

1. The man she married is a scientist. 2. Whosoever arrives first, will win. 3.

Send to my house the tailor who stitched your dress. 4. The man who is standing there is our postman. 5. The boys I was playing with are my classmates. 6. The city in which we live is very modern. 7. He who will work hard, will progress. 8. He who has broken this vase, may come in front. 9. The things that you said, I remember them. 10 The book that Rani is reading, that is very interesting.

Ex. G 33.2 Translate into Hindi:

1. मैं वही करूँगा जो आप कहेंगे। 2. मैं उन्ही को आमंत्रित करूँगा जिन्हें आप चाहेंगे। 3. तुम वही विषय पढ़ो जिनमें तुम्हें रुचि है।4. तुम वही पोशाक पहनो जो तुम्हें पसन्द है। 5. वह उसी काम को करता है जिसे वह ठीक समझता है। 6. मां मुझे उसी के साथ जाने देती है जिस पर वह विश्वास करती हैं। 7. जिसके लिए मैं इस शहर में आया, उसका स्थानान्तरण हो गया। 8. जिन्होंने मेरी सलाह मानी, वे बच गए। 9. जिनके अपने घर कांच के होते हैं, वे दूसरों के घरों पर पत्थर नहीं फेंकते।10. जिनमें आत्मबल होता है, वे अवश्य अपना लक्ष्य प्राप्त करते हैं।

1. maiṁ vahī karūṁgā jo āp kaheṁge.2. maiṁ unhīṁ ko āmantrit karūṁgā jinheṁ āp cāheṁ ge. 3. tum vahī viṣay paṛho jinmeṁ tumheṁ ruchi hai. 4. tum vahī pośāk pahno jo tumheṁ pasand hai. 5. vah usī kām ko kartā hai jise vah ṭhīk samajhtā hai. 6. māṁ mujhe usīke sāth jāne detī hai jispar vah viśvās kartī hai. 7. jiske lie maiṁ is śahar meṁ āyā, uskā sthānāntaraṇ ho gayā. 8. jinhoṁne merī salāh mānī, ve bac gae. 9. jinke apne ghar kāṁc ke hote haiṁ, ve dūsroṁ ke gharoṁ par patthar nahīṁ pheṁkte. 10. jinmeṁ ātmbal hotā hai, ve avaśyā apnā lakṣyā prāpt karte haiṁ.

Ex. G 33.3 Translate into English:

1. यद्यपि वह अमीर है, तो भी वह बहुत विनम्र है। 2. जब तक हम वहाँ पहुँचे, तब तक वे वहाँ से जा चुके थे। 3. जहाँ आप चाहेंगे, वहीं हम चलेंगे। 4. जब आप दिल्ली आएँ, तब हमारे घर ज़रूर आइएगा। 5. जो आप कहेंगे, वह मैं करूँगा। 6. जैसा आप चाहती थीं, वैसा ही हुआ। 7. जितनी मेहनत करोगे, उतनी सफलता पाओगे। 8. वह उतना बुद्धिमान नहीं जितना सब सोचते हैं।

1. yadyapi vah amīr hai, to bhī vah bahut vinamra hai. 2. jab tak ham vahāṁ pahuṁce, tab tak ve vahāṁ se jā cuke the. 3. jahāṁ āp cāheṁge, vahīṁ ham caleṁge. 4. jab āp dillī āeṁ, tab hamāre ghar zarūr āiegā. 5. jo āp kaheṁge, vah

maiṁ karūṁgā. 6. jaisā āp cāhtī thīṁ, vaisā hī huā 7. jitnī mehnat karoge, utnī saphaltā pāoge. 8. vah utnā buddhimān nahīṁ, jitnā sab socte haiṁ.

Key G 33.1

1. जिस आदमी से उसने शादी की, वह वैज्ञानिक है। 2. जो पहले पहुँचेगा, वही जीतेगा। 3. उस दर्जी को मेरे घर भेजिएगा, जिसने आपकी पोशाक सी। 4. जो आदमी वहाँ खड़ा है, वह हमारा डाकिया है। 5. जिन लड़कों के साथ मैं खेल रहा था, वे मेरे सहपाठी हैं। 6. जिस शहर में हम रहते हैं, वह बहुत आधुनिक है। 7. जो परिश्रम करेगा, वह प्रगति करेगा। 8. जिसने यह फूलदान तोड़ा है, वह सामने आए। 9. जो बातें आपने कहीं, वे मुझे याद हैं। 10. जो किताब रानी पढ़ रही है, बहुत रोचक है.।

1. jis ādmī se usne śādī kī, vah vaigyānik hai. 2. jo pahle pahuṁcegā, vahī jītegā. 3. us darzī ko mere ghar bhejiegā, jisne āpkī pośāk sī. 4. jo ādmī vahāṁ khaṛā hai, vah hamārā ḍākiyā hai. 5. jin laṛkoṁ ke sāth maiṁ khel rahā thā, ve mere sahpāṭhī haiṁ. 6. jis śahar meṁ ham rahte haiṁ, vah bahut ādhunik hai. 7. jo priśram baregā, vahī pragati karegā. 8. jisne yah phūldān toṛā hai, vah sāmne āe. 9. jo bāteṁ āpne kahīṁ, ve mujhe yād haiṁ.10. jo kitāb Rānī paṛh rahī hai, bahut rocak hai.

Key G 33.2

1. I will do what you will say. 2. I will invite only those whom you want. 3. Study the subjects that you are interested in. 4. Wear the dress that you like. 5. He does exactly that that he believes is right. 6. Mother lets me go out with him whom she trusts. 7. The one for whom I came into this city, got transferred. 8. Those who listened to my advice, they survived. 9. Those whose own houses of glass, don't throw stones at other peoples homes. 10. Those who have self confidence, certainly attain their goal.

Key G 33.3

1.Although he is rich, he is very polite. 2. By the time we arrived,(by then) they had already left. 3. We will go, where you would desire to. 4. When you come to Delhi, (then) do come to ou house. 5. I will do what you will say. 6. As you desired, exactly that happened. 7. As much hard work you will do, that much success you will get. 8. He is not as intelligent as everybody thinks.

●●●●●

G 34 COMPULSION STRUCTURE

Hindi expresses compultion in three diffent ways:

(1) inner compulsion (2) outer compulsion (3) moral compulsion (pg. 158).

■ Inner Compulsion : v. intransitive

(subj. + को) +	v.inf.	+	होना honā **in the required tense**

1. अब मुझको जाना है। ab mujhko jānā hai. — I must go now.

3. आज उन्हें फ़िल्म देखने जाना था। āj unheṁ film dekhne jānā thā. — They had to go to see a film today.

4. आज मुझे बैंक जाना होगा। āj mujhe baink jānā hogā. — I will have to go to the bank today.

■ Inner compulsion : v. transitive

(subj. + को ko) +	obj. +	v.r. + ना nā ने ne नी nī agree with the N and G of the obj.	+ होना honā in the required tense

1. मुझे यह किताब[f.] पढ़नी है। mujhe yah kitāb paṛhnī hai — I must read this book.

2. उसे अब कपड़े[m.pl.] धोने हैं। use ab kapṛe dhone haiṁ — He/She must wash clothes now.

3. माता जी को खाना m.sg. पकाना था।
mātā jī ko khānā pakānā thā.

Mother had to cook food.

4. कमला को अगले महीने विदेश यात्रा f. करनी होगी।
kamlā ko agle mahīne videś yātrā karnī hogī.

Kamla will have to travel abroad next month.

Outer compulsion : verb intransitive

(Subj. + को ko) + v.inf. + पड़ना parṇā + honā होना in the required tense

1. पिता जी को बहुत बाहर जाना पड़ता है।
pitā jī ko bahut bāhar jānā partā hai

Father has to go out a lot.

2. मुझे हफ़्ते में तीन बार अस्पताल में सोना पड़ता था।
mujhe hafte meṁ tīn bār aspatāl meṁ sonā partā thā.

I used to have to sleep in the hospital three times a week.

3. उसको उस दिन कई मील पैदल चलना पड़ा।
usko us din kaī mīl paidal calnā parā.

She had to walk several miles that day.

4. उनको कुछ दिन होटल में रहना पड़ेगा।
unko kuch din hoṭal meṁ rahnā paṛegā.

They will have to stay in a hotel for a few days.

Outer compulsion : verb transitive

(subj.+ को) + obj. + (v.r. + ना , ने , नी) + पड़ना + होना
nā ne, n ī paṛtā honā
in the required tense
agree with N and G of the obj.

1. मुझे ठंडा दूध[m.] पीना पड़ता है। mujhe ṭhaṇḍā dūdh pīnā paṛtā hai.	I have to drink cold milk.
2. उनको रात्रि में काम[m.] करना पड़ता था। unko rātri meṁ kām karnā paṛtā thā.	They used to have to work at night.
3. मुझे दवाई खानी पड़ी। mujhe davāī khānī paṛī.	I had to take medicine.
4. आज मुझे खाना[m.] पकाना पड़ेगा। āj mujhe khānā pakānā paṛegā	I will have cook food today.

☞ **Be it inner or outer compulsion, when verb transitive is used without mention of the object, use only m.sg. 'आ' ā form of the verb infinitive as well as that of the compound verb पड़ना paṛnā.**

Ex. G 34.1 Translate into English:

1. अब मुझे सोना है। 2. मुझे पुस्तकालय में पुस्तकें लौटानी हैं। 3. बच्चों को इस समय खेलना है। 4. मुझे यह फ़िल्म ज़रूर देखनी है। 5. आपको क्या कहना है? 6. उसे दर्ज़ी से कपड़े सिलवाने हैं। 7. हमें रोज़ सुबह स्कूल जाना पड़ता था। 8. उन्हें हवाई–जहाज़ से जाना पड़ा। 9. आज आपको बाहर खाना पड़ेगा। 10. तुम्हें लखनऊ में गाड़ी बदलनी पड़ेगी।

1. ab mujhe sonā hai. 2. mujhe pustakālay meṁ pustakeṁ lauṭānī haiṁ. 3. baccoṁ ko is samay khelnā hai. 4. mujhe yah film zarūr dekhnī hai. 5. āpko kyā kahnā hai?

6. use darzī se kapṛe silvāne haiṁ. 7. hameṁ roz subah skūl jānā paṛtā thā. 8. unheṁ havāī jahāz se jānā paṛā. 9. āj āpko bāhar khānā paṛegā. 10. tumheṁ Lukhnow meṁ gāṛī badalnī paṛegī.

Ex. G 34.2 Translate into English:

1. Ram has to get up every morning at 5 o'clock. 2. We had to stay in a hotel. 3. I had to learn Hindi before going to India. 4. They had to sleep early today. 5. She will have to go to the doctor's. 6. I have to work ten hours every day. 7. We have to do social service for six months after school. 8. I had to work very hard for the exam. 9. All the countries will have to join together to deal with terrorism. 10. I had to have my watch repaired.

Key G 34 .1

1. I must sleep now. 2. I have to return books to the library. 3. Children must play at this time. 4. I must see this film. 5. What do you have to say ? 6. She has to get clothes stiched by the tailor. 7 We used to have to go to school everyday. 8. They had to go by air-plane. 9. You will have to eat out today. 10. You will have to change trains at Lukhnow.

Key G 34. 2

1. राम को रोज़ सुबह पाँच बजे उठना पड़ता है। 2. हमे होटल मे ठहरना पड़ा। 3. मुझे भारत जाने से पहले हिन्दी सीखनी पड़ी। 4. उन्हें आज जल्दी सोना पड़ा। 5. उसे डाक्टर के पास t kukiMxkA 6. मुझे रोज़ दस घण्टे काम करना पड़ता है। 7. हमें स्कूल के बाद छह महीने समाज सेवा करनी पड़ती है। 8. मुझे परीक्षा के लिए बहुत परिश्रम करना पड़ा। 9. सब देशों को मिलकर आतंकवाद से निबटना पड़ेगा। 10. मुझे अपनी घड़ी ठीक करवानी पड़ी।

1. Ram ko roz subah pāṁc baje uṭhnā paṛtā hai. 2. hameṁ hoṭal meṁ ṭhahrnā paṛā. 3. mujhe bhārat jāne se pahle hindī sīkhnī paṛī. 4. unheṁ āj jaldī sonā paṛā. 5. use ḍaukṭar ke pās jānā paṛegā. 6. mujhe roz das ghaṇṭe kām karnā paṛtā hai. 7. hameṁ skūl ke bād chah mahīne samāj sevā karnī paṛtī hai. 8. mujhe parīkṣā ke lie bahut pariśram karnā paṛā. 9. sab deśoṁ ko milkar ātankvād se nibaṭnā paṛegā. 10. mujhe apnī ghaéī ṭhīk karvānī paṛī.

●●●●●

G 35 PERMISSION

Use of v.r. + ने + देना

subj. + obj. + (v.r. + ने ne) + देना denā

☞ **In the case of transitive activities in the past simple, present and past perfect tense, देना denā agrees with the N and G of the object in all other tenses it agrees with the subject.**

1. आप मुझको जाने दीजिए। āp mujhko jāne dījie.	Please let me go. (Imperative)
2. माता जी हमें खेलने देती है। mātā jī hameṁ śām ko khelne nahīṁ detīṁ.	Mother does not lets us play in the evening. (Present Simple Tense)
3. दादा जी हमें सिनेमा जाने देते थे। dādā jī hameṁ cinemā jāne dete the.	Grandfather used to let us go to the movies. (Past Habitual Tense)
4. अध्यापक ने हमें तैरने दिया। adhyāpak ne hameṁ tairne diyā.	The teacher let us swim in the river. (Past Simple Tense)
5. सविता ने अपने पति को पद–यात्रा पर जाने दिया। savitā ne apne pati ko pad-yātrā par jāne diyā.	Savita let her husband go trekking. (Past Simple Tense)

6. नौकर मेहमानों को अन्दर आने देगा।
naukar mehmānoṁ ko andar āne degā.
The servant will let the guests come in.

7. वे हमें अपने घर में रहने देंगे।
ve hameṁ apne ghar meṁ rahne deṁge.
They will let us stay in their house.

●●●●●

USE OF THE PARTICLE भी bhī

- **When two different subjects do the same activity, भी follows the subject of the second sentence.**

1. Olga speaks Hindi.
ओलगा हिन्दी बोलती है।
olga hindī boltī hai.

Also I speak Hindi.
मैं **भी** हिन्दी बोलती हूँ।
maim bhī hindī boltī huṁ.

2. Robert eats rice.
राबर्ट चावल खाता है।
raubert cāval khātā hai.

Also Tom also eats .
टाम **भी** चावल खाता है।
ṭaum bhī cāval khātā hai.

- **When the same subject does two different activities, भी follows the activity in the second sentence.**

1. Olga speaks Hindi.
ओलगा हिन्दी बोलती है।
olga hindī boltī hai.

Olga speaks English too.
ओलगा अंग्रेज़ी **भी** बोलती है।
olga angrezī bhī boltī hai.

2. Robert eats rice.
राबर्ट चावल खाता है।
raubarṭ cāval khātā hai.

Robert eats roṭī too. .
राबर्ट रोटी **भी** खाता है।
raubarṭ roṭī bhī khātā hai.

G 36 Perfective and Imperfective Participial Constructions

Two much used grammar tools in Hindi are :

(1) the imperfective participial construction and (2) the perfective participial construction abbreviated as IPC and PPC here.

☞ **Both of thes are used as adjective, adverb or noun. When it is used as nouns, it take the place of nouns it modifies**

☞ **Use of हुआ huā, हुए hue, हुई huī is not obligatory**

■ Perfective Participial Construction

v.r.	+	आ, ए, ई +	हुआ, हुए, हुई
		ā, e, ī	huā, hue, huī

1. **फटा हुआ** कुर्ता मत पहनो। (adj.) phaṭā huā kurtā mat pahno. — Don't wear torn 'kurta'.

2. बच्चा **खुली हुई** खिड़की से बाहर कूदा। (adj.) baccā khulī huī khiṛkī se bāhar kūdā. — The child jumped out of the open window.

3. आदमी लेटा हुआ दूरदर्शन देख रहा था। (adverb) ādmī leṭā huā dūrdarśan dekh rahā thā. — The man was watching T.V. lying down.

4. माली फूल **पकड़े हुए** मेरे पास आया। (adverb) — The gardner came to me holding flowers.

mālī phūl pakṛe hue mere pās āyā.

5. **मरों** को मत मारो। (noun) marom̐ ko mat māro. — Don't hit the ones who are (already) dead.

6. **सीखे** को क्या सिखाना! (noun) sīkhe ko kyā sikhānā! — What to teach the one who has already learnt!

- **Hindi also has a repetitive use of the past participle: (v.r. +आ ā, ए e, ई ī) +(v.r. +आ ā, ए e, ई ī) . It is used as adverb.**

7. वह सोई–सोई बोल रही थी। vah soī-soī bol rahī thī. — She was talking in sleep.

8. वह कुछ खोया–खोया लगा। vah kuch khoyā-khoyā lagā. — He looked somewhat lost.

9. मुझको लेटे–लेटे दूरदर्शन देखना पसन्द है। mujhko leṭe leṭe dūrdarśan dekhnā pasand hai. — I like to watch television lying down.

Ex. G 36.1 Translate into Hindi:

1. Please eat these ripe mangoes[m.pl]. 2. Whose is this broken house[m.sg]? 3. Where are the washed clothes[m.pl]? 4. Let the child that got wet (the wet child) come in. 5. I like the words[m.pl] spoken by you[formal]. 6. Whose is this cut kite[f.sg]. 7. Give rest to your tired brain[m.sg.]. 8. I drink very hot boiled milk[m.sg]. 9. Don't eat burnt 'roti'[f.sg.] 10. He is a defeated player[m.sg]. 11. Who could be this dead man? 12. Nobody has the medicine for my broken heart[m.sg].

Ex. G 36.2 Translate into English:

1. मुझे उबला हुआ दूध पसन्द है। 2. वह टूटे हुए मकान में रहता है। 3. थका हुआ कर्मचारी बेहोश हो गया। 4. आप थके–थके लग रहे हैं। 5. मैं बैठी–बैठी ऊब गई हूँ। 6. जला हुआ खाना फेंक दो। 7. फटा हुआ दूध प्रयोग न कीजिए। 8. तुम वहाँ खड़े–खड़े क्या कर रहे हो? 9. आप इन धुले हुए कपड़ों को सुखा दीजिए। 10. मैं ये सूखे कपड़े तहा दूँगी।

1. mujhe ublā huā dūdh pasand hai. 2. vah ṭuṭe hue makān meṁ rahtā hai. 3. thakā huā karmcārī behoś ho gayā. 4.. āp thake-thake lag rahe haiṁ. 5. maiṁ baiṭhī-baiṭhī ūb gaī hūṁ. 6. jalā huā khānā pheṁk do. 7. phaṭā huā dhūdh prayog na kījie. 8. tum vahāṁ khaṛe khaṛe kyā kar rahe ho? 9. āp in dhule hue kapṛoṁ ko sukhā dījie. 10. maiṁ ye sūkhe kapṛe tahā dūṁgī.

Key G 36. 1

1. ये पके हुए आम[m.pl] खाइए। 2. यह टूटा हुआ घर[m.] किसका है? 3. धुले हुए कपड़े[m.pl] कहाँ हैं? 4. भीगे हुए बच्चे[m.sg.obl.] को अन्दर आने दीजिए। 5. आपके कहे हए शब्द[m.pl.] मुझे पसन्द हैं। 6. यह कटी हुई पतंग[f.sg.] किसकी है? 7. अपने थके हए दिमाग[m.sg.] को आराम दीजिए। 8. मैं गरम–गरम उबला हआ दूध[m.] पीती हूँ। 9. जली हुई रोटी[f.sg] मत खाओ। 10. वह हारा हुआ खिलाड़ी[m.sg.] है। 11. यह मरा हुआ आदमी[m.sg] कौन हो सकता है?12. मेरे टूटे हुए दिल[m.sg] की दवाई[f.sg.] किसीके पास नहीं।

1. ye pake hue ām khāie. 2. yah ṭūṭā huā ghaṛ kiskā hai. 3. dhule hue kapṛe kahāṁ haiṁ. 4. bhīge hue bacce ko andar āne dījie. 5. āpke kahe hue śabd mujhe pasand haiṁ. 6. yah kaṭī huī pataṅg kiskī hai? 7. apne thake hue dimāg ko ārām dījie. 8. maiṁ garam-garam ublā huā dūdh pītī hūṁ. 9. jalī huī roṭī mat khāo. 10. vah hārā huā khilāṛī hai. 11. yah marā huā ādmī kaun ho saktā hai? 12. mere ṭūṭe hue dil kī davāī kisīke pās nahīṁ.

Key G 36.2

1. I like boiled milk. 2. He lives in a broken house. 3. The exhausted worker fainted. 4. You look tired. 5. I am bored of sitting. 6.Throw away the burnt food. 7. Don't use the curdled milk. 8. What are you doing standing there? 9. You dry these washed clothed. 10. I will fold these dry clothes.

■ **Imperfective Participial Construction.**

v.r.	+	ता, ते, ती	+	हुआ, हुए, हुई
		tā, te, tī		huā, hue, huī

☞ **English language uses either gerund or relative clause instead.**

1. **चलती हुई** बस[f.] में मत चढ़ो। — Don't get on a moving bus.
caltī huī bas meṁ mat caṛho. (adj.)

2. **भौंकते हुए** कुत्ते को चुप कराओ। bauṁkte hue kutte ko cup karāo. (adj.)	Silence the barking dog.
3. बच्चा[m] **रोता हुआ** आया। baccā rotā huā āyā. (adverb)	The child[m] came crying.
4. औरतें[f.pl.] **गाती हुई** जा रही थीं। aurteṁ gātī huī jā rahī thīṁ. (adverb)	The women were going singing.
5. **जातों** को मत रोको। jātoṁ ko mat roko. (noun)	Dont' stop the ones who are going.
6. बोलती[f] को मत टोको। boltī ko mat toko. (noun)	Don't interrupt the one who is talking.

Repetitive use of present participle

(v.r. + ता tā, ते te, ती tī)+(v.r. + ता tā, ते te, ती tī)

☞ **This is used as adverb.**

7. मैं[m] खबरें सुनते–सुनते चाय पीता हूँ। maiṁ khabreṁ sunte-sunte cāy pītā hūṁ	I drink tea while listening to the news.
8. वे[m.hon.] नाश्ता करते–करते पत्र लिखते हैं। ve nāśtā karte-karte patra likhte haiṁ.	He writes letters while eating breakfast.
9. खाते–खाते मत बोलिए। khāte-khāte mat bolie.	Don't speak while eating.
10. उसने जाते–जाते कहा। usne jāte-jāte kahā.	He said while going.

IMPERFECTIVE PARTICIPIAL CONSTRUCTION

■ **Two very specific uses of IPC are:**

subject + (v.r. + ते te)+(v.r. + ते te,) +बचा bacā, बचे bace, बची bacī
☞ बचा bacā, बचे bace, बची bacī agrees with the N &G of the subj.

1. किताब गिरते–गिरते बची। kitāb girte-girte bacī.	The book almost fell.
2. राबर्ट मरते–मरते बचा। raubarṭ marte-marte bacā.	Robert almost died.
3. हम फिसलते–फिसलते बचे। ham phisalte-phisalte bace.	We almost slipped.
4. दुर्घटना होते–होते बची। durghaṭnā hote-hote bacī.	Accident almost took place.

देखते–ही–देखते dekhte-hī-dekhte = in no time

1. देखते–ही–देखते सब बिक गया। dekhte-hī-dekhte sab bik gayā.	In no time, all got sold.
2. देखते–ही–देखते वहाँ बहुत भीड़ लग गई। dekhte-hī-dekhte bahut bhīṛ lag gaī.	In no time, big crowd gathered there.

Ex. G 36.3 Translate into Hindi:

1. The husband entered the house drinking alcohol. 2. Mother ran after the child scolding. 3. Uncle said while reading the newspaper. 4. The dog came with me waging the tail. 5. She was talking to her neighbor while drying clothes. 6. Viewers stood up clapping. 7. The crowd dispersed while shouting slogans. 8. The girls came up the stage dancing. 9. I just saw a man drowning. 10. The drowning man was shouting for help. 11. The flower vase almost fell. 12. In no time he became a big businessman.

Ex. G 36.4 Translate into English:

1. आदमी बोलता हुआ चल रहा था। 2. धोबी गाता हुआ कपड़े धो रहा था। 3. माँ खाना बनाते हुए बोलीं। 4. क्या किसीने अध्यापक को जाते हुए देखा है? 5. मैंने मकान को जलते हुए देखा । 6. मुझे उड़ती हुई पतंग अच्छी लगती है। 7. बहता हुआ पानी बन्द करो। 8. विद्यार्थी डरते–डरते बोला। 9. बच्चा पढ़ते–पढ़ते सो गया। 10. देखते ही देखते सब कुछ बदल गया। 11. बुढ़िया कार से टकराते–टकराते बची। 12. यह लड़का डूबते–डूबते बचा।

1. ādmī boltā huā cal rahā thā. 2. dhobī gātā huā kapṛe dho rahā thā. 3. māṁ khānā banāte hue bolīṁ. 4. kyā kisīne adhyāpak ko jāte hue dekhā hai? 5. maiṁne makān ko jalte hue dekhā. 6. mujhe uṛtī huī pataṅg acchī lagtī hai. 7. bahtā huā pānī band karo 8. vidyārthī ḍarte-ḍarte bolā. 9. baccā paṛhte-paṛhte so gayā. 10. dekhte-hī-dekhte sab badal gayā. 11. buṛhiyā kār se takrāte-takrāte bacī. 12. yah laṛkā dūbte-dūbte bacā.

Key G 36. 3

1. पति$^{m,sg.}$ शराब पीते हुए घर में घुसा। 2. माँ डाँटते हुए बच्चे के पीछे भागी। 3. चाचा जी ने अख़बार$^{m,sg.}$ पढ़ते–पढ़ते कहा। 4. कुत्ता$^{m,sg.}$ पूँछ हिलाता हुआ मेरे साथ आया। 5. वह कपड़े$^{m,pl.}$ सुखाते–सुखाते अपने पड़ोसी$^{m.}$ से बात कर रही थी। 6. दर्शक$^{m.}$ तालियाँ$^{f.pl.}$ बजाते हुए खड़े हो गए। 7. भीड़$^{f.}$ नारे$^{m,pl.}$ लगाते हुए तितर–बितर हो गई। 8. लड़कियाँ$^{f.pl.}$ नाचती हुई मंच$^{m.}$ पर आईं। 9. मैंने अभी–अभी एक आदमी को डूबते हुए देखा। 10. डूबता हुआ आदमी$^{m.}$ मदद$^{f.}$ के लिए पुकार रहा था। 11. फूलदान$^{m,sg.}$ गिरते–गिरते बचा। 12. देखते–ही–देखते वह बहुत बड़ा व्यापारी$^{m,sg.}$ बन गया।

1. pati śarāb pīte hue ghar meṁ ghusā. 2. māṁ dāṁṭtī huī bacce ke pīche bhāgī. 3.cācā jī ne akhbār paṛhte-paṛhte kahā. 4. kuttā pūṁch hilātā huā mere sāth āyā. 5. vah kapṛe sukhāte- sukhāte apne paṛosī se bāt kar rahī thī. 6. darśak tāliyāṁ bajāte hue khaṛe ho gae.7. bhīṛ nāre lagāte hue titar-bitar ho gaī. 8. laṛkiyāṁ nāctī huī mañc par āīṁ. 9. maiṁne abhī-abhī ek ādmī ko dūbte hue dekhā hai. 10. dūbtā huā ādmī madad ke lie pukār rahā thā. 11. phūldān girte-girte bacā. 12. dekhte-hī-dekhte vah bahut baṛā vyāpārī ban gayā.

Key G 36. 4

1. The man was walking while talking. 2. The washerman was washing clothes while singing. 3. Mother said while preparing food. 4. Has anybody seen the teacher going. 5. I saw the house burning. 6. I like flying kite. 7. Stop the running water. 8. The student spoke while feeling scared. 9. The child fell asleep reading. 10. In no time everything changed. 11. The old woman almost hit against the car. 12. This boy almost drowned.

Use of: मालूम होता है mālūm hotā hai, लगता है lagtā hai — It seems

1. मालूम होता है कल तक बारिश होगी। mālūm hotā hai kal tak bāriś hogī.	It seems it will rain by tomorrow.
2. मालूम होता है इस साल बहुत गर्मी होगी। mālūm hotā hai is sāl bahut garmī hogī.	It seems it will be very hot this year.
3. लगता है वे जल्दी दुबारा आएँगे। lagtā hai ve jaldī dubārā āeṁge.	It seems soon they will come again.
4. लगता है वे आपसे नाराज़ हैं। lagtā hai ve āp se nārāz haiṁ.	It seems they are annoyed with you.

G 37 PROBABILITY

Probability expressions 'शायद' (perhaps), 'हो सकता है' (it is likely), 'संभव है' (it is probable) 'संभवता' (probably) correspond to English 'may', 'might' 'may/might + have + pp' etc.

■ Present probability

probability expression	+ subj. nom. case	+ obj. (if any)	+ v.r. + ता, ते, ती tā, te, tī	+ होउँ, हो, होओ, हों houṁ, ho, ho'o, hoṁ
				agree with the Subj.

1. शायद वह शाम को खेलता हो।
   śāyad vah śām ko kheltā ho.
   Perhaps he plays in the evening.
2. हो सकता है वे रोज़ सुबह घूमने जाते हों।
   ho saktā hai ve roz subah ghūmne jāte hoṁ.
   Its likely they go for a walk every morning.

■ Past probability v.i.

probability expression	+ subj. nom. case	+ v.r	+ आ, ए, ई ā, e, ī	+ होउँ, हो, हों houṁ, ho, hoṁ
				agree with the Subj.

1. हो सकता है वे कल यहाँ आए हों।
   ho saktā hai ve kal yahāṁ āe hoṁ.
   Its likely they came here yesterday.
2. शायद वे उस समय सो रहे हों।
   śāyad ve us samay so rahe hoṁ.
   Perhaps they were sleeping at that time.

Past Probability v.t.

probability expression	+ (subj. + ने)	+ obj.	+ v.r	+ आ, ए, ई ā, e, ī	+ हो, हों, ho, hoṁ
				agree with the object	

1. हो सकता है उन्होंने (hon.sg.) पत्र (m.) लिखा हो।
   ho saktā hai unhoṁne patra likhā ho.
   It could be that he wrote a letter.
2. हो सकता है उसने नई कार ख़रीदी हो।
   ho saktā hai usne naī kār kharīdī ho.
   It is likely he bought a new car.

Future probability

probability expression	+ subj. nom. case	+ obj. (if any)	+ v.r	+ उँ, ए, ओ, एँ ūṁ, e, o, eṁ
				agree with the subject

1. शायद मैं अगले हफ़्ते दिल्ली आऊँ।
   śāyad maiṁ agle hafte dillī āūṁ.
   Perhaps I will come to Delhi next week.

2. हो सकता है आज शाम को बारिश हो।
   ho saktā hai āj śām ko bāriś ho.
   It could be that it rains this evening

3. हो सकता है वे कल यहाँ आए।
   ho saktā hai ve kal yahāṁ āeṁ.
   It is likely they come here tomorrow.

PROBABILITY

Ex. G 37.1 Read and Translate into English:

1. शायद वह $^{m.sg}$ पैदल जाता हो। 2. हो सकता है वे $^{m.hon.}$ दिन में आराम करते हों। 3. शायद उनकी $^{m.hon.}$ गाड़ी समय पर न आई हो। 4. हो सकता है वह $^{m.sg}$ अपने अधिकारी से मिला हो। 5. हो सकता है उन्होंने आपको दावत में न बुलाया हो। 6. शायद मैं देर से पहुँचूँ। 7. हो सकता है आज शाम को हम सिनेमा देखने जाएँ। 8. हो सकता है आज पिता जी देर से घर आएँ। 9. संभवता वह उसी होटल में रुकेगा। 10. शायद आप नहीं जानते कि मैं कौन हूँ। 11. शायद मैं अगले हफ़्ते मुम्बई जाऊँ। 12. हो सकता है मेरी बेटी भी मेरे साथ जाए। 13. संम्भव है कि हम वहाँ समुद्रतट पर जाकर भेलपूरी खाएँ। 14. हो सकता है एक दिन मेरी लाटरी $^{f.sg}$ निकले।

1. śāyad vah $^{m.sg}$ paidal jātā ho. 2. ho saktā hai ve $^{m.hon.}$ din meṁ ārām karte hoṁ. 3. śāyad unkī $^{m.hon}$ gāṛī $^{f.sg}$ samay par na āī ho. 4. ho saktā hai vah $^{m.sg}$ apne adhikārī se milā ho. 5. ho saktā hai unhoṁne āpko dāvat meṁ na bulāyā ho. 6. śāyad maiṁ der se pahuṁcūṁ. 7. ho saktā hai āj śām ko ham 'sinemā' dekhne jāeṁ. 8. ho saktā hai āj pitā jī der se ghar āeṁ. 9. sambhavtā vah usī hoṭal meṁ rukegā. 10. śāyad āp nahīṁ jānte ki maiṁ kaun hūṁ. 11. śāyad maiṁ agle hafte mumbai jāūṁ. 12. ho saktā hai merī beṭī bhī mere sāth jāe. 13. sambhav hai ki ham vahāṁ samudrataṭ par jākar bhelpūrī khāeṁ. 14. ho saktā hai ek din merī lauṭrī $^{f.sg}$ nikle.

Key G 37.1

1. Perhaps he goes on foot. 2. It is likely he rests during the day. 3. Perhaps his train did not come on time. 4. It could be that he met his boss. 5. It could be that they did not invite you to the party. 6. I might arrive late. 7. It could be that we go to see a film this evening. 8. It could be that father comes home late today. 9. Probably he will stay in the same hotel. 10. Perhaps you don't know who I am. 11. I might go to Mumbai next week. 12. My daughter might come with me. 13. It is likey that we go there on the beach and eat 'bhelpoori'. 14. It could be that one day I win a lottery.

●●●●●

G 38 CONDITIONAL

Hindi uses अगर/यदि correspomding to English 'if' at the beginning of conditional caluse, and 'तो' at the beginning of dependant clause.
Sentence structures vary according to the level of proability indicated.

■ **In situations where there is very high probability of fulfilment of the condtion and hence that of the dependant clause, Hindi speakers use simple future tense in both the clauses. It is called the prabable condition.**

1.	अगर मैं[m.sg] दिल्ली आऊँगा, तो मैं आपको ज़रूर मिलूँगा। agar maiṁ[m.sg] dillī āūṁgā, to maiṁ āpko zarūr milūṁgā.	If I come to Delhi, I will certainly meet you.
2.	अगर वेतन[m.sg] अच्छा होगा, तो मैं यह नौकरी स्वीकार करूँगा। agar vetan[m.sg] acchā hogā, to maiṁ yah naukarī svīkār karūṁgā.	If the salary is good, I will accept this job.

■ **In case the probability of fulfilment of the condition and hence that of the dependent clause is somewhat less, Hindi uses past tense in 'if' clause, and simple future in 'तो' clause. It is called Improbable condition.**

1.	यदि/अगर मैं[m.sg] दिल्ली आया, तो आपसे मिलूँगा। yadi /agar maiṁ[m.sg] dillī āyā, to āpse milūṁgā	If I came to Delhi, I would meet you.
2.	यदि बारिश[f.sg] हुई, तो हम घर से बाहर नहीं जाएँगे। yadi bāriś[f.sg] huī, to ham ghar se bāhar nahīṁ jāeṁge.	If it rained, we would not go out of the house.

3. यदि आपने मेहनत$^{f.sg}$ की, तो अवश्य सफल होंगे।
yadi āpne mehnat$^{f.sg}$ kī, to avaśyă saphal homge.
If you worked hard, you would be succesful.

■ **Absurd condition or the very low probability : Use future subjunctive to agree with the subject in both the clauses.**

1. यदि मैं सन्तरा होऊँ, तो गोलं होऊँ।
yadi maiṁ santrā hoūṁ, to gol hoūṁ.
If I were an orange, I would be spherical.

2. यदि मैं मछली होऊँ, तो समुद्र में तैरूँ।
yadi maiṁ machlī hoūṁ, to samudra meṁ tairūṁ.
If I were a fish, I would swim in the ocean.

■ **In situations where the probability for the fulfilment of the dependant clause is nil because the condition failed to realise in the past, Hindi uses past participle of the main verb followed by present participle of honā to agree with the subject or object depending upon the nature of the verb being transitive or intransitive in the conditional clause, and the present pariciple of honā in the dependant clause. It is impossible condition.**

1. अगर आपने टैक्सी$^{f.sg}$ ली होती, तो आपकी गाड़ी$^{f.sg}$ न छूटती।
yadi āpne ṭaiksī$^{f.sg}$ lī hotī, to āpkī gāṛī$^{f.sg}$ na chūṭtī.
If you had taken a taxi, you would not have missed the train.

2. यदि तुम$^{f.sg}$ दावत में आई होतीं, तो सब$^{m.sg}$ बहुत खुश हुए होते।
yadi tum$^{f.sg}$ dāvat meṁ āī hotīṁ, to sab$^{m.sg}$ bahut k͟huś hue hote.
If you had come to the party, everybody would have been very happy.

Ex. G 38.1 Translate into English:

1. यदि मेरे पास पैसे होंगे, तो मैं यह घर ख़रीदूँगी। 2. यदि तुम बुलाओगे, तो वह आएगी। 3. यदि आप उसे ठीक पैसे दें, तो वह आपके यहाँ काम करे। 4. यदि मुझे वीसा मिलेगा, तो मैं आस्ट्रेलिया जाऊँगा। 5. यदि वह मेहनती हो, तो जल्दी काम ख़त्म करे। 6. यदि वह बीमार न होती, तो पहाड़ पर चढ़ी होती। 7. यदि उसने मुझे बताया होता, तो मैंने अवश्य उसकी मदद की होती।

1.yadi mere pās paise hoṁge, to maiṁ yah ghar kharīdūṁgī. 2. yadi tum bulāoge, to vah āegī. 3. yadi āp use ṭhīk paise deṁ, to vah āpke yahāṁ kām kare. 4. yadi mujhe vīsā milegā, to maiṁ austreliā jāūṁgā. 5. yadi vah mehantī ho, to vah jaldī kām khatm kare. 6. yadi vah bīmār na hotī, to pahāṛ par caṛhī hotī. 7. yadi usne mujhe batāyā hotā, to maiṁne avaśyă uskī madad kī hotī.

Ex. G 38. 2 Translate into Hindi:

1. If I had a piano, I (f.) would play it now. 2. If I had a car, I (m.)would show yo u round my city. 3. If we had a television set, we would watch some Hindi serials. 4. If it does not rain this Sunday, I will come to your (hon.) house. 5. If cigarettes became more expensive, he will stop smoking. 6. If he won a lottery, he would do a world tour.

Key G 38.1

1. If I have the money, I will buy this house. 2. If you invite her, She will come. 3. If you paid her well, she would work for you. 4. If I (m.) get visa, I will emigrate to Australia. 5. If she were diligent, she would finish the work. 6. If she had not been sick, she could have climbed up the mountain. 7. If she had told me, I would certainly have helped her.

Key G 38.2

1. **यदि** मेरे पास पिआनो होता, **तो** मैं इस समय बजाती। 2. **यदि** मेरे पास कार होती, **तो** मैं इस समय आपको अपना शहर घुमाता। 3. **यदि** हमारे पास दूरदर्शन यंत्र होता, **तो** हम हिन्दी धारावाहिक देखते। 4. **यदि** इस इतवार को बारिश न हुई, **तो** मैं आपके घर आऊँगा। 5. **यदि** सिगरेट महँगे हो गए, **तो** वह धूम्रपान छोड़ देगा। 6. **यदि** उसकी लाटरी लग गई, **तो** वह विश्वभ्रमण करेगा।

1. yadi mere pās piāno hotā, to maiṁ use is samay bajātī. 2. yadi mere pās kār hotī, to maiṁ is samay āpko apnā śahar ghumātā. 3. yadi hamāre pās dūrdarśan yantra

hotā, to ham hindī dhārāvāhik dekhte. 4. yadi is itvār ko bāriś na huī, to maiṁ āpke ghar āūṁgā. 5. yadi sigreṭ mahṁge ho gae, to vah dhūmrapān chor degā. 6. yadi uskī lauṭrī lag gaī, to vah viśvabhramaṇ karegā.

EXPRESSING WISHES

1.	काश मैं तैर सकती। kāś maiṁ tair saktī.	I wish I could swim!
2.	काश मेरे अधिक मित्र होते। kāś mere adhik mitra hote.	I wish I had more friends!
3.	काश तुम इतनी भुलक्कड़ न होतीं। kāś tum itnī bhulakkaṛ na hotīṁ.	I wish you were not so forgetful!
4.	काश आप मेरे जन्मदिन पर आए होते। kāś āp mere janmdin par āe hote.	I wish you had come to my birthday!
5.	काश मैंने इतना खाना न पकाया होता। kāś maiṁne itnā khānā na pakāyā hotā.	I wish I had not cooked so much food!
6.	काश कल वे मेरे यहाँ न आएँ। kāś kal ve mere yahāṁ na āeṁ.	I wish they don't come to my house tomorrow!
7.	काश कल बारिश न हो। kāś kal bāriś na ho.	I wish it won't rain tomorrow!
8.	काश कल धूप हो। kāś kal dhūp ho.	I wish it would be sunny tomorrow!

●●●●●

G 39 PASSIVE

(subj. + से/के द्वारा) + obj + (v.r. + आ/या, ए, ई) + जाना + होना
ā/yā, e, ī jānā + honā,
in the appropriate tense
to agree with the N and G of object

COMPREHENSION

1. बनारस में हिन्दी$^{f.sg}$ बोली जाती है। banāras meṁ hindī$^{f.sg}$ bolī jātī hai.	Hindi is spoken in Banaras. (present simple passive)
2. डोसा$^{m.sg}$ कैसे बनाया जाता है? dosā$^{m.sg}$ kaise banāyā jātā hai?	How is dosa made? (present simple passive)
3. धोबी के द्वारा कपड़े$^{m.pl.}$ धोए जाते थे। dhobī ke dvārā kapṛe$^{m.pl}$ dhoe gae.	Clothes used to be washed by the washerman. (past habitual passive)
4. महात्मा के द्वारा उपदेश$^{m.sg}$ दिया जाता था। mahātmā ke dvārā updeś$^{m.sg}$ diyā jātā thā.	Sermon used to be delivered by the mahatma. (past habitual passive)
5. बच्चों को मिठाइयाँ$^{f.pl.}$ बाँटी गईं । baccoṁ ko miṭhāiyāṁ$^{m.sg}$ bāṁṭī gaīṁ .	Sweets were distributed among the children. (past simple passive)
6. यह नया पुल$^{m.sg}$ हाल में बनाया गया है। yah nayā pul$^{m.sg}$ hāl meṁ banāyā gayā hai.	This new bridge has been made recently. (present perfect passive)

7.	ये पौधे[m.pl.] कब लगाए गए थे? ye paudhe[m.pl.] kab lagāe gae the?	When were these plants planted?(past perf. passive)
8.	भाषण[m.sg] कहाँ दिया जाएगा? bhāṣaṇ[m.sg] kahāṁ diyā jāegā?	Where will the speech be given? (fut. simple passive)
9.	कल की सभा में आपको भेजा जाएगा? kal kī sabhā meṁ āpko bhejā jāegā.	You will be sent in tomorrow's meeting. (future simple passive)

SOME OTHER USES OF PASSIVE IN HINDI

- **Passive to express inability to do a certain activity:**

(subject + se) + mas. sg. past simple tense of the intransitive verbs + jānā and honā in the required tense.

1.	मुझसे पहाड़ पर नहीं चढ़ा जाता। mujhse pahāṛ par nahīṁ caṛhā jātā.	I can't climb up the mountain. (present simple passive)
2.	उनसे रात भर सोया न गया। unse rāt bhar soyā na gayā.	They could not sleep all night. (past simple passive)
3.	मुझसे पैदल नहीं जाया* जाएगा। mujhse paidal nahīṁ jāyā* jāegā.	I won't be able to go on foot. (future simple passive)

☞ **In this use, the verb जाना jānā changes like a regular verb to जाया jāyā and not गया** gayā।

Subjunctive Passive i.e. main verb in the mas. sg past simple tense followed by जाय jāy. correspondin English usage 'Let's do ....' or 'shall we do...?'

1.	चला जाय। calā jāy.	Let's go. /Shall we go?
2.	खाया जाय। khāyā jāy	Let's eat./Shall we eat?

Ex. G 39.1 Transalate into English:

1. यहाँ बहुत किताबें ख़रीदी जाती हैं। 2. कल शाम को बैंक लूटा गया। 3. उपहार कब ख़रीदा गया? 4. चोर पिछले हफ़्ते पकड़ा गया था। 5.यह पौधा कब लगाया गया था? 6. चाय कितने बजे बनाई जाएगी? 7. भोजन कब तक मेज़ पर लगाया जाएगा? 8. आपकी किताब कब तक छापी जाएगी? 9. उससे बोले बिना नहीं रहा जाता। 10. उनसे इतने छोटे घर में न रहा गया। 11. हमसे इतना तेज़ न दौड़ा जाएगा। 12. मुझसे वहाँ नहीं जाया जाएगा। 13. अब भोजन किया जाए? 14. आज शाम को सिनेमा देखा जाए? 15. चला जाए।

1. yahāṁ bahut kitābeṁ kharīdī jātī haiṁ. 2. kal śām ko baṅk lūṭā gayā. 3. uphār kab kharīdā gayā? 4. cor pichle hafte pakṛā gayā thā. 5. yah paudhā kab lagāyā gayā thā? 6. cāy kitne baje banāī jāegī? 7. bhojan kab tak mez par lagāyā jāegā? 8. āpkī kitāb kab tak chāpī jāegī? 9. usse bole binā nahīṁ rahā jātā. 10. unse itne choṭe ghar meṁ na rahā gayā. 11. hamse itnā tez na dauṛā jāegā. 12. mujhse vahāṁ nahīṁ jāyā jāegā. 13. ab bhojan kiyā jāe? 14. āj śām ko sinemā dekhā jāe? 15. calā jāe.

Ex. G 39.2 Translate into Hindi:

1.The house is cleaned everyday . 2. Food is cooked by mother. 3. Our clothes used to be washed by the washerman. 4. Money used to be earned by father. 5. This bridge was built a long time ago. 6. Your watch has been repaired. 7.Picture has been put up on the wall. 8. Our house will be painted next week. 9. Shall we lay food on the table? 10. Let's go to Agra next week.11. I can't eat spicy food. 12. I won't be able to climb the stairs. 13. The book is taught by the teacher. 14. The books are read by the students. 15. The dress will be sewn by the tailor.

Key G 39.1

1.Many books are bought here. 2. Bank was robbed yesterday evening. 3.when was the gift bought? 4. The thief had been caught last week. 5. When was this plant planted? 6. What time will tea be made? 7. By when will food be laid on the table. 8. By when will your book be printed? 9. He/She can not stay without talking. 10. They could not not live in such a small house. 11. We will not be able to run so fast. 12. I won't be able to go there. 13. Shall we eat now? 14. Let's see a film this evening. 15. Let's go.

Key G 39. 2

1. घर रोज़ साफ़ किया जाता है।2. खाना माँ के द्वारा पकाया जाता है। 3. हमारे कपड़े

धोबी के द्वारा धोए जाते थे। 4. पैसा पिता जी के द्वारा कमाया जाता था। 5. यह पुल बहुत समय पहले बनाया गया था।6. आपकी घड़ी ठीक कर दी गई है। 7. तस्वीर दीवार पर टाँग दी गई है। 8. हमारा घर अगले हफ़्ते रंगा जाएगा।9. मेज़ पर खाना लगाया जाए ? 10. अगले हफ़्ते आगरा चला जाए। 11. मुझसे मसालेवाला खाना नहीं खाया जाता। 12. मुझसे सीढ़ियाँ नहीं चढ़ी जाएँगी। 13. अध्यापक के द्वारा किताब पढ़ाई जाती है। 14. विद्यार्थियों के द्वारा किताबें पढ़ी जाती हैं। 15. दर्ज़ी के द्वारा कपड़ा सिया जाएगा।

1. ghar roz sāf kiyā jātā hai. 2. khānā māṁ ke dvārā pakāyā jātā hai. 3 hamāre kapṛe dhobī ke dvārā dhoe jāte the. 4. paisā pitā jī ke dvārā kamāyā jātā thā. 5. yah pul bahut samay pahle banāyā gayā thā. 6. āpkī ghaṛī ṭhīk kar dī gaī hai. 7. tasvīr dīvār par ṭaṅg dī gaī hai. 8. hamāṛā ghar agle hafte raṅgā jāegā. 9. mez par khānā lagāyā jāe? 10. agle hafte āgrā calā jāe. 11. mujhse masālevālā khānā nahīṁ khāyā jātā. 12. mujhse sīṛhiyāṁ nahīṁ caṛhī jāeṁgī. 13. adhyāpak ke dvārā kitāb paṛhāī jātī hai. 14. vidyārthiyoṁ ke dvārā kitābeṁ paṛhī jātī haiṁ. 15. darzī ke dvārā kapṛā siyā jāegā.

Read khel divas pg. 280

Use of -सा, -से, -सी -sā, -se, -sī :

with noun to express likeness:

बन्दर–सा, –से, –सी	bandar-sā, -se, -sī	like a monkey

with adjective to express 'somewhat like...; very little/ much etc:

लाल–सा, –से, –सी	lāl-sā , -se, -sī	reddish
थोड़ा–सा, –से, –सी	thoṛā sā, -se, -sī	very little
बहुत–सा, –से, –सी	bahut sā , -se, -sī	very many, a lot

-sā, -se, -sī accords with the N and G of the noun it qualifies

G 40 FREQUENTATIVES

☞ **Frequentative form can be used in the imperative, present simple, past habitual and future simple tense. It indicates that the action is taking place more frequently within a certain time-period, under certain conditions.**

☞ **In this structure 'जाना'** jānā **changes to 'जाया'**jāyā

☞ **Put 'नहीं' nahīṁ before (v.r. + आ** ā/**या** yā**), and drop the auxiliary 'होना'** honā **at the end to make negative sentences.**

■ Frequentative Present Simple Tense

subj. +	obj. +	(v.r. + आ ā/या yā) +	करता kartā +	हूँ hūṁ हो ho,
nom. case	(if any)	(invariable)	करते karte	है hai, हैं haiṁ
			करती kartī	
			agree with N and G of the subj.	

जब मैं भारत में होता हूँ, मैं सिर्फ़ हिन्दी बोला करता हूँ।
jab maiṁ bhārat meṁ hotā hūṁ, maiṁ sirf hindī bolā kartā hūṁ.
When I am in India, I speak only Hindi.

■ Frequentative Past Habitual Tense

subj. +	obj. +	(v.r. + आ ā/या yā) +	करता kartā +	था thā थे the,
nom. case	(if any)	(invariable)	करते karte	थी thī, थीं thīṁ
			करती kartī	
			agree with N and G of the subj.	

FREQUENTATIVE COMPOUND

जब मैं भारत में था, मैं सिर्फ़ हिन्दी बोला करता था।
jab maiṁ bhārat meṁ thā , maiṁ sirf hindī bolā kartā thā.
When I was in India, I used to speak only Hindi.

■ Frequentative Imperative

subject	+	object	+	(v.r. आ ā/या yā)	+	करो/कीजिए
तुम tum		(if any)		(invariable)		karo/ kijie
आप āp						करना/कीजिएगा
						karnā /kījiegā

☞ **The imperative frequentative is used to command or request the second person, 'तू', 'तुम' or 'आप' form, to carry out some activity with more regular frequency, in the present or future tense.**

जब आप भारत जाते हैं, आप सिर्फ़ हिन्दी बोला कीजिए।
jab āp bhārat jāte haiṁ, āp sirf hindī bolā kījie.
When you go to India, you speak only Hindi.

■ Frequentative Future Simple Tense

subj.	+	obj.	+	(v.r. आ ā/या yā)	+	करूँगा/ करूँगी, करेगा/करेगी,
nom. case		(if any)		(invariable)		karūṁgā/karūṁgī, karega, karegī,
						करोगे /करोगी, करेंगे / करेंगी
						karoge / karogī, kareṁge / kareṁgī
						agree with N and G of the subject.

जब मैं भारत जाऊँगा, मैं सिर्फ़ हिन्दी बोलूँगा।
jab maiṁ bhārat jāūṁgā, maiṁ sirf hindī bolā karūṁgā.
When I go India, I will speak only Hindi.

Ex. G 40.1 Translate into English:

1. मैं अक्सर यहाँ आया करता हूँ। 2. मेरे दोस्त और मैं कभी–कभी इस भोजनालय में खाया करते हैं। 3. यहाँ एक ढाबा हुआ करता था। 4. हम वहाँ लस्सी पीया करते थे। 5. नदी के किनारे, इस पेड़ पर, एक बन्दर रहा करता था। 6.एक मगरमच्छ रोज़ उसे मिलने आया करता था। 7. बन्दर उसे पेड़ पर से फल फेंका करता था। 8. मगरमच्छ फल लेकर, बहुत खुश होकर पानी में लोटा करता था। 9. वह स्वयं भी भर–पेट खाया करता था, और अपने साथ अपनी पत्नी के लिए भी ले जाया करता था। 10. हम प्रायः तट पर जाया करते थे, और यह सब देखा करते थे।

1 maiṁ aksar yahāṁ āyā kartā hūṁ. 2. mere dost aur maiṁ kabhī-kabhī is bhojanālay meṁ khāyā karte haim. 3. yahāṁ ek ḍhābā huā kartā thā. 4. ham vahāṁ lassī pīyā karte the.5. nadī ke kinare, is peṛ par, ek bandar rahā kartā thā. 6. ek magarmacch roz use milne āyā kartā thā. 7. bandar use peṛ par se phal pheṁkā kartā thā. 8. magarmacch phal lekar, bahut khuś hokar pānī me loṭā kartā thā. 9. vah svayam bhī bhar-peṭ khāyā kartā thā aur apne sāth apnī patnī ke lie bhī le jāyā kartā thā. 10. ham prāyaḥ taṭ par jāyā karte the, aur yah sab dekha karte the.

Ex. G 40.2 Translate into Hindi:

Use the frquentative compound where required.

UNITY IS STRENGTH

Once upon a time, a wise farmer lived in a village. He had four sons.
They kept quarreling among themselves. Poor farmer was very unhappy due to their mutual quarrels.
Once, he became very sick. He had no hopes of survival. He became very worried about the future of his children.
A plan occurred to him. At first he called his four sons. Then he asked one of his sons to bring a bundle of very thin wood sticks.
When the bundle of wood-sticks arrived, he asked them to break it turn by turn. They were not able to break it. Then he asked them to break it together. Even

then they could not manage to break it.
Now he asked them to open the bundle and break the wood sticks one by one. This time they could break them easily. The boys understood, 'unity is strength'. They began to live together lovingly. The wise farmer's worry was over.

Key G 40.1

1. I come here often. 2. My friends and I sometimes eat in this restaurant.. 3. There used to be a 'dhaba' here. 4. We used to have 'lassi' there. 5. A monkey used to live on this tree on the river coast. 6. A crocodile used to come everyday to meet him. 7. The monkey used to throw to him fruit from the tree. 8. The crocodile used to take the fruit, become very happy and roll in water. 9. He used to eat stomachful himself, and also take along for his wife..10. Usually we used to go on the coast and watch all this.

Key G 40.1

Go to page 269.

●●●●●

S 1 डाकिया

डाकिया एक सरकारी कर्मचारी है। वह डाकघर में काम करता है। वह खाकी वर्दी पहनता है। वह हमारे लिए पत्र, 'पार्सल' आदि लाता हैं। हम प्रति दिन उसका इन्तज़ार करते हैं। वह सुबह–सुबह डाकघर आता है। वह पत्र–पेटी से पत्र निकालता है। उनपर मोहर लगाता है। वह घर–घर और दुकान–दुकान पर पत्र, 'पार्सल', 'मनी आर्डर' वगैरा पहुँचाता है। वह सर्दी, गर्मी, बारिश आदि हर मौसम में काम पर जाता है।

ḍākiyā

ḍākiyā ek sarkārī karmcārī hai. vah ḍākghar meṁ kām kartā hai. vah khākī vardī pahntā hai. vah hamāre lie patra, pārsal, ādi lātā hai. ham prati din uskā intzār karte haiṁ. vah subah-subah ḍākghar ātā hai. vah patra-peṭī se patra nikāltā hai. unpar mohar lagātā hai. vah ghar-ghar aur dukān-dukān par patra, 'parcel' aur 'money order' vagairā pahuṁcātā hai. vah sardī, garmī, bāriś ādi har mausam meṁ kām par jātā hai.

WORDS AND PHRASES

डाकिया (m.)	ḍākiyā	postman
सरकारी (adj.)	sarkārī	government
कर्मचारी (m.)	karmcārī	employee
डाकघर (m.)	ḍākghar	postoffice
काम करना (conj. v.t.)	kām karnā	to work
खाकी (adj.)	khākī	khaki color
वर्दी (f.)	vardī	uniform
पहनना (v.t.)	pahnanā	to wear
हमारे लिए	hamāre lie	for us
पत्र (m.)	patra	letter
आदि (adv.)	ādi	etc.
लाना (v.t.)	lānā	to bring
दिन (m.)	din	day
प्रति दिन	prati din	every day

ḍākiyā

इन्तज़ार करना (v.t.)	intzār karnā	to wait
सुबह–सुबह	subah-subah	early morning
पत्र–पेटी (f.)	patra peṭī	letter box
निकालना (v.t.)	nikālnā	to take out
मोहर लगाना (v.t.)	mohar lagānā	to stamp
घर–घर	ghar-ghar	house to house
और (conj.)	aur	and
दुकान–दुकान	dukān-dukān	shop to shop
वगैरा (adv.)	vagairā	etc
पहुँचाना (v.t.)	pahuṁcānā	here: to deliver
सर्दी (f.)	sardī	winter
गर्मी (f.)	garmī	summer
बारिश (f.)	bāriś	rain
हर मौसम में	har mausam meṁ	in every weather
काम पर जाना	kām par jānā	to go to work

■ **Use of Compound postpositions (के 'ke' + ...) Gram. Ref. pg.** 81.

Similarly:

- **हम + के पास = हमारे पास** **ham + ke pās = hamāre pās** near us
- **हम + के पीछे = हमारे पीछे** **ham + ke** pīche = **hamāre** pīche behind us
- **हम + के नीचे = हमारे नीचे** **ham + ke** nīce = **hamāre** nīche below us
- **हम + के लिए = हमारे लिए** **ham + ke lie = hamāre lie** for us

■ **Use of Present form of the verb** होना **'honā' Gram. Ref. pg.** २६

- डाकिया एक सरकारी कर्मचारी है।
ḍākiyā ek sarkārī karmcārī hai. — Postman is a government employee.

Similarly:

1. क्या आप भी सरकारी कर्मचारी हैं? — Are you too a government employee?

ḍākiyā ek sarkārī karmcārī hai.

2. जी, मैं सरकारी कर्मचारी हूँ। jī, maiṁ sarkārī karmcārī hūṁ. — Yes, I am a government employee?

3. जी नहीं, मैं सरकारी कर्मचारी नहीं हूँ? jī nahīṁ, maiṁ sarkārī karmcārī nahīṁ hūṁ. — Yes, I am not a government em ployee?

■ Use of Present Simple Tense Gram. Ref. pg. 95 :

- वह सुबह–सुबह डाकघर आता है। vah subah-subah ḍākghar ātā hai. — He come to the post office early morning.
- वह पत्र–पेटी से पत्र निकालता है। vah patra-peṭī se patra nikāltā hai. — He takes the letters out of the letter box.
- उनपर मोहर लगाता है। unpar mohar lagātā hai. — He stamps them.
- वह .... पहुँचाता है। vah .... pahuṁcātā hai. — He delivers................

■ Use of the conjunct verb इन्तज़ार करना intzār karnā = to wait :

☞ **Regardless of the N and G of the subject who waits, or the object — livng or non-living —awaited, it is always preceded by का kā .**

- हम **उसका इन्तज़ार** करते हैं। ham uskā intzār karte haiṁ. — We wait for him/her.

1. वह **हमारा इन्तज़ार** करता है। vah hamārā intzār kartā hai. — He waits for us.

■ Use of काम पर जाना kām par jānā = to go to one's place of work, office or shop.

1. वह रोज़ काम पर जाता है। vah roz kām par jātā hai — He goes to work every day.
2. आप कितने बजे काम पर जाते हैं? āp kitne baje kām par jāte haiṁ? — What time do you go to work?

●●●●●

S 2 मेरा कुत्ता

मेरे पास एक कुत्ता है। उसका रंग सफ़ेद है। वह एक वर्ष का है। वह रोटी खाता है। वह दूध पीता है। वह मेरे साथ खेलता है। वह मेरे पिता जी के साथ सवेरे और शाम को सैर करता है। वह चिड़ियाओं के पीछे भागता है। उसका नाम शेरू है। वह मेरे घर की रखवाली करता है। मुझे अपना कुत्ता प्यारा लगता है।

merā kuttā

mere pās ek kuttā hai. uskā raṅg safed hai. vah ek varṣ kā hai. vah roṭī khātā hai. vah dūdh pītā hai. vah mere sāth khieltā hai. vah mere pitā jī ke sāth savere aur śām ko sair kartā hai. vah ciṛiyāoṁ ke pīche bhāgtā hai. uskā nām śerū hai. vah mere ghar kī rakhvālī kartā hai. mujhe apnā kuttā bahut pyārā lagtā hai.

WORDS AND PHRASES

कुत्ता (m.)	kuttā	dog
रंग (m.)	raṅg	color
सफ़ेद (adj.)	safed	white
वर्ष (m.)	varṣ	year
खेलना (v.t.)	khelnā	to play
• मेरे पास.... है।	mere pās.... hai	I have....... **(See. pg.81)**
• वह एक वर्ष **का** है।	vah ek varṣ kā hai.	He is one year old.

☞ **का** kā , **के** ke, **की** kī **following वर्ष** varṣ **depends upon the nmber and gender of the subject whose age is being talked of. For example:**

मैं (m.) बीस वर्ष **का** हूँ।	maim bīs varṣ kā hūṁ.	I am twenty years old.
मैं (f.) बीस वर्ष **की** हूँ।	maim bīs varṣ kī hūṁ	I am twenty years old.

☞ **If the subject were twins, both mas. or one mas. and one fem., के would be used.**

हम (m.)बीस वर्ष के हैं ।	ham bīs varṣ ke haiṁ.	I am twenty years old.
• मेरे साथ (ppn.)	mere sāth	with me
• मेरे पिता जी के साथ	mere pitā jī ke sāth	with my father **(See pg 48)**

☞ **plural determiner मेरे has been used because पिता जी is hon. expression.**

सवेरे (adv.)	savere	in the morning
शाम को	śām ko	in the evening
चिड़िया (f.)	ciṛiyā	bird
चिड़ियाओं (f. obl. pl.)	ciṛiyāoṁ	birds
के पीछे (ppn.)	ke pīche	hehind, after
भागना (v.i.)	bhāgnā	to run

■ **Telling or asking names: X kā nām ...... hai.**

☞ **Regardless of the N and G of the subject whose name is being asked or told, का kā precedes नाम 'nām' (m.sg.) see pg. 302**

- उसका नाम शेरू है। uskā nām śerū hai. Its name is Sheru.
  आपका नाम क्या है? āpkā nām kyā hai? What is your name?

■ **Use of the conjunct verb रखवाली करना rakhvālī karnā' = to watch or** guard.☞ **Regardless of the N an G of the object being guarded, always की kī precedes रखवाली rakhvālī (fem. sg.)**

- वह मेरे घर की रखवाली करता/करती है। He/IShe guards my house
  vah mere ghar kī rakhvālī kartā / kartī hai.
  कृपया मेरे घर की रखवाली कीजिए। .Please guards my house!
  kṛpayā mere ghar kī rakhvālī kījie.

■ **(subject+ को ko) + object + प्यारा / अच्छा लगना pyārā / acchā lagnā in the required tense = to find lovely, to like etc. (See pg. 184-185; 139)**

- मुझे अपना कुत्ता बहुत प्यारा लगता है। I find my dog very lovely.
  mujhe apnā kuttā bahut pyārā lagtā hai.
  उसे अपनी बिल्ली बहुत प्यारी लगती है। He/She finds his/her cat lovely.
  use apnī billī bahut pyārī lagtī hai.

●●●●●

S 3 मेरा परिचय

मैं एक औरत हूँ । मेरा नाम जिज्ञासा है। मैं बाईस वर्ष की हूँ । मैं छात्रा हूँ । मैं हिन्दी सीखती हूँ । मैं न्यूयार्क की रहनेवाली हूँ । आजकल मैं दिल्ली में हूँ । दिल्ली भारत की राजधानी है। मेरे पिता जी डाक्टर हैं। मेरे पिता जी का 'क्लिनिक' हमारे घर से तीस मिनट की दूरी पर है। मैं रोज़ शाम को अपने पिता जी के 'क्लिनिक' में जाती हूँ। मेरी माता जी शिक्षिका हैं। मेरी माता जी का स्कूल हमारे घर के पास है। उनके स्कूल में पन्द्रह सौ बच्चे पढ़ते हैं।

merā paricay

maiṁ ek aurat hūṁ. merā nām jigyāsā hai. maiṁ bāīs varṣ kī hūṁ. maiṁ chātrā hūṁ. maiṁ hindī sīkhtī hūṁ. maiṁ 'nyū yaurk' kī rahnevālī hūṁ. ājkal maiṁ dillī meṁ hūṁ. dillī bhārat kī rājdhānī hai. mere pitā jī dauktar haiṁ. mere pitā jī kā 'klinik' hamāre ghar se tīs minaṭ kī dūrī par hai. maiṁ roz śām ko apne pitā jī ke 'klinik' meṁ jātī hūṁ. merī mātā jī śikṣikā haiṁ. merī mātā jī kā skūl hamāre ghar ke pās hai. unke skūl meṁ pandrah sau bacce paṛhte haiṁ.

WORDS AND PHRASES

परिचय (m.)	paricay	introduction
राजधानी (f.)	rājdhānī	capital
तीस मिनट	tīs minaṭ	thirty minutes
पन्द्रह	pandrah	fifteen
सौ	sau	hundred
दूरी (f.)	dūrī	distance
की दूरी पर	ki dūrī par	at a distance of
शिक्षिका (f.)	śikṣikā	teacher

- मैं (f.) बाईस वर्ष की* हूँ । maiṁ bāis varṣ kī hūṁ. I am 22 years old.

☞ का, के, की agrees with the N and G of the subject .**(See pg. 242**)

■ **Use of : रहनेवाला rahnevālā (m.sg.), रहनेवाले rahnevale (m.pl), रहनेवाली rahnevālī (f.sg.) preceded by का kā, के ke, की kī = resident/ residents of. (* का kā, के ke,की kī agrees with the N and G of the**

subject.)

- मैं न्यूयार्क की रहनेवाली हूँ। — I am a resident of New york.
  maiṁ 'nyū yaurk' kī rahnevālī hūṁ.

Similarly:

1. मैं[m.psg] अमरीका का रहनेवाला हूँ। — I am a resident of Amerika.
   maiṁ[m.sg.] amrīkā kā rahnevālā hūṁ.
2. हम[f..pl.] दिल्ली की रहनेवाली हैं। — We are residents of Delhi.
   ham[f.pl.] dillī kī rahnevālī haiṁ .
3. वे[m.pl.] कहाँ के रहनेवाले हैं? — Where are they from?
   ve[m.pl] kahāṁ ke rahnevāle haiṁ?
4. आप[f.hon.] कहाँ की रहनेवाली हैं? — Where are you from?
   āp[f.hon.] kahāṁ kī rahnevālī[f.] haiṁ?

- दिल्ली भारत की राजधानी है। — Delhi is the capital of India.
  dillī bhārat kī rājdhānī hai.

  लंदन इंगलैंड की राजधानी है। London is the capital of England.
  londan inglaind kī rājdhānī hai.

■ की दूरी पर होना **kī dūrī par honā = to be at a distance of /away from:**

- मेरे पिता जी का 'क्लिनिक' हमारे घर से तीस मिनट की दूरी पर है।
  mere pitā jī kā 'klinik' hamāre ghar se tīs minaṭ kī dūrī par hai.
  My father's clinic is 30 minutes away from our house.

Similarly:

1. बस अड्डा मेरे घर से दो मिनट की दूरी पर है।
   bas addā mere ghar se do minaṭ kī dūrī par hai.
   Bus stop is two minutes away from my house.
2. म्यूज़ियम मेरे घर से दस मिनट की दूरी पर है।
   myusiyam mere ghar se das minaṭ kī dūrī par hai.
   museum is ten minutes away from our houe.

3. स्टेशन आपके घर से कितना दूर है?
   sṭeśan āpke ghar se kitnā dūr hai?
   How far is the station from your house?
4. स्टेशन मेरे घर से दस–पन्द्रह मिनट की दूरी पर है।
   sṭeśan mere ghar se das-pandrah minaṭ kī dūrī par hai.
   The station is ten -fifteen minutes away from my house.

Use of Possessive Determiners (See pg.46) and Compound postpositions (See pg. 80-81)

- मेरे पिता जी डाक्टर हैं। — My father is a doctor.
  mere pitā jī daukṭar haiṁ.

  मेरा भाई इन्जीनियर है। — My brother is an engineer..
  merā bhāī ingīniyar hai.

  मेरी बहन परिचारिका हैं। — My sister is a nurse.
  merī bahan paricārikā hai
- मेरी माता जी का स्कूल **हमारे** घर **के पास** है।
  merī mātā jī kā skūl **hamāre** ghar **ke pās** hai
  My mother's school is near our house.
- **उनके** स्कूल में पन्द्रह सौ बच्चे पढ़ते हैं।
  unke skūl meṁ pandrah sau bacce paṛhte haiṁ.
  Fifteen hundred children study in her school.

Similarly:

1. खेल का मैदान **हमारे** घर **के सामने** है।
khel kā maidān hamāre ghar **ke sāmne** hai
The playground is in front of our house.

2. डाकघर **हमारे** घर **के पीछे** है।
ḍākghar hamāre ghar ke pīche hai
The post office is behind our house.

●●●●●

S 4 मेरा प्रिय खेल

मेरा प्रिय खेल क्रिकेट है। यह खेल मैं रोज़ाना स्कूल तथा घर के पास के मैदान में खेलता हूँ । मैं स्कूल की क्रिकेट टीम का कप्तान हूँ । हम हर रविवार को दूसरे स्कूलों की टीमों के साथ मैच खेलते हैं। अधिक रन बनाने के कारण मुझे कई इनाम मिले हैं। मुझे बैट के साथ खेलने में बड़ा आनन्द आता है। मेरे माता–पिता और अध्यापक मेरे इस खेल से बहुत प्रसन्न हैं। मैं बड़ा होकर क्रिकेट का अच्छा खिलाड़ी बनना चाहता हूँ ।

merā priya khel

merā priy ă khel kriket̩ hai. yah khel maiṁ rozānā skūl tathā ghar ke pās ke maidān meṁ kheltā hūṁ. maiṁ skūl kī ṭīm kā kaptān hūṁ. ham har ravivār ko dūsre skūloṁ kī ṭīmoṁ ke sāth maic khelte haiṁ. adhik ran banāne ke kāraṇ mujhe kaī inām mile haiṁ. muje baiṭ ke sāth khelne meṁ baṛā ānand ātā hai. mere mātā pitā aur adhyāpak mere is khel se bahut prasann haiṁ. maiṁ baṛā hokar kriket̩ kā acchā khilāṛī bananā cāhtā hūṁ.

WORDS AND PHRASES

मेरा *	merā	my
प्रिय (adj.)	priyă	favorite
खेल (m.sg.)	khel	sport
रोज़ाना (adv.)	rozānā	daily
तथा (conjunct)	tathā	and
घर (m.sg.)	ghar	house
के पास (ppn)	ke pās	near
मैदान (m.sg.)	maidān	field
खेलना (v.t.)	khelnā	to play
कप्तान (m.)	kaptān	captain
हर (adv.)	har	every
रविवार (m.sg)	ravivār	Sunday

दूसरे (adj.)	dūsre	other
अधिक (adj.)	adhik	more
बनाना (v.t..)	banānā	to make
के कारण (ppn)	ke kāraṇ	because of
कई (adj.)	kaī	several
इनाम (m.sg./pl)	inām	prize(s)
मिलना (v.i.)	milnā	to to get/ to obtain
और (conjunct)	aur	and
अध्यापक (m.sg)	adhyāpak	teacher
प्रसन्न (adj.)	prasann	happy
बड़ा होकर ('kar' conj.)	baṛā hokar	grow up and
खिलाड़ी (m.sg.)	khilāṛī	player
बनना (v.i.)	bananā	to become
चाहना (v.t.)	cāhnā	to want

■ **The verb मिलना milnā in the sense of ' to receive', 'to find' something is used (1) in the required tense, (2) to agree with the N & G of the obj., (3) with (subj.+ को ko):**

- मुझे कई इनाम मिले हैं। — I received several prizes.
  mujhe kaī inām mile haiṁ.
  मुझे रोज़ सौ रुपए मिलते हैं। — I get 100 rupees every day.
  mujhe roz sau rupae milte haiṁ.

■ **The verb आनन्द आना ānand ānā = to enjoy is used with (subj. + को ko):**

- मुझे .... आनन्द आता है। — I enjoy............
  mujhe ....ānand ātā hai.

Similarly:

1. आपको किस चीज़ में आनन्द आता है? — What do you enjoy?
   āpko kis cīz meṁ ānand ātā hai?
2. मुझे किताबें पढ़ने में आनन्द आता है। — I enjoy reading books.

mujhe kitābeṁ paṛhne meṁ ānand ātā hai.

■ **Use of X से प्रसन्न होना X se prasann honā = to be pleased with X:**

- मेरे माता–पिता और अध्यापक मेरे इस खेल से बहुत प्रसन्न हैं।
  mere mātā pitā aur adhyāpak mere is khel se bahut prasann haiṁ.
  My parents and teachers are very pleased with this sport of mine.

Similarly:

1. मैं आपसे बहुत प्रसन्न हूँ । I am very pleased with you.
   maiṁ.āpse bahut prasann hūṁ.

2. वे हमारे काम से बहुत प्रसन्न हैं। They are very pleased with our .work
   ve hamāre kām se bahut prasann haiṁ.

■ **Use of X बनना चाहना X bananā cāhnā = to want to become X:**

- मैं$^{m.}$ बड़ा होकर खिलाड़ी बनना चाहता हूँ ।
  maiṁ$^{m.}$ baṛā hokar khilāṛī bananā cāhtā hūṁ.
  I want to become a sportsman when I grow up.

Similarly:

1. वे$^{f.hon.}$ बड़े होकर क्या बनना चाहती हैं?
   ve$^{f..hon.}$ baṛe hokar kyā bananā cāhtī haiṁ?
   What does she want to become when she grows up?

2. वे$^{f.hon.}$ बड़ी होकर अध्यापिका बनना चाहती है।
   ve$^{f.hon.}$ baṛī hokar adhyāpikā bananā cāhtī hai.
   She wants to become a teacher when she grows up.

●●●●●

S 5 लोभी कुत्ता

एक गाँव में एक कुत्ता रहता था। एक दिन उसे बहुत भूख लगी। भोजन की खोज में वह कसाई की दुकान पर गया। वहाँ से उसने एक मांस का टुकड़ा चुराया। वह उसे अपने मुँह में लेकर फिर अपने गाँव की ओर भागा। रास्ते में एक नदी थी। नदी पर एक पुल था। उसने पुल पर चढ़कर नदी के पानी में झाँका। उसको नदी के पानी में अपनी परछाई दिखाई दी। उसने उस परछाई को ठीक अपने जैसा एक दूसरा कुत्ता समझा। उसने तुरन्त वह टुकड़ा भी लेना चाहा, जो दूसरे कुत्ते के मुँह में था। क़ुत्तों के स्वभाव के अनुसार, उसने गुर्राना शुरू किया। ऐसा करते ही जो टुकड़ा उसके मुँह में था, वह भी नदी में गिर गया। वह बहुत पछताया।

किसीने ठीक ही कहा है : 'लालच बुरी बला है।'

lobhī kuttā

ek gāṁv meṁ ek kuttā rahtā thā. ek din use bahut bhūkh lagī. bhojan kī khoj meṁ vah ek kasāī kī dukān par gayā. vahāṁ se usne ek māṁs kā tukṛā curāyā. vah use apne muṁh meṁ lekar phir apne gāṁv kī or bhāgā. rāste meṁ ek nadī thī. nadī par ek pul thā. usne pul par caṛhkar nadī ke pānī meṁ jhāṁkā. usko nadī ke pānī meṁ apnī parchāī dikhāī dī. us parchāī ko usne ṭhīk apne jaisā ek dusrā kuttā samjhā. usne turant vah ṭukṛā bhī lenā cāhā, jo dūsre kutte ke muṁh meṁ thā. kuttoṁ ke svabhāv ke anusār, usne gurrānā śurū kiyā. aisā karte hī jo ṭukṛā uske muṁh meṁ thā, vah bhī nadī meṁ gir gayā. vah bahut pachtāyā. kisīne ṭhīk hī kahā hai: lālac burī balā hai.

WORDS AND PHRASES

लोभी (adj.)	lobhī	greedy
कुत्ता (m.)	kuttā	dog
गाँव (m.)	gāṁv	village
रहता था। (past habitual)	rahtā thā	used to live
भोजन (m.)	bhojan	food
खोज (f.)	khoj	search

भोजन की खोज में	bhojan kī khoj meṁ	in search of food
कसाई (m.)	kasāī	butcher
दुकान (f.)	dukān	shop
कसाई की दुकान	kasāī kī dukān	shop of butcher
मांस (m.)	māṁs	meat
टुकड़ा (m.)	ṭukṛā	a piece
चुराना (v.t.)	curānā	to steal
अपने मुँह में	apne muṁh meṁ	in its (own) mouth
लेकर (kar-conjunct)	lekar	took and
फिर (adv.)	phir	then
की ओर (ppn.)	kī or	towards
भागना (v.i.)	bhāgnā	to run
रास्ते में	rāste meṁ	on the way
नदी (f.)	nadī	river
पुल (m.)	pul	bridge
चढ़कर (kar-conjunct)	caṛhkar	get on and
झाँकना (v.t.)	jhāṁknā	to peep
जल (m.)	jal	water
अपनी (reflexive adj.)	apnī	his own
परछाई (f.)	parchāī	reflection
दिखाई देना	dekhī denā	to be visible
ठीक (adv.)	ṭhīk	exactly
अपने जैसा	apne jaisā	like himself
दूसरा (adj.)	dūsrā	another
समझना (v.t.)	samjhnā	to understand / to consider
स्वभाव (m.)	svabhāv	nature
के अनुसार (ppn)	ke anusār	according to
गुर्राना (v.i.)	gurrānā	snarl, growl
शुरू (m.)	śurū	beginning

लोभी कुत्ता

करना (v.t.)	karna	to do
किया	kiyā	did
(m.sg. past simple tense of v.t. **करना** to do)		
शुरू किया (v.t.)	śurū kiyā	began
ऐसा (adj.)	aisā	such
करते ही	karte hī	as soon as it did
जो (relative pronoun)	jo....	the ...that
जो टुकड़ा	jo ṭukṛā	the piece that
पछताना	pachtānā	to repent

- किसीने ठीक ही कहा है : Somebody has rightly said:
  kisīne ṭhīk hī kahā hai:
- 'लालच बुरी बला है।' Greed is evil.
  lālac burī balā hai.

■ **Expressing feeling of hunger, thirst:**
(subject+ ko) भूख bhūkh /प्यास pyās lagnā Gram. Ref . 138; See 263

- एक दिन उसे बहुत भूख लगी। One day he felt hungry.
  ek din use bahut bhūkh lagī.

■ **Possessive case endings का, के, की agree with the N and G of the noun following them: Gram. Ref pg:- 46**

- भोजन की खोज[f.] search of food
  bhojan kī khoj[f.] (kī agrees with khoj[f.])
- कसाई की दुकान[f.] shop of butcher
  kasāī kī dukān[f.] (kī agrees with dukān[f.])
- मांस का टुकड़ा[m.] a piece of meat
  māṁs kā tukṛā[m.] (kā agrees with tukṛā [f.])

☞ **However the possessive ending का kā changes to के ke if the object possessed is masculine and is followed by some other postposition. (See Pg. 48)**

For Example:

- नदी का पानी — water of river

  nadī kā pānī **(kā ' agrees with 'pānī' m.sg.)**

  but

  नदी के पानी में — in the water of river

  nadī ke pānī meṁ

☞ **Here as you see, there is postposition 'meṁ' after 'pānī' which is noun masculine. Hence 'kā' preceding 'pānī' changes to' ke'.**
Similarly:

- कुत्तों का स्वभाव — the nature of dogs.

  kuttoṁ kā svabhāv

  but

  कुत्तों के स्वभाव के अनुसार — in accordance with the nature of dogs.

  kuttoṁ ke svabhāv ke anusār

■ **Use of (v.r. + ते te) + ही hī: Gram.Ref. pg:- 179**

- ऐसा करते ही, — As soon as it did so.........

  aisā karte hī

■ **दिखाई देना dikhāī denā = to be visible is used with ((subj. को): pg.134**

- उसको नदी के पानी में अपनी परछाई **दिखाई दी।**

  usko nadī ke pānī meṁ apnī parchāī dikhāī dī.

  His own shadow in the river water was visible to him.

  मुझको एक काली चिड़िया **दिखाई दे रही है।**

  mujhko ek kālī ciṛiyā dikhāī de rahī hai.

  I can see a black bird.

●●●●●

S 6 मिशायल और एमि भारत में

मिशायल तीन महीने से वाराणसी में है। वह अपनी मित्र एमि के साथ रहता है। वे दोनों 'संकटमोचन रोड' पर श्री त्रिपाठी के मकान में रहते हैं। श्रीमती त्रिपाठी उनकी मकान–मालकिन है। उनका घर गंगा से पाँच मिनट की दूरी पर है। सुबह पाँच बजे दोनों पैदल घाट पर जाते हैं। दोनों गंगा में स्नान करते·हैं, सूर्योदय देखते हैं, और कुछ समय घाट पर बैठते है। वे सवा सात बजे लौटकर नाश्ता बनाते हैं। वे साढ़े सात बजे नाश्ता करके विश्वविद्यालय पढ़ने जाते हैं। वे नाश्ते में प्रायः पराठा खाते हैं और लस्सी पीते हैं। कभी–कभी वे कचौरी और जलेबी खाते हैं। दोपहर में वे दोनों कॉलेज के भोजनालय में शाकाहारी भोजन करते हैं। जब वे भारत में रहते हैं, वे मांसाहारी भोजन कभी नहीं करते। हफ़्ते में दो बार वे आइसक्रीम खाते हैं। वे अपराह्न में पुस्तकालय में बैठकर अख़बार और पत्रिकाएँ पढ़ते हैं।

शाम को मिशायल सितार सीखने जाता है। एमि व्यायामशाला में जाती है। वे रात को साढ़े आठ बजे खाना खाते हैं। वे घर का काम मिलकर करते है। मिशायल खाना पकाता है और कपड़े धोता है। एमि बर्तन धोती है और घर साफ़ करती है। सामान्यता वे ११ (ग्यारह) बजे सोते हैं।

miśāyal aur emī bhārat mem

miśāyal tīn mahīne se vārāṇasī meṁ hai. vah apnī mitra emī ke sāth rahtā hai. ve donoṁ saṅkaṭmocan roḍ par śrī tripāṭhī ke makān meṁ rahte haiṁ. śrīmatī tripāṭhī unkī makān-mālkin haiṁ. unkā ghar gaṅgā se pāṁc minat kī dūrī par hai. subah pāṁc baje donoṁ paidal ghāṭ par jāte haiṁ. donoṁ gaṅgā meṁ snān karte haiṁ., sūryoday dekhte haiṁ, aur kuch samay ghāṭ par baiṭhte haiṁ. ve savā sāt baje lauṭkar nāśtā banāte haiṁ. sāṛhe sāt baje nāśta karke viśvavidyālay paṛhne jāte haiṁ. ve nāśte meṁ prāyaḥ parāṭhe khāte haiṁ aur lassī pīte haiṁ. kabhī-kabhī ve kacaurī aur jalebī khāte haiṁ. dopahar meṁ ve donoṁ kaulij ke bhojanālay meṁ śākāhārī bhojan karte haiṁ. jab ve bhārat meṁ rahte haiṁ, ve mānsāhārī bhojan kabhī nahiṁ karte. hafte meṁ do bār ve āiskrīm khāte haiṁ. ve aprāhn meṁ pustakālay meṁ baiṭh kar a<u>kh</u>bār aur patrikāeṁ paṛhte haiṁ.
śām ko miśāyal sitār sīkhne jātā hai. emī vyāyāmśālā meṁ jākar vyāyām kartī hai. ve rāt ko saṛhe āṭh baje khānā khāte haiṁ. ve ghar kā kām milkar karte haiṁ.

miśāyal khānā pākātā hai aur kapṛe dhotā hai. emī bartan dhotī hai aur ghar sāf kartī hai. sāmānyătā ve gyārah baje sote haiṁ.

WORDS AND PHRASES

दोनों (adj.)	donoṁ	both
मकान–मालकिन (f.sg.)	makān-mālkin	landlady
सुबह (f..)	subah	in the morning
पाँच बजे	pāṁc baje	at five o'clock
पैदल (adv)	paidal	on foot
घाट (m.)	ghāṭ	cemented area on the banks of river
घाट पर	ghāṭ par	on the ghat
स्नान करना (v.t.)	snān karnā	to have bath
सूर्योदय (m.sg.)	sūryoday	sunrise
लौटकर (kar-conj.)	lauṭkar	return and
नाश्ता (m.sg.)	nāśtā	breakfast
बनाना (v.t.)	banānā	to make
साढ़े सात बजे	sāṛhe sāt baje	7:30 p.m./a.m.
नाश्ता करके (kar-conj.)	nāśta karke	have breakfast and
विश्वविद्यालय (m.sg./pl.)	viśvavidyālay	university
पढ़ना (v.t.)	paṛhnā	to study/ to read
प्रायः (adv.)	prāyaḥ	usually
कभी–कभी (adv.)	kabhī- kabhī	sometimes
भोजनालय (m.sg./pl.)	bhojanālay	canteen
शाकाहारी (adj.)	śākāhārī	vegetarian
मांसाहारी (adj.)	mānsāhārī	nonvegetarian
कभी नहीं (adv.)	kabhī nahīṁ	never
अपराह्न (m.)	aprāhn	early afternoon
पुस्तकालय (m.sg./pl.)	pustakālay	library
अख़बार (m.sg./pl.)	akhbār	newspaper

मिशायल और एमि भारत में

पत्रिका (f.sg.)	patrikā	magazine
पत्रिकाएँ (f.pl.)	patrikāeṁ	magazines
बैठकर (kar-conjunct)	baiṭhkar	sit and
शाम को	śām ko	in the evening
सीखना (v.t.)	sīkhnā	to learn
व्यायामशाला (f.sg)	vyāyāmśālā	gym
जाकर (kar-conjunct)	jākar	go and
व्यायाम करना (v.t.)	vyāyām karnā	to do exercise
साढ़े आठ बजे	saṛhe āṭh baje	half past eight
मिलकर (kar-conjunct)	milkar	together
पकाना (v.t.)	pākānā	to cook
कपड़े (m.pl.)	kapṛe	clothes
धोना (v.t.)	dhonā	to wash
बर्तन (m.sg./pl.)	bartan	pots and pans
घर (m.sg./pl.)	ghar	house
साफ़ करना (v.t.)	sāf karnā	to clean
सामान्यता (adv.)	sāmānyătā	normally
ग्यारह बजे	gyārah baje	11 o'clock

■ **से 'se' is used in time expressions to mean both 'for a period of time' or ' since a point of time'.**

- मिशायल तीन महीने से वाराणसी में है। misǎyal tīn mahīne se vārāṇasī meṁ hai. — Michael has been in in Varanasi for three months.

Similarly:

1. मैं सोमवार से यहाँ हूँ। maiṁ somvār se yahāṁ hūṁ. — I am here since Monday
2. वह दो हफ़्ते से बीमार है। vah do hafte se bīmār hai. — He has been ill for two weeks.

■ **Reflexive Adjective** अपना, अपने, अपनी apna, apne, apnī : It agrees with the noun that it qualifies. **Gram. ref. pg:- 135**

- वह अपनी मित्र एमि के साथ रहता है। He lives with his friend Amy.
  vah apnī mitra emī ke sāth rahtā hai.

Similarly:

1. तुम अपना नाम बताओ। (You) Tell your name.
   tum apnā nām batāo.
2. तुम अपनी किताब से पढ़ो। Read from your (own) book
   tum apnī kitāb se paṛho.

Present Simple Tense Gram. Ref. pg. 95

- वे दोनों 'संकटमोचन रोड' पर श्री त्रिपाठी के मकान में रहते हैं।

  ve donoṁ saṅkaṭmocan roḍ par śrī tripāṭhī ke makān meṁ rahte haiṁ.

☞ श्री त्रिपाठी का मकान śrī tripāṭhī kā makān house of Mr. Tripathi changes to श्री त्रिपाठी के मकान में śrī tripāṭhī ke makān meṁ. Here का kā has changed to के ke because मकान makān is followed by the postposition में meṁ

- वे सवा सात बजे लौटकर नाश्ता बनाते हैं।

  ve savā sāt baje lauṭkar nāśtā banāte haiṁ.
- वे साढ़े सात बजे नाश्ता करके विश्वविद्यालय पढ़ने* जाते हैं।
  ve sāṛhe sāt baje nāśta karke viśvavidyālay paṛhne* jāte haiṁ

☞ रहते हैं rahte haiṁ, बनाते हैं banāte haiṁ, जाते हैं jāte haiṁ , agree with the subject वे ve.

☞ पढ़ने paṛhne* has been used here as object of the main verb जाना jānā to go. Hindi speakers usually tend to drop the required postposition (in this case it is के लिए ke lie meaning 'for') and just change the ' ना nā - ending' of the verb infinitive to 'ने ne- ending'. (Use of Infinitive as Noun: See pg. 104)

Similarly:

- शाम को मिशायल सितार सीखने (के लिए) जाता है।

  śām ko miśāyal sitār sīkhne (ke lie) jātā hai.

☞ सीखना changes to सीखने because it is used here as the object of the sentence. Though the required postposition has been dropped, the verb infinitive is inflected.

Time Expressions Gram. Ref. pg. 200

• सवा सात बजे	savā sāt baje	at a quarter past seven
• साढ़े सात बजे	sāṛhe sāt baje	at half past seven
• साढ़े आठ बजे	saṛhe āṭh baje	at eight thirty
• 11 (ग्यारह) बजे	gyārah baje	at eleven o'clock

kar-conjunct Gram. Ref. pg. 174

• लौटकर	lauṭkar	here: 'return and'
• बैठकर	baiṭhkar	sit and
• मिलकर	milkar	together
• नाश्ता करके	nāśtā kar ke	have breakfast and

☞ नाश्ता करना nāśta karknā means to have breakfast. **कर kar** is the root of the verb करना (to do) and **के ke** is the contracted form of the कर conjunct Together नाश्ता करके nāśtā karke means 'have breakfast and'.

- उनका घर गंगा से पाँच मिनट की दूरी पर है।
  unkā ghar gaṅgā se pāṁc minaṭ kī dūrī par hai. **(See pg.245)**

Similarly:

1. डाकघर हमारे स्कूल से बीस मिनट की दूरी पर है।
   ḍākghar hamāre skūl se bīs minaṭ kī dūrī par hai.
   The post office is twenty minutes away from our school.
2. बैंक डाकघर से दो मिनट की दूरी पर है।
   bañk ḍākghar se do minaṭ kī dūrī par hai.
   The bank is two minutes away from the post office.

●●●●●

S 7 एक कौवा

एक गाँव^m^ में एक पेड़^m^ पर एक कौवा^m^ रहता था। कौवा^m^ प्यासा^adj.^ था। कौवे ने इधर उधर^adv.^ देखा। कौवे ने एक मटका^m^ देखा। कौवा फ़ौरन^adv.^ मटके के पास गया। मटके का मुँह^m^ बहुत छोटा था। मटके में पानी^m^ बहुत कम था। कौवे ने एक उपाय^m.sg^ सोचा। कोवे ने मटके में छोटे–छोटे कंकड^m.pl^ डाले। पानी^m^ ऊपर आ गया। कौवे ने पानी पिया। कौवे ने अपनी प्यास^f^ बुझाई। कौवा उड़ गया।

ek kauvā

ek gāṁv meṁ ek peṛ par ek kauvā rahtā thā. kauvā pyāsā thā. kauve ne idhar-udhar dekhā. kauve ne ek maṭkā dekhā. kauvā fauran maṭke ke pās gayā. maṭke kā muṁh bahut choṭā thā. maṭke meṁ pānī bahut kam thā. kauve ne ek upāy socā. kauve ne maṭke meṁ choṭe-choṭe kaṅkaṛ ḍāle. pānī ūpar ā gayā. kauve ne pānī piyā. kauve ne apnī pyās bujhāī. kauvā uṛ gayā.

WORD POWER

गाँव (m.)	**gāṁv**	village;
पेड (m.)	peṛ	tree ;
कौवा (m.)	kauvā	crow
रहना (v.i..)	rahnā	to live
रहता था(past hab.)	rahtā thā	used to live
प्यासा(adj.)	pyāsā	thirsty
इधर उधर (adv.)	idhar-udhar	here and there
मटका (m.)	maṭkā	pitcher
देखा	dekhā	saw

(past simple tense of देखना dekhnā v.t. = to see; agrees with the object मटका^m^ maṭkā)

फ़ौरन (adv.)	fauran	instantly
के पास ppn	ke pās	near
गया	gayā	went

(past simple tense of जाना v.i. ; it agrees here with the subject कौवा^m^ kauvā^m^)

ek kauvā

मुँह^m	muṁh	mouth;
कम	kam	less
उपाय(fm.)	upāy	plan
सोचा	socā	thought

(past simple tense of सोचना^v.t. socnā = to think; agrees with the object उपाय^m. upāy)

छोटे–छोटे adj.	choṭe-choṭe	very small
कंकड m.sg./pl.	kaṅkaṛ	stone(s)/pebble(s)
डाले^v.t.	ḍāle	put

(m.pl. past simple tense of v.t. डालना^v.t. ḍālnā = to put; it agrees with the object कंकड़^m.pl kaṅkaṛ^m.pl)

ऊपर आना	ūpar ānā	to come up
आ गया (comp. verb)*	ā gayā	came
पिया	piyā	drank

(past simple tense of पीना pīnā v.t. = to drink; it agrees with the object पानी^m. pānī)

अपनी (reflexive adj.)	apnī	its own
प्यास^f. (f.)	pyās	thirst
बुझाई	bujhāī	extinguished

(past simple tense of बुझाना bujhānā v.t. = to extinguish/ here: to quench; it agrees with the object प्यास^f. pyās)

उडना^v.i.	uṛnā	to fly
उड़ गया (comp.verb)*	uṛ gayā	flew away.

***Compound verbs : Gram. Ref. pg:- 187**

●●●●●

S 8 अंगूर खट्टे हैं

किसी वन में एक लोमड़ी रहती थी। एक दिन उसे बहुत भूख लगी। भोजन की खोज में वह एक बाग़ में पहुँची। वहाँ उसने उँचाई पर अंगूरों की बेल लटकी हुई देखी। उनको पाने के लिए वह बहुत उछली और कूदी। किन्तु उसके पंजे वहाँ तक न पहुँच पाए। वह बहुत निराश होकर आगे बढ़ गई। चलते–चलते उसने कहा : 'अंगूर बहुत खट्टे हैं।'

aṅgūr khaṭṭe haiṁ

kisī van meṁ ek lomṛī rahtī thī. ek din use bahut bhūkh lagī. bhojan kī khoj meṁ vah ek bāg meṁ pahuṁcī. vahāṁ usne uṁcāī par aṅgūroṁ kī bel laṭkī huī dekhī. unko pāne ke lie vah bahut uchlī aur kūdī. kintu uske pañje vahāṁ tak na pahuṁc pāe.₁ vah nirāś hokar āge baṛh gaī. calte-calte usne kahā: 'aṅgūr khaṭṭe haiṁ'

WORDS AND PHRASES

अंगूर (m.)	aṅgūr	grapes
खट्टे (adj.)	khaṭṭe	sour
किसी (pronoun)	kisī	some
(obl. of indefinite pronoun कोई koī)		
वन (m.)	van	forest
लोमड़ी (f.)	lomṛī	fox
भूख (f.)	bhūkh	hunger
भोजन (m.)	bhojan	meal
खोज (f.)	khoj	search
पहुँचना (v.i.)	pahuṁcnā	to arrive
उँचाई (f.)	uṁcāī	height
बेल (f.)	bel	creeper, vine
अंगूरों की बेल (f.)	aṅgūroṁ kī bel	grape vine
लटकी हुई (PPC)	laṭkī huī	hanging
देखना (v.t.)	dekhnā	to see

aṅgūr khaṭṭe haiṁ

वहाँ तक	vahāṁ tak	upto a certain point of space
पहुँचने के लिए	pahuṁcne ke lie	for reaching
उछली	uchlī	sprang (f.sg. past

simple tense of v.i. उछलना uchlnā = to jump; agrees with लोमड़ी^f. lomṛī^f.)

कूदी	kūdī	jumped (f.sg. past

simple tense of v.i. कूदना kūdnā = to spring/ jump; agrees with लोमड़ी^f.) lomṛī^f..)

किन्तु (conj.)	kintu	but
पंजे (m.pl)	pañje	paws
पाना (here: v.i.)	pānā	to be able to manage
निराश (adj.)	nirāś	disappointed
होकर (kar-conj.)	hokar	become and
आगे (adv.)	āge	ahead, further on
बढ़ना (v.i..)	baṛhnā	**here:** to move on
बढ़ गई (comp.verb)	baṛh gaī	went ahead.
कहना (v.t.)	kahnā	to say
चलते–चलते (IPC)	calte-calte	while moving

■ **कर - conjunct Gram. Ref. pg:- 174**

निराश होकर	nirāś hokar	become disappointed and

Similarly:

जाकर	jākar	go and
बैठकर	baiṭhkar	sit and
खुश होकर	khuś hokar	be happy and

■ **PPC : Gram. Ref. pg:- 217; See pg. 267**

उसने उँचाई पर अंगूरों की बेल **लटकी हुई** देखी।
usne uṁcāī par aṅgūroṁ kī bel laṭkī huī dekhī.
She saw a grape vine hanging high up.

Similarly:

1. **टूटा हुआ** फूलदान उठाइए। — Pick up the broken vase!
   ṭūṭā huā phūldān uṭhāie.
2. **फटा हुआ** कुर्ता मत पहनिए। — Don't wear torn 'kurta'!
   phaṭā huā kurtā mat pahnie.

■ **Use of the sense verb lagnā to express feeling of hunger, thirst etc.: Gram Ref. Pg. 138; See pg. 252**

- उसे बहुत भूख लगी। — She felt very hungry.
  use bahut bhūkh lagī.

Similarly:

मुझे बहुत प्यास लगी है। — I am feeling very thirsty.
mujhe bahut pyās lagī hai.

■ **(v.r. + te) + (v.r. + te) = IPC: Gram.Ref. pg. 219**; See 267

- चलते–चलते उसने कहा। — **While moving she said:**
  calte-calte usne kahā.

Similarly:

1. पिता जी जाते–जाते बोले। — Father spoke while leaving.
   pitā jī jāte-jāte bole.
2. लोग चिल्लाते हुए जा रहे थे। — People were going while shouting.
   log cillāte hue jā rahe the.

●●●●●

S 10 चालाक लोमड़ी

किसी जंगल में एक लोमड़ी रहती थी। वह बहुत चालाक थी। एक दिन उसे बहुत भूख लगी। भोजन की खोज में वह एक बाग़ में पहुँची। वहाँ उसने एक पेड़ पर एक कौवे को बैठे हुए देखा। उसकी चोंच में पनीर का टुकड़ा था। कौवे की चोंच में पनीर का टुकड़ा देखकर उसके मुँह में पानी आ गया। उसे एक उपाय सूझा। उसने कौवे की झूठी प्रशंसा करते हुए कहा : ' कौवे भाई, तुम बहुत सुन्दर हो। तुम्हारा रंग कोयल की तरह काला है। तुम्हारी आवाज़ भी कोयल की आवाज़ की तरह बहुत मीठी होगी। कृपया, कुछ गाकर सुनाओ।'

कौवा चुप रहा।

चालाक लोमड़ी फिर बोलीः 'अफ़सोस ! तुम गूंगे हो !'

कौवे को गुस्सा आया। उसने बोलने के लिए अपनी चोंच खोली। पनीर का टुकड़ा ज़मीन पर गिर पड़ा। लोमड़ी ने झट से पनीर अपने मुँह में लिया और भाग गई।

कौवा देखता रह गया।

cālāk lomṛī

kisī jaṅgal meṁ ek lomṛī rahtī thī. vah bahut cālāk thī. ek din use bahut bhūkh lagī. bhojan kī khoj meṁ vah ek bāg meṁ pahuṁcī. vahāṁ usne ek peṛ par ek kauve ko baiṭhe hue dekhā. uskī coṁc meṁ ek panīr kā ṭukṛā thā. kauve kī coṁc meṁ panīr kā ṭukṛā dekhkar uske muṁh meṁ pānī ā gayā. use ek upāy sūjhā. usne kauve kī jhūṭhī praśaṁsā karte hue kahā: 'kauve bhāī, tum bahut sundar ho. tumhārā raṅg 'koyal' kī tarah kālā hai. tumhārī āvāz bhī koyal kī āvāz kī tarah mīṭhī hogī. kṛpayā kuch gākar sunāo na. kauvā cup rahā.'

cālāk lomṛī phir bolī: 'afsos! tum gūṅge ho!'

kauve ko gussā āyā. usne bolne ke lie apnī coṁc kholī. panīr kā ṭukṛā zamīn par gir paṛā. lomṛī ne jhaṭ se panīr apne muṁh meṁ liyā aur bhāg gaī.

kauvā dekhtā rah gayā.

WORDS AND PHRASES

किसी *	kisī	some/ any

***indefinite pronoun; oblique of कोई 'koī')**

जंगल (m.)	jaṅgal	forest
लोमड़ी (f.)	lomṛī	fox
चालाक (adj.)	cālāk	cunning
रहती थी। (past habitual)	rahtī thī	used to live
भूख लगना	bhūkh lagnā.	to feel hungry
भोजन (m.)	hojan	meal
खोज (f.)	khoj	search
बाग (m.)	bāg	park
पहुँची	pahuṁcī.	arrived

(past simple tense fem. form of the v.i. पहुँचना pahuṁcnā = to arrive; agrees with लोमड़ी lomṛī n.f.)

वहाँ	vahāṁ	there
कौवा (m.)	kauvā	crow
पेड़ (m.)	peṛ	tree
बैठे हुए (PPC)	baiṭhe hue	seated
देखा (v.t.)	dekhā.	saw

(past simple tense masc.sg.form of the v.t. देखना dekhnā = to look/to see)

चोंच (f.)	coṁc	beak
पनीर (m.)	panīr	cheese
टुकड़ा (m.)	ṭukṛā	piece
देखकर ('kar' conj.)	dekhkar	saw and
मुँह में पानी आना	muṁh meṁ pānī ānā.	mouth to water
उपाय (m.)	upāy	plan
सूझा (v.t..)	sūjhā.	occurred

(past simple tense masc.sg. of the v.i. सूझना sūjhnā ; it agrees here with masc. sg. उपाय upāy .)

झूठी (adj.)	jhūṭhī	false
प्रशंसा (f.)	praśaṁsā	praise
करते हुए (IPC)	karte hue	while doing
कहा	kahā	said

cālāk lomṛī

(past simple tense masc.sg. of the v.t. कहना kahnā = to say)

रंग (m.)	rang	color
कोयल (f.)	koyal	a bird known
for its melodious musical voice		
बहुत (adv.)	bahut	very
सुन्दर (adj.)	sundar	beautiful
की तरह (ppn.)	kī tarah	like
आवाज (f.)	āvāz	voice
भी (adv.)	bhī	also
मीठी (adj.)	mīṭhī	sweet
कृपया (adv.)	kṛpayā	please
गाकर (kar conj.)	gākar	sing and
सुनाओ	sunāo	sing
(imperative 'tum' form of the v.t. सुनाना sunānā =here: to sing)		
न (adv.)	na	here : please
चुप रहना (v.i.)	cup rahnā	to keep quiet.
फिर (adv.)	phir	again
बोली	bolī	spoke
(past simple tense masc.sg. of the verb बोलना bolnā* = to say) (*see pg. 124)		
अफ़सोस	afsos!	Sad!
गूंगा (adj.)	gūṅgā	dumb
खोली	kholī.	opened
(past simple tense masc. sg form of खोलना kholnā v.t. = to open ; agrees with		
चोंच f.sg.)	coṁc	beak
ज़मीन (f.)	zamīn	ground/ floor
झट से (adv.)	jhaṭ se	quickly
लिया	liyā	took
(m. sg. past simple tense of the v.t. लेना lenā=to take; agrees with टुकड़ा[m.sg.] ṭukṛā[m.sg.] =piece)		

- **PPC Gram. Ref. pg.217; See pg. 262**

- उसने एक पेड़ पर एक कौवे को **बैठे हुए** देखा।
  usne ek peṛ par ek kauve ko baiṭhe hue dekhā.
  She saw a crow sitting on the tree.

- **IPC Gram. Ref. pg. 219; See pg. 263**

- उसने कौवे की झूठी प्रशंसा करते हुए कहा:
  usne kauve kī jhūṭhī praśaṁsā karte hue kahā:
  Doing false praise of the crow, she said:

- **Compound Verbs: Gram. Ref. pg. 187-191**

- उसके मुँह में पानी आ गया। Her mouth watered.
  uske muṁh meṁ pānī ā gayā.

- लोमड़ी .... भाग गई। The fox .... ran away.
  lomṛī .... bhāg gaī.

- पनीर का टुकड़ा ज़मीन पर गिर पड़ा। The piece of cheese fell down
  panīr kā ṭukṛā zamīn par gir paṛā.

- **Establishing likeness between two objects:**

  Use of : X की तरह X kī tarah = like X Ref. pg. 80-81

- तुम्हारा रंग कोयल की तरह काला है।
  tumhārā raṅg 'koyal' kī tarah kālā hai.
  Your complexion is black like the 'koyal'

Similarly:

1. मैं आपकी तरह अमीर नहीं।
   maiṁ āpkī tarah amīr nahīṁ.
   I am not rich like you.

- **Presumptive Sructure: Gram. Ref. pg. 202**

- तुम्हारी आवाज़ भी बहुत मीठी होगी।
  tumhārī āvāz bhī ....bahut mīṭhī hogī.
  You voice must also be very sweet.

■ **Use of the verbs (1) गुस्सा आना gussā ānā = to become angry; (2) सूझना sūjhnā = to occur to somebody:**

☞ **These verb always go with subject in the oblique case followed by the postposition को 'ko'**

• कौवे को गुस्सा आया। kauve ko gussā āyā.	The crow became angry

Similarly:

1. मुझको को गुस्सा आया। mujh ko gussā āyā.	I became angry.
2. उसको एक उपाय सूझा। usko ek upāy sūjhā .	A plan occured to him.
3. मुझे इस समय कुछ नहीं सूझ रहा। mujhe is samay kuch nahīṁ sūjh rahā .	At this moment nothing is occuring to me.

■ **Use of the verb** रहना rahnā **to continuatively remain in a certain state. Gram. Ref. pg:-198**

• कौवा चुप रहा। kauvā cup rahā.	The crow remained silent.

Similarly:

आदमी पेड़ के नीचे लेटा रहा। ādmī peṛ ke nīce leṭā rahā.	The man remained lying under the tree.

■ **देखता रह गया, देखते रह गए, देखती रह गई**
dekhtā rah gayā, dekhte rah gae, dekhtī rah gaī = **remained looking.**

☞ **This expression is used wnen one stands agape, awestruck, left helpless, unable to cope with a situation that popped up unexpectedly.**

• कौवा देखता रह गया। kauvā dekhtā rah gayā.	The crow remained looking.

●●●●●

S 10 एकता में बल

एक समय की बात है। एक गाँव में एक बहुत समझदार किसान रहता था। उसके चार बेटे थे। वे सब आपस में लड़ते झगड़ते रहते थे। बेचारा किसान उनके आपसी झगड़ों से बहुत दुखी था।

एक बार वह बहुत बीमार हो गया। उसे अपने बचने की कोई उम्मीद न रही। उसको अपने बेटों के भविष्य की बहुत चिन्ता हुई।

उसको एक तरकीब सूझी। पहले उसने अपने चारों बेटों को बुलाया। फिर उसने अपने एक बेटे को पतली–पतली लकड़ियों का एक गट्ठर लाने को कहा।

जब लकड़ियों का एक गट्ठर आ गया, तो उसने उनको बारी–बारी से उसे तोड़ने को कहा। यद्यपि उन्होंने अपनी–अपनी पूरी ताकत लगाई, वे फिर भी उसे न तोड़ पाए। फिर उसने उनको मिलकर उसे तोड़ने को कहा। वे फिर भी उसे न तोड़ पाए।

अब उसने उनको गट्ठर खोलकर, एक एक करके, लकड़ियाँ तोड़ने को कहा। इस बार वे आसानी से लकड़ियाँ तोड़ सके।

लड़के समझ गए कि एकता में बल होता है। वे प्यार से मिलकर रहने लगे। समझदार बूढे किसान की चिन्ता दूर हो गई।

ektā meṁ bal

ek samay kī bāt hai. ek gāṁv meṁ ek bahut samajhdār kisān rahtā thā. uske cār beṭe the. ve sab āpas meṁ laṛte-jhagaṛte rahte the. becārā kisān unke āpsī jhagṛoṁ se bahut dukhī thā.

ek bār vah bahut bīmār ho gayā. use apne bacne kī koī ummīd na rahī. usko apne cāroṁ beṭoṁ ke bhaviṣyă kī bahut cintā huī

usko ek tarkīb sūjhī. pahle usne apne beṭoṁ ko bulāyā. phir usne apne ek beṭe ko patlī-patlī lakṛiyoṁ kā gaṭṭhar lāne ko kahā.

jab lakṛiyoṁ kā gaṭṭhar ā gayā, to usne unko bārī-bārī se use toṛne ko kahā. yadyăpi unhoṁne apnī -apnī pūrī tākat lagāī, ve phir bhī use na toṛ pāe. phir usne unko milkar use toṛne ko kahā. ve phir bhī use na toṛ pāe.

ab usne unko gaṭṭhar kholkar, ek-ek karke, lakṛiyāṁ toṛne ko kahā. is bār ve āsānī se lakṛiyāṁ toṛ sake.

laṛke samajh gaye ki ektā meṁ bal hotā hai. ve pyār se milkar rahne lage. samajhdār būṛhe kisān kī cintā dūr ho gaī.

WORDS AND PHRASES

एकता[f.sg]	ektā	unity
बल[m.sg]		bal strength
गाँव[m.sg]	gāṁv	village
समझदार[adj.]	samajhdār	wise
किसान[m.sg]	kisān	farmer
आपस में	āpas meṁ	mutually
लडना झगडना[v.i.]	laṛnā-jhagaṛnā	to quarrel
बेचारा[adj.]	becārā	poor
झगडा[m.sg]	jhagaṛā	dispute
दुखी[adj.]	dukhī	unhappy
एक बार	ek bār	once
बचने की	bacne kī	of survival
उम्मीद[f.sg]	ummīd	hope
भविष्य[m.sg]	bhaviṣya	future
चिन्ता[f.sg]	cintā	worry
तरकीब[f.sg]	tarkīb	plan
सूझी	sūjhī	occured

(past simple tense of v.i. सूझना sūjhnā to occure; it agrees with तरकीब[f.sg] tarkīb)

चारों (adj.	cāroṁ	all four
पतली–पतली[adj.]	patlī-patlī	very thin
लकडी[f.sg]	lakṛī	wood
गट्ठर[m.sg]	gaṭṭhar	bundle
बारी–बारी से[adv.]	bārī-bārī se	turn by turn
तोड़ना[v.t.]	toṛnā	break

मिलकर (conj.verb)	milkar	together
एक एक करके	ek-ek karke	one by one
आसानी से[adv.]	āsānī se	easily
चिन्ता[f.sg]	cintā	worry
दूर हो जाना	dūr ho jānā	to get removed.

■ **Continuative Compound Gram. Ref. pg:-198**

- वे सब आपस में **लड़ते–झगड़ते रहते थे।**
  ve sab āpas meṁ **laṛte-jhagaṛte rahte the.**
  They used to keep fighting among themselves.

Similarly:

1. व्यापारी ख़रीदते–बेचते **रहते हैं।** The businessmen keep buying and selling.
   vyāpārī kharīdte-becte rahte haiṁ.
2. लड़कियां **नाचती**–गाती रहती **हैं।** The girls keep dancing and singing.
   la ṛkiyāṁ nācti- gatī rahtī haiṁ.

■ **Use of the Verb सूझना sūjhnā See pg:-268**

- उसको एक तरकीब सूझी। A plan occured tohim/her.
  usko ek tarkīb sūjhī.

■ **Compound Verbs: Gram Ref. pg:- 187**

- एक बार वह बहुत बीमार हो गया। Once he became very ill.
  ek bār vah bahut bīmār ho gayā.
- लकड़ियों का एक गट्ठर आ गया। The bundle of wood arrived.
  lakṛiyoṁ kā ek gaṭṭhar ā gayā.

('आ गया ā gayā' is compound verb with the nuance of completion of action).

- किसान की चिन्ता दूर हो गई। Farmer's worry got removed.
  kisān kī cintā dūr ho gaī.

■ **To ask someone(=X*) to do something(=Y*):**

subject + (X* को ko) + Y* + (v.r. + ने ne) +को ko + कहना kahnā:

- उसने उनको ...... उसे तोड़ने को कहा। He asked them..... to break it.
  usne unko .... use toṛne ko kahā.
- उसने अपने एक बेटे को .... गट्ठर लाने को कहा।
  usne apne ek beṭe ko................. gaṭṭhar lāne ko kahā.
  He asked his one son to bring bundle of wood-sticks.

Similarly:

1. उसने मुझे जाने को कहा। He asked me to1. go.
   usne mujhe jāne ko kahā.
2. माँ ने हमें जल्दी सोने को कहा। Mother asked us to sleep early.
   māṁ ne hameṁ jaldī sone ko kahā.
3. नौकर को चाय बनाने को कहो। Tell the servant to make tea.
   naukar ko cāy banāne ko kaho!

■ **Use of verbs सकना/पाना 'saknā'/ pānā= can**

Gram Ref. pg:- 154

- वे उसे न तोड़ पाए। They were not able to break it.
  ve use na toṛ pāe.
- इस बार वे आसानी से लकड़ियाँ तोड़ सके। This time they could break the woods easily.
  is bār ve āsānī se lakṛiyāṁ toṛ sake.

■ **yadyăpi........phir bhī यद्यपि...... फिर भी...... although..even then..**

- यद्यपि उन्होंने अपनी पूरी ताकत लगाई, वे फिर भी उसे न तोड़ पाए। Although they used all their energy, even then they could not break it.
  yadyăpi unhoṁne apnī purī tākat lagāī, ve phir bhī use na toṛ pāe.

Similarly:

1. यद्यपि वह बहुत अमीर नहीं, फिर भी बहुत उदार है। Although he is not very rich, even then he is very generous.
   yadyăpi vah bahut amīr nahīṁ, phir bhī vah bahut udār hai.

2. यद्यपि पेट्रोल बहुत महँगा है, **फिर भी** मुझे कार से जाना पड़ता है। — Although petrol is very expensive, even then I have to go by car.
3. यद्यपि वह ज्योतिष में विश्वास नहीं करता, **फिर भी** वह दैनिक भविष्यवाणी पढ़ता है। — Although he does not believe in astrology, even then he reads daily forecast.

■ Use of the present habitual tense for all time truth: Gram Ref. pg. 95

- एकता में बल होता है। — Unity is strength.
  ektā meṁ bal hotā hai.

Similarly:

1. सत्य की जीत होती है। — Truth wins.
   satya kī jīt hotī hai.
2. सूर्य पूर्व से निकलता है। — The Sun rises in the east.
   sūrya pūrv se nikaltā hai.

■ Use of (v.r.+ 'ne') + lagnā = to begin to do something. Gram.Ref. pg:- 140

- वे प्यार से मिलकर रहने लगे। — They began to live togther with love.
  ve pyār se milkar rahne lage.

Similarly:

1. बच्चे मिलकर राष्ट्रगाण गाने लगे। — The children began to sing the national anthem together.
   bacce milkar rāṣṭragāṇ gāne lage.
2. सुबह–सुबह पक्षी कलरव करने लगेंगे। — Early morning, the birds will begin to chirp.
   subah-subah pakṣī kalrav karne lageṁge.

●●●●●

S12 घमण्डी का सिर नीचा होता है

एक समय की बात है। किसी जंगल में एक सिरफिरा खरगोश रहता था। यह खरगोश स्वभाव से नटखट था। उसे अपनी तेज़ गति पर बहुत घमण्ड था। एक बार इस सिरफिरे और, घमण्डी खरगोश ने किसी कछुए को मन्द गति से जाते हुए देखा। वह, उसे धीरे– धीरे चलते हुए देखते ही, उसपर हँसने लगा। कछुआ उसकी हँसी सुनकर रुक गया, और पीछे मुड़कर देखने लगा। उसे रुका हुआ देखते ही खरगोश ने उसे अपने साथ दौड़ने के लिए ललकारा। कछुआ समझदार था। वह जानता था, 'सहज पके सो मीठा होय'। उसने खरगोश की चुनौती स्वीकार कर ली।

दोनों ने वहाँ से लगभग एक कोस दूर एक मज़ार पर मिलने का निश्चय किया।

खरगोश उछलता–कूदता बहुत जल्दी काफ़ी आगे निकल गया। उसे अपनी गति पर कुछ ज़्यादा ही भरोसा था। उसे पूरा विश्वास था कि वह कछुए को पीछे छोड़कर वह स्वयं आगे निकल जाएगा। उसने थोड़ी देर सुस्ताने का निश्चय किया। उसे नींद आ गई। कछुआ मन्द गति से चलते–चलते मज़ार पर पहुँचकर खरगोश का इन्तज़ार करने लगा। आँख खुलते ही खरगोश ने दौड़ना शरू किया। वहाँ पहुँचकर, कछुए को पहले से ही वहाँ पहुँचा हुआ देखकर वह चकित हो गया।

उसका सिर शर्म से झुक गया। वह कछुए से आँख न मिला सका।

किसीने ठीक ही कहा है : 'घमण्डी का सिर नीचा होता है।'

ghamaṇḍī kā sir nīcā hotā hai

ek samay kī bāt hai. kisī jaṅgal meṁ ek sirphirā khargoś rahtā thā. yah khargoś svabhāv se naṭkhaṭ thā. use apnī tez gati par bahut ghamaṇḍ thā. ek bār is sirphire aur ghamaṇḍī khargoś ne kisī kachue ko mand gati se jāte hue dekhā. vah use dhīre-dhīre calte hue dekhte hī, us par haṁsne lagā. kachuā uskī haṁsī sunkar ruk gayā, aur pīche muṛkar dekhne lagā. use rukā huā dekhte hī khargoś ne use apne sāth dauṛne ke lie lalkārā. kachuā samajhdār thā. vah jāntā thā 'sahaj pake so mīṭhā hoy'. usne khargoś kī cunautī svīkār kar lī. donoṁ ne vahāṁ se lagbhag ek kos dūr ek mazār par milne kā niścay kiyā.

khargoś uchaltā- kūdtā jaldī kafī age nikal gayā. use apnī gati par kuch zyādā hī bharosā thā. use pūra viśvās thā ki vah kachue ko pīche choṛkar svayam āge nikal jāegā. usne thoṛī der sustāne kā niścay kiyā. use nīṁd ā gaī. kachuā mand gati se

calte-calte mazār par pahuṁc kar khargoś kā intzār karne lagā. āṁkh khulte hī khargoś ne dauṛnā śurū kiyā. vahāṁ pahuṁc kar, kachue ko pahle se hī vahāṁ pahuṁcā huā dekhkar vah cakit ho gayā. uskā sir śarm se jhuk gayā. vah kachue se āṁkh na milā sakā.
kisī ne ṭhīk hī kahā hai: ghamaṇḍī kā sir nīcā hotā hai."

WORDS AND PHRASES

एक समय की बात है।	ek samay kī bāt hai.	once upon a time
किसी (pron.)	kisī	some, any
जंगल (m.)	jaṅgal	forest
(oblique of indefinite pron. कोई koī)		
सिरफिरा (adj.)	sirphirā	crazy
खरगोश (m.)	khargoś	rabit
स्वभाव से (adv.)	svabhāv se	tempramentally
नटखट (adj.)	naṭkhaṭ	naughty
अपनी (reflexive adj.)	apnī	one's own
तेज़ (adj.)	tez	fast
गति (f.)	gati	speed
घमण्ड (m.)	ghamaṇḍ	arrogance
घमण्डी (adj.)	ghamaṇḍī	arrogant
कछुआ (m.)	kachuā	tortoise
मन्द (adj.)	mand	slow
जाते हुए (IPC)	jāte hue	while going
धीरे धीरे (adv.)	dhīre dhīre	slowly
चलते हुए (IPC)	calte hue	while walking
देखते ही	dekhte hī	as soon as …saw
हँसी (f.)	haṁsī	laughter
सुनकर (kar-conjunct)	sunkar	heard and
रुक गया (comp.verb)	ruk gayā	stopped
पीछे मुड़कर (kar-conj.)	pīche muṛkar	turned back and

ghamaṇḍī kā sir nīcā hotā hai

रुका हुआ (PPC)	rukā huā	stopped
अपने साथ	apne sāth	with him
दौड़ने के लिए	dauṛne ke lie	for a race
ललकारना (v.t.)	lalkārnā	to challange
समझदार (adj.)	samajhdār	wise
जानना (v.t.)	jānanā	to knew
चुनौती (f.)	cunautī	challenged
स्वीकार (m.)	svīkār	acceptance
स्वीकार कर लेना	svīkār kar lenā	to accept
दोनों (adj.)	donoṁ	both
लगभग (adv.)	lagbhag	approximately
कोस (m.)	kos	2 miles
मज़ार (m.)	mazār	tomb
मिलना (v.i.)	milnā	to meet
उछलता–कूदता (IPC)	uchaltā- kūdtā	jumping
बहुत जल्दी	bahut jaldī	very soon
काफ़ी (adv.)	kāfī	quite
निकल जाना (comp. verb)	nikal jānā	to go
कुछ ज़्यादा ही (adv.)	kuch zyādā hī	a bit too much
भरोसा (m.)	bharosā	faith
पूरा (adj.)	pūrā	complete
विश्वास (m.)	viśvās	trust
पीछे छोड़कर	pīche choṛkar	leave behind and
थोड़ी देर (f.)	ṭhoṛī der	a short while
सुस्ताना (v.i.)	sustānā	to rest
का निश्चय करना	kā niścay karnā	to resolve
को नींद आना /आ जाना	ko nīṁd ānā/ā jānā	to fall asleep
आँख खुलते ही	āṁkh khulte hī	as soon as ..woke up
दौड़ना शुरू किया	dauṛnā śurū kiyā.	began to run

पहुँचकर (kar-conj.)	pahuṁckar	arrived and
पहले से ही (adv)	pahle se hī	already
पहुँचा हुआ (PPC)	pahuṁcā huā	arrived
चकित होना/हो जाना	cakit honā/ ho jānā	to be surprised
शर्म से	śarm se	with shame
झुक जाना	jhuk jānā	to bend low
• हँसने लगना	haṁsne lagā	begin to laugh
• देखने लगा	dekhne lagā.	began to look
• इन्तज़ार करने लगना	intzār karne lagnā.	to begin to wait
• मिलने का निश्चय किया	milne kā niścay kiyā	resolved to meet
• आगे निकल जाना	āge nikal jānā	to overtake
• से आँख न मिला सकना	se āṁkh na milā saknā.	to be unable to look in the eyes
• सहज पके सो मीठा होय	sahaj pake so mīṭhā hoy	slow and steady wins the race

• किसीने ठीक ही कहा है : 'घमण्डी का सिर नीचा होता है।'
kisī ne ṭhīk hī kahā hai: ghamaṇḍī kā sir nīcā hotā hai."
somebody has rightly said: " The arrogant brings downfall."

• खरगोश ने किसी कछुए को मन्द गति से जाते हुए देखा।
khargoś ne kisī kachue ko mand gati se jāte hue dekhā.
The rabit saw some tortoise going at low speed.
जाते हुए jāte hue while going (**Gram. Ref. pg. 219**)

• वह, उसे धीरे–धीरे चलते हुए देखते ही, उसपर हँसने लगा।
vah use dhīre-dhīre calte hue dekhte hī, us par haṁsne lagā.
As soon as it (rabbit) saw it(tortoise) moving slowly, it (rabbit) began to laugh.
चलते हुए calte hue while walking **Gram. Ref. IPC pg. 219**
देखते ही dekhte hī as soon as he saw **Gram. Ref. pg. 179**
हँसने लगा haṁsne lagā began to laugh **Gram. Ref. pg. 145**

- कछुआ उसकी हँसी सुनकर कछुआ रुक गया, और पीछे मुड़कर देखने लगा।
  kachuā uskī haṁsī sunkar ruk gayā, aur pīche muṛkar dekhne lagā.
  The tortoise heard its laughter, stopped, turned back and began to look.
  हँसी सुनकर haṁsī sunkar heard laughter and
  पीछे मुड़कर pīche muṛkar turned back and
  देखने लगा dekhne lagā. **Gram. Ref.(v.r. +ने ne + लगना lagnā) pg. 145**
- रुका हुआ देखते ही खरगोश ने उसे अपने साथ दौड़ने के लिए ललकारा।
  use rukā huā dekhte hī khargoś ne use apne sāth dauṛne ke lie lalkārā.
  As soon as it (the rabbit) saw it (the tortoise) stopped at one place, it (the rabbit) challenged it (the tortoise) to ruṇ a race with him.
  रुका हुआ rukā huā stopped **(PPC Gram. Ref. 217)**
  देखते ही dekhte hī as soon as he saw **(See above)**
- खरगोश उछलता–कूदता बहुत जल्दी ही काफ़ी आगे निकल गया।
  khargoś uchaltā- kūdtā jaldī hī kafī age nikal gayā.
  The rabbit, jumping ans leaping went much ahead vry soon.

  उछलता–कूदता uchaltā- kūdtā **(IPC Gram. Ref. pg:- 220)**
  निकल गया। nikal gayā. **(compound verb 187)**
- कछुआ मन्द गति से चलते–चलते मज़ार पर पहुँचकर खरगोश का इन्तज़ार करने लगा।
  kaċhuā mand gati se calte-calte mazār par pahuṁc kar khargoś kā intzār karne lagā.
  The tortoise, walking continuouslyat low speed arrived at the tomb and began to wait for the rabbit.
  चलते–चलते calte-calte walking continuously
  IPC : (v.r. +ते te) + (v.r. + ते te) Gram. Ref. pg:- 220
  पहुँचकर pahuṁckar arrived and **(कर kar- conj. Gram. Ref. 174)**

  इन्तज़ार करने लगा intzār karne lagā. **(v.r. + ne)** + lagnā **Gram. Ref . pg. 140**
- आँख खुलते ही खरगोश ने दौड़ना शरू किया।
  āṁkh khulte hī khargoś ne dauṛnā śurū kiyā.
  As soon as the rabbit woke up, it began to run.

आँख खुलते ही āṁkh khulte hī **Gram. Ref. (v.r. +ते te + ही hī pg. 179)**

- वहाँ पहुँचा हुआ देखकर वह चकित हो गया।
  vahāṁ pahuṁcā huā dekhkar vah cakit ho gayā.
  Seeing (the tortoise) already arrived there, it (the rabbit) was astonished.

  पहुँचा हुआ already arrived **(PPC Gram. Ref. 217)**
  देखकर dekhkar saw and **(कर kar- conjunct Gram. Ref. 174)**
  चकित हो गया। cakit ho gayā was astonished **(compound verb pg. 187)**

- उसका सिर शर्म से झुक गया।
  uskā sir śarm se jhuk gayā.
  His head bent low in shame./ He looked down in shame.
  झुक गया jhuk gayā bent down **(comp. verb Gram. Ref. pg. 187)**

●●●●●

S 13 खेल दिवस

हमारे स्कूल में हर साल चौदह नवम्बर को खेल दिवस मनाया जाता है। इस दिन के लिए बहुत पहले से तैयारियाँ शुरू की जाती हैं। जो बच्चे जीतते हैं, उन्हें इनाम दिए जाते हैं।

हर साल की तरह, इस साल भी, चौदह नवम्बर को खेल दिवस मनाया गया। क्रिकेट के जाने–माने खिलाड़ी सचिन तेंदुलकर को मुख्य अतिथि के रूप में बुलाया गया था। खेल का मैदान सजाया गया था। चारों ओर रंग–बिरंगी झंडियाँ लगाई गई थीं। महमानों और दर्शकों के लिए शामियाने और कुर्सियाँ भी लगाई गई थीं।
दोपहर दो बजे हमारे मुख्य अतिथि लाए गए। खेल शुरू किए गए। खेलों का कार्यक्रम तीन घण्टे चला। मुख्य अतिथि के द्वारा जीतनेवाले बच्चों को इनाम दिए गए। अन्त में स्कूल के बच्चों और उपस्थित दर्शकों के द्वारा मिलकर राष्ट्रगाण गाया गया।

khel divas

hamāre skūl meṁ har sāl caudah navambar ko khel divas manāyā jātā hai. is din ke lie bahut pahle se taiyāriyāṁ śurū kī jātī haiṁ. jo bacce jītate haiṁ, unheṁ inām die jāte haiṁ.

har sāl kī tarah, is sāl bhī, caudah navambar ko khel divas manāyā gayā. kriket ke Ãne-m Áne khilÁéí Sachin Tendulkar ko m ukhyă atithi ke rūp meṁ bulāyā gayā thā. khel kā maidān sajāyā gayā thā. cāroṁ or raṅg-biraṅgī jhaṇḍiyāṁ lagāī gaī thīṁ. mahmānoṁ aur darśakoṁ ke lie śāmiyāne aur kursiyāṁ bhī lagāī gaī thīṁ. dopahar do baje hamāre mukhyă atithi lāe gae. khel śuru kie gae. kheloṁ kā kāry/kram tīn ghaṇṭe calā. mukhyă atithi ke dvārā jītnevāle bacc̄oṁ ko inām die gae. ant meṁ skūl ke baccoṁ aur upasthit darśakoṁ ke dvārā milkar rāṣṭragāṇ gāyā gayā.

WORDS AND PHRASES

हर साल	har sāl	every year
चौदह	caudah	fourteen
खेल दिवस (m.)	khel divas	sports day
मनाना (v.t.)	manānā	to celebrate

बहुत पहले से	bahut pahle se	from long before
तैयारियाँ (f.pl.)	taiyāriyāṁ	preparations
शुरू करना (v.t.)	śurū karnā	to begin
जो (relative pronoun)	jo	those who
इनाम (m.sg./pl.)	inām	prize(s)
इस साल भी	is sāl bhī	this year too
जाने–माने (adj.)	jāne-māne	well known
खिलाड़ी (m.)	khilāṛī	sportsman
मुख्य अतिथि (m.)	mukhyă atithi	chief guest
के रूप में	ke rūp meṁ	as/ in the form of
सजाना (v.t.)	sajānā	to decorate
चारों ओर	cāroṁ or	all round
रंग–बिरंगी (adj.)	raṅg-biraṅgī	multicolored
झंडियाँ (f.pl.)	jhaṇḍiyāṁ	flags
बुलाना (v.t..)	bulānā	to call/ to invite
जीतना (v.t./v.i)	jītnā	to win
जीतनेवाले (adj.)	jītnevāle	the winning ones
उपस्थित (adj)	upasthit	those who were present
के द्वारा (ppn)	ke dvārā	by (passive)
मिलकर (kar-conj.)	milkar	together
राष्ट्रगाण (m.)	rāṣṭragāṇ	national song
गाना (v.t./ n.)	gānā	song
• खेल का मैदान (m.)	khel kā maidān	sports field
• हर साल की तरह	har sāl kī tarah	like every year
• तीन घण्टे चला।	tīn ghaṇṭe calā	lasted three hours

■ Present Passive: Gram. Ref. pg 231

• खेल दिवस मनाया जाता है। — Sports Day is celebrated.
khel divas manāyā jātā hai.

khel divas

• तैयारियाँ शुरू की जाती हैं। taiyāriyāṁ śurū kī jātī haiṁ.	Preparations are begun.
• इनाम दिए जाते हैं। inām die jāte haiṁ.	Prizes are given.

Present Passive: Gram. Ref. pg 231

• खेल दिवस मनाया गया। khel divas manāyā gayā	Sports Day was celebrated.
• सचिन तेंदुलकर को बुलाया गया था। Sachin Tendulkar ko bulāyā gayā thā	Sachin Tendulkar was invited invited.
• खेल का मैदान सजाया गया था। khel kā maidān sajāyā gayā thā.	The playground was decorated.
• रंग–बिरंगी झंडियाँ लगाई गई थीं। raṅg-biraṅgī jhaṇḍiyāṁ lagāī gaī thīṁ.	Colorful frill was put up all round.
• मुख्य अतिथि लाए गए। m ukhyă atithi lāe gae.	The chief guest was brought.
• खेल शुरू किए गए। khel śuru kie gae	Games were begun.
• राष्ट्रगाण गाया गया। rāṣṭragāṇ gāyā gayā.	National anthem was sung

●●●●●

S 13 धनतेरस

धनतेरस का त्योहार दीवाली से दो दिन पहले आता है। धनतेरस के दिन, लोग धनवन्तरी पूजा करते हैं। धनवन्तरी भगवान विष्णु का एक अवतार माने जाते हैं। वे देवताओं के चिकित्सक और आयुर्वेद के गुरू हैं। वे समुद्र मंथन के समय अमृत का कलश लिए हुए प्रकट हुए थे।

एक पौराणिक कथा के अनुसार हिमराज के सोलह वर्ष का पुत्र था। उसकी जनम कुंडली के अनुसार उसकी उम्र छोटी थी। ज्योतिषियों के अनुसार उसकी मृत्यु उसकी शादी के चौथे दिन होनी थी। उसकी सुन्दर पत्नी ने एक तरकीब सोची। उसने अपने पति के सोने के कमरे के बाहर एक बहुत बड़ा सोने चाँदी का ढेर लगाया। उसपर बहुत दीये जलाकर रख दिए। वह सारी रात नाचती–गाती रही। उसने अपने पति को सोने नहीं दिया।

जब यमराज साँप बनकर आए, उन्हें दीयों की रोशनी और सोने चाँदी की चमक में कुछ दिखाई नहीं दिया। वे सारी रात उसं ढेर पर बैठे रहे और मधुर संगीत सुनते रहे। वे ध्यान मग्न हो गए और भूल गए कि वे उसे यमलोक ले जाने के लिए आए थे। सुबह होते ही वे खुशी–खुशी अपने घर लौट गए।

इस तरह एक सुन्दर, युवा पत्नी ने अपने पति को मृत्यु के चंगुल से बचाया था।

आज भी इस दिन यमराज की पूजा की जाती है। पति के ऐश्वर्य और लम्बी आयु की प्रार्थना की जाती है। यमराज को प्रसन्न करने के लिए दीये जलाए जाते हैं। ये दीये सारी रात जलते रहते हैं। इसीलिए धनतेरस / धनत्रयोदशी को यमदीपदान भी कहते हैं।

dhanteras

dhanteras kā tyohār divālī se do din pahle ātā hai. dhanteras ke din log dhanvantrī pūjā karte haiṁ. dhanvantrī bhagvān viṣnu kā avtār māne jāte haiṁ. ve devtāoṁ ke cikitsak aur āyurved ke guru haiṁ. ve samudra manthan ke samay amṛit kā kalaś lie hue prakaṭ hue the.

ek paurāṇik kathā ke anusār himrāj ke solah varṣ kā putra thā. uskī janam kuṇḍlī ke anusār uskī umra choṭī thī. jyotiṣiyoṁ ke anusār uskī mṛtyu uskī śādī ke cauthe din honī thī. uskī sundar patnī ne ek tarkīb socī. usne apne pati ke sone ke kamre

ke bāhar ek bahut baṛā sone-cāndī kā ḍher lagāyā. uspar bahut dīye jalākar rakh die. vah sārī rāt nāctī-gātī rahī. usne apne pati ko sone nahīṁ diyā.
jab yamrāj sāṁp bankar āe, unheṁ dīyoṁ kī rośnī aur sone- cāṁdī kī camak meṁ, kuch dikhāī nahīṁ diyā. ve sārī rāt us ḍher par baiṭhe rahe aur madhur saṅgīt sunte rahe. ve dhyān magna ho gae, aur bhūl gae ki ve use yamlok le jāne ke lie āe the. subah hote hī ve khuśī-khuśī apne ghar lauṭ gae.
is tarah ek sundar yuvā patnī ne apne pati ko mṛtyu ke caṅgul se bacāyā thā.
āj bhī is din yamrāj kī pujā kī jātī hai. pati ke aiśvaryă aur lambī āyu kī prārthnā kī jātī hai. yamrāj ko prasann karne ke lie dīye jalāe jāte haiṁ. ye dīye sārī rāt jalte rahte haiṁ.
isīlie dhanteras/dhantryodaśī ko yamdīpdān bhī kahte haiṁ.

WORDS AND PHRASES

त्योहार (m.)	tyohār	festival
भगवान विष्णु	bhagvān viṣnu	the sustainer of the universe (one of the Hindu Trinity)
अवतार (m.)	avtār	incarnation
माने जाते हैं (passive)	māne jāte haiṁ.	is believed to be
देवता (m.)	devtā	god
चिकित्सक (m.)	cikitsak	doctor
आयुर्वेद (m.)	āyurved	ayurveda
समुद्र मंथन (m.)	samudra manthan	churning of the Ocean
अमृत (m.)	amṛit	nectar
कलश (m.)	kalaś	pitcher
प्रकट होना (v.i.)	prakaṭ honā	to appear
पौराणिक कथा (f.)	paurāṇik kathā	classical scriptural story
के अनुसार (ppn.)	ke anusār	according to
हिमराज	himrāj	name of a King in ancient India
वर्ष (m.)	varṣ	year

धनतेरस

पुत्र (m.)	putra	son
जनम कुंडली (f.)	janam kuṇḍlī	horoscope
उम्र (f.)	umra	age
ज्योतिषि (m.)	jyotiṣi	astrologer
मृत्यु (f.)	mṛityu	death
चौथे दिन	cauthe din	on the fourth day
होनी थी (compulsion str)	honī thī	had to take place
तरकीब (f.)	tarkīb	plan
सोची	socī	thought

(f. form of the past simple tense of v.t. सोचना socnā to think; it agrees here with तरकीब tarkīb f.)

सोने का कमरा (m.)	sone kā kamrā	bedroom
बाहर (adv.)	bāhar	outside;
बहुत बड़ा (adj.)	bahut baṛā	very big
सोना (m.)	sonā	gold
चाँदी (f.)	cāṁdī	silver
ढेर (m.)	ḍher	pile/ heap
जलाना (v.t.)	jalānā	ignite
जलाकर (kar-conj.)	jalākar	ignite and
सारी रात (f.)	sārī rāt	all night
नाचना–गाना (v.t.)	nācnā-gānā	dance and sing
पति (m.)	pati	husband.
यमराज (m.)	yamrāj	god of death
साँप (m.)	sāṁp	snake
दीया (m.)	dīyā	lamp
रोशनी (f.)	rośnī	light
चमक (m.)	camak	light
दिखाई देना	dikhāī denā	to be visible
ध्यान मग्न (adj.)	dhyān magna	engrossed
भूलना (v.i.)	bhulnā	to forget

यमलोक (m.)	yamlok	the world of the dead
खुशी–खुशी (adv.)	khuśī-khuśī	happily
अपने घर	apne ghar	to one's own house
लौटना (v.i..)	lauṭnā	to return
चंगुल (m.)	caṅgul	clutches
बचाना (v.t..)	bacānā	save
ऐश्वर्य (f.)	aiśvaryă	glory
लम्बी आयु (f.)	lambī āyu	long life
प्रार्थना (f.)	prārthnā	prayer, request
यमदीपदान (m.)	yamdīpdān	offering lamps to the Lord of death
बर्तन (m.)	bartan	utensil.

■ **Passive voice: Gram Ref. pg:- 231**

- धनवन्तरी भगवान विष्णु का एक अवतार माने जाते हैं। dhanvantrī bhagvān viṣṇu kā avtār māne jāte haiṁ. — Dhanvantri is believed to be Lord Vishnu reincarnate.
- आज भी इस दिन यमराज की पूजा की जाती है। āj bhī is din yamrāj kī pūjā kī jātī hai. — Even today on this day 'yamrāj' is worshipped.
- पति के लिए ऐश्वर्य और लम्बी आयु की प्रार्थना की जाती है। pati ke lie aiśvaryă aur lambī āyu kī prārthnā kī jatī hai. — Prayers are offered for glory and long life of the husband.
- यमराज को प्रसन्न करने के लिए दीये जलाए जाते हैं । yamrāj ko prasann karne ke lie dīye jalāe jāte haiṁ. — Lamps are lit to please Yamraj.

Continuative compound: Gram Ref. pg:- 198; See pg. 271

- वे सारी रात उस ढेर पर बैठे रहे और मधुर संगीत सुनते रहे।
  ve sārī rāt us ḍher par baiṭhe rahe aur madhur saṅgīt sunte rahe.
  All night, he kept sitting on that pile and listening to sweet music.
- वह सारी रात नाचती–गाती रही।
  vah sārī rāt nāctī-gātī rahī.
  She kept dancing and singing all night.
- ये दीये सारी रात जलते रहते हैं।
  ye dīye sārī rāt jalte rahte haiṁ.
  These lamps stay lit all night.

Use of 'X को ko Y कहना kahna'

- इसीलिए धनतेरस / धनत्रयोदशी **को यमदीपदान भी कहते हैं।**
  isīlie dhanteras/dhantryodaśī **ko yamdīpdān bhī kahte haiṁ.**
  Therefore dhanteras /dhantryodashi is also called 'yamdeepdan'.

Similarly:

1. **'buttermilk'** को हिन्दी में क्या कहते हैं।
   'buttermilk' ko hindī meṁ kyā' kahte haiṁ.
   What is buttermilk called in Hindi.
2. **buttermilk'** को हिन्दी में लस्सी कहते हैं।
   'buttermilk' is called 'lassī' in Hindi.
   Buttermilk is called 'lassi' in Hindi.

•••••

S 14 दीवाली

दीवाली हिन्दुओं का प्रमुख त्योहार है। यह कार्तिक महीने की कृष्ण चतुर्दशी को होता है। इसे दीयों का त्योहार भी कहते हैं। इस दिन भगवान राम ने लंका के राजा रावण को हराया था। वे चौदह वर्ष के वनवास के बाद अयोध्या लौटे थे और वहाँ के राजा बने थे। अयोध्यावासी बहुत खुश हुए थे। उन्होंने अपने घरों और अपनी दुकानों की सजावट की थी और सब जगह दीये जलाए थे। उन्होंने नए कपड़े पहने थे और स्वादिष्ट पकवान बनाए थे। उन्होंने आपस में मिठाइयाँ बाँटी थीं। वे एक दूसरे के घरों में गए थे और एक दूसरे से गले मिले थे। आज भी भारतवासी यह त्योहार बहुत धूमधाम से मनाते हैं। वे अपने घरों की सजावट करते हैं। वे अच्छे–अच्छे पकवान अपने–अपने घरों में बनाते हैं, और बाज़ार से भी ख़रीदते हैं। स्वयं भी खाते हैं और मित्रों को भी खिलाते हैं। एक दिन धनवंतरी पूजा होती है। लोग नए बर्तन ख़रीदते हैं। शाम को सपरिवार लक्ष्मी पूजा करते हैं। इस दिन व्यापारी वर्ग अपना नया साल शुरू करता है। बच्चे–बूढ़े मिलकर पटाख़े चलाते हैं। एक दूसरे के यहाँ मिलने जाते हैं। आपसी मनमुटाव दूर हो जाता है। घर–घर में खुशी की लहर दौड़ जाती है। यह सच में खुशियों का त्योहार है।

dīvālī

dīvālī hinduoṁ kā pramukh tyohār hai. yah kārtik mahīne kī kṛṣṇa caturdaśī ko hotā hai. ise dīyoṁ kā tyohār bhī kahte haiṁ. is din bhagvān rām ne laṅkā ke rājā rāvaṇ ko harāyā thā. ve caudah varṣ ke vanvās ke bād ayodhyā lauṭe the, aur vahāṁ ke rājā bane the. ayodhyāvāsī bahut k͟huś hue the. unhoṁne apne gharoṁ aur apnī dukānoṁ kī sajāvaṭ kī thī, aur sab jagah dīye jalāe the. unhoṁne nae kapṛe pahne the, aur svādiṣṭ pakvān banāe the. unhoṁne āpas meṁ miṭhāiyāṁ bāṁṭī thīṁ. ve ek dūsre ke gharoṁ meṁ gae the, aur ek dūsre se gale mile the.
āj bhī bhāratvāsī yah tyohār bahut dhūmdhām se manāte haiṁ. ve apne gharoṁ kī sajāvaṭ karte haiṁ. ve acche-acche pakvān apne-apne gharoṁ meṁ banāte haiṁ, aur bāzār se bhī k͟harīdte haiṁ. svayam bhī khāte haiṁ aur mitroṁ ko bhī khilāte haiṁ. ek din dhanvantarī pūjā hotī hai.
log nae bartan k͟harīdte haiṁ. śām ko saparivār lakṣmī pūjā karte haiṁ. is din vyāpārī varg apnā nayā sāl śurū kartā hai . bacce-būṛhe milkar paṭākhe calāte haiṁ. ek dūsre ke yahāṁ milne jāte haiṁ. āpsī manmuṭāv dūr ho jātā hai. ghar-ghar meṁ k͟huśī kī lahar dauṛ jātī hai. yah sac meṁ k͟huśīyoṁ kā tyohār hai.

WORDS AND PHRASES

प्रमुख (adj.)	pramukh	main, chief
त्योहार (m.)	tyohār	festival(s)
कार्तिक	kārtik	the 8th month of Hindu Calendar
कृष्ण चतुर्दशी	krisna caturdaśī	14th day of the dark half of the month
दीया (m.)	dīyā	oil lamp
भगवान राम	bhagvān rām	Lord Ram
रावण	rāvaṇ	demon king of Sri lanka
हराना v.t.	harānā	to defeat
चौदह	caudah	fourteen
वर्ष (m.)	varṣ	year
वनवास (m.)	vanvās	exile
लौटना v.i.	lauṭnā	to return
राजा (m.)	rājā	king
बनना v.i.	bananā	to be made
अयोध्यावासी (m.)	ayodhyāvāsī	resident(s) of Ayodhya;
अपने (ref. adj.)		apne
	here: their own	
सजावट (f.)	sajāvaṭ	decoration
जलाना (v.t.)	jalānā	to burn/ to light
पहनना v.t.	pahnanā	to wear
सवादिष्ट (adj.)	svādiṣṭ	delicious
अच्छे–अच्छे (adj.)	acche-acche	very good
पकवान (m.)	pakvān	sweets and other delicacies
बनाना (v.t..)	banānā	to make

dīvālī

आपस में (adv.)	āpas meṁ	among them selves
मिठाइयाँ (f.pl.)	miṭhāiyāṁ	sweets
बाँटना (v.t.)	bāṁṭnā	to distribute
भारतवासी (m.)	bhāratvāsī	residents of India
धूमधाम (f.)	dhūmdhām	splendour
मनाना (v.t.)	manānā	to celebrate
स्वयं (adv.)	svayam	oneself
मित्र (m.)	mitra	friend
खिलाना (v.t.)	khilānā	to feed; to offer to eat
बर्तन (m.)	bartan	utensil;
सपरिवार	sa-parivār	with family
लक्ष्मी (f.)	lakṣmī	the goddess of wealth
आपसी (adj.)	āpsī	mutual
मनमुटाव (m.)	manmuṭāv	differences
इस दिन	is din	on this day
व्यापारी वर्ग (m.)	vyāpārī varg	business community
नया साल (m.)	nayā sāl	new year
शुरू होना (v.i.)	śurū honā	to begin
बच्चे–बूढ़े (m.pl.)	bacce-būṛhe	young and old
मिलकर (kar-conj.)	milkar	together
पटाख़ा (m.)	paṭākhā	firecracker
सच में (adv.)	sac meṁ	truly
लहर (f.)	lahar	wave

- एक दूसरे के गले मिलना — ek dūsre ke gale milnā — to embrace each other;
- खुशियों का त्योहार m.sg — khuśīyoṁ kā tyohār — festival of joys

- दीवाली हिन्दुओं का प्रमुख त्योहार है।
  dīvālī hinduoṁ kā pramukh tyohār hai.
  Diwali is chief festival of India.
- यह सच में खुशियों का त्योहार है। — This is truly a festival of joys.

yah sac meṁ khuśīyoṁ kā tyohār hai.

- आपसी मनमुटाव दूर हो जाता है। Mutual diff rences go away.
  āpsī manmuṭāv dūr ho jātā hai.
- घर–घर में खुशी की लहर दौड़ जाती है। A wav.e of joy runs through every home.
  ghar-ghar meṁ khuśī kī lahar dauṛ jātī hai

Use of Past Perfect Tense: Gram. Ref. Pg. 130

- राम ने .... रावण को हराया था।
  rām ne .... rāvan ko harāyā thā.
  Ram had defeated Ravana.
- वे अयोध्या **लौटे थे** और वहाँ के राजा **बने थे।**
  ve ayodhyā lauṭe the, aur vahāṁ ke rājā bane the.
  He had returned to Ayodhya and become the king there.
- अयोध्यावासी **खुश हुए थे।**
  ayodhyāvāsī bahut **khuś hue the.**
  Residents of Ayodhya had become happy.
- उन्होंने .... **सजावट की थी** और सब जगह **दीये जलाए थे।**
  unhoṁne........ .... **sajāvaṭ kī thī**, aur sab jagah **dīye jalāe the.**
  They had decorated........ .... and lit lamps at all places.
- उन्होंने नए कपड़े **पहने थे** और स्वादिष्ट **भोजन बनाए थे।**
  unhoṁne nae **kapṛe pahne the** aur svādiṣṭ **bhojan banāe the.**
  They had worn new clothes and prepared good food.
- उन्होंने आपस में मिठाइयाँ **बाँटी थीं।**
  unhoṁne āpas meṁ miṭhāiyāṁ bāṁṭī thīṁ.
  They **had distributed** sweets among themselves.
- वे एक दूसरे के घरों में **गए थे** और एक दूसरे से **गले मिले थे।**
  ve ek dūsre ke gharoṁ meṁ **gae the**, aur ek dūsre se **gale mile the.**
  They had gone to each other's home and emraced each other.

Use of Present Simple Tense: Gram. Ref. Pg:- 95

dīvālī

- इसे दीयों का त्योहार भी कहते हैं।
  ise dīyoṁ kā tyohār bhī kahte haiṁ.
  It is also called a festival of lights.
- आज भी भारतवासी यह त्योहार बहुत धूमधाम से मनाते हैं
  aj bhī bhāratvāsī yah tyohār bahut dhūmdhām se manāte haiṁ.
  Even today the residents of India celebrate this festival with much pomp and show.
- वे अपने घरों की सजावट करते हैं।
  ve apne gharoṁ kī sajāvaṭ karte haiṁ.
  They decorate their homes.

■ **Use of** अपना **apnā,** अपने **apne,** अपनी **apnī : Gram. Ref. Pg:- 135**

- उन्होंने अपने घरों और अपनी दुकानों की सजावट की थी
  unhoṁne apne gharoṁ aur apnī dukānoṁ kī sajāvaṭ kī thī.
  They had decorated their homes and their shops.
- वे अच्छे–अच्छे पकवान अपने–अपने घरों में बनाते हैं,
  ve acche-acche pakvān apne-apne gharoṁ meṁ banāte haiṁ.
  They prepare special foods in their respective homes
- इस दिन व्यापारी अपना नया साल शुरू करते हैं।
  is din vyāpārī apnā nayā sāl śurū karte haiṁ.
  On this day, the businessmen begin their new year.

●●●●●

S 15 भक्ति की परीक्षा

एक समय की बात है। नारद ऋषि धरती से स्वर्ग को जा रहे थे।
लोग जानते शे कि वे भगवान से अवश्य मिलेंगे।
एक साधु उनके पास आकर बोलाः कृपया भगवान से पूछिएगा कि मुझे मुक्ति कब मिलेगी।
कुछ दूर जाने पर एक और साधु उनको मिला। उसने भी वही बात कही।
कुछ दिनों बाद नारद जी धरती पर लौटे। पहलावाला साधु उनको मिला।
उन्होंने इस पहलेवाले साधु को बताया कि अभी उसको चार जनम और तपस्या करनी है।
साधु रोने लगा। वह बोला, 'अभी और चार जनम ! यह कैसे होगा? यह मुझसे नहीं होगा।'
नारद ऋषि मुस्कराते हुए आगे बढ़ गए।
कुछ दूर जाने पर दूसरावाला साधु भी उन्हें मिला।
नारद जी ने उसे बतायाः 'मेरे पास आपके लिए बहुत अच्छी खबर नहीं है। भगवान ने कहा है कि जितने उस पेड़ पर पत्ते हैं, अभी आपको उतने साल और तपस्या करनी होगी।'
ख़बर सुनकर दूसरेवाले साधु की खुशी का ठिकाना न रहा।
वह खुशी से नाचने लगा। उसके अन्दर उम्मीद की किरण जागी।
भगवान उस पर प्रसन्न हुए। उन्होंने उसको तुरन्त मुक्त कर दिया।

bhakti kī parīkṣā

ek samay kī bāt hai. nārad ṛṣi dhartī se svarg ko jā rahe the.
log jānte the ki ve bhagvān se avaśyă mileṁge.
ek sādhu unke pās ākar bolā: 'kṛpayā bhagvān se puchiegā ki mujhe mukti kab milegī.'
kuch dūr jāne par ek aur sādhu unko milā. usne bhī vahī bāt kahī.
kuch dinoṁ bād nārad jī dhartī par lauṭe. pahlāvālā sādhu unko milā.
unhoṁne is pahlevāle sādhu ko batāyā ki abhī usko cār janam aur tapasyā karnī hai.
sādhu rone lagā. vah bolā, ' abhī aur cār janam! yah kaise hogā? yah mujhse nahīṁ hogā.'
nārad ṛṣi muskarāte hue āge baṛh gae.
kuch dūr jāne par, dūsrāvālā sādhu bhī unheṁ milā

bhakti kī parīkṣā

nārad jī ne usko batāyā: 'mere pās āpke lie bahut acchī khabar nahīṁ hai. bhagvān ne kahā hai ki jitne us peṛ par patte haiṁ, abhī āpko utne sāl aur tapasyā karnī hogī.'
khabar sunkar dūsrevāle sādhu kī khuśī kā ṭhikānā na rahā.
vah khuśī se nācne lagā. uske andar ummīd kī kiraṇ jāgī.
bhagvān us par prasann hue. unhoṁne usko turant mukt kar diyā.

WORD POWER

भक्ति परीक्षा (f.)	bhakti parīkṣā	test of devotion
नारद	nārad	name of a sage
ऋषि (m.)	ṛṣi	sage
धरती (f.)	dhartī	earth
स्वर्ग (m.)	svarg	heaven
भगवान (m.)	bhagvān	God
अवश्य	avaśyă	certainly
साधु (m.)	sādhu	mendicant
मुक्ति (f.)	mukti	salvation
जनम (m.)	janam	birth; here: life
और (conj.)	aur	more
तपस्या (f.)	tapasyā	penance
करनी है (compulsion.)	karnī hai	have to do
मुस्कराते हुए (IPC)	muskarāte hue	while smiling
आगे बढ़ जाना	āge baṛh jānā	to move on
दूर	dūr	far
खबर (f.)	khabar	news
जितने (adj.)	jitne	as many
पत्ते (m.pl)	patte	leaves
उतने (adj.)	utne	that many
साल (m.sg./pl.)	sāl	year (s)

करनी होगी (compulsion)	karnī hogī	will have to do
खुशी से (adv.)	khuśī se	happily
नाचने लगा	nācne lagā	began to dance
उम्मीद (f.)	ummīd	hope
किरण (f.)	kiraṇ	ray
प्रसन्न (adj.)	prasann	happy

- एक समय की बात है। ek samay kī bāt hai. — once upon a time
- मुझे मुक्ति कब मिलेगी। mujhe mukti kab milegī. — when will I get salvation?
- कुछ दूर जाने पर, ... kuch dūr jāne par — on going ahead some distance,...
- मेरे पास आपके लिए बहुत अच्छी खबर नहीं है। mere pās āpke lie bahut acchī khabar nahīṁ hai — I don't have very good news. for you
- उसके अन्दर उम्मीद की किरण जागी। uske andar ummīd kī kiraṇ jāgī. — A ray of hope woke up in him.

■ **X की खुशी का ठिकाना न रहना X kī khuśī kā ṭhikānā na rahnā.**
X's joy to know no bounds :

☞ **की kī precedes खुशी khuśī (f.) regardless of the N and G of the subject X**

☞ **का kā precedes ठिकाना ṭhikānā (m.) regardless of the N and G of the subject X**

☞ **rahnā agrees with ṭhikānā.**

- दूसरेवाले साधु की खुशी का ठिकाना न रहा।
  dūsrāvāle sādhu kī khuśī kā ṭhikānā na rahā.
  The second sadhu's joy knew no bounds.

Similarly:

1. मुझको देखकर उसकी खुशी का ठिकाना न रहा।
   mujhko dekhkar uskī khuśī kā ṭhikānā na rahā.
   On seeing me, his joy knew no bounds.

■ **Use of future imperative : Gram. Ref. Pg:- 91**

- कृपया भगवान से पूछिएगा
  kṛpayā bhagvān se puchiėgā
  Please ask God,

■ **Suffix: वाला vālā, वाले vāle, वाली vālī : Gram. Ref. Pg:-167**

- पहलावाला साधु उनको मिला।
  pahlāvālā sādhu unko milā.
  The first sadhu met him.
- उन्होंने इस पहलेवाले साधु को बताया
  unhoṁne is pahlevāle sādhu ko batāyā
  He told the first sadhu.
- उन्हें दूसरावाला साधु भी मिला।
  unheṁ dūsrāvālā sādhu bhī milā
  The second sadhu met him too.

■ **Use of the Verb मिलना milnā :**

☞ **to find some living or non-living object:**

(subject + को ko) + object + मिलना milnā to agree with the N and G of the object:

1. आपको यहाँ शान्ति मिलेगी।
   āpko vahāṁ śānti milegī.
   You will find peace there.
2. मुझको एक कुत्ता घर के सामने मिला।
   mujhko yah kuttā ghar ke sāmne milā.
   I found a dog in front of the house.
3 मुझको यह बच्चा मंदिर में मिला।
   usko yah baccā mandir meṁ milā.
   He/ She found this baby in the temple.

☞ **to meet somebody:**

subject + (object = ko) + मिलना milnā to agree with the N and G of the subject:

1. हम उनको रोज़ मिलते हैं। ham unko roz milte haiṁ.	We meet them every day.
2. वह मुझको डाकघर में मिली। vah mujhko ḍākghar meṁ milī.	She met me in the post office.
3. मैं आपको पाँच बजे मिलूँगा/मिलूँगी। maiṁ āpko pāṁc baje milūṁgā / milūṁgī.	I will meet you at 5 o'clock.

■ **Use of (v.r.+ ne ने) + लगना lagnā: Gram. Ref. Pg:-140**

• साधु रोने लगा। sādhu rone lagā.	Sadhu began to cry.
• वह खुशी से नाचने लगा। vah khuśī se nācne lagā.	Sadhu began to dance for joy.

■ **Use of (Inner-) Compulsion Structure: Gram. Ref. Pg. 211**

उसको तपस्या करनी है। usko.... .... tapasyā karnī hai.	He has to do penence.
आपको तपस्या करनी होगी। āpko.... .... tapasyā karnī hogī.	You will have to do penence.

●●●●●

Neighbors Introducing Themselves To Each Other

D 1 Neighbors Meet

Rishabh and Pragya recently moved from New Delhi to South India. One of the neighbors, Mr. Piush, approaches Pragya in front of her house:

पियूषः नमस्ते। मेरा नाम पियूष है। मैं यहीं रहता हूँ। आपको पहले कभी नहीं देखा।

प्रज्ञाः नमस्ते। हम हाल में यहाँ आए हैं।

पियूषः तब तो हम पड़ोसी हैं। हमारे शहर में आपका स्वागत है।

प्रज्ञाः धन्यवाद।

पियूषः आपका नाम क्या है?

प्रज्ञाः मेरा नाम प्रज्ञा है।

पियूषः आप दिल्ली से हैं न!

प्रज्ञाः जी, मैं दिल्ली की रहनेवाली हूँ।

पियूषः दिल्ली कैसा शहर है?

प्रज्ञाः बहुत बड़ा और बहुत सुन्दर।

पियूषः आप अकेली हैं?

प्रज्ञाः जी नहीं, मेरे पति मेरे साथ हैं। इनसे मिलिए, ये हैं मेरे पति, श्री ऋषभ। ऋषभ, आप इनसे मिले हैं? ये हमारे पड़ोसी हैं, श्री पियूष।

रिषभः नमस्ते! आपसे मिलकर बहुत खुशी हुई।

पियूषः मुझे भी। आपके घर में और कौन–कौन हैं?

प्रज्ञाः हमारे घर में दो कुत्ते और तीन बिल्लियाँ हैं।

पियूषः आपके बच्चे हैं?

प्रज्ञाः जी, एक लड़का, एक लड़की। लड़का बीस (20) साल का है। वह कॉलिज में पढ़ता है।

पियूषः आपके बेटे का नाम क्या है?

प्रज्ञाः मेरे बेटे का नाम वेद है?

पियूषः वह आपके साथ यहीं रहता है?

प्रज्ञाः जी नहीं, वह छात्रवास में रहता है।

प्रज्ञाः मेरी बेटी बाईस (22) साल की है। उसका नाम जिज्ञासा है। वह विवाहित है। उसका पति पच्चीस (25) साल का है। उसका नाम क्षितिज है। वह कॉलिज में

अध्यापक है।
पियूषः तब तो आप नानी भी होंगी?
प्रज्ञाः जी नहीं, अभी तक नहीं। अभी मेरी बेटी के बच्चे नहीं हैं।
पियूषः आप गृहणी हैं?
प्रज्ञाः जी नहीं, मैं भी विश्वविद्यालय में अध्यापिका हूँ।

piyūṣ: namaste! merā nām piyūṣ hai. maiṁ yahīṁ rahtā huṁ. āpko pahle kabhī nahīṁ dekhā.
pragya: ham hāl meṁ yahāṁ āe haiṁ.
piyūṣ: tab to ham parosī haiṁ. hamāre śahar meṁ āpkā svāgat hai.
pragya: dhany*f*vad.
piyūṣ: āpkā nām kyā hai?
pragya: merā nām pragyā hai.
piyūṣ: āp dillī se haiṁ na?
pragya: jī, maiṁ dillī kī rahnevālī hūṁ.
piyūṣ: dillī kaisā śahar hai?
pragya: bahut baṛā aur bahut sundar.
piyūṣ: āp akelī haiṁ?
pragya: jī nahīṁ, mere pati mere sāth haiṁ. inse milie. ye haiṁ mere pati, śrī ṛiṣabh. ṛiṣabh, āp inse mile haiṁ? ye hamāre paṛosī haiṁ, śrī piyūṣ.
ṛiṣabh: namaste. āpse milkar bahut khuśī huī.
piyūṣ: mujhe bhī. āpke ghar meṁ aur kaun-kaun haiṁ?
pragya: hamāre ghar meṁ do kutte aur tīn billiyāṁ haiṁ.
piyūṣ: āpke bacce haiṁ?
pragya: jī hāṁ, ek laṛkā, ek laṛkī. laṛkā bīs (20) sāl kā hai. vah kaulij meṁ paṛhtā hai.
piyūṣ: āpke beṭe kā nām kyā hai?
pragya: hamāre beṭe kā nām ved hai.
piyūṣ: vah āpke sāth yahīṁ rahtā hai?
pragya: ji nahīṁ, vah chātrāvās meṁ rahtā hai. merī beṭī bāis (22) sāl kī hai. uskā nām jigyāsā hai. vah vivāhit hai. uskā pati paccīs (25) sāl kā hai. uskā nām kṣitij hai. vah kaulij meṁ adhyāpak hai.
piyūṣ: tab to āp nānī bhī hoṁgī?
pragya: jī nahīṁ, abhī tak nahīṁ. abhī merī beṭī ke bacce nahīṁ haiṁ.
piyūṣ: āp gṛhaṇī haiṁ?

Neighbors Introducing Themselves To Each Other

pragya: jī nahīṁ, maiṁ bhī viśvavidyālay meṁ adhyāpikā hūṁ.

WORDS & PHRASES

पहले (adv.)	pahle	earlier
हाल में (adv.)	hāl meṁ	recently
पड़ोसी (m.)	paṛosī (m.)	neighbor(s)
शहर (m.)	śahar	city
स्वागत (m.)	svāgat	welcome
बड़ा (adj.)	baṛā	big
सुन्दर (adj.)	sundar	beautiful
अकेली (adj.)	akelī	alone
पति (m.)	pati	husband
कुत्ते (m.pl.)	kutte	dogs
बिल्लियाँ (f.pl)	billiyāṁ	cats
बेटा (m.)	beṭā	son
यहीं (adv.)	yahīṁ	here (emphatic)
बेटी (f.)	beṭī	daughter
विवाहित (adj.)	vivāhit	married
साल (m.)	sāl	year
छात्रवास (m.)	chātrāvās	students' hostel
अध्यापक (m.)	adhyāpak	teacher
नानी (f.)	nānī	grandmother
गृहणी (f.)	gṛhaṇī	housewife
विश्वविद्यालय (m.)	viśvavidyālay	university
अध्यापिका (f.)	adhyāpikā	teacher(f.)

■ **Have never seen somebody or something before:**

☞ **In the past simple tense, when both the subject and the object are followed by postposition, verb always has आ ā- ending. Gram. Ref. pg. 128**

- मैंने आपको पहले कभी नहीं देखा। I have never seen you bef.ore.
  maiṁne āpko pahle kabhī nahīṁ

dekhā.

1. मैंने उनको पहले कभी नहीं देखा। maiṁne unko pahle kabhī nahīṁ dekhā. — I have never seen them bef.ore
2. मैंने यह पहले कभी नहीं देखा। maiṁne yah pahle kabhī nahīṁ dekhā. — I have never seen this bef.ore

■ X has come to a place recently:

☞ **In the present perfect tense, , when verb intransitive is used , it agrees with the subject. Gram. Ref. pg. 133**

- हम **(m.pl.)** हाल में यहाँ आए हैं। ham hāl meṁ yahāṁ āe haiṁ. — **We have come here recently**

1. वे **(m.pl.)** हाल में यहाँ आए हैं। ve hāl meṁ yahāṁ āe haiṁ. — **They have come here recently.**
2. वह **(f.)**हाल में यहाँ आई है। vah hāl meṁ yahāṁ āī hai. — **She has come here recently.**
3. मैं **(m.)** हाल में यहाँ आया हूँ। maiṁ hāl meṁ yahāṁ āyā hūṁ. — **I have come here recently.**

■ How to welcome someone : X का स्वागत होना kā svāgat honā

- हमारे शहर में आपका स्वागत है। hamāre śahar meṁ āpkā svāgat hai. — **You are wecome in our city.**

1. आपका स्वागत है। āpkā svāgat hai. — **You are wecome.**
2. हमारे घर में आपका स्वागत है। hamāre ghar meṁ āpkā svāgat hai. — **You are wecome in our house.**

■ Asking and telling name:

☞ **Regardless of the gender of the person whose name is being asked or told, the expression is always का नाम 'kā nām'.**

- आपका नाम क्या है? āp kā nām kyā hai? — What is your name?

Neighbors Introducing Themselves To Each Other

- मेरा नाम प्रज्ञा है। — My name is Pragya.
  merā nām Pragya hai?

■ **Asking ' where is somebody from?' See pg. 245**

☞ **का, के, की** kā, ke, kī **agrees with the N and G of the subject .**

- जी, मैं दिल्ली की रहनेवाली हूँ। — I am resident of Delhi.
  jī, maiṁ dillī kī rahnevālī hūṁ.

■ **What kind of.....? कैसा kaisā, कैसे kaise, कैसी kaisī**

- दिल्ली कैसा शहर है? — What kind of city is Delhi?
  dillī kaisā śahar hai?

■ **Confirming somebody's identity: Use of न 'na' at the end of a sentence corresponds to question tags such as 'isn't it', etc. in English):**

- आप दिल्ली से हैं न? — You are from Delhi, aren't you?
  āp dillī se haiṁ na?

■ **Introducing People:**

1. **इनसे मिलिए।** — Meet him/her(hon.).
   inse / āpse se milie.

■ **Asking if they already know each other:**

- ऋषभ, आप इनसे मिलें हैं? — Rishabh, have you met him?
  ṛiṣabh āp inse mile haiṁ

☞ **Expressing pleasure at meeting somebody:**

- आपसे मिलकर बहुत खुशी हुई। — I am very pleased to meet you.
  āpse milkar bahut khuśī huī.

☞ **Responding to somebody's expressing pleasure at meeting you:**

- मुझे भी। — Me too.
  mujhe bhī.
- मुझे भी आपसे मिलकर बहुत — I am pleased to meet you too.

खुशी हुई।

mujhe bhī.āpse milkar bahut
khuśī huī.

■ **Asking someone if something or somebody belongs to him/her.**

☞ का, के, की kā, ke, kī **depends upon the number and gender of the object , living or non-living, possessed, and not on the N and G of the owner.**

1. आपके बच्चे हैं? — Do you have children?
   āpke bacce haiṁ?

■ **Asking and telling about somebody's age?**

☞ **Possessive case endings** का kā, के kī, की kī **depend upon the N and G of the subject whose age is being talked about.**

- लड़का बीस साल का है। — The boy is 20 years old.
  laṛkā bīs sāl kā hai.
- लडकी बाईस साल की है। — The girl is 22 years old.
  laṛkī bāis sāl kī hai.

Ex. D 1.1 Say in Hindi:

1. Where are you(f. informal) from? 2. Where are you(m. formal) from? 3. Where is Robert from? 4. Where is this professor (m.) from. 5. Where are these students from?

Ex. D 1.2 Say in Hindi:

1. He(honorific) is Mr. Kapoor, isn't he? 2. He is Anil, isn't he? 3.Yes, he is Anil. 4. No, he is not Anil. 5. This woman is Indian, isn't she? 6. Yes, this woman is Indian. 7. No, she is not Indian. 8. That man is Indian, isn't he? 9. Yes, that man is Indian. 10. No, that man is not Indian.

Ex. D 1.3 Say in Hindi:

1. How is he related to you? 2. He is my brother. 3. How is she (hon.) related to you? 4. She is my aunt (mother's sister).

Ex. D 1.4 Say in Hindi:

1. Meet my nephew/teacher(m.)/boss/ fiance. 2. Have you met my boss/ my son/

Mr. Sharma. 3. Meet my fiance. 4. Yes we have met before. 5. No, we have not met before. 6. I am pleased to meet you too.

Ex. D 1.5 Translate into English:

1. यह आपका घर है?	yah āpkā ghar hai?
2. जी, यह मेरा घर है।	jī , yah merā ghar hai.
3.जी नहीं, ये मेरा घर नहीं हैं।	.jī nahīṁ, yah merā ghar nahīṁ hai.
4.यह आपका बेटा है?	yah āpkā beṭā hai?
5.जी, यह मेरा बेटा है।	.jī, yah merā beṭā hai
6. जी नही, यह मेरा बेटा नहीं है।	jī nahīṁ, yah merā beṭā nahīṁ hai.
7.यह आपकी बेटी है?	yah āpkī beṭī hai?
8.जी, यह मेरी बेटी है।	jī, yah merī beṭī hai.
9.जी नहीं, यह मेरी बेटी नहीं है।	jī nahīṁ, yah merī beṭī nahīṁ hai.

Ex. D 1.6 Say in Hindi:

1. Where is my room? 2. Your(formal) roomis here/there. 3.Where is my book? 4. Your book is in that room. 5. Where are our children? 6. Where is his/her son? 7. Where ishis/her daughter? 8. Where are his/her children? 9. Where are your (formal) books? 10. Where are your (formal) keys?

Ex. D 1.7 Say in Hindi:

1.How old is this man? 2. The man is 42 years old. 3. How old is the girl? 4. The girl is 35 years old. 5. How old Mr. Kapoor? 6. Mr Kapoor is 50 years old. 7. How old is Mrs.Kapoor 8. Mrs Kapoor is 45 years old. 9. How old are you(m. formal) 10. I (m.) am 70 years old.

Key: D 1.1

1. तुम कहाँ की रहनेवाली हो?	tum kahāṁ kī rahnevālī ho?
2. आप कहाँ के रहनेवाले हैं?	āp kahāṁ ke rahnevāle haiṁ?
3. राबर्ट कहाँ का रहनेवाला है?	raubarṭ kahāṁ kā rahnevālā hai?
4. यह प्रोफ़ेसर कहाँ का रहनेवाला है?	yah profaisar kahāṁ kā rahnevālā hai?
5. ये छात्र कहाँ के रहनेवाले हैं?	ye chātra kahāṁ ke rahnevāle haiṁ?

Neighbors Introducing Themselves To Each Other

Key: D 1.2

1. वे श्री कपूर हैं न?	ve śrī kapūr haiṁ na?
2. वह अनिल है न?	vah anil hai na?
3. जी, वह अनिल है।	jī, vah anil hai?
4. जी नहीं, वह अनिल नहीं है।	jī nahīṁ, vah anil nahīṁ hai?
5. यह महिला भारतीय है न?	yah mahilā bhārtīyă hai na?
6. जी, यह महिला भारतीय है	jī , yah mahilā bhārtīyă hai.
7. जी नहीं, यह महिला भारतीय नहीं है	jī nahīṁ, yah mahilā bhārtīyă nahīṁ hai
8. वह आदमी भारतीय है न?	vah ādmī bhārtīyă hai na?
9. जी, वह आदमी भारतीय है।	jī , vah ādmī bhārtīyă hai.
10. जी नहीं, वह आदमी भारतीय नहीं है।	jī nahīṁ, vah ādmī bhārtīyă nahīṁ hai.

Key D 1.3

1. वह आपका क्या लगता है?	vah āpkā kyā lagtā hai?
2. वह मेरा भाई लगता है।	vah merā bhāī lagtā hai. .
3. वे आपकी क्या लगती हैं?	ve$^{f.}$ apkī kya lagtī haiṁ?
4. वे मेरी मौसी लगती हैं।	ve$^{f.}$ merī mausī lagtī haiṁ?

Key D 1.4

1. मेरे भतीजे / अध्यापक / अधिकारी/ मंगेतर से मिलिए। 2. क्या आप मेरे अध्किारी/ बेटे/ श्री शर्मा से मिले हैं? 3. मेरे/मेरी मंगेतर से मिलिए। 4. हां हम पहले मिले हैं। 5. जी नहीं, हम पहले नहीं मिले। 6. मुझे आप से मिलकर खुशी हुई।

Key D 1.5

1. Is this your house? 2. Yes, this is my house. 3. No, this is not my house. 4. Is he your son? 5. Yes, he is my son. 6. No, he is not my son. 7. Is she your daughter? 8.Yes, she is my daughter. 9. No, she is not my daughter.

Key D 1.6

1. मेरा कमरा कहाँ है?	merā kamrā kahāṁ hai?
2. आपका कमरा यहाँ/वहाँ है।	āpkā kamrā yahāṁ/vahāṁ hai
3. मेरी किताब कहाँ है?	merī kitāb kahāṁ hai?
4. आपकी किताब उस कमरे में है।	āpkī kitāb us kamre meṁ hai?

5. हमारे बच्चे कहाँ है?	hamāre bacce kahāṁ haiṁ?
6. उसका बेटा कहाँ है?	uskā beṭā kahāṁ hai?
7. उसकी बेटी कहाँ है?	uskī beṭī kahāṁ hai?
8. उसके बच्चे कहाँ हैं?	uske bacce kahāṁ haiṁ?
9. आपकी किताबें कहाँ हैं?	āpkī kitābeṁ kahāṁ haiṁ?
10. आपकी चाभियाँ कहाँ हैं?	āpkī cābhiyāṁ kahāṁ haiṁ?

Key D 1.7

1. यह आदमी कितने साल का है?	yah ādmī kitne sāl kā hai?
2. यह आदमी ब्यालीस साल का है	yah ādmī bayālīs sāl kā hai.
3. यह औरत कितने साल की है?	yah aurat kitne sāl kī hai?
4. यह औरत पैंतीस साल की है।	yah aurat paiṁtīs sāl kī hai.
5. श्री कपूर कितने साल के हैं?	śrī kapur kitne sāl ke haiṁ?
6. श्री कपूर पचास साल के हैं।.	śrī kapur pacās sāl ke haiṁ.

●●●●●

D 2 Piyush Invites Rishabhs

Mr. Piyush comes to Mr Rishabh's house to invite them to a meal in their house.

पियूषः नमस्ते! आप लोग कैसे हैं?
रिषभः हम मज़े में हैं। और आप?
पियूषः मैं भी ठीक हूँ। आपको यहाँ कैसे लग रहा है?
रिषभः हमें अच्छा लग रहा है। लेकिन यहाँ गर्मी बहुत है।
पियूषः क्या यहाँ दिल्ली से ज़्यादा गर्मी है?
रिषभः जी, दिल्ली की तुलना में यहाँ बहुत ज़्यादा गर्मी है।
पियूषः दिल्ली में आजकल कैसा मौसम चल रहा है?
रिषभः दिल्ली में आजकल बहुत सुहावना मौसम चल रहा है। न ज़्यादा गर्मी, न ज़्यादा सर्दी।
पियूषः आप रविवार शाम को हमारे यहाँ भोजन कीजिए। मैं अपनी पत्नी और बच्चों को आपसे मिलाना चाहता हूँ। उन्हें आपसे मिलकर बहुत खुशी होगी।
रिषभः धन्यवाद। हम अवश्य आएँगे। कितने बजे?
पियूषः आप लगभग सात बजे तक आ जाइएगा।
रिषभः जी, ज़रूर। हम सात बजे तक पहुँच जाएँगे।
पियूषः अब मैं चलता हूँ। रविवार को मिलेंगे। नमस्ते।
रिषभः नमस्ते।

piyūṣ: namaste. āp log kaise haiṁ?
ṛṣabh: ham maze meṁ haiṁ. aur āp?
piyūṣ: maiṁ bhī ṭhīk hūṁ. āpko yahāṁ kaise lag raha hai?
ṛṣabh: hameṁ acchā lag rahā hai. lekin yahāṁ garmī bahut hai.
piyūṣ: kyā yahāṁ dillī se zyādā garmī hai.
ṛṣabh: Ji, dillī kī tulnā meṁ yahāṁ bahut zyādā garmī hai.
piyūṣ: dillī meṁ ājkal kaisā mausam cal rahā hai?
ṛṣabh: dillī meṁ ājkal bahut suhāvnā mausam cal rahā hai. na zyādā garmī, na zyādā sardī.
piyūṣ: āp ravivār śām ko hamāre yahāṁ bhojan kījie. maiṁ apnī patnī aur

baccoṁ ko āpse milānā cāhtā hūṁ. unheṁ āpse milkar bahut khuśī hogī.
r̥ṣabh: dhanyăvād. ham avaśyă āeṁge. kitne baje?
piyūṣ: āp laghbhag sāt baje tak ā jāiegā.
r̥ṣabh: Ji, zarūr. ham sāt baje tak pahuṁc jāeṁge.
piyūṣ: ab maiṁ caltā hūṁ. ravivār ko mileṁge. namaste.
r̥ṣabh: namaste.

WORDS AND PHRASES

मज़ा (m.)	mazā	enjoyment
मज़े में होना	maze meṁ honā	to be fine
ठीक (adj.)	ṭhīk	here: fine
गर्मी (f.)	garmī	heat
आजकल (adv.)	ājkal	these days
मौसम (m.)	mausam	weather
सुहावना (adj.)	suhāvnā	pleasant
न... ... न (conj.)	na......na.....	neither.... nor...
भोजन (m.)	bhojan	meal
पत्नी (f.)	patnī	wife
मिलाना (v.t.)	milānā	here: to introduce
धन्यवाद (m.)	dhanyăvād	thanks
ज़रूर (adv.)	zarūr	certainly
रविवार (m.)	ravivār	Sunday
अवश्य	avaśyă	certainly
लगभग	laghbhag	approximately
• हम मज़े में हैं।	ham maze meṁ haiṁ	We are fine.
• मैं भी ठीक हूँ।	maiṁ bhī ṭhīk hūm.	I am fine too.

■ **Use of the sense verb लगना 'lagna': Gram Ref. 139**

• आपको यहाँ कैसे लग रहा है? — How do you like it here?
āpko yahāṁ kaise lag raha hai?

• हमें यहाँ अच्छा लग रहा है। — We like it here.

hameṁ yahāṁ acchā lag rahā hai.

Practice with: उनको, उसको, तुमको, आपके परिवार को, आपकी माता जी को
unko, usko, tumko, āpke parivar ko, āpkī mātā jī ko

■ Comparative Adjective : Gram. Ref. pg. 41

- क्या यहाँ दिल्ली से ज़्यादा गर्मी है? kyā yahāṁ **dillī se zyādā** garmī hai? — Is it hotter here than Delhi?
- यहाँ दिल्ली की तुलना में बहुत ज़्यादा गर्मी है। dillī **kī tulnā meṁ** yahāṁ bahut zyādā garamī hai. — Yes it is much hotter here compared to Delhi.

■ Expressing desire to introduce 'X' to 'Y'.

☞ **Subject + (X को ko Y से se मिलाना* milānā* + चाहना cāhnā + होना honā):**

* **मिलाना milānā is invariable, where as चाहना cāhnā + होना honā agree with the N and G of the subject. Gram. Ref. 150**

- मैं अपनी पत्नी और बच्चों को आपसे मिलाना चाहता हूँ। maiṁ apnī patnī aur baccoṁ ko āpse milānā cāhtā hūṁ. — I would like to introduce my wife and children to you.

1. मैं अपनी बहन को आपसे मिलाना चाहता हूँ। maiṁ apnī bahan ko āpse milānā cāhtā hūṁ. — I (m.) want to introduce my sister to you.
2. मैं अपने भाई को आपसे मिलाना चाहती हूँ। maiṁ apne bhāī ko āpse milānā cāhtā hūṁ. — I (f.) want to lintroduce my brother to you.

Piyush Invites Rishabhs

■ Expressing pleasure at meeting somebody

☞ **(subj. + को ko) + Y से se + मिलकर milkar + खुशी होना <u>kh</u>uśī honā**

उन्हें आपसे मिलकर बहुत खुशी हुई। unheṁ āpse milkar bahut <u>kh</u>uśī huī. — They were very pleased to meet you.

मुझे आपसे मिलकर बहुत खुशी होगी। mujhe āpse milkar bahut <u>kh</u>uśī hogī. — I will be very pleased to meet you.

■ Expressing pleasure at doing something:

☞ **(subj. + को ko) + obj. + (v.r.+ कर kar) + खुशी होना <u>kh</u>uśī honā**

आपको यह पुस्तक पढ़कर बहुत खुशी होगी। āpko yah pustak paṛhkar bahut <u>kh</u>uśī hogī. — You will be very pleased to read this book.

■ At A Certain Time: Gram Ref. 200

- आप लगभग सात बजे तक आ जाइएगा। āp laghbhag sāt baje tak pahuṁc jāiegā. — Please come around 7 p.m.
- जी, ज़रूर। हम सात बजे तक पहुँच जाएँगे। ji, zarūr. ham sāt baje tak pahuṁc jāeṁge. — Certainly. We shall be there by 7.

■ On A Certain Day: Gram Ref. pg 34

- आप रविवार को रात का भोजन हमारे यहाँ कीजिए। āp ravivār ko rāt kā bhojan hamāre yahāṁ kījie. — Please have dinner at our place on Sunday.
- आप सोमवार शाम को हमारे यहाँ आइए। āp somvār śām ko hamāre yahāṁ aīie. — Please come to our place on Monday in the evening.
- आप शनिवार को सुबह नाश्ता — Please have breakfast with us

हमारे साथ कीजिए। āp ravivār ko rāt kā bhojan hamāre yahāṁ kījie.	on Saturday morning.
• वे बुधवार को अपराह्न ढाई बजे तक आएंगे। ve budhvār ko aprāhn dhāī baje tak āeṁge.	They will come by 2:30 n the afternoon.

■ **Parting Sentences:**

• अब मैं चलता हूँ।	ab maiṁ caltā hūṁ	I shall get going now.
• रविवार को मिलेंगे।	ravivār ko mileṁge.	We shall meet on Sunday.

Ex. D 2 . Say in Hindi

1. How are you people? 2. We are fine? 3. How do you like it here? 4. We like it here. 5. It is colder here than New York. 6. The weather is very pleasant here. 7. I would like to introduce my daughter to you. 8. Please have lunch with us on wednesday. 9. We shall certainly come. 10. We shall get going now.

Key D 2 .

1.	आप लोग कैसे हैं?	āp log kaise haiṁ?
2.	हम मज़े में हैं।	ham maze meṁ haiṁ.
3.	आपको यहाँ कैसे लग रहा है?	āpko yahāṁ kaise lag raha hai?
4.	हमें अच्छा लग रहा है।	hameṁ acchā lag rahā hai.
5.	यहाँ न्यू यार्क से ज्यादा सर्दी है।	yahāṁ New York se zyādā sardī hai.
6.	यहाँ मौसम बहुत सुहावना है।	yahāṁ mausam bahut suhāvnā hai.
7.	मैं अपनी बेटी को आपसे मिलाना चाहता हूँ।	maiṁ apnī beṭī ko āpse milānā cāhtā hūṁ.
8.	आप बुधवार दिन में हमारे यहाँ भोजन कीजिए।	āp budhvār ko din meṁ hamāre yahāṁ bhojan kījie
9.	हम अवश्य आएँगे।	ham avaśyă āeṁge.
10.	अब हम चलते है।	ab ham calte haiṁ.

●●●●●

D 3 Rishabh Seeks Neighbor's Help

रात के बारह बजे हैं। द्वार पर घण्टी बजती है।
पियूष और उनकी पत्नी सो रहे हैं।
(आवाज़ सुनकर)
'इस समय कौन हो सकता है!'
वे उठकर दरवाज़े पर जाती हैं, और दरवाज़ा खोलकर देखती हैं।
(श्री ऋषभ को देखकर)
'आप! इस समय? आपका चेहरा उतरा हुआ लग रहा है। सब ठीक तो है न?'

ऋषभ: क्षमा कीजिए! इतनी रात गए आपको कष्ट दे रहा हूँ। मेरी पत्नी गिर गई हैं। उनके पैर में मोच आ गई लगती है। उन्हें बहुत दर्द हो रहा है। यहाँ पास में कोई डॉक्टर मिलेगा?

पियूष: डॉक्टर तो कई मिलेंगे। लेकिन मैं सोचता हूँ, हमें उन्हें अस्पताल ले जाना चाहिए। हो सकता है कि उनकी हड्डी टूट गई हो। चलिए! मैं भी आपके साथ चलता हूँ।

ऋषभ: आप परेशान न हों। मैं उन्हें ले जाऊँगा।

पियूष: इसमें परेशानी की कोई बात नहीं। चलिए, जल्दी चलें।

ऋषभ: धन्यवाद। जैसा आप ठीक समझें। चलिए। धन्यवाद।

rāt ke bārah baje haiṁ. dvār par ghaṇṭī bajtī hai.
piyūṣ aur unkī patnī so rahe haiṁ.
(āvāz sunkar, piyūṣ kī patnī kahtī haiṁ)
' is samay kaun ho saktā hai!
ve uṭhkar darvāze par jātī haiṁ, aur darvāzā kholkar dekhtī haiṁ.
ṛṣabh ko dekhkar kahtī haiṁ:
' āp! is samay? āpkā cehrā utarā huā lag rahā hai. sab ṭhīk to hai na?

ṛṣabh: kṣamā kījie. itnī rāt gae āpko kaṣṭ de rahā hūṁ. merī patnī gir gaī haiṁ. unke pair meṁ moc ā gaī lagtī hai. unheṁ bahut dard ho rahā hai. yahāṁ pās meṁ koī acchā ḍaukṭar milegā?

piyūṣ: ḍaukṭar to kaī mileṁge. lekin maiṁ soctā hūṁ hameṁ unheṁ aspatāl le jānā cāhie. ho saktā hai ki unkī haḍḍī ṭūṭ gaī ho. calie maiṁ bhī āpke sāth caltā hūṁ.

ṛṣabh: āp pareśān na hoṁ. maiṁ unheṁ le jāuṁgā.

piūṣ: ismeṁ pareśānī kī koī bāt nahīṁ. calie, jaldī caleṁ.

ṛṣabh: jaisā āp ṭhīk samjheṁ. calie. dhanyăvād.

WORDS & PHRASES

द्वार (m.)	dvār	door
घण्टी (f.)	ghanṭī	bell
बजना (v.i.)	bajnā	to ring
आवाज़ (f.)	āvāz	sound/voice
सुनकर (kar-conj.)	sunkar	hear and
खोलना (v.t.)	kholnā	to open
खोलकर (kar-conj.)	kholkar	open and
देखकर (kar-conj.)	dekhkar	see and
चेहरा (m.)	cehrā	face
उतरना (v.i.)	utarnā	to climb down
चेहरा उतरना	cehrā utarnā	face to look pale
उतरा हुआ (PPC)	utrā huā	pale
कष्ट (m.)	kaṣṭ	trouble
कष्ट देना (v.t.)	kaṣṭ denā	to trouble
गिर जाना (comp.v.i.)	gir jānā	to fall down
दर्द होना (conj.v.i.)	dard jānā	to have pain
ले जाना (comp.v.i.)	le jānā	to take along
हड्डी (f.)	haḍḍī	bone
हड्डी टूटना	haḍḍī ṭūṭnā	bone to be fractured

• क्षमा कीजिए	kṣamā kījie	excuse me!
• इतनी रात गए	itnī rāt gae	so late in the night
• हो सकता है	ho saktā hai	it could be
• चलिए!	calie	let's go!

Rishabh Seeks Neighbor's Help

- मैं सोचता हूँ — I think...
  maiṁ soctā hūṁ
- मैं भी आपके साथ चलता हूँ। — I will come with you too.
  maiṁ bhī āpke sāth caltā hūṁ.
- आप परेशान न हों। — Please don't trouble yourself.
  āp pareśān na hoṁ.
- इसमें परेशानी की कोई बात नहीं। — This is no problem!
  ismeṁ pareśānī kī koī bāt nahīṁ.
- जैसा आप ठीक समझें। — As you say.
  jaisā āp ṭhīk samjheṁ.

■ **Use of the sense verb लगना lagnā to seems: Gram Ref. pg. 139, 412-419**

- आपका चेहरा उतरा हुआ लग रहा है। — You look pale.
  āpkā cehrā utrā huā lag rahā hai.
- उनके पैर में मोच आ गई लगती है। — She seems to have sprained her ankle.
  unke pair meṁ moc ā gaī lagtī hai.

■ **Asking About Availability: Use the verb मिलना milnā: See pg. 422**

- यहाँ पास में कोई डॉक्टर मिलेगा? — Will a doctor be available nearby?
  yahāṁ pās meṁ koī acchā ḍaukṭar milegā.
- डॉक्टर तो कई मिलेंगे। — Several doctors will be available.
  ḍaukṭar to kaī mileṁge.

■ **Present Progressive: Gram. Ref. pg. 110**

- इतनी रात गए आपको कष्ट दे रहा हूँ। — I am troubling you so late in the night.
  itnī rāt gae āpko kaṣṭ de rahā hūṁ.

- उन्हें बहुत दर्द हो रहा है। She is having much pain.
  unheṁ bahut dard ho rahā hai.

■ **Present Perfect Tense: Gram. Ref. pg. 128**

- मेरी पत्नी गिर गई हैं। My wife has fallen.
  merī patnī gir gaī haiṁ.

■ **Moral Obligation: Gram. Ref. pg. 158**

हमें उन्हें अस्पताल ले जाना चाहिए। We ought to take her to the hospital.
hameṁ unheṁ aspatāl le jānā cāhie.

■ **Probability : Gram. Ref. pg. 224**

- हो सकता है कि उनकी हड्डी टूट गई हो। It is likely she fractured the bone.
  ho saktā hai ki unkī haḍḍī ṭūṭ gaī ho.
- हो सकता है कि उनके पैर में मोच आ गई हो। It is likely that she sprained her ankle.
  ho saktā hai ki unke pair mem moc ā gaī ho.

●●●●●

D 4 Rishabhs Thank Piyūṣ for Help

ऋषभ और उनकी पत्नी प्रज्ञा अपने पड़ोसी पियूष और उसकी पत्नी जिज्ञासा के बहुत आभारी हैं। वे उन्हें मदद के लिए धन्यवाद देने के लिए उनके घर जाते हैं।

ऋषभः नमस्ते। क्षमा कीजिए। आज हमारा 'टेलिफ़ोन' ख़राब है; इसलिए आपको बिना बताए चले आए।

पियूषः अरे! यह तो हमारा सौभाग्य है।.हमें बहुत खुशी हुई कि आपने हमें याद किया। आइए, आइए, अन्दर आइए। स्थान ग्रहण कीजिए।
(अपनी पत्नी से)
जिज्ञासा! यहाँ आओ। देखो तो कौन आया है!

जिज्ञासाः अरे ऋषभ जी, प्रज्ञा जी, आप लोग! आप थोड़ी देर पियूष से बात कीजिए, मैं चाय लेकर आती हूँ।

ऋषभः आज हम कुछ जल्दी में हैं। वास्तव में हम आपको न्योता देने आए हैं।

पियूषः नहीं, नहीं। अभी नहीं। खाना बनाने के लिए आपको खड़े रहना पड़ेगा; यह आपके पैर के लिए ठीक नहीं। अभी आपको आराम करना चाहिए।

ऋषभः ऐसा कुछ नहीं होगा। हम बाहर किसी 'रेस्टराँ' में खाएँगे।

पियूषः तब ठीक है। हम अवश्य चलेंगे।

ऋषभः आप क्या पसन्द करेंगे, दक्षिण का खाना या कुछ उत्तर भारत का।

पियूषः दक्षिण का खाना तो हम रोज़ ही खाते हैं; आपके साथ कुछ पंजाबी खाएँगे।

ऋषभः आप कहाँ खाना पसन्द करेंगे, 'शेरे पंजाब' में या 'टेस्ट ऑफ़ इंडिया' में?

पियूषः 'शेरे पंजाब' का खाना भी अच्छा है। लेकिन हमने सुना है कि 'टेस्ट ऑफ़ इंडिया' का खाना 'शेरे पंजाब' के खाने से ज़्यादा अच्छा है। 'टेस्ट ऑफ़ इंडिया' में चला जाय।

Rishabhs Thank Piyush For Help

ऋषभः बहुत बढ़िया। शनिवार को शाम को सात बजे 'टेस्ट ऑफ़ इंडिया' में मिलते हैं। जी, ठीक है। धन्यवाद।

ऋषभः चलता हूँ। नमस्ते।

पियूषः नमस्ते।

ṛṣabh aur uskī patnī pragyā apne paṛosī piūṣ aur uskī patnī jigyāsā ke bahut ābhārī haiṁ. ve unheṁ madad ke lie dhanyavād dene ke lie unke ghar īte haiṁ.

ṛṣabh: namaste. kṣamā kījie. āj hamārā ṭailifon kharāb hai; islie āpko binā batāe cale āe.

piūṣ: are! yah to hamārā saubhāgyă hai. hameṁ bahut <u>kh</u>uśī huī ki āpne hameṁ yād kiyā. āie, āie, andar āie. sthān grahaṇ kījie.
(apnī patnī se)
jigyāsā! yahāṁ āo, dekho to kaun āyā hai!

jigyāsā: are, ṛṣabh jī, pragyā jī, āp log! āp thoṛī der piūṣ se bāt kījie, maiṁ cāy lekar ātī hūṁ

ṛṣabh: āj ham kuch jaldī meṁ haiṁ. vāstav meṁ, ham āpko nayotā dene āe haiṁ.

piūṣ: nahīṁ, nahīṁ. abhī nahīṁ. khānā banāne ke lie āpko khaṛe rahnā paṛegā; yah āpke pair ke lie ṭhīk nahīṁ. abhī āpko ārām karnā cāhie.

ṛṣabh aisā kuch nahīṁ hogā. ham bāhar kisī 'raisṭrāṁ' meṁ khāeṁge.

piūṣ: tab ṭhīk hai. ham avaśyă caleṁge.

ṛṣabh āp kyā pasand kareṁge, dakṣiṇ kā khānā, ya kuch uttar bhārat kā?

piūṣ: dakṣiṇ kā khānā to ham roz hī khāte haiṁ; āpke sāth kuch punjābī khāeṁge.

ṛṣabh: āp kahāṁ khānā pasand kareṁge, 'śere panjāb' meṁ, yā 'ṭesṭ auf inḍiā' meṁ?

piūṣ: 'śere panjāb' kā khānā bhī acchā hai. lekin hamne sunā hai ki 'ṭesṭ auf inḍiā' kā khānā 'śere panjāb' ke khāne se zyādā acchā hai. 'ṭesṭ auf inḍiā' meṁ calā jāy.

ṛṣabh: bahut baṛhiyā. śanivār ko śām ko sāt baje 'ṭesṭ auf inḍiā' meṁ milte haiṁ.

piūṣ: jī ṭhīk hai, dhanyăvād

ṛṣabh: caltā hūṁ. namaste.

piūṣ: namaste

Rishabhs Thank Piyush For Help

WORDS & PHRASES

क्षमा कीजिए	kṣamā kījie	excuse me
बिना बताए	binā batāe	without announcing
चला आना	calā ānā	to come over
सौभाग्य (m.)	saubhāgyă	good luck
याद करना (conj. verb.)	yād karnā	ro remember
स्थान (m.)	sthān	place/seat
स्थान ग्रहण करना	sthān grahaṇ karnā	to take a seat
थोड़ी देर	thoṛī der	for a short while
लेकर (kar.conj.)	lekar	here:bring
जल्दी में	jaldī meṁ honā	to be in a hurry
वास्तव में (adv.)	vāstav meṁ	in fact
न्योता (m.)	nayotā	invitation
न्योता देना (v.t.)	nayotā denā	to invite
अभी नहीं	abhī nahīṁ	not yet
खड़े रहना (v.i.)	khaṛe rahnā	to keep standing
आराम (m.)	ārām	rest
करना चाहिए	karnā cāhie	ought to do
दक्षिण (m.)	dakṣiṇ	south
उत्तर (m.)	uttar	north
अवश्य (adv.)	avaśyă	certainly
पसन्द करना	pasand karnā	to like
से ज़्यादा	se zyādā	more than

- यह तो हमारा सौभाग्य है। This is our good fortune.
  yah to hamārā saubhāgyă hai.
- स्थान ग्रहण कीजिए। Please be seated.
  sthān grahaṇ kījie.

- देखो तो कौन आया है!   Look, who has come!
  dekho to kaun āyā hai!
- हम आपको न्योता देने आए हैं   we have come to invite you.
  ham āpko nayotā dene āe haiṁ.
- आज हम कुछ जल्दी में हैं।   We are somewhat in a hurry today.
  āj ham kuch jaldī meṁ haiṁ.
- हम आपको न्योता देने आए हैं   we have come to invite you.
  ham āpko nayotā dene āe haiṁ.
- ऐसा कुछ नहीं होगा।   No such thing will happen.
  aisā kuch nahīṁ hogā.
- अब चलता हूँ।   I get going now!
  ab caltā hūṁ.

■ **X का आभारी होना   X kā ābhārī honā   to be grateful to X**

का kā, **के** ke, **की** kī agrees with the N and G of the subject.

- वे उनके बहुत आभारी हैं।   They are very grateful to them.
  ve unke bahut ābhārī haiṁ.

  मैं (f.) आपकी आभारी हूँ।   I am grateful to you.
  maiṁ (f.)āpkī ābhārī hūṁ.

■ **पसन्द करना pasand karnā = to like: Gram. Ref. pg. 184**

- आप क्या पसन्द करेंगे?   What would you like?
  āp kyā pasand kareṁge?

  आप कहाँ खाना पसन्द करेंगे?   Where would you like to eat?
  āp kahāṁ khānā pasand kareṁge?

■ **Outer compulsion: Gram Ref. pg. 212**

- आपको खड़े रहना पड़ेगा।   You will have to keep standing.
  āpko khaṛe rahnā paṛegā

Rishabhs Thank Piyush For Help

Moral Compulsion: Gram Ref. pg. 158

- आपको आराम करना चाहिए। You ought to rest.
  āpko ārām karnā cāhie.

Adjective-base form: Gram. Ref. pg. 35

- शेरे पंजाब' का खाना भी **अच्छा है।** Shere Punjab food is good too.
  śere panjāb' kā khānā bhī acchā hai.

Adjective - comparative: Gram. Ref. pg. 41

- टेस्ट आफ़ इंडिया' का खाना 'शेरे पंजाब' के खाने **से ज़्यादा अच्छा है।**
  'ṭesṭ auf inḍiā' kā khānā 'śere panjāb' ke khāne se zyādā acchā hai.
  Food of Taste of India is tastier than the food of Shere Punjab.

Subjunctive Passive: Gram. Ref. pg. 233

- टेस्ट आफ़ इंडिया' में चला जाय। Let's go to Taste of India.
  'ṭesṭ auf inḍiā' meṁ calā jāy.

Ex. D 4. Say in Hindi:

1. Your house is big. 2. His house is bigger than yours. 3. I am clever. 4. She is cleverer than me. 5. Yesterday was warm. 6. Today is warmer than yesterday. 7. I like Indian food. 8. I like Indian food more than japanese food. 9. I like this dress. 10. I like that dress more than this one.

Key D 4.

1. आपका घर बड़ा है। 2. उसका घर आपके घर से बड़ा है।3. मैं होशियार हूँ 4. वह मुझसे होशियार है। 5. कल गर्म था।6. आज कल से गर्म है। 7. मुझे भारतीय खाना पसन्द है। 8. मुझे भारतीय खाना जापानी खाने से ज़्यादा पसन्द है। 9. मुझे यह पोशाक पसन्द है। 10. मुझे वहवाली पोशाक इसवाली से ज़्यादा पसन्द है।

1. āpkā ghar baṛā hai. 2. uskā ghar āpke ghar se baṛā hai. 3. maiṁ hośiyār hūṁ. 4. vah mujhse hośiyār hai. 5. kal garm thā. 6. āj kal se garm hai. 7. mujhe bhārtīyă khānā pasand hai. 8. mujhe bhārtīyă khānā jāpānī khāne se zyādā pasand hai. 9. mujhe yah pośāk pasand hai. 10. mujhe vahvālī pośāk isvālī se zyādā pasand hai.

●●●●●

D 5 The Friends At The Restaurant

ऋषभः आपके यहाँ कोई खाली मेज़ है?

परिचरः कितने लोगों के लिए?

ऋषभः चार लोगों के लिए।

परिचरः जी। आइए, इस ओर , यहाँ बैठिए। आप क्या लीजिएगा?

ऋषभः धन्यवाद। कृपया 'मेन्यु' लाइए।

परिचरः जी, यह लीजिए।

ऋषभः देखें, क्या–क्या है ! साग–पनीर, भठूरे–छोले, नान और बिरयानी। हाँ तो आप लोग क्या–क्या लेंगे?

जिज्ञासाः आज मुझे बहुत भूख नहीं है। (परिचारक से) आपके पास उबला चावल और सादा दही होगा?

परिचरः जी।

जिज्ञासाः तो फिर मेरे लिए सिर्फ़ उबला चावल और सादा दही लाइए।

पियूषः भई, मुझे तो बहुत भूख लगी है। मैं तो साग–पनीर, नान और खीरे का रायता लूँगा।

परिचरः और पीने के लिए?

पियूषः मुझे बहुत प्यास भी लगी है। मेरे लिए तो 'मिनरल वॉटर' लाइए। और जिज्ञासा, तुम्हारे लिए?

जिज्ञासाः मेरे लिए भी 'मिनरल वॉटर'

ऋषभः प्रज्ञा, मैं तो छोले–भठूरे खाने की सोच रहा हूँ। तुम क्या लोगी?

प्रज्ञाः मैं छोले–भठूरे नहीं लूँगी। आप तो जानते हैं कि कुछ दिनों से मेरा वज़न बहुत बढ़ रहा है। मैं सादी रोटी, दही, और कोई सब्ज़ी लूँगी।

(कुछ समय बाद)

पियूषः मुटा तो मैं भी रहा हूँ। फिर भी मैं तो अच्छे से खाऊँगा। (परिचर से) सुनिए। दो नान और एक बोतल पानी और लाइए।

ऋषभः आपके पास मीठे में क्या–क्या है?

परिचरः जी। इमरती, गुलाबजामुन, गाजर का हलवा, आइसक्रीम।

The Friends At The Restaurant

ऋषभः आप लोग मीठा क्या लीजिएगा?
पियूषः मैं कुछ नहीं लूँगा। मुझे मीठा खाना मना है।
ऋषभः मैं गुलाबजामुन लूँगा।
जिज्ञासाः मेरे लिए एक आइसक्रीम लाइए।
प्रज्ञाः मेरे लिए भी। कृपया बिल भी लाइए।
परिचरः जी, यह लीजिए आपका बिल। और कुछ?
ऋषभः (पैसे देते हुए) धन्यवाद। बाकी आप रखें।

ṛṣabh: āpke yahāṁ koī khālī mez hai?
paricar: kitne logoṁ ke lie?
ṛṣabh: cār logoṁ ke lie.
paricar: jī, āie, iṣ or, yahāṁ baiṭhie. āp kyā lījiegā?
ṛṣabh: dhanyăvād, kṛpayā 'menyu' lāie.
paricar: jī, yah lījie.
ṛṣabh: dekheṁ, kyā-kyā hai! sāg-panīr, bhaṭhūre chole, nān aur biriyānī. hāṁ to āplog kyā-kyā leṁge?
jigyāsā: mujhe bahut bhūkh nahīṁ hai.
(paricar se)
āpke pās ublā cāval aur sādā dahī hogā?
paricar: Jī.
jigyāsā: to phir mere lie sirf ublā cāval aur sādā dahī lāie.
piūṣ: bhaī, mujhe to bahut bhūkh lagī hai. maiṁ to sāg-panīr, nān aur khīre kā rāyatā lūṁgā.
paricar: aur pīne ke lie?
piyūṣ: mujhe bahut pyās bhī lagī hai. mere lie to 'minral vauṭar' lāie. aur jigyāsā, tumhāre lie?
jigyāsā: mere lie bhī 'minral vauṭar'.
ṛṣabh: pragyā, maiṁ to chole bhaṭhūre khāne kī soc rahā hūṁ. tum kyā logī?
pragyā: maiṁ chole bhaṭhūre nahīṁ lūṁgī. āp to jānte haiṁ ki kuch dinoṁ se merā vazan bahut baṛh rahā hai. maiṁ sādī roti, dahī, aur koī sabzī lūṁgī.
(kuch samay bād)
piyūṣ: muṭā to maiṁ bhi rahā hūṁ. phir bhī maiṁ to acche se khāūṁgā.

(paricar se) sunie, do nān aur ek botal pānī aur lāie.

ṛṣabh: āpke pās mīṭhe meṁ kyā.-kyā hai?

paricar: Jī, imartī, gulāb jāmun, gājar kā halvā, āiskrīm.

ṛṣabh: āplog mīṭhā kyā lījiegā?

piūṣ: maiṁ kuch nahīṁ lūṁgā. mujhe mīṭhā khānā manā hai.

ṛṣabh: maiṁ gulābjāmun lūṁgā.

jigyāsā: mere lie ek āiskrīm lāie.

pragyā: mere lie bhi. kṛpayā 'bil' bhī lāie.

paricar: jī, yah lījie āpkā 'bil'. aur kuch?

ṛṣabh: (paise dete hue) dhanyăvād. bākī āp rakheṁ.

WORDS & PHRASES

खाली मेज़	khālī mez	free table
कितने लोग	kitne log	how many people
कृपया	kṛpayā	please
साग–पनीर	sāg-panīr	spinach and cottage cheese
भठूरे–छोले	bhaṭhūre chole	fried bread served with chickpeas
नान	Rān	baked bread
सादा	sādā	plain
उबला	ublā	boiled
वज़न	vazan	weight
बढना	baṛhnā	grow
खाने की सोचना	khāne kī socnā	to think of eating
सब्ज़ी	sabzī	vegetable
मीठा	mīṭhā	dessert
परिचर	paricar	waitor

- इमरती, गुलाबजामुन, गाजर का हलवा — Indian sweets
  imartī, gulāb jāmun, gājar kā halvā
- आपके यहाँ कोई खाली मेज़ है? — Do you have a table free?
  āpke yahāṁ koī khālī mez hai?

The Friends At The Restaurant

• आप क्या लीजिएगा? āp kyā lījiegā?	What would you like to have?
• यह लीजिए। yah lījie.	Here you are.
• देखें, क्या–क्या है। dekheṁ, kyā-kyā hai?	Let's see, what all they have.
• हाँ, तो आप लोग क्या–क्या लेंगे? hāṁ, to āp log kyā-kyā leṁge?	What would you like to have?
• आज मुझे बहुत भूख नहीं है। āj mujhe bahut bhūkh nahīṁ hai.	I am not very hungry today.
• भई, मुझे तो बहुत भूख लगी है। bhaī, mujhe to bahut bhūkh lagī hai.	Well, I am very hungry indeed
• मैं तो छोले–भठूरे खाने की सोच रहा हूँ। maiṁ to chole bhaṭhūre khāne kī soc rahā hūṁ.	I am thinking of eating bhathure-chole.
• मेरा वज़न बढ़ रहा है। merā vazan baṛh rahā hai.	I am gaining weight.
• सुनिए। sunie!	Excuse me! (literally: Listen!)
• दो नान और एक बोतल पानी और लाइए। do nān aur ek botal pānī aur lāie.	Please bring two nans and one more bottle of water.
• आप लोग मीठा क्या लीजिएगा? āplog mīṭhā kyā lījiegā?	What would you have for a dessert.
• मुझे मीठा खाना मना है। mujhe mīṭhā khānā manā hai.	I am not allowed to eat sweets.
• आपके पास मीठे में क्या–क्या है? āpke pās mīṭhe meṁ kyā.-kyā hai?	What all do you have in desserts.
• इमरती, गुलाबजामुन, गाजर का हलवा imartī, gulābjāmun, gājar kā halvā	different Indian sweets
• आइसक्रीम	icecream

āīskrīm

- बाकी आप रखें। — You may keep the balance.
  bākī āp rakheṁ.

Ex D 5. Say in Hindi:

1. What will you have? 2. What will she have? 3. What will the kids have? 4. What do you have in desserts.5. What do you have in drinks. 6. What do you have in snacks. 7. What will you have to drink. 8. What will you have for dessert. 9. What would you like to have, rice or roti? 10. I shall have 'roti'. 11. She will have rice. 12. My husband will have 'nan'. 13. I am not allowed to eat spicy food. 14. I am not allowed to eat fats. 15. I am not allowed any milk products. 16. I am gaining weight. 17. I am losing weight. 18. Bring two more 'rotis' please! 19.Bring me a knife and a fork please. 20. Bring me an empty bowl please. 21.Bring the bill please?

Key D 5.

1.	तुम क्या लोगे?/आप (m.) क्या लेंगे?	tum kyā loge?/āp (m.) kyā leṁge?
2.	वह क्या लेगी?	vah kyā legī?
3.	बच्चे क्या लेंगे?	bacce kyā leṁge?
4.	आपके पास मीठे में क्या–क्या है?	āpke pās mīṭhe meṁ kyā-kyā hai?.
5.	आपके पास पीने के लिए क्या–क्या है?	āpke pās pīne ke lie kyā-kyā hai?
6.	आपके पास जलपान में क्या–क्या है?	āpke pās jalpān meṁ kyā-kyā hai?
7.	आप पीने में क्या लेंगे?	āp pīne meṁ kyā leṁge?
8.	आप मीठे में क्या लेंगे?	āp mīṭhe meṁ kyā leṁge?
9.	आप क्या लेंगे, रोटी या चावल?	āp kyā leṁge, roṭī yā cāval?
10.	मैं रोटी लूँगा।	maiṁ 'roṭī'lūṁgā.
11.	वह चावल लेगी।	vah cāval legī.
12.	मेरे पति नान लेंगे।	mere pati 'nān leṁge'.
13.	मुझे तीता खाना मना है।	mujhe tītā khānā manā hai.
14.	मुझे घी–तेल खाना मना है।	mujhe ghī-tel khānā manā hai.
15.	मुझे दूध से बनी चीज़ें खाना मना है।	mujhe dūdh se banī cīzeṁ khānā

	manā hai.
16. मेरा वज़न बढ़ रहा है।	merā vazan baṛh rahā hai.
17. मैं मुटा रहा /रही हूँ । (informal)	maiṁ muṭā rahā/rahī hūṁ.
18. कृपया दो और रोटियाँ लाइए।	kṛpayā do aur 'roṭiyāṁ lāie.
19. कृपया एक चाकू और एक काण्टा लाइए।	kṛpayā ek 'cākū' aur ek 'kāṇṭā' lāie.
20. कृपया एक खाली कटोरी लाइए।	kṛpayā ek khālī kaṭorī lāie.
21. कृपया बिल लाइए।	kṛpayā bil lāie.

•••••

D 6 At The Railway Station

Piyūṣ Buying Ticket

पियूषः नई दिल्ली के लिए अगली गाड़ी कितने बजे है?
▣ जी, शाम को छह बजे।
पियूषः कृपया दो टिकट दीजिए।
▣ कौन–सी श्रेणी में?
पियूषः जी, वातानुकूलित थ्री टियर में।
▣ आने–जाने के या सिर्फ़ जाने के?
पियूषः जी, आने–जाने के।
▣ कृपया यह 'फ़ारम' भर दीजिए। यह लीजिए आपके आने–जाने के दो टिकट।
पियूषः धन्यवाद। कितने पैसे हुए?
▣ जी, चार सौ पचास रुपए।
पियूषः आपके पास पाँच सौ का छुट्टा होगा?
▣ जी। यह लीजिए पचास रुपए। धन्यवाद।

piyūṣ: naī dillī ke lie aglī gāṛī kitne baje hai?
▣ jī, śām ko chah baje.
piyūṣ: kṛpayā do ṭikaṭ dījie.
▣ kaun-sī śreṇī meṁ?
piyūṣ: jī, vātānukūlit thrī ṭiyar meṁ.
▣ āne-jāne ke yā sirf jāne ke?
piyūṣ: jī, āne-jāne ke .
▣ kṛpayā yah 'fāram' bhar dījie. yah lījie āpke āne-jāne ke do ṭikaṭ
piyūṣ: dhanyăvād! kitne paise hue?
▣ jī, cār sau pacās rupae.
piyūṣ: āpke pās pāṁc sau kā chuṭṭā hogā?
▣ jī. yah lījie pacās rupae. dhanyăvād.

Piyūṣ At The Railway Station

WORDS AND PHRASES

कृपया (adv.)	kṛpayā	please
अगला,अगले,अगली (adj.)	aglā, agle, aglī	next
(agrees with the following noun)		
अगली गाड़ी (f.)	aglī gāṛī	next train
शाम को	śām ko	in the evening
छह बजे	chah baje	at 6 o'clock
कौन–सी (adj.)	kaun-sī	which one
श्रेणी (f.)	śreṇī	class
वातानुकूलित (adj.)	vātānukūlit	airconditioned
थ्री टियर	thrī ṭiyar	three tier
फ़ारम (m.)	fāram	form
भरना (v.t.)	bharnā	to fill
आने–जाने का	āne-jāne kā	to and fro
सिर्फ़ जाने का	sirf jāne kā	only for going
चार सौ पचास	cār sau pacās	four hundred and fifty
छुट्टा (m.)	chuṭṭā	small money

- कितने पैसे हुए? kitne paise hue? — How much does it come to?
- जी, शाम को छह बजे jī, śām ko chah baje. — At 6.00 p.m., sir.
- कौन सी श्रेणी में? kaun-sī śreṇī meṁ? — In which class?
- जी, वातानुकूलित थ्री–टियर में। jī, vātānukūlit thrī ṭiyar meṁ. — In airconditioned three tier.
- आने–जाने का या सिर्फ़ जाने का? āne-jāne kā yā sirf jāne kā? — Return ticket or one way?
- कृपया यह 'फ़ारम' भर दीजिए। — Please fill in this form.

kṛpayā yah 'fāram' bhar dījie.

▣ आपके पास पाँच सौ का छुट्टा होगा? āpke pās pāṁc sau kā chuṭṭā hogā? — Do you have change for five hundred.

▣ कृपया दो टिकट दीजिए। kṛpayā do ṭikaṭ dījie. — Please give me two tickets.

Piyūṣ On The Train

▣ कृपया अपना टिकट दिखाइए।
पियूषः जी। ये हैं हमारे टिकट। कृपया बताएँ, गाड़ी कितने बजे नई दिल्ली पहुँचेगी?
▣ जी, कल सुबह सात बजकर पचास मिनट पर।
पियूषः क्या इस गाड़ी में चाय मिलेगी?
▣ जी, इस गाड़ी में चाय मिलेगी; और इस गाड़ी में खाना भी मिलेगा।

▣ kṛpayā apnā ṭikaṭ dikhāie.
piyūṣ: jī. ye haiṁ hamāre ṭikaṭ. kṛpayā batāeṁ, gāṛī kitne baje naī dillī pahuṁcegī?
▣ jī, kal subah sāt bajkar pacās minaṭ par.
piyūṣ: kyā is gāṛī meṁ cāy milegī?
▣ jī, is gāṛī meṁ cāy milegī aur is gāṛī meṁ khānā bhī milegā.

WORDS AND PHRASES

कृपया	kṛpayā	please
बताएँ (subjunc. imper.)	batāeṁ	please tell
कितने बजे	kitne baje	what time
पहुँचना (v.i.)	pahuṁnā	to arrive
पहुँचेगी	pahuṁcegī	will arrive

▣ कृपया अपना टिकट दिखाइए। kṛpayā apnā ṭikaṭ dikhāie. — Please show me your ticket.

▣ नई दिल्ली के लिए अगली गाड़ी — What time is the next train to New

	कितने बजे है? naī dillī ke lie aglī gāṛī kitne baje hai?	Delhi.
▣	कल सुबह सात बजकर पचास मिनट पर kal subah sāt bajkar pacās minaṭ par	tomorrow at 7:30 a.m.
▣	क्या इस गाड़ी में चाय मिलेगी? kyā is gāṛī meṁ cāy milegī?	Will tea be available on this train?

At the Destination

पियूष : क्षमा कीजिए, मुझे पहाड़गंज जाना. है। यहाँ टैक्सी कहाँ मिलेगी?

▣ इस समय कोई खाली टैक्सी नहीं है। आप चाहें तो इन्तज़ार कर सकते हैं; आप चाहें तो बस से भी जा सकते हैं।

पियूष : बस कहाँ मिलेगी?

▣ बस अड्डा वहाँ सामने है।

पियूष : कौन–सी बस जाएगी?

▣ बस नम्बर पाँच सौ आठ।

पियूष : वहाँ आस–पास कोई अच्छा होटल मिलेगा?

▣ जी, बस अड्डे के पास कई काफ़ी अच्छे होटल हैं। ये बहुत महँगे भी नहीं हैं।

पियूष : जानकारी के लिए धन्यवाद।

▣ कोई बात नहीं। यह तो मेरा कर्तव्य था।

piyūṣ: kṣamā kījie, mujhe pahāṛgañj jānā hai. yahāṁ ṭaiksī kahāṁ milegī?

▣ muje khed hai ki is samay koī khālī ṭaiksī nahīṁ hai. āp cāheṁ to intzār kar sakte haiṁ. āp cāheṁ to bas se bhī jā sakte haiṁ.

piyūṣ: bas kahāṁ milegī?

▣ bas aḍḍā vahāṁ sāmne hai.

piyūṣ: kaun-sī bas jāegī?

▣ bas nambar pāṁc sau āṭh.

piyūṣ: vahāṁ ās-pās koī acchā hoṭal milegā?

▣ Ji, bas aḍḍe ke pās kaī kāfī acche hoṭal haiṁ. ye bahut mahṁge bhī nahīṁ haiṁ.

□ jānkārī ke lie dhanyăvād.

- koī bāt nahīṁ. yah to merā kartavyă thā.

WORDS AND PHRASES

मिलेगी	milegī	will be available.
खाली (adj.)	khālī	free
इन्तज़ार करना (v.t.)	intzār karnā	to wait
सामने (adv.)	sāmne	in front
जाएगी	jāegī	will go
पाँच सौ आठ	pāṁc sau āṭh	five hundred and eight
आस–पास (adv.)	ās-pās	nearby
महँगे (adj.)	mahṁge	expensive
जानकारी (f.)	jānkārī	information
कर्तव्य (m.)	kartavyă	duty
• क्षमा कीजिए (imper.)	kṣamā kījie	Excuse me!
• मुझे खेद है	muje khed hai	I am sorry
• आप चाहें तो	āp cāheṁ to	if you like,...

- कोई खाली टैक्सी नहीं है। — There isn't any free taxi?
  koī khālī ṭaiksī nahīṁ hai?
- बस कहाँ मिलेगी? — Where could I get a bus?
  bas kahāṁ milegī?
- जानकारी के लिए धन्यवाद। — Thanks for the information.
  jānkārī ke lie dhanyăvād.
- कोई बात नहीं। — You are welcome!
  koī bāt nahīṁ.
- यह तो मेरा कर्तव्य (m.) था। — This was my duty.
  yah to merā kartavyă thā.

■ **Compulsion Structure : Gram. Ref. pg: 211**

- मुझे पहाड़गंज जाना है । — I have togo to paharganj.
  mujhe pahāṛgañj jānā hai.

At The Destination

■ **Use of सकना 'can'/be able to : Gram. Ref. pg: 154**

- आप चाहें तो इन्तज़ार कर सकते है। — If you like, you may wait for one.
  āp cāheṁ to intzār kar sakte haiṁ.
- आप चाहें तो बस से भी जा सकते हैं। — If you like you could go by bus too.
  āp cāheṁ to bas se bhī jā sakte haiṁ.

Ex D 6. 1 Say in Hindi:

1. How much do I owe you?
2. What time is the next bus to Connaught Place?
3. What time is the next train to Varanasi?
4. What time is the next flight to Nepal.
5. 2:30 p.m; 7:30 p.m.;8:15 p.m..
6. in the morning; in the afternoon; in the evening; at night
7. In which class?
8. In the sleeper coach
9. In first class
10. Return ticket or one way?
11. One way ticket
12. Return ticket.
13. Do you have change for 100 rupee bill?
14. Do you have change for a thousand?
15. Do you have change for ten?

Key D 6. 1

1.	कितने पैसे हुए?	kitne paise hue?
2.	कन्नाट प्लेस के लिए अगली बस कितने बजे है?	kannāt ples ke lie aglī bas kitne baje hai?
3.	वाराणसी के लिए अगली गाड़ी कितने बजे है?	Varanasi ke lie aglī gāṛī kitne baje hai?
4.	नेपाल के लिए अगली उड़ान कितने बजे है?	Nepal ke lie aglī uṛān kitne baje hai?

5.	अपराहन् ढाई बजे	aprāhn ḍhāī baje
	शाम को साढ़े सात बजे	śām ko sāṛhe sāt baje
	शाम को सवा आठ बजे	śām ko savā āṭh baje
6.	सुबह	subah
	अपराहन् में	aprāhn meṁ
	शाम को	śām ko
	रात को	rāt ko
7.	कौन सी श्रेणी में?	kaun-sī śreṇī meṁ?
8.	सामान्य शयन श्रेणी में	sāmānyă śayan śreṇī meṁ
9.	प्रथम श्रेणी मे	pratham śreṇī meṁ
10.	आने–जाने का या सिर्फ़ जाने का?	āne-jāne kā yā sirf jāne kā?
11.	इकतरफ़ा टिकट	iktarfa ṭikaṭ
12.	वापसी टिकट	vapsī ṭikaṭ
13.	आपके पास सौ का छुट्टा होगा?	āpke pās sau kā chuṭṭā hogā?
14.	आपके पास हज़ार का छुट्टा होगा?	āpke pās hazār kā chuṭṭā hogā?
15.	आपके पास दस का छुट्टा होगा?	āpke pās das kā chuṭṭā hogā?

Ex D 6. 2 Say in Hindi:

1. Please give one dozen bananas. (dozen = दर्जन darjan ; bananas = केले kele)
2. Please give two kilos potatoes. (potatoes =आलू alū)
3. Please give ten one rupee tickets.
   ten one rupee tickets = दस एक रुपए के टिकट das ek rupae ke ṭikaṭ
4. Please tell me when the bus will arrive at connaught Place?
5. Please tell me when the airplane will arrive in Nepal?
   (airplane = हवाई जहाज havāī jahāz)
6. Please tell me what time will the rikshaw arrive at the temple?
   (temple= मंदिर mandir)
7. 8:50 a.m. ; 9:15 a.m. ;1p.m.; 2:40 a.m. ; 3:10 a.m. ; 6 p.m.
8. Will food be available on this train?

9. Yes, tea will be available on this train.
10. Yes, food will be available on this on this train.

Key D 6. 2

1. कृपया एक दर्जन केले दीजिए।	kṛpayā ek darjan kele dījie.
2. कृपया दो किलो आलू दीजिए।	kṛpayā do kilo ālū dījie.
3. कृपया दस एक रुपए के टिकट दीजिए।	kṛpayā das ek rupae ke ṭikaṭ dījie.
4. कृपया बताएँ, बस क्नाट प्लेस कितने बजे पहुँचेगी?	kṛpayā batāeṁ, bas kannāṭ ples kitne baje pahuṁcegī?
5. कृपया बताएँ, हवाई जहाज़ नेपाल कितने बजे पहुँचेगा?	kṛpayā batāeṁ, havāī jahāz kitne baje Nepal pahuṁcegā?
6. कृपया बताएँ, रिक्शा कितने बजे मंदिर पहुँचेगा?	kṛpayā batāeṁ, rikshā kitne baje mandir pahuṁcegā?
7. सुबह नौ बजने में दस मिनट पर	subah nau bajne meṁ das minaṭ par
सुबह सवा नौ बजे	subah savā nau baje
दोपहर एक बजे	dopahar ek baje
रात को तीन बजने में बीस मिनट पर	rāt ko tīn bajne meṁ bīs minaṭ par
रात को तीन बजकर दस मिनट पर	rāt ko tīn bajkar das minaṭ par
शाम को छह बजे	śām ko chah baje
8. क्या इस गाड़ी में खाना मिलेगा?	kyā is gāṛī meṁ khānā milegā?
9. जी, इस गाड़ी में चाय मिलेगी।	jī, is gāṛī meṁ cāy milegī?
10. जी, इस गाड़ी में खाना मिलेगा।	jī, is gāṛī meṁ khānā milegā.

●●●●●

D 7 Tired of Walking!

रिषभः मैं दिन भर चलते–चलते थक गया हूँ। मेरा चाय पीने को मन हो रहा है। यहाँ रुककर कुछ चाय पी जाय।

प्रज्ञाः ज़रूर।
(परिचर को आवाज़ लगाते हुए)

रिषभः सुनिए।

परिचरः जी। आप क्या लेंगे?

रिषभः मेरे लिए एक गर्म–गर्म चाय लाइए।

परिचरः जी। दूध और चीनी के साथ?

रिषभः दूध के साथ, परन्तु चीनी के बिना। मुझे कुछ कड़क–सी चाय पसन्द है। प्रज्ञा, तुम क्या लोगी?

प्रज्ञाः मैं कुछ ठण्डा लूँगी। आपके पास ठण्डे में क्या है?

परिचरः जी, लस्सी, मिल्क–शेक, नींबू–पानी।

प्रज्ञाः ठीक है, मेरे लिए ठण्डी मीठी लस्सी लाइए।

परिचरः जी, और कुछ खाने के लिए?

प्रज्ञाः धन्यवाद। मुझे और कुछ नहीं चाहिए। बस, ज़रा जल्दी लाइए। हम कुछ जल्दी में हैं।

ṛṣabh:: maiṁ din bhar calte-calte thak gayā hūṁ. merā cāy pīne ko man ho rahā hai. yahāṁ rukkar kuch cāy pī jāy.

pragya: zarūr.
(paricar ko āvāz lagāte hue)

ṛṣabh: sunie!

paricar jī, āp kyā leṁge?

ṛṣabh: mere lie ek garm-garm cāy lāie

paricar jī. dūdh aur cīnī ke sāth?

ṛṣabh: dūdh ke sāth, parantu cīnī ke binā. mujhe kuch kaṛak-sī cāy pasand hai.pragya, tum kyā logī?

pragya: maiṁ kuch ṭhaṇḍā lūṁgī. āpke pās ṭhaṇḍe meṁ kyā hai?

paricar jī, lassī, milk-shake, nīmbū-pānī.

pragya: ṭhīk hai mere lie ṭhaṇḍī mīṭhī lassī lāie.
paricar: jī, aur kuch khāne ke lie?
pragya: dhanyăvād. mujhe aur kuch nahīṁ cāhie. bas! zarā jaldī laie. ham kuch jaldī meṁ haiṁ

.WORDS AND PHRASES

दिन भर	din bhar	all day
चलते–चलते (IPC)	calte-calte	walking continuously
थक गया हूँ	thak gayā hūṁ	have become tired.
रुककर (kar-conj.)	rukkar	stop and
ज़रूर (adv.)	zarūr.	certainly
परिचर (m.)	paricār	waitor
आवाज़ लगाते हुए (IPC)	āvāz lagāte hue	calling
गर्म–गर्म (adj.)	garm-garm	very hot
लाइए	lāie	please bring
(polite imperative of the v.t. लेना lenā to take)		
दूध के साथ	dūdh ke sāth	with milk
चीनी के बिना	cīnī ke binā	without sugar
परन्तु	parantu	but
कड़क–सी चाय	kaṛak-sī cāy	rather strong tea
पसन्द करना	pasand karnā	to like
कुछ	kuch	something
ठण्डा	ṭhaṇḍā	cold
लूँगी	lūṁgī.	will have
(f.sg. future simple of the v.t. लेना lenā to take ; it agrees with the subject 'maiṁ')		
को पसन्द होना	ko pasand honā	to like
और कुछ	aur kuch	anything else
खाने के लिए	khāne ke lie	for eating

■ बस ! — that's all!
bas!

- ज़रा जल्दी लाइए। — Please bring soon.
  zarā jaldī lāie.
- हम कुछ जल्दी में हैं। — We are a bit in a hurry.
  ham kuch jaldī meṁ haiṁ.

IPC (v.r.+te)+(v.r.+te): Gram. Ref. 219-220

- मैं दिन भर **चलते-चलते** थक गया हूँ। — I am tired of walking all day.
  maiṁ din bhar calte-calte thak gayā hūṁ.
  मैं दिन भर **पढ़ते-पढ़ते** ऊब गया हूँ। — I am bored of reading all day.
  maiṁ din bhar paṛhte-paṛhte ūb gayā hūṁ.

(v.r. + ने) को मन होना to feel like doing something:

- मेरा चाय पीने को मन हो रहा है। — I feel like drinking tea.
  merā cāy pīne ko man ho rahā hai.
  आज हमारा हिन्दी फ़िल्म देखने को मन हो रहा है। — Today we feel like watching hindi- movie.
  āj hamārā hindī film dekhne ko man ho rahā hai.

'Let's do .....' Passive subjunctive: Gram. Ref. 233

- कुछ चाय पी जाय — Let's have tea.
  kuch cāy pī jāy.
  कुछ काम किया जाय — Let's do some work.
  kuch kām kiyā jāy.

पसन्द होना: to like (used with subject + **को** 'ko') **Gram. Ref. 185**

- मुझे कुछ कड़क–सी चाय पसन्द है। — I like somewhat strong tea.
  mujhe kuch kaṛak-sī cāy pasand hai.

1. मुझे दूरदर्शन देखना पसन्द है। — I like to watch television
   mujhe dūrdarśan dekhnā pasand hai.
2. मुझे संगीत सुनना काफ़ी पसन्द है। — I quite like to watch television

mujhe saṅgīt sunanā kāfī pasand hai.

3. मुझे फ़िल्म देखना **कोई ख़ास** पसन्द नहीं।
mujhe film dekhnā koī khās pasand nahīṁ.
I don't quite like to watch movies.

■ **Asking about availability:**

- आपके पास ठण्डे में क्या है?
āpke pās ṭhaṇḍe meṁ kyā hai?
What do you have in cold?

■ **Ordering food:**

- मेरे लिए एक गर्म-गर्म चाय लाइए।
mere lie ek garm-garm cāy lāie
Please bring me a very hot tea.

Similarly:

......................एक नींबू पानी .... ।
......................ek nīmbū panī..................
......................lemon-drink...............

......................एक आईस-क्रीम.................. ।
......................ek āīs krīm.........................
......................ice cream...............

......................एक ठण्डा कोकाकोला.............. ।
.....................ek ṭhaṇḍā kokā kolā...........
..................a cold cocacola...............

■ **Asking others what they would like to have:**

- आप क्या लेंगे?
āp kyā leṁge/ leṁgī?
What would you(formal) like to have?

1. तुम क्या लोगे/लोगी?
tum kyā loge/ logī?
what would you(informal) like to have?

2. वे क्या लेंगे?
ve kyā leṁge/ leṁgi?
What would they(formal) like to have?

Ex. D 7. Say In Hindi:

1.I am bored watching TV . 2. We are fed up eating the same food every day. 3. We feel like sleeping. 4. They feel like eating out. 5. Mother feels like resting. 6.

Let's rest. 7. Let's go for a walk. 8. What do you have in dessert? 9. What do you have in hot? 10. He likes playing football. 11. They like swimming. 12. What do you like? 13. .Please bring me a cold sweet 'lassi'. 14. Please bring for her/him mineral water. 15. .Please bring for them biryani.

Key: D 7.

1.	मैं टी वी देखते–देखते ऊब गई हूँ	maiṁ ṭīvī dekhte-dekhte ūb gaī hūṁ.
1.	हम वही खाना रोज़ खाते–खाते तंग आ गए हैं।	ham vahī khānā roz khāte-khāte tang ā gae haiṁ.
3.	हमारा सोने को मन हो रहा है।	hamārā sone ko man ho rahā hai.
4.	उनका बाहर खाने को मन हो रहा है।	unkā bāhar khāne ko man ho rahā hai.
5.	माता जी का आराम करने को मन हो रहा है।	mātā ji kā ārām karne ko man ho rahā hai.
6.	आराम किया जाय।	ārām kiyā jāy.
7.	सैर करने चला जाय।	sair karne calā jāy.
8.	आपके पास मीठे में क्या है?	āpke pās mīṭhe meṁ kyā hai?
9.	आपके पास गर्म में क्या है?	āpke pās garm mec kyā hai.
10.	उसको 'फुटबाल' खेलना पसन्द है।	usko 'fuṭbaul' khelnā pasand hai.
11.	उनको तैरना पसन्द है।	unko tairnā pasand hai.
12.	आप क्या पसन्द करते हैं?	āp kyā pasand karte haiṁ?
13.	मेरे लिए ठण्डी मीठी लस्सी लाइए।	mere lie ṭhaṇḍī mīṭhī lassī lāie.
14.	उसके लिए 'मिनरल वाटर' लाइए।	uske lie 'mineral vauṭar' lāie.
15.	उनके लिए बिरयानी लाइए।	unke lie biryānī lāie.

●●●●●

D 8 Window Shopping

प्रज्ञा: मैंने कल बाहर खिड़की में एक साड़ी टंगी हुई देखी थी। मुझे बहुत पसन्द आई थी। लेकिन आज वहाँ नहीं है।

दुकानदार: यह कैसी थी?

प्रज्ञा: यह गहरे नील–से रंग की थी। किनारे और पल्लू पर सुनहरी ज़री और गुलाबी धागे का काम था।

दुकानदार: जी, अब मुझे याद आ रहा है। वह साड़ी आज ही सुबह बिक गई। ठीक वैसी ही साड़ी तो और हमारे पास नहीं है। परन्तु हमारे पास और, उससे भी कहीं अधिक सुन्दर साड़ियाँ हैं। यदि आप चाहें तो मैं आपको उससे मिलती–जुलती दिखा सकता हूँ।

प्रज्ञा: जी नहीं, धन्यवाद। अभी रहने दीजिए। फिर कभी। नमस्ते।

दुकानदार: नमस्ते। अवश्य फिर आइएगा।

pragya: maiṁne kal bāhar khiṛkī meṁ ek sāṛī ṭaṁgī huī dekhī thī. mujhe bahut pasand āī thī. lekin āj vahāṁ nahīṁ hai.

dukāndār: yah kaisī thī?

pragya: yah gahre nīle-se raṅg kī thī. kināre aur pallū par sunaharī zarī aur gulābī dhāge kā kām thā.

dukāndār: jī, ab mujhe yād ā rahā hai. vah sāṛī āj hī subah bik gaī. ṭhīk vaisī hī sāṛī to aur hamāre pās nahīṁ hai. parantu hamāre pās aur, usse bhī kahīṁ adhik sundar sāṛiyāṁ haiṁ. yadi āp cāheṁ to maiṁ āpko usse miltī-jultī dikhā saktā hūṁ.

pragya: jī nahīṁ, dhanyăvād. abhī rahne dījie. phir kabhī. namaste.

dukāndār: namaste. avaśyă phir āiegā.

WORDS AND PHRASES

गाहक (m.)	gāhak	customer
बाहर (adv.)	bāhar	ouside
खिड़की (f.)	khiṛkī	window
टंगी हुई (PPC)	ṭaṁgī huī	hanging

पसन्द आना	pasand ānā	to like
दुकानदार (m.)	dukāndār	shopkeeper
गहरा (m.)	gahrā	deep
नीला–सा	nīlā-sā	blue-ish
रंग (m.)	raṅg	color
किनारा (m.)	kinārā	border
पल्लू (m.)	pallū	the part of a sari that goes on the shoulder
सुनहरी (adj.)	sunaharī	golden
ज़री (f.)	jarī	gold thread
गुलाबी	gulābī	pink
धागा (m.)	dhāgā	thread
बिकना (v.i.)	biknā	to get sold
बिक जाना (comp.verb)	bik jānā	to get sold (comp.verb)
ठीक वैसी (adj.)	ṭhīk vaisī	exactly alike
फिर कभी (adv.)	phir kabhī	some other time
मिलती–जुलती (adj.)	miltī-jultī	similar

- अवश्य फिर कभी आइएगा। avaśyă phir āiegā. — Certainly come again sometime.
- यदि आप चाहें तो yadi āp cāheṁ to — If you like...
- अभी रहने दीजिए। abhī rahne dījie — Let it be, for now.
- हमारे पास नहीं है। hamāre pās nahīṁ hai. — We don't have.

■ सा, से, सी sā, se, sī with adjective or noun to express 'somewhat like...; very little/ much etc: See pg. 235, 359

Pragya Went Window Shopping

यह गहरे नील–से रंग की थी। yah gahre nīle-se raṅg kī thī.	It was of dark bluish color.

■ **ठीक वैसा, वैसे, वैसी ही ṭhīk vaisā, vaise, vaisī hī = exatly like that: vaisā, vaise, vaisī agrees with the subject whose likeness or unlikeness to some object is being established.**

•	ठीक वैसी ही साड़ी (f.) तो और हमारे पास नहीं है। ṭhīk vaisī hī sārī (f.) to aur hamāre pās nahīṁ hai.	We don't have another *sari* exactly like that one.
1.	ठीक वैसा ही फूलदान (m.sg.) तो और हमारे पास नहीं है। ṭhīk vaisā hī 'phūldān' (m.) to aur hamāre pās nahīṁ hai.	We don't have another flower vase exactly like that one.
2.	ठीक वैसे ही कुर्ते (m.) तो और हमारे पास नहीं है। ṭhīk vaisā hī 'kurte' (m.pl) to aur hamāre pās nahīṁ hai.	We don't have another 'kurta' exactly like that one.

■ **Perfective Participial Construction: Gram. Ref. pg. 217**

•	मैंने .... एक साड़ी[f.] **टंगी हुई** देखी थी। maiṁne .... ek sārī[f.] **ṭaṁgī huī** dekhī thī.	I had seen a *sari* hanging.
1.	मैंने .... एक दुपट्टा[m.] **टंगा हुआ** देखा था। maiṁne .... ek dupaṭṭā[m.] **ṭaṁgā hu**ā dekhā thā.	I had seen a *dupaṭṭa* hanging.

■ **पसन्द आना pasand ānā = 'to like' is always used with subject + को 'ko', which agrees with the N and G of the object.** **See pg. 185**

■ **To describe color use:**

Subj.+ **रंग का, के, की** raṅg **kā, ke, kī'+ होना honā: to agree with the N and G of the subject in the required tense.**

- यह गहरे नीले रंग की है। It was of dark blue color.
  yah gahre nīle raṅg kī thī.

1. कुर्ता (m.)पीले रंग का था। kurta was of yellow color.
   kurtā (m.) pīle raṅg kā thā.

■ **Use of medio-passive** बिक जाना **'bik jānā' to get sold .**

- वह साड़ी आज सुबह बिक गई। That sari was sold off.
  vah sārī āj subah bik gaī.

  Similarly:

1. सब सामान एक घण्टे में बिक गया। Everything got sold off in one hour.
   sab sāmān ek ghaṇṭe meṁ bik gayā.

■ **याद आना yād ānā = to recall/ to remember is always used with oblique subject followed by the postposition को 'ko'.**

- अब मुझे याद आ रहा है। I recall now.
  ab mujhe yād ā rahā hai.

  Similarly:

1. याद आया? Do you recall?

   yād āyā?

■ **Comparative Adjective: Gram. Ref. pg. 41**

- उससे भी कहीं अधिक सुन्दर much more beautiful than that
  usse bhī kahīṁ adhik sundar

Ex. D 8. Say in Hindi:

Use 'pasand ana':

1. Did you like the book? 2. I liked this book very much. 3. My sister did not like it.

Pragya Went Window Shopping

Use future imperative:

4. Tell me the truth! 5. Come to my place on Sunday. 6. Do visit our shop again sometime.

Use PPC

7. I saw a man lying in front of our house. 8. We saw a dress hanging in the window.

Use the verb 'bik jānā'

9. That dress got sold. 10. All the books got sold. 11. That table cover got sold.

Use the verb 'yād honā'/ 'yād ānā'

11.Do you recall anything? 12.I recall now. 13.I don't recall anything.

Key D 8.

1. आपको किताब पसन्द आई ?	āpko kitāb pasand āī.
2. मुझको यह किताब बहुत पसन्द आई ?	mujhko yah kitāb bahut pasand āī.
3. मेरी बहन को यह किताब पसन्द नहीं आई ?	merī bahan ko yah kitāb pasand nah īṁ āī.
4. मुझे सच बताना।/बताइएगा।	mujhe sac batānā/batāiegā
5. रविवार को मेरे यहाँ आना/आइएगा।	ravīvār ko mere yahāṁ ānā / āiegā.
6. हमारी दुकान पर फिर अवश्य आइएगा।	hamārī dukān par phir avaśyă āiegā.
7. मैंने अपने घर के सामने एक आदमी को लेटे हुए देखा।	maiṁne apne ghar ke sāmne ek ādmī ko leṭe hue dekhā
8. हमने खिड़की में एक पोशाक टंगी हुई देखी।	hamne khiṛkī meṁ ek pośāk ṭaṅgī huī dekhī.
9. वह पोशाक बिक गई।	vah pośāk bik gaī.
10.सब किताबें बिक गईं।	sab kitābeṁ bik gaīṁ.
11.वह मेज़पोश बिक गया।	vah mezpoś bik gayā.
12. आपको कुछ याद है?	āpko kuch yād hai?
13.मुझको अब याद आया	mujhko ab yād āyā.
14. मुझको कुछ याद नहीं ।	mujhko kuch yād nahīṁ.

●●●●●

D 9 Unknown Visitor!

परिचरः	साहिब, एक युवक आपसे मिलने आया था। वह कह रहा था कि एक समय वह आपका विद्यार्थी हुआ करता था।
महमानः	उसने अपना कोई नाम–पता छोड़ा?
परिचरः	जी नहीं। उसने आपके बारे में पूछा। जब मैंने उसे बताया कि आप अभी यहाँ नहीं हैं, तो वह बिना कुछ और कहे–सुने चला गया।
महमानः	वह देखने में कैसा था?
परिचरः	जहाँ तक मुझे याद है, नाटा–सा, कुछ भारी बदन का, रंग गोरा, होंठ पतले, आँखें बड़ी–बड़ी।
महमानः	अजीबो गरीब हुलिया है। क्या उम्र रही होगी? मैं तो ऐसे किसी आदमी को नहीं जानता।
परिचरः	जी यही कोई तीस–पैंतीस साल।
महमानः	जाने दीजिए। यदि वह फिर कभी आए, तो उसका नाम–पता पूछ लीजिएगा। उसे मेरा दूरभाष नम्बर दे दीजिएगा। और उसे बता दीजिएगा कि वह शाम को छह बजे के बाद जब चाहे मुझसे बात कर सकता है।
परिचरः	जी साहिब।

Attendant:	sāhib ek yuvak āpse milne āyā thā. vah kah rahā thā ki ek samay vah āpkā vidyārthī huā kartā thā.
Guest:	usne apnā koī nām-patā choṛā?
Attendant:	jī nahīṁ. usne āpke bāre meṁ pūchā. jab maiṁne use batāyā ki āp abhī yahāṁ nahīṁ haiṁ, to vah binā kuch aur kahe-sune calā gayā.
Guest:	vah dekhne meṁ kaisā thā?
Attendant:	jahāṁ tak mujhe yād hai, nāṭā-sā , kuch bhārī badan kā, raṅg gorā, hoṁṭh patle, aṁkheṁ baṛī-baṛī.
Guest:	ajībo-gariīb huliyā hai. uskī kyā umra rahī hogī? maiṁ to aise kisī ādmī ko nahīṁ jāntā.
Attendant:	jī yahī koī tīs paiṁtīs sāl.
Guest:	jāne dījie. yadi vah phir kabhī āe, to uskā nām patā pūch lījiegā.

use merā dūrbhāṣ nambar de dījiegā. aur use batā dījiegā ki śām ko chah baje ke bād, jab cāhe, mujhse bāt kar saktā hai.

Attendant: jī sāhib.

WORDS AND PHRASES

परिचर (m.)	paricar	attendant/waitor
साहिब (m.)	sāhib	sir
युवक (m.)	yuvak	young man
मिलना (v.i.)	milnā	to meet
विद्यार्थी (m.)	vidyārthī	student
हुआ करता था (hab.past)	huā kartā thā	used to be
महमान (m.)	mahmān	guest
नाम–पता (m.)	nām-patā	name and address
चला गया (past simple)	calā gayā	went away
देखने में (adv.)	dekhne meṁ	to look at
याद होना (v.i.)	yād honā	to remember
नाटा–सा (adj.)	nāṭā-sā	somewhat short
भारी (adj.)	bhārī	heavy
बदन (m.)	badan	body
रंग (m.)	raṅg	complexion
गोरा (adj.)	gorā	fair
होंठ (m.)	hoṁṭh	lips
पतले (adj.)	patle	thin
आँखे (f.pl.)	aṁkheṁ	eyes
बड़ी–बड़ी (adj.)	baṛī-baṛī	very big
अजीबो ग़रीब (adj.)	ajībo-garīb	strange
हुलिया (m.)	huliyā	description
उम्र (f.)	umra	age
रही होगी (presumptive)	rahī hogī	must have been
तीस–पैंतीस	tīs paiṁtīs	thirty-thirtyfive
साल (m.)	sāl	year

दूरभाष नम्बर (m.) dūrbhāṣ nambar telephone number

- बिना कुछ और कहे–सुने without saying any thing else
  binā kuch aur kahe-sune

- जहाँ तक मुझे याद है as far as I remember
  jahāṁ tak mujhe

■ **(v.r. + ने ne) + देना denā : GramRef. pg. 215**

- जाने दीजिए। Let it be.
  jāne dījie !

■ **Use of : मिलने जाना milne jānā to go to meet; मिलने आना milne ānā to come to meet.**

☞ **Regardless of the N and G of the person who goes or comes to meet, or N and G of the person whom he/ she meets, 'milne' is invariable. jānā or ānā agrees with the N and G of the subject.**

- एक युवक आपसे मिलने आया था। A young man had come to meet you.
  ek yuvak āpse milne āyā thā

1. वे कल आपसे मिलने आएँगे। They will come to meet you tomorrow.
   ve kal āpse milne āeṁge.

■ **Frequentative Past Habitual: Gram. Ref. pg. 236**

- वह आपका विद्यार्थी हुआ करता था। He used to be your student.
  vah āpkā vidyārthī huā kartā thā.

1. हम रोज़ समुद्रतट पर जाया करते थे। We used to go on the beach every day.
   ham roz samudrataṭ par jāyā karte the.

■ **Presumptive: Gram. Ref. pg. 202**

- क्या उम्र रही होगी? What age could he be?
  kyā umra rahī hogī?

■ **Conditional: Gram. Ref. pg. 227**

- यदि वह फिर कभी आए, If he comes again sometime
  yadi vah phir kabhī āe,

Unknown Visitor!

- **Use of the verb to know = जानना janană , मालूम होना mālum honā, पता होना patā honā : Gram. Ref. pg. 145**

- मैं तो ऐसे किसी आदमी को नहीं जानता। — I don't know any such man.
- maiṁ to aise kisī ādmī ko nahīṁ jāntā.

- **Imperative future: Graṁ. Ref. pg. 91**

- उसका नाम–पता पूछ लीजिएगा। — Ask him his name and address.
  uskā nām patā pūch lījiegā.
- उसे मेरा दूरभाष नम्बर दे दीजिएगा। — Give him my phone number.
  use merā dūrbhāṣ numbar de dījiegā.
- और उसे बता दीजिएगा.... — And tell him....
  aur use batā dījiegā....

Ex. D 9. Say in Hindi:

1. He went without eating anything. 2. I^{m} slept without turning the light off.

3.They go to meet their children every Monday. 4. He came to meet me yesterday. 5. Soon we$^{m.pl.}$ will come to meet you. 6. It used to snow there every day. 7. He used to be my teacher. 8. A young woman had come to meet him /her. 9. Give them my address.

Use 'jānanā'/ mālūm honā patā honā, ānā: Gram.Ref. 145

10. I know. 11.Do you$^{m.hon.}$ know? 12.I know how to speak Hindi. 13.But I don't know how to read or write Hindi. 14.I know Robert. 15 I know Robert is sick these days.

Key D 9.

1. वह बिना कुछ खाए चला गया।	vah binā kuch khāe calā gayā.
2. मैं बिना बत्ती बुझाए सो गया।	maiṁ binā battī bujhāe so gayā.
3. वे प्रति सोमवार को अपने बच्चों से मिलने जाते हैं।	ve prati somvār ko apne baccoṁ se milne jāte haiṁ.
4. वह कल मुझे मिलने आया।	vah kal mujhe milne āyā.

5. हम जल्दी आपसे मिलने आएँगे।	ham jaldī āpse milne āeṁge.
6. वहाँ रोज़ बर्फ़ पड़ा करती थी।	vahāṁ roz barf paṛā kartī thī.
7. वह मेरा अध्यापक हुआ करता था।	vah merā adhyāpak huā kartā thā.
8. एक युवती उसे मिलने आई थी।	ek yuvatī use milne āyī thī.
9. उन्हें मेरा पता दे दीजिएगा।	unheṁ merā patā de dījiegā.
10. • मैं जानता हूँ।	maiṁ jāntā hūṁ.
• मुझको पता है।	mujhko patā hai.
• मुझको मालूम है।	mujhko mālūm hai.
11. • क्या आप जानते/जानती हैं?	kyā āp jānte haiṁ?
• क्या आपको पता है?	kyā āpko patā hai?
• क्या आपको मालूम है?	kyā āpko mālūm hai?
12. • मैं हिन्दी बोलना जानता/जानती हूँ।	maiṁ hindī bolnā jāntā hūṁ.
• मुझको हिन्दी बोलनी आती है।	mujhko hindī bolnī ātī hai.
13. • लेकिन मैं हिन्दी पढ़ना और लिखना नहीं जानता/जानती ।	lekin maiṁ hindī paṛhnā aur likhnā nahīṁ jāntā / jāntī.
• लेकिन मुझको हिन्दी पढनी और लिखनी नहीं आती।	lekin mujhko hindī paṛhnī aur likhnī nahīṁ ātī.
14. मैं राबर्ट को जानता / जानती हूँ।	maiṁ raubarṭ ko jāntā / jāntī hūṁ
15. • मैं जानता / जानती हूँ कि राबर्ट आजकल बीमार है।	maiṁ jāntā / jāntī hūṁ ki raubarṭ ājkal bīmār hai.
• मुझे मालूम/पता है कि राबर्ट आजकल बीमार है।	mujhe mālūm hai ki raubarṭ ājkal bīmār hai.

●●●●●

D 10 The City Has Changed Much!

(piyūṣ and Jigyasa visit their home town after a long time.)

पियूषः यह शहर कितना बदल गया है! कितनी बड़ी–बड़ी, **चमचमाती हुई** नई ईमारतें बन गई हैं! जहाँ तक मुझे याद है, यहाँ तो **एक ढाबा हुआ करता था।** हम लगभग रोज़ उसमें चाय पीने आया करते थे। यहाँ एक पान की **दुकान हुआ करती थी।** हम लोग आते–जाते वहाँ रुककर **पान खाया करते थे।**

जिज्ञासाः मैं तो इस बात पर हैरान हूँ कि इतने सालों के बाद भी तुम्हें यह सब याद है।

पियूषः बिल्कुल याद है। मुझे उस ढाबे के समोसे, चाट और कुलचे–छोले सब आज भी याद हैं। सच पूछो तो उनकी याद भर से मेरे मुह में पानी आ रहा है।

जिज्ञासाः एक बात बताओ। इन दुकानों का क्या हुआ होगा?

पियूषः तुम भी कभी–कभी अजीब बात करती हो। सब लोग प्रगति कर रहे हैं। वह सामने बड़ा–सा होटल देख रही हो न, यह वही पुरानावाला ढाबा है। वह पानवाला अब बहुत बड़ा व्यापारी बन गया है। वह विदेशों में भांति–भांति के पान और पान मसाले भेजता है।

piyūṣ: yah śahar kitnā badal gayā hai. kitnī baṛī-baṛī camcamātī huī imārteṁ ban gaī haiṁ! jahāṁ tak mujhe yād hai yahāṁ ek ḍhābā huā kartā thā. ham lagbhag roz usmeṁ cāy pīne āyā karte the. yahāṁ ek pān kī dukān huā kartī thī. ham log āte-jāte vahāṁ rukkar pan khāyā karte the.

jigyasa: maiṁ to is bāt par hairān hūṁ kī itne sāloṁ bād bhī tumheṁ yah sab yād hai.

piyūṣ: bilkul yād hai. mujhe us ḍhābe ke samose , chāṭ aur kulce-chole sab āj bhī yād haiṁ. sac pūcho to unkī yād bhar se mere muṁh meṁ pānī ā rahā hai.

jigyasa: ek bāt batāo. in dukānoṁ kā kyā huā hogā?

piyūṣ: tum bhī kabhī-kabhī ajīb bāt kartī ho! sab log pragati kar rahe haiṁ. vah sāmne baṛā- sā hoṭal dekh rahī ho na, yah vahī purānāvālā ḍhābā hai. vah panvālā ab bahut baṛā vyāpārī ban gayā hai. vah videśoṁ meṁ bhāṁti-bhāṁti ke pān aur pān-masāle bhejtā hai.

WORDS AND PHRASES

शहर (m.)	śahar	city
कितना (adj.)	kitnā	how much
चमचमाती हुई (PPC)	camcamātī huī	glittering
ईमारतें (f.pl.)	imārteṁ	monuments
ढाबा (m.)	ḍhābā	small roadside eating shop
लगभग (adv.)	lagbagh	approximately
पान (m.)	pān	betel leaf
पान की दुकान (f.)	pān kī dukān	shop selling 'pan'
आते–जाते (IPC)	āte-jāte	passing by
रुकना (v.i.)	ruknā	to stop
रुककर (kar-conj.)	rukkar	stop by and
प्रगति (f.)	pragati	progress
कभी–कभी (adv.)	kabhī-kabhī	some times
अजीब (adj.)	ajīb	strange
वही (pron./adj.)	vahī	that very
पुरानावाला (adj.)	purānāvālā	the old one
पानवाला (m.)	pānvālā	betel leaf seller
व्यापारी (m.)	vyāpārī	businessman
बन जाना (comp.verb)	ban jana	to become

- □ बदल गया है! badal gayā hai. — has changed
- हुआ करता था huā kartā thā — used to be
- जहाँ तक मुझे याद है jahāṁ tak mujhe yād hai — as far as I remember
- वह अब बहुत बड़ा व्यापारी **बन** गया है। vah ab bahut baṛā vyāpārī ban — He **has become** a big businessman now.

gayā hai.

- हम वहाँ पान खाया करते थे। — We used to eat betel leaf there.
  ham vahāṁ pān khāyā karte the.
- X की याद भर से — just by the thought of X
  X kī yād bhar se
- मेरे मुह में पानी आ रहा है। — my mouth is watering
  mere muṁh meṁ pānī ā rahā hai

■ **Use of I PC: (v.r.+ ता tā / ते te/ ती tī)+ हुआ huā / हुए hue/हुई huī Gram.Ref. pg. 219**

- कितनी बड़ी–बड़ी, **चमचमाती हुई** नई ईमारतें बन गई हैं! — So many huge glittering new buildings have been constructed.
  kitnī baṛī-baṛī **camcamātī huī** imārtaeṁ ban gaī haiṁ!

■ **Past Habitual Frequentative: Gram ref. pg.** 239
(v.r. +) **आ** ā /**या** yā + **करता/करते/करती था/थे/थी/थीं।**

- यहाँ तो एक ढाबा हुआ करता था। — There used to be a Dhaba here.
  yahāṁ to ek ḍhābā huā kartā thā.
- .हम लगभग रोज़ उसमें चाय पीने आया करते थे। — We used to come almost daily to have tea there.
  ham lagbhag roz usmeṁ cāy pīne āyā karte the.
- यहाँ एक पान की दुकान हुआ करती थी। — There used to be a pan shop here.
  yahāṁ ek pān kī dukān huā kartī thī.
- हम लोग आते–जाते वहाँ रुककर पान खाया करते थे। — Passing by, we used to stop there and have pan.
  ham log āte-jāte vahāṁ rukkar pān khāyā karte the.

■ **Use of the suffix सा sā, से se, सी sī : Gram ref. pg- 235, 348**

बड़ा–सा	baṛā-sā	rather big
छोटा–सा	choṭā-sā	rather small
थोड़ा–सा	thoṛā-sā	very little
कौन–सा	kaun-sā	which one
कोई–सा	koī-sā	any one (out of a number of possibilities)
फूल–सा	phūl-sā	like a flower

■ **Use of the suffix न 'na' at the end of the sentence is used as a question tag usually expecting confirmation of the statement: See pg. 306, 362**

- वह सामने **बड़ा-सा** होटल देख रही हो **न**, यह वही **पुरानावाला** ढाबा है।
  vah sāmne **baṛā- sā** hoṭal dekh rahī ho **na**, yah vahī **purānāvālā** ḍhābā hai.
  You see that rather big hotel in front, this is the same old 'ḍhābā'.
- मैं ठीक कह रहा हूँ न? — I am right, isn't it?
  maiṁ ṭhīk kah rahā hūṁ na?
  आप जापान की रहनेवाले हैं न? — You are a resident of Japan, aren't you?
  āp jāpān ke rahnevāle haiṁ na?

■ **वाला vālā/ वाले vāle/ वाली vālī: Gram ref. pg. 167**

- पुरानावाला purānāvālā — the old one
- पानवाला pānvālā — betel leaf seller

Ex. D 10.1 Test your comprehension!

1. हमारे पुरानेवाले घर में पीले गुलाब की बेल हुआ करती थी। — hamāre purānevāle ghar meṁ ek pīle gulāb kī bel huā kartī thī.
2 हमारे सामनेवाले 'फ़्लैट' में एक मूछोंवाला आदमी रहा करता था। — hamāre sāmnevāle 'flaiṭ' meṁ ek mūchoṁvālā ādmī rahā kartā thā.
3. मैं अक्सर यहाँ आया करता हूँ । — maiṁ aksar yahāṁ āyā kartā hūṁ.
4. छात्र रोज़ पीछेवाले मैदान में खेला करते हैं। — chātra roz pīchevāle maidān meṁ khelā karte haiṁ.
5. आप रोज़ सैर किया कीजिए। — āp roz sair kiyā kījie.

6. आप इसवाली व्यायामशाला में आया कीजिए।	āp isvālī vyāyāmśālā meṁ āyā kījie.
7. अबसे मैं हमेशा हिन्दी बोला करूँगा।	abse maiṁ hameśā hindī bolā karūṁgā.
8. अबसे मैं दूरदर्शन पर हिन्दी के धारा–वाहिक देखा करूँगा।	abse maiṁ hindī ke dhārāvāhik dekhā karūṁgā.
9. यह आपकी किताब है न?	yah āpkī kitāb hai na?
10. मकानमालिक का नाम श्रीधर है न?	makānmālik kā nām śridhar hai na?
11. आज रविवार है न?	āj ravivār hai na?
12. मुझको बहुत थोड़ा-सा दीजिए।	mujhko bahut thoṛā-sā dījie.
13. मुझको कोई-सा दीजिए।	mujhko koī-sā dījie.
14. हमने उनको अपना आभार प्रकट किया।	hamne unko apnā ābhār prakaṭ kiyā.
15. उसने हम सबको बधाई दी।	usne ham sab ko badhāī dī.
16. बधाई हो।	badhāī ho.
17. आपका दिन मंगलमय हो।	āpkā din maṅgalmay ho.
18. आपकी यात्रा मंगलमय हो।	āpkī yātrā maṅgalmay ho.

Key D 10.1

1. There used to be a creeper of yellow roses in our old house. 2. A man with mustaches used to live in the flat across from us. 3.I often come here. 4. Students play every day in the field behind. 5. Go for a walk every day. 6. Come to this gym. 7. Now on, I will always speak Hindi. 8. Now on I will watch Hindi serials on TV. 9. This is your book, isn't it? 10. The name of the landlord is Shridhar, isn't it. 11. Today is Sunday, isn't it? 12. Give me very little. 13. Give me any. 14. We expressed our gratitude to them. 15. He congratulated us all. 16. Congratulation! 17. Have a good day! 18. Wish you a safe journey!

●●●●●

D 11 Pragya and Jigyasa in Sari Shop

प्रज्ञा और जिज्ञासा साड़ी की दुकान में

दुकानदार : कहिए, मैं आपकी क्या सेवा कर सकता हूँ?

जिज्ञासा : धन्यवाद। अभी हम देख रही हैं।
(थोड़ी देर बाद, दुकानदार से)
सुनिए। कृपया कुछ अच्छी सिल्क की साड़ियाँ दिखाइए।

दुकानदार : जी, आप इधर आइए। आप मुझे कुछ बताएँ कि आप कैसे अवसर के लिए साड़ी चाहती हैं।

प्रज्ञा : (दुकानदार से) सामान्य प्रयोग में आनेवाली, परन्तु सुन्दर और आधुनिक साड़ियाँ दिखाइए। (जिज्ञासा से) आप चयन में मेरी सहायता कीजिएगा न!

जिज्ञासाः अवश्य!

प्रज्ञा : (साड़ियाँ देखते ही) मुझे वहवाली पसन्द है।

दुकानदारः कौन–सी वाली?

प्रज्ञा : वह पीले रंग की, हरे किनारेवाली।
(जिज्ञासा से) आपको कैसी लगी?

जिज्ञासा : मुझे भी बहुत पसन्द है। आपपर बहुत अच्छी लगेगी।

प्रज्ञा : धन्यवाद।
(दुकानदार से) यह कितने की है?

दुकानदार : पन्द्रह सौ रुपए की।

प्रज्ञा : इस पर कोई छूट?

दुकानदार : जी नहीं। हमारी दुकान पर दाम अन्य दुकानों से कम होते हैं।

प्रज्ञा : ठीक है। दे दीजिए। क्या इसके साथ मिलता–जुलता पेटीकोट और ब्लाउज़ का का कपड़ा भी यहाँ मिलेगा?

दुकानदार : जी, यह देखिए। क्या यह रंग चलेगा? कुछ उन्नीस–बीस का फ़र्क तो है; फिर भी काफ़ी मिलता–जुलता है।

प्रज्ञा : चलेगा। यह भी दे दीजिए। कुल कितने पैसे हुए।

दुकानदार : कुल मिलाकर साढ़े सत्तरह सौ रुपए हुए।

प्रज्ञा : आप 'चैक' स्वीकार करते हैं?

Pragya And Jigyasa In Sari Shop

दुकानदार : जी। (चैक लेते हुए) धन्यवाद! नमस्ते।
प्रज्ञा : नमस्ते।

dukāndār: kahie. maiṁ āpkī kyā sevā kar saktā hūṁ?
jigyāsā: dhany/vād. abhī ham dekh rahī haiṁ.
(thoṛī der bād, dukāndār se)
sunie. kṛpayā kuch acchī silk kī sāṛiyāṁ dikhāie.
dukāndār: jī, āp idhar āie. āp mujhe kuch batāeṁ ki āp kaise avsar ke lie sāṛī cāhtī haiṁ.
Pragya: (dukāndār se) sāmāny/ prayog meṁ ānevālī, parantu sundar aur ādhunik sāṛiyāṁ dikhāie.
(jigyasa se) āp cayan meṁ merī sahāytā kījiegā na!
jigyasa: avaśy/.
Pragya: (sāṛiyāṁ dekhte hī) mujhe yahvālī pasand hai.
Jigaya: kaun-sī vālī?.
Pragya: vah pīle raṅg kī, hare kinārevālī.
(jigyasa se) āpko kaisī lagī?
Jigyasa: mujhe bhī bahut pasand hai? āppar bahut acchī lagegī.
Pragya: dhany/vād.
(dukāndār se) yah kitne kī hai?
dukāndār: pandrah sau rupae kī.
Pragya: ispar koī chūṭ?
dukāndār: jī nahīṁ. hamārī dukān par dām any/ dukānoṁ se kam hote haiṁ.
Pragya: ṭhīk hai. de dījie. kyā iske sāth miltā-jultā 'peṭikoṭ' aur 'blāus' kā kapṛā bhī yahāṁ milegā?
dukāndār: jī yah dekhie. kyā yah raṅg calegā? kuch unnīs-bīs kā fark to hai; phir bhī kāfī miltā-jultā hai.
pragya: calegā. yah bhī de dījie. kul kitne paise hue?
dukāndār: kul milākar sāṛhe sattrah sau rupae hue.
pragya: āp 'caik' svīkār karte haiṁ?
dukāndār: jī.('caik' lete hue) dhany/vād. namaste.
pragya: namaste.

Pragya And Jigyasa In Sari Shop

WORDS AND PHRASES

दिखाना (v.t..)	dikhānā.	to show
बताना (v.t.)	batānā	to tell
अवसर (m.)	avsar	opportunity
चाहना (v.t.)	cāhnā	to desire/to want
सामान्य (adv.)	sāmānyă	normal
प्रयोग (m.)	prayog	use
आनेवाली (adj./n.)	ānevālī	the one that comes
परन्तु (conj.)	parantu	but
सुन्दर (adj.)	sundar	beautiful
आधुनिक (adj.)	ādhunik	modern
चयन (m.)	cayan	selection
कीजिएगा (fut. imper.)	kījiegā	Please do
अवश्य! (adv.)	avaśyă	certainly
वहवाली (adj./pron.)	vahvālī	that one
कौन–सी वाली?(adj..)	kaun-sī vālī?.	which one
मिलता–जुलता (IPC adj.)	miltā-jultā	matching
रंग (m.)	raṅg	color
हरे किनारेवाली (adj./n)	hare kinārevalī	the one with green border
फिर भी (adv.)	phir bhī	even then
स्वीकार करना (v.t.)	svīkār karnā	to accept

- मैं आपकी क्या सेवा कर सकता हूँ? — May I help you, Sir/Ma'm
  maiṁ āpkī kyā sevā kar saktā hūṁ?
- आपको कैसी लगी? — How do like it?
  āpko kaisī lagī?
- अभी हम देख रही हैं। — We are looking.
  abhī ham dekh rahī haiṁ.
- इस पर कोई छूट? — Any discount on it?

ispar koī chūṭ?

- क्या यह रंग चलेगा? — Will this color do?
  kyā yah raṅg calegā?
- काफ़ी मिलता–जुलता है; — It is quite similar.
  kāfī miltā-jultā hai.
- उन्नीस–बीस का फ़र्क है। — There is negligible difference.
  unnīs-bīs kā fark hai.
- चलेगा। — This will do.
  calegā.
- यह भी दे दीजिए। — Please give this too.
  yah bhī de dījie
- कुल कितने पैसे हुए? — How much does it come to?
  kul kitne paise hue?
- कुल मिलाकर साढ़े सत्तरह सौ रुपए हुए। — All together it is seventeen hundred and fifty rupees.
  kul milākar sāṛhe sattrah sau rupae hue.
- आप 'चैक' स्वीकार करते हैं? — Do you accept checks.
  āp 'caik' svīkār karte haim?

■ **Imperative Present: Gram.Ref. pg. 87**

- कहिए! (pres.imper.) kahie — **here:** Yes! **literally:** please say
- कृपया कुछ अच्छी सिल्क की साड़ियाँ दिखाइए।
  kṛipayā kuch acchī silk kī sāṛiyāṁ dikhāie.
  Please show me some good saris.
- सामान्य प्रयोग में आनेवाली साड़ियाँ.........................दिखाइए।
  sāmānyǎ prayog meṁ ānevālī......................... sāṛiyāṁ dikhāie.
  Please show me daily use saris.

■ **Imperative Subjunctive: Gram.Ref. pg. 94**

- आप मुझे कुछ बताएँ .... — Please tell me something.......

āp mujhe kuch batāeṁ ....

- **Imperative Future: Gram.Ref. pg. 91**

- आप चयन में मेरी सहायता कीजिएगा। Please help me in selection.
  āp cayan meṁ merī sahāyatā kījiegā.

- **Use of the verb चाहना cāhnā = to desire/towant Gram.Ref. pg. 150**

- आप कैसे अवसर के लिए साड़ी चाहती हैं। For what occasion you want a sari.
  āp kaise avsar ke lie sārī cāhtī haiṁ.

- **Use of the Suffix वाला, वाले, वाली vālā, vāle, vālī Gram:Ref. pg. 167**

- सामान्य प्रयोग में आनेवाली — that is of daily use
  sāmānyă prayog meṁ ānevālī
- मुझे वहवाली पसन्द है। — I like that one.
  mujhe yahvālī pasand hai.
- कौन–सी वाली? — which one
  kaun-sī vālī?
- हरे किनारेवाली। — the one with a green border
  hare kinārevalī.

- **Use of the Verb लगना 'lagna' Gram:Ref. pg. 139**

- आपको कैसी लगी? — How do like it?
  āpko kaisī lagī?
- आपपर बहुत अच्छी लगेगी। — It will look good on you.
  āppar bahut acchī lagegī.

- **Comparative Adjective Gram:Ref. pg. 41**

- हमारी दुकान पर दाम अन्य दुकानों से कम होते है। — The prices at our shop are less than other shops.
  hamārī dukān par dām anyă dukānoṁ se kam hote haiṁ.

Pragya And Jigyasa In Sari Shop

■ **Gram:Ref. (v.r. + ता/त/ती) + हआ, हुए, हुई pg. 219**

- चैक लेते हुए — while taking checks
  'caik' lete hue

D 11. Say in Hindi:

1. May I help you? 2. What can I do for you? 3. What kind of dress do you like? 4. He said while going out. 5. He was singing while having a bath. 6. Grand mother fell asleep while narrating a story. 7. How old is this shop? 8. This is the oldest shop in town. 9. I need your help. 10. The saris at our shop are more modern than at other shops. 11. Please show me some T-shirt to go with these pants. 12. Please tell me in detail.

Key D 11.

1. मैं आपकी मदद करूँ ? 2. मैं आपके लिए क्या कर सकता हूँ? 3. आप कैसी पोशाक पसन्द करती हैं। 4. उसने बाहर जाते हुए कहा। 5. वह नहाते हुए गा रहा था। 6. दादी माँ कहानी सुनाते–सुनाते सो गई। 7. यह दुकान कितनी पुरानी है? 8.यह शहर में सब से पुरानी दुकान है। 9. मुझे आपकी सहायता चाहिए। 10. हमारी दुकान पर साड़ियाँ अन्य दुकानों से आधुनिक हैं। 11. कृपया इस पैण्ट के साथ मिलता–जुलता कोई टी शर्ट दिखाइए। 12. कृपया मुझे विस्तार से बताइए।

1. maiṁ āpkī madad karūṁ? 2. maiṁ āpke lie kyā kar saktā hūṁ? 3. āp kaisī pośāk pasand kartī haiṁ. 4. usne bāhar jāte hue kahā. 5. vah nahāte hue gā rahā thā. 6 . dādī jī kahānī sunāte-sunāte so gaīṁ.7. yah dukān kitnī purānī hai? 8. yah śahar meṁ sabse purānī dukān hai. 9. mujhe āpkī sahāyatā cāhie. 10. hamārī dukān par sāṛiyāṁ anyă dukānoṁ se ādhunik haiṁ. 11. kṛpayā is paiṇṭ se miltā-jultā koī ṭī-śarṭ dikhāie.12. kṛpayā mujhe vistār se batāie.

●●●●●

D 12 An Excellent Bargain!

विपाषाः इतनी सुन्दर मूर्तियाँ ! कहाँ मिलीं?

विपुलः आज मंगल–बाज़ार लगा हुआ है। वहीं पटरी पर एक बूढ़ा मूर्तिकार दुकान लगाकर बैठा हुआ था। मुझे मूर्तियाँ बहुत पसन्द आईं। सच पूछो तो, उस मूर्ति–कार को इतनी धूप में बैठे हुए देखकर मुझे बहुत दया आई। पूछने पर मुझे दाम भी ठीक–ठीक लगे। मैंने बिना ज़्यादा सोचे, उससे सब मूर्तियाँ ख़रीद लीं। तुम्हें कैसी लगीं?

विपाषाः मुझे भी बहुत अच्छी लगी हैं। कितने में मिलीं?

विपुलः बहुत नहीं। सब मिलाकर तीन सौ रुपए में।

विपाषाः बहुत बढ़िया सौदा!

विपुलः मैंने कोई मोल–भाव नहीं किया। उसने जितने पैसे मांगे, उतने मैंने दे दिए।

विपाषाः और क्या ख़रीदा?

विपुलः कुछ ख़ास नहीं। अपनी माता जी के लिए एक कड़ा। यह अष्टधातु का बना हुआ है। दुकानदार ने बताया कि जिन लोगों को जोड़ों में दर्द होता है, उनको इससे बहुत लाभ होता है। यह देखने में सुन्दर है, और बहुत महँगा भी नहीं। मात्र पच्चीस (25)रुपए में। मुझे विश्वास है कि उन्हें अवश्य पसन्द आएगा।

विपाषाः अब?

विपुलः अब बहुत भूख लगी है। चलो, कुछ खाया जाय।

विपाषाः चलो।

vipāśā: itnī sundar mūrtiyāṁ kahāṁ milīṁ?

vipul: āj maṅgal bāzār lagā huā thā. vahīṁ paṭrī par ek būṛhā mūrtikār dukān lagākar baiṭhā huā thā. mujhe mūrtiyāṁ bahut pasand āīṁ. sac pūcho to, us mūrtikār ko itnī dhūp meṁ baiṭhe hue dekhkar mujhe bahut dayā āī. pūchne par mujhe dām bhī ṭhīk-ṭhīk lage. maiṁne binā zyā-dā soce, usse sab mūrtiyāṁ kharīd līṁ. tumheṁ kaisī lagīṁ?

vipāśā: mujhe bhī bahut acchī lagī haiṁ. kitne meṁ milīṁ?

vipul: bahut nahīṁ. sab milākar tīn sau rupae meṁ.

vipāśā: bahut baṛhiyā saudā!

vipul: maiṁne koī mol-bhāv nahīṁ kiyā. usne jitne paise māṁge, utne

	maiṁne de die.
vipāśā:	aur kyā kharīdā?
vipul:	kuch khās nahīṁ. apnī mātā jī ke lie ek kaṛā. yah aṣṭdhātu kā banā huā hai. dukāndār ne batāyā ki jin logoṁ ko joṛoṁ meṁ dard hotā hai, unko isse bahut lābh hotā hai. yah dekhne meṁ sundar hai, aur bahut mahṁgā bhī nahīṁ hai. mātra paccīs (25) rupae meṁ. mujhe viśvās hai ki unheṁ avaśyă pasand āegā.
vipāśā:	ab?
vipul:	ab mujhe bahut bhūkh lagī hai. calo, kuch khāyā jāy.
vipāśā:	calo.

WORDS AND PHRASES

मूर्तियाँ (f.pl.)	mūrtiyāṁ	statues
मंगल–बाज़ार (m.)	maṅgal bāzār	Tuesday-market
बाज़ार लगा होना	bāzār lagā honā	market to be arranged
मूर्तिकार (m.)	mūrtikār	sculptor
दुकान लगाना	dukān lagānā	to put up a shop
धूप (f.)	dhūp	sunshine
दाम (m.)	dām	price(s)
ठीक–ठीक	ṭhīk-ṭhīk	just right
कड़ा (m.)	kaṛā	bangle
जोड़ (m.)	joṛ	joints
दर्द (m.)	dard	pain
लाभ (m.)	lābh	gain
मात्र (adv.)	mātra	only

- कहाँ मिलीं?
  kahāṁ milīṁ — where did you find them?
- मुझे ....पसन्द आई
  mujhe .. pasand āīṁ. — I liked them
- सच पूछो तो
  sac pūcho to — to tell you the truth
- मुझे बहुत दया आई

mujhe bahut dayā aī	I felt much pity
• मुझे भी बहुत अच्छी लगी हैं। mujhe bhī bahut acchī lagīṁ haiṁ.	I too like them.
• कुछ ख़ास नहीं। kuch khās nahīṁ.	Nothing special.
• यह अष्टधातु का बना हुआ है। yah aṣṭdhātu kā banā huā hai.	It is made of eight metals.
• यह देखने में सुन्दर है। yah dekhne meṁ sundar hai.	It is beautiful to look at.
• मुझे विश्वास है कि...... mujhe viśvās hai ki......	I trust that......
• उन्हें अवश्य पसन्द आएगा। unheṁ avaśyă pasand āegā.	She/He (hon.) will certinly like it.
• मुझे बहुत भूख लगी है। mujhe bahut bhūkh lagī hai.	I am very hungry.
• चलो, कुछ खाया जाय। calo, kuch khāyā jāy.	Come, let's eat something!
• चलो। calo.	Come!
• वहीं पटरी पर एक बूढ़ा मूर्तिकार दुकान लगाकर बैठा हुआ था। vahīṁ paṭrī par ek būṛhā mūrtikār dukān lagākar baiṭhā huā thā.	An old sculptor put up a shop on the pavement and was sitting there.

Use of the Verb लगना 'lagna' : Gram. Ref. pg. 144.

• आज मंगल–बाज़ार लगा हुआ है। āj maṅgal bāzār lagā huā thā.	Today there was Tuesday market.
• मुझे दाम भी ठीक–ठीक लगे। mujhe dām bhī ṭhīk-ṭhīk lage.	I found the prices just right too.

An Excellent Bargain!

■ **Exclamatory opinion:**

- इतनी सुन्दर मूर्तियाँ ! — Such beautiful statues!
  itnī sundar mūrtiyāṁ

1. इतनी भव्य इमारतें! — Such splendid monuments!
   itnī bhavyă imārteṁ!
2. इतना सुहावना मौसम ! — Such pleasant weather!
   itnā suhāvnā mausam!
3. इतने प्यारे बच्चे ! — Such lovely children!
   itne pyāre bacce!
4. इतने महँगे ! — So expensive!
   itne mahṁge!

■ **Use of पिछला/पिछले/पिछली: Grammar Ref. pg. 125**

1. मैं पिछले मंगलवार को यहाँ पहुँचा/ पहुँची। — I arrived here last Tuesday.
   maiṁ pichle maṅgalvār ko yahāṁ pahuṁcā/ pahuṁcī
2. वह पिछले महीने भारत गया/गई। — He/ She went to India last month.
   maiṁ pichle mahīne bhārat gayā.
3. पिता जी पिछले साल बीमारी के कारण दफ़्तर नहीं गए। — Last year, father did not go to office because of illness.
   pitā jī pichle sāl bīmārī ke kāraṇ daftar nahīṁ gae.

4 .हमने पिछले हफ़्ते नया घर ख़रीदा।
hamne pichle hafte nayā ghar kharīdā.
We bought a new house last week.

■ **Use of some other past related time expressions:**

1. वह **परसों** छात्रावास गया / गई।

vah **parsoṁ** chātrāvās gayā / gaī.
He / She went to the hostel the day before yesterday.

2. मैं उसे **घण्टा भर पहले** मिला था / मिली थी।
maiṁ use **ghaṇṭā bhar pahle** milā thā / milī thī.
I met him/her just an hour ago.

3. वह मेरे यहाँ **महीना भर हुआ** आया था/आई थी।
vah mere yahāṁ **mahinā bhar hu** āyā thā ./ āī thī.
He/She came to my place a month ago.

■ **To express liking something after having experienced something: Grammar Ref.: pg. 185**

- मुझे मूर्तियाँ पसन्द आईं। — I liked the statues.
mujhe mūrtiyāṁ pasand āīṁ.

1. उन्हें अवश्य पसन्द आएगा। — She (hon.) will certinly like it.
unheṁ avaśyă pasand āegā.

2. हमें यहाँ का शाकाहारी भोजन हमेशा पसन्द आता है। — We always like the vegetarian. food here.
hameṁ yahāṁ kā śakāhārībhojan
hameśā pasand ātā hai.

■ **Use of the compound verb 'banā honā': Asking & Telling what/where something is made of:**

- यह किस धातु का बना हुआ है? — What metal is this made of?
yah kis dhātu kā banā huā hai?

1. यह कुर्ता किस कपडे का बना है? — What material is this 'kurta' made of?
yah 'kurtā' kis kapṛe kā banā hai?

2. यह कुर्ता 'सिल्क' का बना है। — This 'kurta'is made of silk.
yah 'kurtā' 'silk' kā banā hai.

3. यह चूड़ी किस धातु की बनी है? — What metal is this bangle made of?

yah cūṛī kis dhātu kī banī haī.

4. यह अष्टधातु की बनी हुई है। yah aṣṭdhātu kī banī huī hai. — This is made of eight metals.

5. यह घड़ी कहाँ की बनी है? yah ghaṛī kahāṁ kī banī haī? — Where was this made?

6. यह घड़ी भारत की बनी है? yah ghaṛī bhārat kī banī haī? — Where was this made?

Use of the Verb मिलना milā : Asking & Tellingwhere one found something?

- आपको ये मूर्तियाँ कहाँ मिलीं? āpko ye mūrtiyāṁ kahāṁ milīṁ? — Where did you get these statues?
- मुझे ये मूर्तियाँ पटरी पर एक मूर्तिकार से मिलीं? mujhe ye mūrtiyāṁ paṭrī par ek mūrtikār se milīṁ. — I got them at the pavement from a sculptor.

1. आपको यह बच्चा कहाँ मिला? āpko yah baccā kahāṁ milā? — Where did you find this child?

2. मुझे यह बच्चा मंदिर के सामने मिला। mujhe yah baccā mandir ke sāmne milā. — I found this child in front of the temple.

Another way of saying the same thing.

- मैंने ये मूर्तियाँ पटरी पर एक मूर्तिकार से ख़रीदीं? maiṁne ye mūrtiyāṁ paṭrī par ek mūrtikār se kharīdīṁ. . — I bought these statues from a sculptor on the pavement

2. मैंने यह बच्चा मंदिर के सामने पड़ा हुआ पाया? — I found this child lying in front of the temple.

maiṁne yah baccā mandir ke
sāmne paṛā huā pāyā.

Ex D 12.1. Say in Hindi:

1. Where did you find this watch? 2. Where did you find these gloves? 3. I got them from a vendor. 4. I found these gloves in Tuesday market. 5. This bangle is made of five metals. 6. This is made in Sweden. 7. I bought these clothes in the Monday market. 8. I think you are mistaken. 9.You are right. 10. Such delicious food! 11. So inexpensive! 12. So stupid!

Key D 12.1

1. आपको यह घड़ी कहाँ मिली?	āpko yah ghaṛī kahāṁ milī?
2. आपको ये दस्ताने कहाँ मिले?	āpko ye dastāne kahāṁ mile?
3. मुझे ये जुराबें एक ठेलेवाले से मिलीं।	mujhe ye jurābeṁ ek ṭhelevāle se milīṁ.
4. मुझे ये दस्ताने मंगल–बाज़ार में मिले।	mujhe ye dastāne maṅgal bāzār meṁ mile.
5. यह चूड़ी पँचधातु की बनी है।	yah cūṛī paṁcdhātu kī banī hai?
6. यह घड़ी स्वीडन की बनी है।	yah ghaṛī sweden kī banī hai?
7. मैंने यह कपड़े सोम–बाज़ार में ख़रीदे?:	maiṁne ye kapṛe som- bāzār meṁ kharīde.
8. मेरे खयाल में तुम्हें गलती लगी है।	mere khayāl meṁ tumheṁ galtī lagī hai.
9. आप ठीक कह रहे हैं।	ap ṭhīk kah rahe haiṁ.
10. इतना स्वादिष्ट भोजन!	itnā svādiṣṭ bhojan !
11. इतना सस्ता	itnā sastā !
12. इतना मूर्ख !	itnā mūrkh!

●●●●●

D 13 Think Before You Accuse

विपुलः (परिचर से) मेरी घड़ी यहाँ छूट गई थी। क्या किसीने देखी?

परिचरः जी, मैंने कुछ देर पहले एक आदमी को यहाँ से घड़ी लेकर जाते हुए देखा था। अरे! अभी–अभी तो यहीं था। कहाँ चला गया? इस समय तो कहीं दिखाई नहीं दे रहा।

विपुलः वह देखने में कैसा था?

परिचरः यही कोई बीस पच्चीस साल का युवक। लाल कमीज़ और नीली जीन्स पहने हुए था। देखिए, वह रहा, वहाँ, उस मेज़ पर बैठा हुआ कुछ पी रहा है।

विपुलः चलिए। वहीं चलकर पूछते हैं।
(युवक के पास जाकर)
सुनिए। मेरी घड़ी वहाँ, उस मेज़ पर, छूट गई थी। लगता है कि आप उसे गलती से उठा लाए हैं।

युवकः जी, मैं आपकी घड़ी के बारे में कुछ नहीं जानता। यह तो मेरी अपनी घड़ी है। मैंने इसे पिछले महीने ही ख़रीदा था।

विपुलः ज़रा दिखाइए। मेरी घड़ी पर न्यु यॉर्क की दुकान का नाम–पता भी लिखा है। और मेरे पास उसकी रसीद भी है।

युवकः मैंने आपसे कहा न कि यह मेरी अपनी घड़ी है। अपना और मेरा समय ख़राब न करें। जाइए। जाकर अपनी घड़ी कहीं और देखिए।

विपुलः लगता है आप ऐसे नहीं मानेंगे। आप सीधे से दिखा दीजिए वरना,

युवकः वरना क्या?

विपुलः वरना हमें पुलीस को बुलाना पड़ेगा।

युवकः ठीक है, बुलाइए पुलीस को; संयोग से, मेरे पास अपनी रसीद भी है।
पहले तो अपनी चीज़ संभालकर नहीं रखते; फिर आ जाते हैं, दूसरों पर चोरी का इल्ज़ाम लगाने।
(घड़ी उतारकर दिखाते हुए) यह लीजिए, पहचानिए, क्या यह आपकी है?

विपुलः (लज्जित होते हुए) देखिए। मैं मानता हूँ कि मुझसे बहुत बड़ी भूल हुई है।

मेरी भूल आसानी से क्षमा के लायक नहीं है। फिर भी मेरी आप से हाथ जोड़ कर प्रार्थना है कि कृपया मुझे क्षमा करें।

युवकः ठीक है। आगे से अपनी चीज़ें संभाल कर रखें। बिना वजह न स्वयं परेशान हों, न दूसरों को परेशान करें।

विपुलः आप ठीक कह रहे हैं। नमस्ते।

युवकः नमस्ते।

vipul: (paricār se) merī gharī yahāṁ chūṭ gaī thī. kyā kisīne dekhī?

paricār: jī, maiṁne kuch der pahle ek ādmī ko yahāṁ se gharī lekar jāte hue dekhā thā. Are! abhī-abhī to yahīṁ thā. is samay to kahīṁ dikhāī nahīṁ de rahā.

vipul: vah dekhne meṁ kaisā thā?

paricār: yahī koī bīs-paccīs sāl kā yuvak. lāl kamīz pahne hue thā. dekhie! vah rahā, vahāṁ us mez par baiṭhā huā kuch pī rahā hai.

vipul: calie, vahīṁ calkar pūchte haiṁ.
(yuvak ke pās jākar)
sunie! merī gharī vahāṁ, us mez par, chūṭ gaī thī. lagtā hai ki āp use galtī se uṭhā lāe haiṁ.

yuvak: jī maiṁ āpkī gharī ke bare meṁ kuch nahīṁ jāntā. yah to merī apnī gharī hai. maiṁne ise pichle mahīne hī kharīdā thā.

vipul: zarā dikhāie. merī gharī par nyu yaurk kī dukān kā nām-patā bhī likhā hai. aur mere pās uskī rasīd bhī hai.

yuvak: maiṁne āpse kahā na ki yah merī apnī gharī hai. apnā aur merā samay kharāb na kareṁ. jāie! jākar apnī gharī kahīṁ aur dekhie.

vipul; lagtā hai āp aise nahīṁ māneṁge. āp sīdhe se dikhā dījie, varnā,....

Yuvak: varnā kyā?

vipul: varnā hameṁ pulīs ko bulānā paṛegā.

yuvak: ṭhīk hai, bulāie pulīs ko! saṁyog se, mere pās bhī apnī rasīd hai. ek to apnī cīz saṁbhālkar nahīṁ rakhte, phir ā jāte haiṁ dūsroṁ par corī kā ilzām lagāne.
(gharī utārkar dikhāte hue) yah lījie, pahcānie, kyā yah āpkī hai?

vipul: (lajjit hote hue) maiṁ māntā hūṁ ki mujh se bahut baṛī bhūl huī hai. merī bhūl āsānī se kṣamā ke lāyak nahīṁ hai. phir bhi merī āpse hāth joṛkar prārthnā hai ki kṛpayā mujhe kṣamā kareṁ.

yuvak: ṭhīk hai. āgese apnī cīzem saṁbhālkar rakheṁ. binā vajah na svayam pareśān hoṁ, na dūsroṁ ko pareśān kareṁ.

Think Before You Accuse!

vipul: āp ṭhīk kah rahe haiṁ. namaste.
yuvak: namaste.

WORDS AND PHRASES

घड़ी (f.)	gharī	watch/ time clock
छूट गई थी	chūṭ gaī thī	got left
अभी–अभी	abhī-abhī	just now
लेकर (kar-conj.)	gharī lekar	take and
जाते हुए (IPC.)	jāte hue	going
अरे!	are!	exclamation!
दिखाई देना	dikhāī denā	to be visible
युवक	yuvak	young man
पहने हुए PPC	pahne hue	having worn
बैठा हुआ PPC	baiṭhā huā	seated
चलकर kar-conj.	calkar	go and
पूछना	pūchnā	to ask
गलती से	galtī se	by mistake
जानना (v.t.)	jānnā	to know
पिछले महीने	pichle mahīne	last month
ही	hī (emphatic)	
नाम–पता	nām-patā	address
रसीद (f.)	rasīd	receipt
मेरी अपनी	merī apnī	my own
मेरा समय	merā samay	my time
कहीं और	kahīṁ aur	somewhere else
ऐसे	aise	like this/so easily
सीधे से (adv.)	sīdhe se	without hassle straight away
वरना	varnā	or else

बुलाना पड़ेगा	bulānā paregā	will have to call
ठीक है	ṭhīk hai	okay!
संयोग से (adv.)	saṁyog se	luckily
एक तो	ek to	on the one hand
अपनी चीज़	apnī cīz	one's own stuff
संभालकर रखना	saṁbhālkar rakhnā	keep safely
फिर	phir	then
आ जाते हैं	ā jāte haiṁ	(they) come
(here: spoken with some contempt)		
दूसरों पर	dūsroṁ par	on others
चोरी (f.)	corī	theft
इल्ज़ाम (m.)	ilzām	blame
का इल्ज़ाम लगाना	kā ilzām lagānā	to blame for
उतारना (v.i.)	utārnā	to remove
उतारकर (kar-conj.)	utārkar	remove and
दिखाते हुए (IPC)	dikhāte hue	while showing
आसानी से	āsānī se	easily
क्षमा के लायक	kṣamā ke lāyak	worthy of being forgiven
आगे से	āge se	in future
दूसरों को	dūsroṁ ko	to others
अपनी चीज़ें	apnī cīzeṁ	one's own stuff
संभालकर	saṁbhālkar	carefully/ safely
न...... न......	na...na..	neither ...nor..
बिना वजह	binā vajah	without reason
स्वयं	svayam	oneself
परेशान	pareśān	upset/ troubled

- कुछ देर पहले — a short while ago
  kuch der pahle

Think Before You Accuse!

• वह रहा vah rahā	there he is
• चलिए। calie	come!
• लगता है lagtā hai	it seems
• वरना क्या? varnā kyā?	or else what?
• वह देखने में कैसा था? vah dekhne meṁ kaisā thā?	How was he to look at.?
• कोई बीस पच्चीस साल का koī bīs-paccīs sāl kā	About twent to twent-five years old
• युवक के पास जाकर yuvak ke pās jākar	Go near the man and
• आप ऐसे नहीं मानेंगे। āp aise nahīṁ maneṁge	You won't listen to me so easily.
• मैं मानता हूँ। maiṁ māntā hūṁ	I admit.
• मुझसे भूल हुई है। mujhse bhūl huī hai.	I made a mistake.
• मेरी आपसे हाथ जोड़कर प्रार्थना है। merī āpse hāth joṛkar prārthnā hai.	I beg you with folded hands.
• आप ठीक कह रहे हैं। āp ṭhīk kah rahe haiṁ.	You are right!

■ **Use of the compound verb** छूट जाना **'chūṭ janā' in the sense of: (1) departure of a train, bus etc (2) missing a train, bus etc. (3)leaving something somewhere inadvertently.**

• मेरी घड़ी यहाँ छूट गई थी।	I left my watch here.

merī gharī yahāṁ chūṭ gaī thī.

1. मेरी गाड़ी छूट गई । — I missed my train .
merī gāṛī chūṭ gaī .

☞ **Use of the v.i. छूटना 'chūṭnā' in the sense of 'departure' of train, bus etc.**

2. गाड़ी कितने बजे छूटेगी? — What time will the train leave?
gāṛī kitne baje chūṭegī.

3. गाड़ी छूटनेवाली है। — The train is about to leave?
gāṛī chūṭnevālī hai.

■ **(subject + को ko) + दिखाई देना dikhāī denā : See pg. 134, 253.**

• इस समय तो कहीं दिखाई नहीं दे रहा।
is samay to kahīṁ dikhāī nahīṁ de rahā.

At this time he is not visible anywhere./
I cannot see him anywhere at this time'

Similary:

1. मुझको एक आदमी दिखाई दे रहा है। — I can see a man.
mujhko ek ādmī dikhāī de rahā hai.

2. आपको क्या दिखाई दे रहा है? — What can you see?
āpko kyā dikhāī de rahā hai?

3. मुझको कुछ दिखाई नहीं दे रहा। — I cannot see anything.
mujhko kuch dikhāī nahīṁ de rahā.

■ **Outer Compulsion Structure: Gram Ref. pg. 213**

• वरना हमें पुलीस को बुलाना पड़ेगा। — Or else we will have to call the police.
varnā hameṁ pulīs ko bulānā paṛegā.

■ **Use of the conjunct verb 'लायक होना lāyak honā: Be worthy of.....**
(1) noun + के लायक होना ke lāyak honā; Example 1,2
(2) (verb root + ne) + लायक होना lāyak honā: Example 3, 4.

Think Before You Accuse!

1. मेरी भूल आसानी से क्षमा के लायक नहीं है
merī bhūl āsānī se kṣamā ke lāyak nahīṁ hai.
My mistake is not worth forgiving easily.

2. आपकी पसन्द प्रशंसा के लायक है।
āpkī pasand praśaṁsā ke lāyak hai
Your choice is worthy of praise.

3. यह शहर देखने लायक है।
yah śahar dekhne lāyak hai.
This city is worth seeing.

4. यह किताब पढ़ने लायक है।
yah kitāb paṛhne lāyak hai.
This book is worth reading.

■ **Use of Perfective Participial Construction- adverbial use: Gram. Ref. pg. 217**

- लाल कमीज़ और नीली जीन्स पहने हुए था।
lāl kamīz aur nīlī jīns pahne hue thā.
He wore red shirt and blue jeans.

1. वहाँ, उस मेज़ पर बैठा हुआ कुछ पी रहा है।
vahāṁ us mez par baiṭhā huā kuch pī rahā hai.
There, sitting at that table, he is drinking something.

■ **Use of Imperfective Participial Construction- adverbial use: Gram. Ref. pg. 219**

- लज्जित होते हुए
lajjit hote hue
while feeling embarrassed

■ **Use of Present Imperative: Gram. Ref. pg. 87**

- ज़रा दिखाइए
zarā dikhāie
Just show me please!

- चलिए।
come!

calie!

- सुनिए। — Listen!
  sunie.
- जाइए। जाकर अपनी घड़ी कहीं और देखिए। — Go and look for your watch somewhere else.
  jāie! jākar apnī gharī kahīṁ aur dekhie.
- आप सीधे से दिखा दीजिए वरना,.... — Show me straight away, or else...
  āp sīdhe se dikhā dījie, varnā,....
- यह लीजिए। — Here you are!
  yah lījie.
- पहचानिए। — Identify it!
  pahcānie

■ Use of Subjunctive Imperative: Gram. Ref. pg. 94

- अपना और मेरा समय ख़राब न करें। — Don't waste your own and my time.
  apnā aur merā samay kharāb na kareṁ.
- कृपया मुझे क्षमा करें। — Please forgive me!
  kṛpayā mujhe kṣamā kareṁ.
- आगे से अपनी चीज़ें संभाल कर रखें। — In future take care of your stuff.
  āge se apnī cīzeṁ saṁbhālkar rakheṁ.
- बिना वजह न स्वयं परेशान हों, न दूसरों को परेशान करें। — For no reason, neither be troubled yourself, not trouble others.
  binā vajah na svayam pareśān hoṁ, na dūsroṁ ko pareśān kareṁ.

●●●●●

D 14 Exploring The City!

- क्षमा कीजिए, यहाँ पास में कोई डाकघर है?
- जी, इस सड़क पर तो नहीं है, लेकिन गाँधी मार्ग पर एक डाकघर है।
- गाँधी मार्ग कहाँ है?
- आप इसी सड़क पर लगभग पचास मीटर सीधे जाइए। पहले चौराहे पर दाएँ मुड़िए। सीधे चलते जाइए। यह सड़क काफ़ी लम्बी है। कुछ आगे, सड़क की दायीं ओर एक बहुत बड़ा होटल है। डाकघर ठीक उसकी बगल में है।
- धन्यवाद! क्या यहाँ से बहुत दूर है?
- जी नहीं, यहाँ से बहुत दूर नहीं है। पैदल सिर्फ़ पाँच–सात मिनट का रास्ता है।
- एक और बात। क्या यहाँ पास में कोई बैंक भी है?
- जी, ठीक वहीं, होटल की एक ओर डाकघर है, और दूसरी ओर बैंक है।
- बैंक कितने बजे खुलता है?
- बैंक सुबह दस बजे खुलता है।
- और डाकघर?
- डाकघर भी सुबह दस बजे खुलता है।
- बैंक कितने बजे तक खुला रहता है?
- बैंक सुबह दस बजे से दोपहर दो बजे तक खुला रहता है।
- और डाकघर?
- डाकघर सुबह दस बजे से शाम को पाँच बजे तक खुला रहता है।
- धन्यवाद! नमस्ते।

- kṣamā kījie. yahāṁ pās meṁ koī ḍākghar hai?
- jī, is saṛak par to nahīṁ hai, lekin gāṁdhī mārg par ek ḍākghar hai.
- gāṁdhī mārg kahāṁ hai?
- āp is saṛak par lagbhag pacās mīṭar sīdhe jāie. pahle caurāhe par dāeṁ muṛie.
  sīdhe calte jāie. yah saṛak kāfī lambī hai. kuch āge, saṛak kī dāyīṁ or ek bahut baṛā hoṭal hai. dākghar ṭhīk uskī bagal meṃ hai.
- dhanyăvād. kyā yahāṁ se bahut dūr hai?

- jī nahīṁ, yahāṁ se bahut dūr nahīṁ hai?
- paidal sirf pāṁc-sāt minaṭ kā rāstā hai.
- ek aur bāt. kyā yahāṁ pās meṁ koī baiṅk bhī hai?
- jī, ṭhīk vahīṁ, hoṭal kī ek or ḍākghar hai, aur dūsrī or baiṅk.
- baiṅk kitne baje khultā hai?
- baiṅk subah das baje khultā hai
- aur ḍākghar?
- ḍākghar bhī subah das baje khultā hai.
- baiṅk kitne baje tak khulā rahtā hai?
- baiṅk subah das baje se dopahar do baje tak khulā rahtā hai.
- aur ḍākghar?
- ḍākghar subah das baje se śām ko paṁc baje tak khulā rahtā hai
- dhanyăvād. namaste.

Ex. D 14.1 Say in Hindi:

1. Is the bank open? 2. Yes, the bank is open. 3. No, the bank is not open. 4. Wat time does the bank open? 5. The bank opens at 10 o'clock. 6. Until when does the bank remain open? 7. The bank remains open from 10 a.m. to 2 p.m.? 8. Is the post office open? 9. Yes, the post office is open. 10. No, the post office is not open. 11.What time does the post office open? 12.The post office also opens at 10 o'clock. 13. Until when is the post office open? 14. The post office is open from 10 o'clock in the morning to 5 o'clock in the evening.

Key D 14.1

1. बैंक खुला है?	baiṅk khulā hai?
2. जी, बैंक खुला है।	jī, baiṅk khulā hai?
3. जी नहीं, बैंक खुला नहीं है?	jī nahīṁ, baiṅk khulā nahīṁ hai?
4. बैंक कितने बजे खुलता है?	baiṅk kitne baje khultā hai?
5. बैंक दस बजे खुलता है।	baiṅk das baje khultā hai?
6. बैंक कितने बजे तक खुला रहता है?	baiṅk kitne baje tak khulā rahtā hai?
7. बैंक सुबह दस बजे से दोपहर दो बजे तक खुला रहता है।	baiṅk subah das baje se dopahar do baje tak khulā rahtā hai?
8. डाकघर खुला है?	ḍākghar khulā hai?

9. जी, डाकघर खुला है।	jī, ḍākghar khulā hai.
10. जी नहीं, डाकघर खुला नहीं है	jī nahīṁ, ḍākghar khulā nahīṁ hai?
11. डाकघर कितने बजे खुलता है?	ḍākghar kitne baje khultā hai?
12. डाकघर भी सुबह दस बजे खुलता है।	ḍākghar bhī subah das baje khultā hai.
13. डाकघर कितने बजे तक खुला रहता है?	ḍākghar kitne baje tak khulā rahtā hai?
14. डाकघर सुबह दस बजे से शाम को पाँच बजे तक खुला रहता है।	ḍākghar subah das baje se śām ko paṁc baje tak khulā rahtā hai.

Practice with these cues:

दवाई की दुकान(f.) pharmacy,

चिड़ियाघर (m.)	zoo
मंदिर (m.)	temple
पुस्तकालय (m.)	library

●●●●●

D 15 Plan An Evening Together!

प्रज्ञा: आप शनिवार शाम को क्या कर रहे हैं?

दक्ष: मैं एक संगीत समारोह में जाऊँगा। यह हनुमान जयन्ती पर संकट मोचन मंदिर में होता है। यह बनारस का सबसे बड़ा संगीत सम्मेलन है। इसमे भारत के कोने–कोने से बड़े–बड़े संगीतकार आते हैं। आप मेरे साथ चलना चाहेंगी?

प्रज्ञा: क्यों नहीं? सहर्ष चलूँगी। मैं शुक्रवार शाम को दफ़्तर के काम से बाहर जाऊँगी परन्तु शनिवार दोपहर तक लौट आऊँगी। समारोह कितने बजे होगा?

दक्ष: समारोह रात को दस बजे शुरू होगा।

प्रज्ञा: तब ठीक है। हम कहाँ मिलेंगे?

दक्ष: मंदिर के सामने, फूलवाले की दुकान के पास।

प्रज्ञा: बहुत बढ़िया। तो फिर लगभग आठ–साढ़े आठ बजे मिलते हैं। तब तक के लिए, नमस्ते।

दक्ष: नमस्ते।

Pragya: āp śanivār śām ko kyā kar rahe haiṁ?

Daksh: maiṁ ek saṅgīt samāroh meṁ jāūṁgā. yah hanumān jayanti par saṅkaṭ mocan mandir meṁ hotā hai. yah banāras kā sab se baṛā saṅgīt sammelan hai. ismeṁ deś ke kone-kone se baṛe-baṛe saṅgītkār āte haiṁ. āp mere sāth calnā cāheṁgī?

Pragya: kyoṁ nahīṁ? saharṣ calūṁgī. maiṁ śukravār śām ko daftar ke kām se bāhar jāūṁgī; parantu śanivār dopahar tak lauṭ āūṁgī. samāroh kitne baje hogā?

Daksh: samāroh rāt ko das baje śurū hogā.

Pragya: tab ṭhīk hai. ham kahāṁ mileṁge?

Daksh: mandir ke sāmne, phūlvāle kī dukān ke pās.

Pragya: bahut baṛhiyā! to phir lagbhag āṭh-saṛhe āṭh baje milte haiṁ. tab tak ke lie, namaste.

Daksh: namaste.

Plan An Evening Together!

WORDS AND PHRASES

संकट मोचन मंदिर (m.)	saṅkaṭ mocan mandir	Hanuman temple in Varanasi
संगीत समारोह (m.)	saṅgīt samāroh	music festival
हनुमान (m.)	Hanuman	monkey God of Hindus
जयन्ती (f.)	jayanti	birthday celebrations
हनुमान जयन्ती	hanumān jayanti	birthday of Lord Hanuman
कोना (m.)	konā	corner
कोने–कोने से	kone-kone se	from far and wide
बड़े–बड़े (f.)	baṛe-baṛe	very big
संगीतकार (m.)	saṅgiīkār	musician
सहर्ष (adv.)	saharṣ	with pleasure
परन्तु (conj.)	parantu	but
लौटना/लौट आना (v.i.)	lauṭnā/lauṭ ānā	to return
लौट आऊँगी	lauṭ āūṁgī	I will return
शुरू होना (v.i..)	śurū honā	to begin
फूलवाला (m.)	phūlvālā	florist
फूलवाले की दुकान (f.)	phūlvāle kī dukān	flower shop

- आप शनिवार शाम को क्या कर रहे हैं ? What are you doing Saturday evening?
  āp śanivār śām ko kyā kar rahe haiṁ?
- यह हनुमान जयन्ती पर होता है। This takes place on Hanuman Jayanti.
  yah hanumān jayanti par hotā hai.

■ **Use of Future Simple: Gram. Ref. pg. 105**

- संगीत सम्मेलन कितने बजे होगा? What time will the music meet take place?
  sañgīt sammelan kitne baje hogā?
- संगीतसम्मेलन रात को दस बजे शुरू Music meet will begin at 10 p.m.

होगा।
sañgīt sammelan rāt ko das baje śurū hogā.

- आप मेरे साथ चलना चाहेंगी? āp mere sāth calnā cāheṁgī? — Would you like to come with me?
- सहर्ष चलूँगी। saharṣ calūṁgī. — I will come gladly.

Ex. D 15. Say in Hindi:

1. What are you doing Sunday afternoon? 2. Annual Function will take place on 14th of November. 3. This happens every year on Ram Navami. 4. What time will the sports begin? 5. The sports will begin the day after tomorrow at 11 a.m. 6. When will Vijay Dashmi be this year? 7. I will not be able to attend the meeting. 8. They will be very happy to meet you.

Key D 15.

1. आप रविवार अपराह्न में क्या कर रहे/रही हैं ? — āp ravivār aprāhn meṁ kyā kar rahe/rahī haiṁ?
2 वार्षिक समारोह चौदह नवम्बर को होगा। — vārṣik samāroh caudah 'navambar' ko hogā?
3. यह हर साल राम नवमी पर होता है। — yah har sāl rām navamī par hotā hai.
4. खेल कितने बजे शुरू होंगे। — khel kitne baje śurū hoṁge?
5. खेल परसों सुबह ग्यारह बजे शुरू होंगे। — khel parsoṁ subah gāyarah baje śurū hoṁge?
6. इस वर्ष विजय दशमी कब होगी? — is varṣ vijay daśmī kab hogī?
7. मैं गोष्ठी में नहीं आ पाऊँगी। — maiṁ goṣthī meṁ nahīṁ ā pāūṁgī.
8. वे आपसे मिलकर बहुत खुश होंगे। — ve āpse milkar bahut khuś hoṁge.

●●●●●

D 16 Phone An Old Friend

श्रोताः हैलो!

विपुलः हैलो! पियूष घर पर हैं?

श्रोताः जी, मैं उन्हें अभी बुलाता हूँ। लीजिए, बात कीजिए।

पियूषः हैलो! कहिए। मैं पियूष बोल रहा हूँ। आप कौन बोल रहे हैं?

विपुलः हैलो पियूष, मैं विपुल बोल रहा हूँ। यहाँ दफ़्तर के काम से आया था। सोचा, तुमसे भी मिल लूँ। तुम कल क्या कर रहे हो?

पियूषः शाम को पाँच बजे तक अपने दफ़्तर में; उसके बाद खाली रहूँगा। यदि तुम भी खाली हो, तो मेरे यहाँ आ जाना। साथ बैठकर भोजन करेंगे; उसके बाद कुछ पुरानी यादें ताज़ी करेंगे और एक–दो बाज़ी शतरंज खेलेंगे। वैसे तुम कब तक यहाँ हो?

विपुलः मैं अगले रविवार तक यहाँ हूँ। कल दफ़्तर के बाद मैं भी खाली हूँ। मैं शाम को छह–साढ़े छह बजे तक तुम्हारे यहाँ पहुँच जाऊँगा।

पियूषः बहुत बढ़िया। चलो फिर, कल मिलते है। तब तक के लिए, नमस्ते।

विपुलः नमस्ते!

śrotā: Hailo!

vipul: Hailo! piyūṣ ghar par haiṁ?

śrotā: Jī, maiṁ unheṁ abhī bulātā hūṁ. lījie, bāt kījie.

piyūṣ: hailo! kahie. maiṁ piyūṣ bol rahā hūṁ. āp kaun bol rahe haiṁ?

vipul: hailo, maiṁ vipul bol rahā hūṁ. yahāṁ daftar ke kām se āyā thā ; socā, tumse bhī mil lūṁ.tum kal kyā kar rahe ho?

piyūṣ: śām ko paṁc baje tak apne daftar meṁ; uske bād khālī rahūṁgā. yadi tum bhī khālī ho, to mere yahāṁ ā jānā. sāth baiṭhkar bhojan kareṁge; uske bād kuch purānī yādeṁ tāzī kareṁge, aur ek - do bāzī śatrañj kheleṁge. vaise tum kab tak yahāṁ ho?

vipul: maiṁ agle ravivār tak yahāṁ hūṁ. kal daftar ke bad maiṁ bhī khālī hūṁ. maiṁ śām ko chah-sāṛhe chah baje tak tumhāre yahāṁ pahuṁc

jāūṁgā.
piyūṣ: bahut baṛhiyā ! calo phir, kal milte haiṁ. tab tak ke lie, namaste.
vipul: namaste!

WORDS AND PHRASES

कहिए। (imperative)	kahie!	Yes!
सोचना (v.t.)	socnā	think
उसके बाद (adv)	uske bād	after that
खाली रहना (v.i.)	khāli rahnā	to be free.
यदि (conditional)	yadi	if
आ जाना (comp.verb) tive)	ā jānā.	come.(future impera-
साथ बैठकर (kar-conj.)	sāth baiṭhkar	sit together and
भोजन करना (v.t.)	bhojan karnā	to eat
बातचीत करना (v.t.)	bātcīt karnā	to talk
एक–दो (adj.)	ek - do	a couple of
बाज़ी (f.)	bāzī	turn in a game
शतरंज खेलना (v.t.)	śatrañj khelenā	to play chess.
बहुत बढ़िया	bahut baṛhiyā	very good
पहुँच जाना (comp.verb)	pahuṁc jānā	to arrive.
तब तक के लिए (adv.)	tab tak ke lie	untill then

- छह– साढ़े छह बजे तक
  chah- saṛhe chah baje tak
  By six- six thirty
- मैं उन्हें अभी बुलाता हूँ।
  maiṁ unheṁ abhī bulātā hūṁ.
  I shall get him on the line right away.
- आप कौन बोल रहे हैं?
  āp kaun bol rahe haiṁ?
  Who is speaking?

Phone An Old Friend

■ यदि **yadi.......तो to.... : Conditional Structure:**

Gram. Ref. pg. 227

- यदि तुम भी खाली हो, तो मेरे यहाँ आ जाना।
  yadi tum bhī khālī ho, to mere yahāṁ ā jānā.
  If you are free too, then come to my place.

■ **Plans to meet : 'When, Where, What time?'**

- हम कहाँ /कब/कितने बजे मिलेंगे?
  ham kahāṁ/ kab/ kitne baje mileṁge?
  Where/When/ What time shall we meet?
- हमें कहाँ /कब/कितने बजे मिलना होगा?
  hamem kahāṁ/ kab/ kitne baje milnā hogā?.
  Where/When/ What time will we have to meet?

■ **Setting up to meet : at a certain time, on a certain day, in a certain month, at a certain place etc.:**

- हम सोमवार को, अपराह्न दो बजे मेरे दफ़्तर में मिलेंगे।
  ham somvār ko aprāhn do baje mere daftar meṁ mileṁge.
  We will meet at 2 o'clock in the afternoon in my office.
- आप आज शाम को पाँच –साढ़े पाँच बजे के बीच मुझे मेरे घर में मिलिएगा।
  āp āj śām ko pāṁc - sāṛhe pāṁc baje ke bīc mujhe mere ghar meṁ miliegā.
  You meet me in the evening between 5-5:30 in my house.
- वे हमें जनवरी की दो तारीख़ को, रात को सवा नौ बजे, सिनेमाघर के सामने मिलेंगे।
  ve hameṁ janvarī kī do tārīkh ko, rat ko savā nau baje, sinemāghar ke sāmne mileṁge.
  They will meet us on the second of January, at a quarter past nine p.m., in front of the cinema hall.
- हम कल सुबह पौने चार बजे बागीचे में मिलेंगे।
  ham kal subah paune cār baje bāgīce meṁ mileṁge.
  We will meet at a quarter to four tommorrow morning in the garden.

Talking about future plans: use of अगला aglā, अगले agle, अगली aglī, next.

- मैं अगले सोमवार को भारत जाऊँगा। maiṁ agle somvār ko bhārat jāūṁgā. — Next Monday, I will go to India.
- वे अगली गर्मी में पहाड़ पर जाएँगे। ve aglī garmī meṁ pahāṛ par jāeṁge. — Next summer, they will go to the mountains.
- आप अगली गर्मी में क्या करेंगे? ap aglī garmī meṁ kyā kareṁge? — What will you do next summer?
- वह अगले साल जनवरी में विदेश जाएगा। vah agle sāl janvarī meṁ videś jāegā. — He will go abroad next year.

Ex. D 16. Say in Hindi:

1. Meet me tomorrow afternoon at 3 p.m. 2. He will meet me in India on 14th January.3. What will she do next winter? 4. Do you agree with them? 5. I agree with them. 6. Next Thursday is a public holiday. 7. Are you free this evening? 8. I am free tomorrow evening. 9. I am usually free on Saturdays. 10. Next week we will go to the zoo. 11. I am here till next Sunday. 12. If you wish, we could see a film on next Friday. 13. If you eat so much, you will become fat. 14. If he does not stop smoking, he will become sick. 15. If you work hard, you will certainly be succesful. 16. If possible, I will certainly go to Bazar to day. 17. If you had invited me, I would have come. 18. If they had said, I would have done. 19. How nice it would have been, if exam had not taken place today. 20. If you had come to the party, everybody would have become happy.

Key: D 16.

1.	कल अपराह्न तीन बजे मुझे मिलना/ मिलिएगा।	kal aprāhn tīn baje mujhe milnā./ miliegā.
2.	वह मुझे चौदह नवम्बर को भारत में मिलेगा।	vah mujhe caudah navambar ko bhārat meṁ milegā.
3.	वह अगली सर्दी में क्या करेगी?	vah aglī sardī meṁ kyā karegī?

4.	क्या आप उनसे सहमत हैं?	kyā āp unse sahmat haiṁ?
5.	जी, मैं उनसे सहमत हूँ।	ji, maiṁ unse sahmat hūṁ.
6.	अगले गुरुवार को सार्वजनिक छुट्टी है।	agle guruvār ko sārvjanik chuṭṭī hai.
7.	क्या आप आज शाम को खाली हैं?	kyā āp āj śām ko khālī haiṁ?
8.	मैं कल शाम को खाली हूँ।	maiṁ. kal śām ko khālī hūṁ.
9.	मैं अक्सर शनिवार को खाली रहता हूँ।	maiṁ aksar śanivār ko khālī rahtā hūṁ.
10.	हम अगले हफ़्ते चिड़ियाघर जाएँगे।	ham agle hafte ciṛiyāghar jāeṁge.
11.	मैं अगले रविवार तक यहाँ हूँ।	maiṁ agle ravivār tak yahāṁ hūṁ.
12.	यदि आप चाहें तो हम अगले शुक्रवार को फ़िल्म देख सकते हैं।	yadi āp cāheṁ to ham agle śukra-vār ko film dekh sakte haiṁ.
13.	यदि तुम इतना ज़्यादा खाओगे, तो मोटे हो जाओगे।	yadi tum itnā zyāda khāoge, to moṭe ho jāoge.
14.	यदि वह धूम्रपान नहीं छोड़ेगा, तो बीमार होगा।	yadi vah dhūmrapān nahīṁ choṛe-gā, to bīmār hogā.
15.	यदि आपने मेहनत की, तो अवश्य सफल होंगे।	yadi āpne mehnat kī, to avaśyă saphal hoṁge.
16.	यदि सम्भव हुआ, तो मैं आज बाज़ार जाऊँगी।	yadi sambhav huā, to maiṁ āj bāzār jāūṁgī.
17.	यदि आप बुलाते, तो मैं आती।	yadi āp bulāte, to maiṁ ātī.
18.	यदि वे कहते, तो मैं करती।	yadi ve kahte, to maiīṁ kartī.
19.	यदि आज परीक्षा न हुई होती, तो कितना अच्छा होता।	yadi āj parīksā na huī hotī, to kitnā acchā hotā.
20.	यदि तुम दावत में आई होती, तो सब बहुत खुश हुए होते।	yadi tum dāvat meṁ aī hotīṁ, to sab bahut khuś hue hote.

●●●●●

D 17 Banaras The City Of Shiva

ऋषभः आप यहाँ कब से हैं?

पौलः लगभग दो महीने से।

ऋषभः तब तो आपने सारा भारत देख लिया होगा।

पौलः भारत विशाल देश है। एक बार में सारा भारत देखना सम्भव नहीं। हमने कुछ दक्षिण भारत और कुछ राजस्थान में यात्रा की है।

ऋषभः आप यहाँ और कहाँ–कहाँ जाएँगे।?

पौलः हम तो सारा भारत देखना चाहते हैं, परन्तु खेद है कि हमारे पास समय नहीं है। हमें अगले हफ़्ते अपने देश लौटना है। शायद कोई एक और स्थान देख सकते हैं। आपकी राय में हमें कहाँ जाना चाहिए?

ऋषभः भई मेरी राय में तो प्रत्येक विदेशी यात्री को उत्तर प्रदेश में बनारस अवश्य जाना चाहिए। यह गंगा नदी के तट पर स्थित है। यह विश्व का सबसे पुराना नगर माना जाता है। इसे भगवान शिव का नगर भी कहा जाता हैं। यह शहर बहुत आधुनिक तो नहीं है, परन्तु यहाँ के कोने–कोने में कोई छोटा–बड़ा मंदिर मिलता है। यह मंदिर वास्तुकला की दृष्टि से बहुत रोचक नहीं, परन्तु हर मंदिर के साथ जुड़ी हुई कोई–न–कोई रोचक पौराणिक कहानी है।

पौलः हम बनारस अवश्य जाएँगे। वास्तव में मेंने फ़ैसला कर लिया है कि बिना बनारस देखे हम अपने देश नहीं लौटेंगे।

ऋषभः बहुत बढ़िया! इसी बात पर हो जाय एक–एक मिठाई; और आज की शाम हमारी दोस्ती के नाम!

ṛṣabh: āp yahāṁ kab se haiṁ?

Paul : lagbhag do mahīne se.

ṛṣabh: tab to āpne sārā bhārat dekh liyā hogā?

Paul : bhārat viśāl deś hai. ek bār meṁ sārā bhārat dekhnā sambhav nahīṁ. hamne kuch dakṣiṇ bhārat, aur kuch rājasthān meṁ yātrā kī hai.

ṛṣabh: āp yahāṁ aur kahāṁ-kahāṁ jāeṁge?

Paul : ham to sārā bhārat dekhnā cāhte haiṁ, parantu khed hai ki hamāre pās samay nahīṁ hai. hameṁ agle hafte apne deś lauṭnā hai. śāyad koī ek aur sthān dekh sakte haiṁ. āpkī rāy meṁ hameṁ kahāṁ jānā cāhie?

ṛṣabh: bhaī merī rāy meṁ to pratyek videśī yātrī ko uttar pradeś meṁ banāras avaśyă jānā cāhie. yah gaṅgā nadī ke taṭ par sthit hai. yah viśva kā sab se purānā nagar mānā jātā hai. ise bhagvān śiva kā nagar bhī kahā jātā hai. yah śahar bahut ādhunik to nahīṁ hai, parantu yahāṁ ke kone-kone meṁ koī choṭā-baṛā mandir miltā hai. yah mandir vāstukalā kī driṣṭi se bahut rocak nahīṁ, parantu har mandir ke sāth juṛī huī koī-na-koī rocak paurāṇik kahānī hai.

Paul : ham banāras avaśyă jāeṁge. vāstav meṁ maiṁne faislā kar liyā hai ki binā banāras dekhe ham apne deś nahīṁ lauṭeṁge.

ṛṣabh: bahut baṛhiyā! isī bāt par ho jāe ek-ek miṭhāī aur āj kī śām hamārī dostī ke nām.

WORDS AND PHRASES

विशाल (adj.)	viśāl	big
देश (m.)	deś	country
सारा (adj.)	sārā	entire
एक बार में	ek bār meṁ	in one go
सम्भव (adj.)	sambhav	possible
दक्षिण (n./adj.)	dakṣiṇ	south
तो (/conj./adv.)	to	here: indeed
खेद (m.)	khed	regret
अवश्य (adv.)	avaśya	certainly
वास्तव में (adv.)	vāstav meṁ	actually
कहाँ–कहाँ (adv.)	kahāṁ-kahāṁ	where all
शायद (adv.)	śāyad	perhaps
राय (f.)	rāy	opinion
प्रत्येक (adj.)	pratyek	every
विदेशी यात्री (m.)	videśī yātrī	foreign traveler
स्थित होना (v.i.)	sthit honā	to be situated
विश्व (m.)	viśva	world
सबसे पुराना (adj.)	sab se purānā	the oldest

नगर (m.)	nagar	city
आधुनिक (adj.)	ādhunik	modern
कोने–कोने में	kone-kone meṁ	in every nook and corner
वास्तुकला (f.)	vāstukalā	architecture
रोचक (adj.)	rocak	interesting
पौराणिक (adj.)	paurāṇik	classical
कहानी (f.)	kahānī	story
फ़ैसला (m.)	faislā	decision
• माना जाता है (passive.)	mānā jātā hai	is considered
• की दृष्टि से	kī driṣṭi se	from the point of view of
• के साथ जुड़ी हुई	ke sāth juṛī huī	connected with
• खेद है कि	khed hai ki	(I) am sorry
• मेरी राय में	merī rāy meṁ	in my opinion

Present Perfect Tense,Compound Verb: Gram. Ref. pg. 129, 187

- मैंने फ़ैसला कर लिया है। — I have already decided.
  maiṁne faislā kar liyā hai.

Presumption: Gram. Ref. pg. 216

- आपने सारा भारत देख लिया होगा। — You must have seen the whole of India.
  āpne sārā bhārat dekh liyā hogā?
- उन्हों ने नाश्ता कर लिया होगा। — They must have had breakfast.
  unhoṁne nāśtā kar liyā hogā?.

के पास होना ke pās honā = to have: Gram. Ref. pg. 81

- हमारे पास समय नहीं है। — We don't have time.
  hamāre pās samay nahīṁ hai.
- उसके पास बहुत धन है। — He/She has much money.

unke pās bahut dhan hai.

Inner Compulsion Gram. Ref. pg. 211

- हमें अगले हफ़्ते अपने देश लौटना है।
  hameṁ agle hafte apne deś lauṭnā hai.
  We must return to our country next week.

Moral Compulsion चाहिए cāhie: Gram. Ref. pg. 158

- प्रत्येक विदेशी यात्री को .... जाना चाहिए।
  pratyek videśī yātrī ko............... jānā cāhie.
  Every foreign traveler ought to go to.............

Passive : Gram. Ref. pg. 231, 286, 287, 292

- यह विश्व का सबसे पुराना नगर माना जाता है।
  yah viśva kā sab se purānā nagar mānā jātā hai.
  It is believed to be the oldest city of the world.
- इसे भगवान शिव का नगर भी कहा जाता है।
  ise bhagvān śiva kā nagar bhī kahā jātā hai.
  It is also called the city of Lord Shiva.

Use of मिलना milnā = to be found:see pg. 296

- यहाँ के कोने–कोने में कोई छोटा–बड़ा मंदिर मिलता है।
  yahāṁ ke kone-kone meṁ koī choṭā-baṛā mandir miltā hai.
  In every nook and corner of this place, some small or big temple is found.

Subjunctive use 'हो जाय ho jāy = let there be/ let's have :

- इसी बात पर **हो जाय** एक–एक मिठाई;
  isī bāt par ho jāy ek-ek miṭhāī
  At this, let's have a piece of sweet each.
- और हो जाय आज की शाम, हमारी दोस्ती के नाम!
  aur ho jāy āj kī śām, hamārī dostī ke nām!
  and let's celebrate the evening in the name of our friendship!

D 18 From Newpapers अख़बारों से

Education

उच्च शिक्षा प्राप्त करने का अच्छा साधन है मुक्त शिक्षा प्रणाली
ucca śikśā prāpt karne kā acchā sādhan hai mukt śikśā praṇālī

उच्च	ucca	high (1)
शिक्षा	śikśā	education
प्राप्त करना	prāpt karmā	to obtain
करने का	karne kā	of obtaining
अच्छा	acchā	good
साधन	sādhan	mode
है	hai	is
मुक्त	mukt	free/open
शिक्षा प्रणाली	shiksha praṇālī	education system

Open education system is a good mode of getting higher education.

महिलाओं की शिक्षा से होगा देश का विकास
mahilāoṁ k ī śikśā se hogā deś kā vikās

महिलाओं की	mahilāoṁ k ī	of women
शिक्षा से	śikśā se	by education
होगा	hogā	will be

देश m.sg. का	deś kā	of the country
विकास m.sg.	vikās	development

Development of the country will be through women's education

छात्र आत्मविश्वास के साथ काम करें
chātra ātmaviśvās ke sāth kām kareṁ

छात्र m.sg.	chātra	students
आत्मविश्वास m.sg.	ātmaviśvās	self confidence
के साथ ppn	ke sāth	with
काम m.sg.	kām	work
करें (imper.subjun.)	kareṁ	may do

May the students work with self confidence!

कामयाबी का मूलमंत्र: धैर्य, कठिन परिश्रम व आत्मविश्वास
kāmyābī kā mūlmantra dhairya, kaṭhin pariśram va ātmaviśvās

कमयाबी f.sg.	kāmyābī	success
मूलमंत्र m.sg.	mūl mantra	basic 'mantra'
धैर्य m.sg.	dhairyă	patience
कठिन adj.	kaṭhin	hard/difficult
परिश्रम m.sg.	pariśram	hardwork
व (conj.)	va	and
आत्मविश्वास m.sg.	ātmaviśvās	self confidence

basic 'mantra' of success: patience, hard work and self confidence

प्रतिभा हो तो मुकाम खुद–ब–खुद मिल जाता है।
pratibhā ho to mukām khud-ba-khud mil jātā hai.

प्रतिभा f.sg.	pratibhā	talent
हो (v.)	ho	be
तो	to	then
मुकाम m.sg.	mukām	destination
खुद–ब–खुद	khud-ba-khud	by itself
मिलना (v.)	milnā	to get
मिल जाता है	mil jātā hai	is attained.

Destination is automatically attained if there is talent.

Terrorism

प्रदेश में श्रृंखलाबद्ध विस्फोट, तेरह की मौत, तिरपन घायल।
prades mem śrinkhlābadh visphoṭ, terah kī maut, tirpan ghāyal

प्रदेश m.sg.	pradeś	State
श्रृंखलाबद्ध adj.	śrinkhlābadh	serial
विस्फोट m.sg.	visphoṭ	blast
तेरह adj.	terah	thirteen
मौत f.	maut	death
तिरपन	tirpan	fifty-three
घायल	ghāyal	injured

Serial blasts in the State, 13 died, 53 injured.

भारी मात्रा में विस्फोट बरामद
bhārī mātrā meṁ visphoṭ barāmad

भारी adj.	bhārī	huge
मात्रा f.sg.	mātrā	quantity
विस्फोट m.sg.	visphoṭ	explosives
बरामद pp	barāmad	seized/ recovered

Explosives recoverred in large quantities.

आतंकियों का मुकाबला जन साहस से ही संभव
ātankiyoṁ kā mukāblā jan sāhas se hī sambhav

आतंकी m.sg.	ātankī	terrorist
मुकाबला m.sg.	mukāblā	confrontation
जन साहस m.sg.	jan sāhas	people's courage
संभव adv.	sambhav	possible

Encountering terrorists possible only by the courage of the people.

आतंकवादियों की चुनौती का माकूल जवाब देंगे।
ātankvādiyoṁ kī cunautī kā mākūl javāb deṁge.

आतंकवादी m.sg.	ātankvādī	terrorist
चुनौती f.sg.	cunautī	challenge
माकूल adj.	mākūl	appropriate
जवाब m.sg.	javāb	reply

We will give appropriate reply to the challenge of the terrorists.

आज आतंकवादी हर संभव रास्ते से देश में प्रवेश कर रहे हैं। आतंकियों ने बड़ी तादाद में देश में घुसपैठ करके अपना व्यापक जाल बिछा लिया है। आतंकवादी सीमा पार घुसपैठ करने के बाद स्थानीय लोगों से इतने घुलमिल गए हैं कि उनकी पहचान कर पाना कठिन ही नहीं, नामुमकिन हो गया है। इतना ही नहीं, आतंकियों ने राशन कार्ड और अन्य पहचान पत्र भी हासिल कर लिए हैं। उनकी जड़ें इतनी गहरी हैं कि वे आसानी से अपने नापाक मंसूबों को अंजाम देने में कामयाब हो जाते हैं।

āj ātankvādī har sambhav rāste se deś meṁ praveś kar rahe haiṁ. ātankiyoṁ ne baṛī tādād meṁ ghuspaiṭh karke apnā vyāpak jāl bichā liyā hai. ātankvādī sīmā pār ghuspaiṭh karne ke bād sthānīyă logoṁ meṁ itne ghulmil gae haiṁ ki unkī pahcān kar pānā kaṭhin hī nahīṁ, nāmumkin ho gayā hai. itna hī nahīṁ, ātankiyoṁ ne rāśankārd aur anyă pahcān patra bhī hāsil kar lie haiṁ. unkī jaṛeṁ itnī gahrī haiṁ ki ve āsānī se apne nāpāk mansūboṁ ko anjām dene me kāmyāb ho jāte haiṁ.

आतंकवादी m.sg.	ātankvādī	terrorist
हर संभव	har sambhav	every possible
रास्ता m.sg.	rāstā	path, route
देश m.sg.	deś	country
प्रवेश m.sg.	praveś	entry
आतंकी m.sg.	ātankī	terrorist(s)
तादाद f.sg.	tādād	quantity, number
घुसपैठ f.sg.	ghuspaiṭh	infiltration
घुसपैठ करना v.t.	ghuspaiṭh karknā	infiltrate into
घुसपैठ करके	ghuspaiṭh karke	infiltrating and
अपना reflexive	apnā	one's own
व्यापक adj.	vyāpak	extensive

जाल m.sg.	jāl	network
जाल बिछाना v.t.	jāl bichānā	to spread the network
–बिछा लिया है।	-bichā liyā hai.	have spread the network
सीमा f.sg.	sīmā	border
सीमा पार adv.	sīmā pār	across the border
स्थानीय adj.	sthānīyă	local
लोग m.pl.	log	people
इतने adv.	itne	so much
घुलमिल जाना v.i.	ghulmil jānā	mingle
पहचान f.sg.	pahcān	identification
पहचान करना v.t.	pahcān karnā	to identify
पहचान कर पाना v.i.	pahcān kar pānā	to be able to identify
कठिन adj.	kaṭhin	difficult
कठिन **ही नहीं**	kaṭhin **hī nahīṁ**	**not only** difficult
नामुमकिन adj.	nāmumkin	impossible
इतना **ही नहीं**	itnā **hī nahīṁ**	**not only** this
राशन कार्ड m.sg.	rāśankārd	ration card
अन्य adj.	anyă	other
पहचान पत्र m.sg.	pahcān patra	ID
भी	bhī	also
हासिल करना v.t.	hāsil karnā	to procure
जड़ें f.pl.	jaṛeṁ	roots
इतनी adv.	itnī	so
गहरी adj.	gahrī	deep
आसानी से adv.	āsāni se	easily
अपने reflexive	apne	one's own
नापाक adj.	nāpāk	dirty, impure, undesirable
मंसूबा m.sg.	mansūbā	intention
अंजाम देना v.t.	anjām denā	to carry out
कामयाब adj.	kāmyāb	successful

The terrorists have infilterated into the country in large numbers and have extended their network. After crossing the border, the terrorists have mingled with the local people to an extent that it is difficult to identify them. Not only this, the terrorists have obtained ration cards and other identity papers too. Their roots are so deep that they are successful in executing their evil plans with ease.

Bureaucracy

नौकरशाही के कामकाज में सुधार की आवश्यकता
naukarśāhī ke kāmkāj meṁ sudhār kī āvaśyaktā

नौकरशाही f.sg.	naukaśāhi	bureaucracy
कामकाज m.sg.	kāmkāj	work, tasks
सुधार m.sg.	sudhār	improvement
आवश्यकता f.sg.	kāmyāb	necessity

There is need to improve the functioning of bureaucracy.

नौकरशाही की मांसिकता में परिवर्तन का समय आ गया है।
naukarśāhī kī mānsiktā meṁ parivartan kā samay ā gayā hai.

मांसिकता f.sg.	mānsiktā	mentality
परिवर्तन m.sg.	parivartan	change
परिवर्तन का समय m.sg.	parivartan kā samay	time for change
आ गया है।	ā gayā hai	has come

It is time now to change the mentality of bureoucracy.

नौकरशाही के कामकाज की निगरानी की जाएगी।
naukarśāhī ke kāmkāj kī nigrānī kī jāegī.

कामकाज m.sg.	kāmkāj	tasks
निगरानी f.sg	·nigrānī	supervision
निगरानी करना v.t.	nigrānī karna	to supervise
निगरानी की जाएगी। passive	nigrānī kī jaegī	will be supervised

The functioning of bureaucracy will be under vigilance.

नौकरशाह बनें जन समस्याओं के प्रति सजग और संवेदनशील!
naukarśāh banem̐ jan samasyāom̐ ke prati sajag aur sam̐vedanśīl

नौकरशाह m.sg.	naukarśāh	bureaucrats
बनें subjunctive	banem̐	should become
जन समस्या f.sg.	jan samasyā	people's problem
के प्रति ppn	ke prati	towards
सजग adj.	sajag	vigilant
संवेदनशील adj.	sam̐vedanśīl	compassionate

The bureaucrats should be vigilant and compassionate towards the problems of the people!

•••

P 1 EVERYDAY PHRASES

all time greeting.	नमस्ते / नमस्कार	namaste/ namaskār
good morning	शुभ प्रभात	śubh nrabhāt
good night	शुभ रात्रि	ś ubh râtri
good evening	शुभ सन्ध्या	śubhsandhyā
greeting used both at the time of meeting as vell as parting, particulary used as a mark of respect:	प्रणाम	praṇām
Thanks.	धन्यवाद / शुक्रिया	dhanyăvād/ śukriyā
Excuse me.	क्षमा कीजिए/ माफ़ काजिए	kṣamā kījie/ māf kījie
I am grateful to you.	मैं आपका/आपकी आभारी हूँ ।	maiṁ āpkā / āpkī ābhārī hūṁ.
You are welcome!	कोई बात नहीं	koī bāt nahīṁ
Wish you a happy journey!	आपकी यात्रा मंगलमय हो।	āp kī yātrā mangalmay ho!
See you again.	फिर मिलेंगे	phir milemge.
Hearty congratulations to you!	आपको हार्दिक बधाई हो।	āpko hārdik badhāī ho!
Yes	हाँ	hāṁ
No	नहीं।	nahīṁ
lunch	दिन का खाना	din kā khānā
dinner	रात का खाना	rāt kā khānā
May I sit here?	क्या मैं यहाँ बैठ सकता हूँ ?	kyā maiṁ yahāṁ baiṭh saktā hūṁ?
Be seated!	बैठिए।	baiṭhie
It is natural!	यह स्वभाविक है।	yah svabhāvik hai!

Everyday Phrases

Absolutely	बिलकुल	bilkul
Perhaps	शायद	śāyad
It could be	हो सकता है	ho saktā hai
Certainly	ज़रूर	zarūr
Do you agree?	आप सहमत हैं?	āp sahmat haiṁ?
Yes I agree.	जी, मैं सहमत हूँ।	ji, maiṁ sahmat hūṁ

■ **Giving Directions:**

Go straight!	सीधे चलो।.	sīdhe calo!
Turn right!	दायें मुड़ो।	dāyeṁ muṛo!
Turn left!	बायें मुड़ो।	bāyeṁ muṛo!
Stop at the crossing.	चौराहे पर रुकिए।	cāurahe par **rukie**!

(if you are asking someone to stop)

Stop here!	यहाँ रोकिए।	yahāṁ **rokie**!

(if you are asking someone to stop some vehicle)

■ **Asking and telling name:**

☞ **Regardless of the gender of the person whose name is being asked or told, the expression is always का नाम 'kā nām'.**

What is your name?	आपका नाम क्या है?	āp kā nām kyā hai?
My name is Rama.	मेरा नाम रमा है।	merā nām Rama hai?
What is her / his name?	उसका नाम क्या है?	uskā nām kyā hai?
Her name is Sarita.	उसका नाम सरिता है।	uskā nām Sarita hai?

■ **Asking ' where somebody is from.'** **See pg. 245**

☞ **का, के, की** kā, ke, kī **agrees with the N and G of the subject .**

1. Where is he from? — वह कहाँ का रहनेवाला है?
vah kahāṁ kā rahnevālā hai ?

2. He is a resident of Delhi. — वह दिल्ली का रहनेवाला है।
vah dillī kā rahnevālā hai ?

3. Where is she from? — वह कहाँ की रहनेवाली है?
vah kahāṁ kī rahnevālī hai?

4. She is a resident of London — वह लंदन की रहनेवाली है।
vah London kī rahnevālī hai.

5. Where is he(hon.) / they from? — वे कहाँ के रहनेवाले है?
ve kahāṁ ke rahnevāle haiṁ?

■ What kind of.....? कैसा kaisā, कैसे kaise, कैसी kaisī

1. What kind of woman is she? — वह कैसी औरत है?
vah kaisī aurat hai?

2 What kind of people are they? — वे कैसे लोग हैं?
ve kaise log haiṁ?

3. What kind of food do they eat? — वे कैसा खाना खाते हैं?
ve kaisā khānā khāte haiṁ?

4. What kind of clothes do they wear? — वे कैसे कपड़े पहनते हैं?
ve kaise kapṛe pahnte haiṁ?

5. What kind of houses do they live in? — वे कैसे घरों में रहते हैं?
ve kaise gharoṁ meṁ rahte haiṁ?

■ How ? कैसा kaisā, कैसे kaise, कैसी kaisī

1. How are you? — आप कैसे हैं?
āp kaise haiṁ?

2. How is your health? — आपकी सेहत कैसी है?
āpkī sehat kaisī hai?

3. How is he/she? — वह कैसे है?
vah kaise hai?

4. How is his/her family. — उसका परिवार कैसे हैं?
uskā parivār kaise hai?

5 .How was the film? — फ़िल्म कैसी थी?
film kaisī thī?

■ **Asking who somebody is?**

Who are you (formal)? — आप कौन हैं?
āp kaun haiṁ?

I am............................ — मैं.............................हूँ।
maiṁ ....hūṁ?

Who are they? — वे कौन हैं?
ve kaun haiṁ?

They are............................ — वे.............................हैं।
ve ....haiṁ.

Who is he/she? — वह कौन है?
vah kaun hai?

She / He is .... — वह.............................है।
vah ....hai?

For answers, use any one of the words given below:
छात्र chātra (m. sg./pl.) student(s) ; छात्रा chātrā (f.sg.) student; छात्राएँ chātrāeṁ (f.pl.) students; गाहक gāhak (m. sg./pl.) customer(s); दुकानदार dukāndār (m. sg./pl.) shopkeeper (s); मरीज़ marīz (m. sg./pl.) patient (s); बच्चा baccā (m.sg.) child; बच्चे bacce (m.pl.) children; लड़का laṛkā (m.sg.) boy; लड़के laṛke (m.pl.) boys; लड़की laṛkī (f.sg.) girl; लड़कियाँ laṛkiyāṁ (f.pl.) girls.

■ **Confirming somebody's identity: Use of न 'na' at the end of a sentence corresponds to question tags such as 'isn't it', etc. in English):**

You are from Delhi, aren't you? — आप दिल्ली से हैं न?
āp dillī se haiṁ na?

You are Mr. Kapoor, aren't you? — आप श्री कपूर हैं न?
āp śrī kapūr haiṁ na?

■ Finding out about mutual relationships:

☞ **Use of the possessive endings का, के, की depends upon the N and G of the person with whom relationship is asked about.**

How is she related to you? — यह/ वह आपकी क्या लगती है?
yah/vah āpkī kyā lagtī hai?

She is my sister. — यह / वह मेरी बहन लगती है।
yah/vah merī bahan lagtī hai.

How are they related to you? — ये/वे आपके क्या लगते हैं ?
ye[m.pl.]/ve[m.pl.] āpke kyā lagte haiṁ?

They are my friends. — ये/वे मेरे मित्र हैं ?
ye[m.pl.]/ve[m.pl.] mere mitra haiṁ?

■ Introducing People

1. Meet him/her(hon.). — **इनसे मिलिए।**
inse / āpse se milie.

2. Meet my wife. — मेरी पत्नी से मिलिए।
merī patnī se milie

3. Meet my friend. — मेरे दोस्त से मिलिए।
mere dost se milie.

4. Meet Mr. Kapoor. — श्री कपूर से मिलिए।
śrī kapūr se milie.

5. Meet my husband. — मेरे पति से मिलिए।
mere pati se milie.

■ Asking if they already know each other:

1. Have you met him/her? — आप इनसे मिलें हैं?
āp inse mile haiṁ

2. Have you met my wife Amy? — आप मेरी पत्नी एमी से मिले हैं?
āp merī patnī Amy se mile haiṁ?

3. Yes we have met before. — जी, हम पहले मिले हैं।
jī, ham pahle mile haiṁ?

4. We have never met before. — जी, हम पहले कभी नहीं मिले।
jī ham pahle kabhī nahīṁ mile.

☞ **Expressing pleasure at meeting somebody:**

I am very pleased to meet you. — आपसे मिलकर बहुत खुशी हुई।
āpse milkar bahut khuśī huī.

☞ **Responding to somebody's expressing pleasure at meeting you:**

Me too. — मुझे भी।
mujhe bhī.

I am pleased to meet you too. — मुझे भी आपसे मिलकर बहुत खुशी हुई।
mujhe bhī.āpse milkar bahut khuśī huī.

■ **Asking about nationality:**

☞ **Regardless of the gender of the person whose nationality is being asked the expression is always 'की राष्ट्रीयता' kī rāṣṭrīyatā.**

What is is his /her nationality. — उसकी राष्ट्रीयता क्या है?
uskī rāṣṭrīyatā kyā hai?

What is is your (formal) nationality. — आपकी राष्ट्रीयता क्या है?
āpkī rāṣṭrīyatā kyā hai?

What is is your (informal) nationality? — तुम्हारी राष्ट्रीयता क्या है?
tumhārī rāṣṭrīyatā kyā hai?

What is is their nationality? — उनकी राष्ट्रीयता क्या है?
unkī rāṣṭrīyatā kyā hai?

He/she is Indian. — वह भारतीय है।
vah bhārtiyă hai.

I am Japanese. — मैं जापानी हूँ।
maiṁ jāpānī hūṁ.

They are Russians.. — वे रूसी हैं।
ve rūsī haiṁ.

■ **Asking and telling about somebody's age?**

☞ **Possessive case endings** का kā, के kī, की kī **depend upon the N and G of the subject whose age is being talked about.**

The boy is 20 years old.	लड़का बीस साल का है। laṛkā bīs sāl kā hai.
The girl is 22 years old.	लडकी बाईस साल की है। laṛkī bāīs sāl kī hai.
How old are you(f. formal)?	आप (f.) कितने साल की हैं? āp (f. formal) kitne sāl kī haiṁ?
I (f.) am 60 years old.	मैं (f.) साठ साल की हूँ। maiṁ sāṭh sāl kī hūṁ.

■ **Suggesting to do something:**

Shall we watch televion?	दूरदर्शन देखा जाय? dūrdarśan dekhā jāy?
Shall we see some movie in the evening?	आज शाम को कोई फ़िल्म देखी जाय? āj śām ko koī film dekhī jāy?
After that , shall we eat out somewhere?	उसके बाद कहीं बाहर भोजन किया जाय। uske bād kahīṁ bāhar bhojan kiyā jāy?
Why not stay at home today?	क्यों न आज घर पर रहा जाय। kyoṁ na āj ghar par rahā jāy?

■ **Expressions about having or not having free time:**

Are you free?/Do you have free time	क्या आप खाली हैं? kyā āp khālī haiṁ?
Yes, I am free.	जी, मैं खाली हूँ। jī, maiṁ khālī hūṁ.

I am sorry, I am not free at the moment	मुझे खेद है, मैं इस समय खाली नहीं हूँ। jī, maiṁ is samay khālī nahīṁ hūṁ
When are you free?	आप कब खाली होते हैं?

☞ **Asking or telling what one does in one's free time :**

What do you do in your free time?	आप अपने खाली समय में क्या करते/ करती हैं? āp apne khālī samay meṁ kyā karte/kartī haiṁ?
I sleep until late.	मैं देर तक सोता/सोती हूँ। maiṁ der tak sotā/ sotī hūṁ.
I watch television.	मैं दूरदर्शन देखता/देखती हूँ। maiṁ dūrdarśan dekhtā /dekhtī hūṁ.
I listen to music	मैं गाने सुनता/सुनती हूँ। maiṁ gāne suntā/suntī hūṁ.
I read novels.	मैं उपन्यास पढ़ता/पढ़ती हूँ। maiṁ upanyās paṛhtā / paṛhtī hūṁ

Similarly practice with वे ve, तुम tum, कौन kaun, हम ham, अध्यापक adhyāpak etc.

■ **Expressing fondness for some thing, object or activity:**
(subject + को ko) + noun or (v.r.+ ने ne) + का शौक है kā śauk hai ।

I am fond of good clothes.	मुझे अच्छे कपड़ों का शौक है। mujhe acche kapṛoṁ kā śauk hai.
I am fond of traveling in foreign countries.	मुझे विदेशों मे घूमने का शौक है। mujhe videśoṁ meṁ ghūmne kā śauk hai.
I am fond of watching cricket.	मुझे क्रिकेट देखने का शौक है। mujhe kriket dekhne kā śauk hai.

I am fond of gardening.	मुझे बागवानी का शौक है। mujhe bāgvānī kā śauk hai.
What are you fond of?	आपको किस चीज़ का शौक है। āpko kis cīz kā śauk hai?
What are they fond of?	उनको किस चीज़ का शौक है। unko kis cīz kā śauk hai?

■ **Telling that something does not agree with you:**

(subject + को ko) **+ object + (माफ़िक** māfik) **+ नहीं आता/आते/आती**

nahīṁ ātā, āte, ātī.

☞ **आता/आते/आती ātā, āte, ātī agrees with N and G of the object.**

Coffee does not agree with me.	मुझे कॉफ़ी[f] माफ़िक नहीं आती। mujhe kaufī[f] māfik nahīṁ ātī.
Cold things don't agree with me	मुझे ठण्डी चीज़ें[f.pl.] माफ़िक नहीं आतीं। mujhe ṭhaṇḍī cīzeṁ[f.pl.] māfik nahīṁ ātīṁ.
Hot climate does not agree with me.	मुझे गर्मी का मौसम[m.] माफ़िक नहीं आता। mujhe garmī kā mausam[m.] māfik nahīṁ ātā.

■ **Telling that something does not look good on you or someone other than you.:**

noun + (subject + पर par) + (ठीक ṭhīk/अच्छा acchā, अच्छे acche, अच्छी acchī,) + नहीं लगता/लगते/लगती nahīṁ lagtā, lagte, lagtī

This color doesnot look good on you.	तुमपर यह रंग ठीक/अच्छा नहीं लगता। tumpar yah raṅg ṭhīk /acchā nahīṁ lagtā.

Tight clothes don't look good on me.	मुझपर तंग कपड़े ठीक/अच्छे नहीं yxrÅ mujhpar taṅg kapṛe ṭhīk/ acche nahīṁ lagte.
Foreign dresses look good on her.	उसपर विदेशी पोशाकें अच्छी लगती हैं। uspar videśī pośākeṁ acchī lagtī haiṁ.
Sari suits you very well.	तुमपर साड़ी बहुत अच्छी लगती है। tumpar sāṛī bahut acchī lagtī hai.

■ **Asking /telling if one knows how to do something.** **see pg. 147**

Do you know how to swim?	तुमको तैरना आता है। tumko tairnā ātā hai?
Yes I know how to swim.	जी हां, मुझको तैरना आता है। jī hāṁ, mujhko tairnā ātā hai.
No, I don't know how to swim.	जी नहीं, मुझको तैरना नहीं आता। jī nahīṁ, mujhko tairnā ātā hai.
Does he know how to speak Hindi?	उसको हिन्दी बोलनी आती है? usko hindi bolnī ātī hai?
Yes he knows how to speak Hindi	जी हां, उसको हिन्दी बोलनी आती है। jī hāṁ, usko hindi bolnī ātī hai?
No, he doesn't know how to speak. Hindi.	जी नहीं, उसको हिन्दी बोलनी नहीं आती। jī nahīṁ, usko hindi bolnī nahīṁ ātī .

•••

P 2 WEATHER TALK

Use of है = is, होता है = is habitually, रहता है = remains

Gram. Ref.

How is the weather today?	आज मौसम कैसा है? āj mausam kaisā hai?
The weather is good today.	आज मौसम अच्छा है। āj mausam acchā hai
Weather is bad today.	आज मौसम ख़राब है। āj mausam kharāb hai
It is very hot today.	आज बहुत गरम है। āj bahut garam hai.
It is very cold today.	आज ठण्ड है। āj ṭhaṇḍ hai.
Today it is very sunny outside.	आज बहुत तेज़ धूप है। āj bahut tez dhūp hai.
It is very windy today.	आज बहुत हवा है। āj bahut havā hai.
It is very foggy today.	आज बहुत कुहरा है। āj bahut kuhrā hai.
The sky is clear.	आसमान साफ़ है। āsmān sāf hai.
There is hail storm.	ओले पड़ रहे हैं। ole paṛ rahe haiṁ.
It is drizzling.	बूँदा–बाँदी हो रही है। būṁdā-bāṁdī ho rahī hai.
There is lightning.	बिजली चमक रही है। bijlī camak rahī hai.

Weather Talk

How is the weather in Delhi.	दिल्ली में मौसम कैसा होता है? dillī meṁ mausam kaisā hotā hai?
It is very hot during summer season in Delhi.	दिल्ली में गर्मी के मौसम में बहुत गरमी होती है। dillī meṁ garmī ke mausam meṁ bahut garmī hotī hai.
It is very cold during winter season in Delhi.	दिल्ली में सर्दी के मौसम बहुत ठण्ड होती है। dillī meṁ sardī ke mausam meṁ bahut ṭhaṇḍ hotī hai.
It rains much in Delhi.	दिल्ली में बहुत बारिश होती है। dillī meṁ bahut bāriś hotī hai.
It remains very hot in Delhi from April to August.	दिल्ली में अप्रैल से अगस्त तक बहुत गर्मी रहती है। dillī meṁ aprail se agast tak bahut garmī rahatī hai.
It remains very cold in Delhi from December to February.	दिल्ली में दिसम्बर से फ़रवरी तक बहुत ठण्ड रहती है। dillī meṁ disambar se farvarī tak bahut ṭhaṇḍ rahatī hai.
It remains very humid in Delhi from August to October.	दिल्ली में अगस्त से अक्तूबर तक बहुत उमस रहती है। dillī meṁ agast se aktūber tak bahut umas rahatī hai.
How is the weather in Delhi these days.	दिल्ली में आजकल कैसा मौसम चल रहा है? dillī meṁ ājkal kaisā mausam cal rahā hai?
Weather in Delhi is very pleasant these days.	दिल्ली में आजकल बहुत सुहावना मौसम चल रहा है? dillī meṁ ājkal bahut suhāvnā mausam cal rahā hai?

It is very hot /cold here these days.	यहाँ आजकल बहुत गरमी/ठण्ड हो रही है। yahāṁ ājkal bahut garmī/ṭhaṇḍ ho rahī hai.
It is very humid here these days.	यहाँ आजकल बहुत उमस हो रही है। yahāṁ ājkal bahut umas ho rahī hai.
It is raining much here these days.	यहाँ आजकल बहुत बारिश हो रही है। yahāṁ ājkal bahut bāriś ho rahī hai.
It is cloudy.	बादल छाए हुए हैं। bādal chāe hue haiṁ.
It is somewhat misty outside.	आज बाहर कुछ धुंधला है। āj bāhar kuch dhundhlā hai.
There are showers with thunder and lightning.	गरज–चमक के साथ छींटे पड़ रहे हैं। garaj-camak ke sāth chīṁṭe paṛ rahe haiṁ.
Last night there was heavy storm here.	कल रात को यहाँ बहुत तेज़ आंधी आई। kal rāt ko yahāṁ bahut tez āṁdhī āī.
What is the temperature today?	आज तापमान क्या है? āj tāpmān kyā hai?
two degrees below zero?	शून्य से दो अंश कम śūnyă se do aṁś kam.
The highest temperature today will be 53 degrees.	आज का उच्चतम तापमान तरेपन अंश होगा। āj kā uccatam tāpmān tarepan aṁś hogā.

*** Weather related vocabulary see pg. 78**

P3 DAYS AND MONTHS

DAYS OF THE WEEK

सोमवार^{m}	somvār	Monday	मंगलवार^{m}	maṅgalvār	Tuesday
बुधवार^{m}	budhvār	Wednesday	गुरुवार^{m}	guruvār	Thursday
शुक्रवार^{m}	śukravār	Friday;	शनिवार^{m}	śanivār	Saturday
रविवार^{m}	ravivār	Sunday.			

- **All days of the week are masculine.**
- **The Hindi expression corresponding to English 'on a certain day' requires the use of 'ko' before the name of the day. For instance:**

on Monday	सोमवार को	somvār ko
on Tuesday	मंगलवार को	maṅgalvār ko
on Wednesday	बुधवार को	budhvār ko **and so on.**

Use of next and last with a certain day of the week:

next + day of the week = अगले agle + the day of the week e.g.

next Wenesday = अगले बुधवार (को) agle budhvār ko. When 'day of the week' is preceded by

last + day of the week = पिछले pichle + the day of the week e.g.

last Wenesday = पिछले बुधवार (को) pichle budhvār ko

☞ When day of the week is preceded by अगले 'agle' or पिछले 'pichle', use of को 'ko' is not obligatory. In fact it is usually dropped by navive speakers.

What day of the week something takes place?

On which day are you going to India?	आप भारत किस दिन जा रहे/रही हैं? āp bhārat kis din jā rahe/rahī haiṁ?
I am going to India on Monday.	मैं सोमवार को भारत जा रहा/रही हूँ। maiṁ somvār ko bhārat jā rahā/rahī hūṁ.

On which day do you go to the mosque?	आप मस्जिद किस दिन जाते/जाती हैं? āp masjid kis din jāte/jātī haiṁ?
I go to mosque on Friday.	मैं शुक्रवार को मस्जिद जाता/जाती हूँ। maiṁ śukravār ko masjid jātā/ jātī hūṁ.
Which day of the week do you worship Lord Shiva ?	आप लोग हफ़्ते में किस दिन भगवान शिव की पूजा करते/करती हैं? āp log hafte meṁ kis din bhagvān śhiv kī pūjā karte/kartī haiṁ?
We worship Lord Shiva every Monday.	हम लोग प्रति सोमवार को भगवान शिव की पूजा करते/करती हैं? ham log prati somvār ko bhagvān śhiv kī pūjā karte/kartī haiṁ.
I learn Hindi twice a week, on Monday and Friday.	मैं हफ़्ते में दो दिन, सोमवार और शुक्रवार को, हिन्दी सीखता/सीखती हूँ। maiṁ hafte meṁ do din, somvār aur śukravār ko hindī sīkhtā/sīkhtī hūṁ.
He will come to the US in January.	वह जनवरी में अमरीका आएगा। vah janvarī meṁ amrīkā āegā.
On what date of January will come to the US?	वह जनवरी की कौन–सी तारीख़ को अमरीका आएगा। vah janvarī kī kaun-sī tārīkh ko amrīkā āegā.
He will come to the US on 2nd of January.	वह जनवरी की दो तारीख़ को अमरीका आएगा। vah janvarī kī do tārīkh ko amrīkā āegā.
.... on 10th of October.............	.......अक्तूबर की दस तारीख को....... ....aktūbar kī das tārīkh ko........

●●●

P4 HEALTH TALK

■ General questions and answers about one's health:

You look pale.	आपका चेहरा उतरा हुआ लग रहा है। āpkā cehrā utrā huā lag rahā hai.
What's the matter?	क्या बात है? kyā bāt hai?
Hope all is well!	सब ठीक तो है न? sab ṭhīk to hai na?
Yes, all is well.	जी, सब ठीक है। jī , sab ṭhīk hai.
I am fine.	जी, मैं ठीक हूँ। Ji, maim ṭhīk hūṁ.
I am not feeling well today.	आज मेरी तबीयत ठीक नहीं है। āj merī tabīyat ṭhīk nahīṁ hai.
I am feeling slightly unwell today.	आज मेरी तबीयत कुछ ख़राब है। āj merī tabīyat kuch <u>kh</u>arāb hai
How are you feeling today?	आज आपको कैसा लग रहा है? āj āpko kaisā lag rahā hai?
I am better.	अब मैं पहले से ठीक हूँ। ab maiṁ pahle se ṭhīk hūṁ.
Worse.	और भी ख़राब। aur bhī <u>kh</u>arāb.

■ Enquiring about second person's specific health problem:

Do you have fever?	क्या आपको बुखार है? kyā āpko bukhār hai?
Does it hurt anywhere?	क्या कहीं दुख रहा है? kyā kahīṁ dukh rahā hai?

Where does it hurt?	कहाँ दुख रहा है? kahāṁ dukh rahā hai?
Where do you have the pain?	आपको कहाँ दर्द हो रहा है? āpko kahāṁ dard ho rahā hai?

■ Telling about one's own specific health problem:

I feel slightly feverish.	मुझे हल्का बुख़ार लग रहा है। mujhe halkā bukhār lag rahā hai.
My whole body is paining.	मेरा सारा बदन दुख रहा है। merā sārā badan dukh rahā hai.
I am perspiring much.	मुझे बहुत पसीना आ रहा है। mujhe bahut pasīnā ā rahā hai.
I feel nausea.	मेरा जी मिचला रहा है। merā jī miclā rahā hai.
My lips are drying.	मेरे होठ सूख रहे हैं। mere hoṭh sūkh rahe haiṁ.
I have stomach ache.	मेरा पेट दुख रहा है। merā peṭ dukh rahā hai.
I have head ache.	मेरा सिर दुख रहा है। merā sir dukh rahā hai.
My foot hurts.	मेरा पैर दुख रहा है। merā pair dukh rahā hai.
I have slightly heavy head.	मेरा सिर कुछ भारी है। merā sir kuch bhārī hai.
My arm hurts.	मेरी बाँह दुख रही है। merī bāṁh dukh rahī hai.
My arms are hurting.	मेरी बाँहें दुख रही हैं। merī bāṁheṁ dukh rahī haiṁ.
My feet are hurting.	मेरे पैर दुख रहे हैं। mere pair dukh rahe haiṁ.

Health Talk

Another way to talk about one's ailment:

I sprained my foot.	मेरे पैर में मोच आ गई है। mere pair meṁ moc ā gaī hai.
I hurt my foot.	मेरे पैर में चोट लग गई है। mere pair meṁ coṭ lag gaī hai.
My foot/feet is hurtingly badly.	मेरे पैर /पैरों में बहुत दर्द हो रहा है। mere pair/pairoṁ meṁ bahut dard ho rahā hai.
My bone seems to have broken.	मेरी हड्डी टूट गई लगती है। merī haḍḍī ṭūṭ gaī lagtī hai
I have a bad stomach ache.	मेरे पेट में बहुत दर्द हो रहा है। mere peṭ meṁ bahut dard ho rahā hai.
I have head ache.	मेरे सिर में बहुत दर्द हो रहा है। mere sir meṁ bahut dard ho rahā hai.
I feel slight heaviness in my head.	मेरे सिर में कुछ भारीपन लग रहा है। mere sir meṁ kuch bhārīpan lag rahā hai.
My arm/arms is hurting.	मेरी बाँह/बाँहों में दर्द हो रहा है। merī bāṁh / bāṁhoṁ meṁ dard ho rahā hai.
I cannot sleep well.	मुझे ठीक से नींद नहीं आ रही। mujhe ṭhīk se nīṁd nahīṁ ā rahī.

Enquiring about third person's specific health problem:

What is your son suffering from?	आपके बेटे को क्या तकलीफ़ है? āpke beṭe ko kyā taklīf hai?
Does your son have fever?	क्या आपके बेटे को बुखार है? kyā āpke beṭe ko bukhār hai?

Does it hurt your son somewher?	क्या आपके बेटे को कहीं दुख रहा है? kyā āpke beṭe ko kahīṁ dukh rahā hai?
Where does it hurt him/her?	इन्हें कहाँ दुख रहा है? inheṁ kahāṁ dukh rahā hai?
Where exactly does he have pain?	इन्हें कहाँ दर्द हो रहा है? inheṁ kahāṁ dard ho rahā hai?

Practice with varied subjects:

(आपकी बेटी को, आपके पति को, आपकी बहन को, आपके दोस्त को)
(āpkī beṭī ko, āpke pati ko, āpkī bahan ko, āpke dost ko)

■ Telling about third person's specific health problem:

My child seems to have low fever.	मेरे बच्चे को हल्का बुख़ार लग रहा है। mere bacce ko halkā bukhār lag rahā hai.
My child has cough and high fever.	मेरे बच्चे को खाँसी और तेज़ बुखार है। mere bacce ko khāṁsī aur tez bukhār hai.
His/ Her fever is gradually increasing.	इसका बुख़ार बढ़ता जा रहा है। iskā bukhār baṛhtā jā rahā hai.
His/ Her condition is gradually deteriorating.	इसकी हालत बिगड़ती जा रही है। iskī hālat bigaṛtī jā rahī hai.
His/ Her forehead is very hot.	इसका माथा तप रहा है। iskā māthā tap rahā hai.
He/She hurt his/her foot.	इसके पैर में चोट लगी है। iske pair meṁ coṭ lagī hai.
My son has stomach ache.	मेरे बेटे का पेट दुख रहा है। mere beṭe kā peṭ dukh rahā hai.

My daughter has head ache.	मेरी बेटी का सिर दुख रहा है। merī beṭī kā sir dukh rahā hai.
My mother has nausea.	मेरी माता जी का जी मिचला रहा है। merī mātā jī kā jī miclā rahā hai.
My husband has back ache.	मेरे पति की पीठ दुख रही है। mere pati kī pīṭh dukh rahī hai.
My brother's feet are hurting.	मेरे भाई के पैर दुख रहे हैं। mere bhāī ke pair dukh rahe haiṁ.

■ **Another way of describing third person's health problem:**

My son has ear ache.	मेरे बेटे के कान में दर्द हो रहा है। mere beṭe ke kān meṁ dard ho rahā hai.
Mydaughter has head ache.	मेरी बेटी के सिर में दर्द हो रहा है। merī beṭī ke sir meṁ dard ho rahā hai.
My husband has back ache.	मेरे पति की पीठ में दर्द हो रहा है। mere pati kī pīṭh meṁ dard ho rahā hai.
My brother has tooth ache.	मेरे भाई के दाँत में दर्द हो रहा है। mere bhāī ke dāṁt meṁ dard ho rahā hai.
My child's hands and feet are becoming cold.	मेरे बच्चे के हाथ–पैर ठण्डे हो रहे हैं। mere bacce ke hāth-pair ṭhaṇḍe ho rahe haiṁ.

■ **Asking the chemist if he could recommend some medicine.**

Could you recommend some medicine for headache?	क्या आप सिर दर्द के लिए कोई दवाई बता सकेंगे? kyā āp sir dard ke lie koī davāī batā sakeṁge?

Could you recommend some ointment to apply on this injury.	क्या आप चोट पर लगाने के लिए कोई मरहम बता सकेंगे? kyā āp coṭ par lagāne ke lie koī marham batā sakeṁge?
Could you recommend some digestive.	क्या आप हाज़मे की कोई दवाई बता सकेंगे? kyā āp hāzme kī koī davāī batā sakeṁge?

■ Asking the chemist to give you some medicine:

Please give me some sleeping pill.	कृपया कोई नींद की गोली दीजिए। kṛpayā koī nīṁd kī golī dījie.
Please give me cotton and bandage.	कृपया मुझे रुई और पट्टी दीजिए। kṛpayā mujhe ruī aur paṭṭī dījie.
Please give me aspirin.	कृपया मुझे एसपिरिन दीजिए। kṛpayā mujhe aspirin dījie.

■ The doctor might say:

Yes, what are you suffering from?	कहिए, आपको क्या तकलीफ़ है? kahie, āpko kyā taklīf hai?
Open your mouth, please.	मुह खोलिए। muṁh kholie.
Sit straight.	सीधे बैठिए। sīdhe baiṭhie.
Remove your shirt please.	अपनी कमीज़ उतारिए। apnī kamīz utārie.
Deep breathe please.	लम्बी सांस लीजिए। lambī sāṁs lījie.
Hold your breath!	सांस रोकिए। sāṁs rokie.
Lie down, please!	लेट जाइए।

let jāie.

Put your shirt on! कमीज़ पहन लीजिए। kamīz pahan lījie.

WORDS AND PHRASES

to sprain	मोच आना	moc ānā
to hurt oneself	चोट लगना	coṭ lagnā
to pain	दर्द होना	dard honā
bone fracture	हड्डी टूटना	haḍḍi ṭūṭnā
feel heaviness	भारीपन लगना	bhārīpan lagnā
to suffer from something	तकलीफ़ होना	taklīf honā
to suffer from fever	बुखार होना	bukhār honā
to hurt/to pain	दुखना	dukhnā
to have slight fever	हल्का बुख़ार आना	halkā bukhār ānā
cough	खाँसी	khāṁsī
high	तेज़	tez
to gradually increase	बढ़ता जाना	baṛhtā jānā
to gradually deteriorate	बिगड़ता जाना	bigaṛtā jānā
fore head to be very hot	माथा तपना	māthā tapnā
to become cold	ठण्डा होना	ṭhaṇḍā honā
ointment	मरहम	marham
sleeping pill	नींद की गोली	nīṁd kī golī
cotton	रुई	ruī
bandage	पट्टी	paṭṭī
injection	सुई	suī
to give injection	सुई लगाना	suī lagnā

●●●

P 5 EATING OUT

■ Reserving table in advance at a restaurant:

I would like to reserve a table for four people for 7:30 p.m. tomorrow.
maiṁ kal śām sāṛhe sāt baje cār vyaktiyoṁ ke lie mez ārakṣit krānā cāhtā hūṁ
मैं कल शाम साढ़े सात बजे चार व्यक्तियों के लिए मेज़ आरक्षित कराना चाहता हूँ।

in the corner	kone meṁ	कोने में
near the window	khiṛkī ke pās	खिड़की के पास
away from the entrance door	praveś dvār se haṭ ke	प्रवेश द्वार से हट के
day after tomorrow	parsoṁ	परसों
(on Monday)	(somvār ko)	(सोमवार को)

☞ **If you go without advance reservation, the manager will say:**

For how many people do you need a table?
āpko kitne logoṁ ke lie mez cāhie?
आपको कितने लोगों के लिए मेज़ चाहिए।

☞ **You could say:**

A table for five, please. — kṛpayā pāṁc logoṁ ke lie.
कृपया पाँच लोगों के लिए।

■ Ordering food:

I would like a cup of lemon tea with sugar please.
mere lie cīnīvalī nimbū kī cāy lāie.
मेरे लिए चीनीवाली नींबू की चाय लाइए।

I would like a glass of lassī, please.
mere lie ek glās lassī lāie.
मेरे लिए एक ग्लास लस्सी लाइए।

I would like a coffe without milk and sugar please.
mere lie binā dūdh aur cīnī ke ek kaufī lāie.

Food Talk

मेरे लिए बिना दूध और चीनी के एक कॉफ़ी लाइए।

■ **If you want to tell the waiter what more you require, you say:**

May I have a knife please.	मुझको चाकू चाहिए। mujhko cāku.cāhie.
I would like some spoons please.	मुझको कुछ चमच चाहिए। mujhko kuch camac cāhie.
I would like more roti pleasė.	मुझको और रोटी चाहिए। mujhko aur roṭī cāhie.
We would like rice pudding please.	कृपया हमारे लिए खीर लाइए। kṛpayā hamāre lie khīr lāie.
He (hon.) would like a glass of water.	इनको एक गलास पानी चाहिए। inko ek glās pānī cāhie.

■ **How do you tell the waitor your problem with the food he served:**

This is cold.	yah ṭhaṇḍā hai	यह ठण्डा है।
It is overdone.	yah bahut zyādā pakā/galā huā hai.	यह बहुत ज़्यादा पका/गला हुआ है।
It tastes burnt.	yah jalā huā lag rahā hai	यह जला हुआ लग रहा है।
It tastes too salty.	ismeṁ namak bahut zyādā hai	इसमें नमक बहुत ज़्यादा है।
It tastes too sweet.	ismeṁ mīṭhā bahut zyādā hai.	यह बहुत ज़्यादा मीठा है।
It is hard.	yah bahut kaṛā hai.	यह बहुत कड़ा है।
It is too spicy.	yah bahut tītā hai.	यह बहुत तीता है।
It is bitter.	yah kuch kaṛuvā hai.	यह कुछ कड़ुवा है।
The plate is dirty.	pleṭ/thālī gandī hai.	प्लेट / थाली गन्दी है।
The cup is dirty.	pyālā gandā hai.	प्याला गन्दा है।

■ **Praising food :**

What a meal! kyā khānā thā!

	क्या खाना था !
What service!	kyā 'service'/sevā thī! क्या 'सर्विस'/सेवा थी !
What an excellent food!	kyā baṛhiyā khānā thā! क्या बढ़िया खाना था !
What a delicious sweet!	kyā svādiṣṭ miṭhāī thī! क्या स्वादिष्ट मिठाई थी !
What delicious 'lassi'.	kyā svādiṣṭ lassī thī! क्या स्वादिष्ट लस्सी थी !

Describing your food habits:

I am vegetarian.	maiṁ śākāhārī hūṁ. मैं शाकाहारी हूँ।
I cannot take any dairy products.	maiṁ dūdh kī koī cīz nahīṁ le saktā/saktī. मैं दूध की कोई चीज़ नहीं ले सकता/सकती।
I like food with much fiber.	मुझे बहुत रेशेदार खाना अच्छा लगता है। mujhe bahut reśedār khānā acchā lagtā hai.

.........with less oil..	.....kam ciknāīvālā......	..........कम चिकनाईवाला......
.........with less salt...	..........kam namakvālā.....	..........कम नमकवाला
......without sugar.....	..........binā cīnī kā...........	..........बिना चीनी का..........
..........without salt......	.........binā namak kā.......	........बिना नमक का..........

I am on diet.	मैं 'डायटिंग'कर रहा/रही हूँ। maiṁ ḍāyaṭing kar rahā/ rahī hūṁ.
I eat everything	मैं सबकुछ खाता हूँ। maiṁ sabkuch khātā /khātī hūṁ.

P 6 SHOPPING

■ Finding Out:

- **About availability in general:**

1. Where can one get English Newspaper here? — यहाँ अंग्रेज़ी का अख़बार कहाँ मिलेगा?
   yahāṁ angrezī kā akhbār kahāṁ milegā?
2. Where can one get milk and yogurt here? — यहाँ दूध, दही कहाँ मिलेगा?
   yahāṁ dūdh, dahī kahāṁ milegā?
3. Where can one get shoes here? — यहाँ जूते कहाँ मिलेगें?
   yahāṁ jūte kahāṁ mileṁge?
4. Where can one get clothes here? — यहाँ कपड़े कहाँ मिलेगें?
   yahāṁ kapṛe kahāṁ mileṁge?

- **If something is available at a certain place.**

1. Can one get English newspaper here? — क्या यहाँ अंग्रेज़ी का अख़बार मिलता है?
   kyā yahāṁ angrezī kā akhbār miltā hai?
2. Can one get milk and yogurt here? — क्या यहाँ दूध, दही मिलता है?
   kyā yahāṁ dūdh, dahī miltā hai?
3. Can one get shoes here? — क्या यहाँ जूते मिलते हैं?
   kyā yahāṁ jūte milte haiṁ?

■ Asking the price: का kā , के ke, , की kī: depends upon the number and gender of the object

How much is this? — यह कितने का है?
yah kitne kā hai?

How much are these. — ये कितने के हैं?
yah kitne ke haiṁ?

How much is this. — यह कितने की है?
yah kitne kī hai?

How much is this book? — यह किताब कितने की है?
yah kitāb kitne kī hai?

How much is this newpaper? — यह अख़बार कितने का है?
yah akhbār kitne kā hai?

Use vah वह instead of yah यह in case the object is in the singular and away from the speaker.
Use ve वे instead of ye ये in case the object is in the plural and away from the speaker.

■ Telling the price:

ten rupees a kilo — दस रुपए किलो
das rupae kilo

twenty-five rupees per meter — पचीस रुपए प्रति मीटर
pacīs rupae prati mīṭar

one rupee and fifty paisae each — डेढ़ रुपए का एक
ḍeṛh rupae kā ek

two rupees and fifty paisa for three — ढाई रुपए के तीन
ḍhāī rupae ke tīn

Rs.7.50 paisa for one dozen — साढ़े सात रुपए के एक दर्जन
sāṛhe sāt rupae ke ek darjan

■ Telling the shopkeeper to give you:

Please give me five kilos. — कृपया मुझे पाँच किलो दीजिए।
kṛpayā muje pāṁc kilo dījie.

.... five kilos............. — ....सवा किलो............
............savā kilo.............

........three fourth of a kilos...... — ....पौन किलो ....
.... paun kilo ....

........two and a half kilos......... — .... ढाई किलो ....

	............ḍhāī kilo ....
Please give fifteen meters	कृपया मुझे पंद्रह मीटर दीजिए।
	kṛpayā mujhe pandrah mīṭar dījie.
........one and a half meter......	............डेढ मीटर................
	............ḍeṛh meter...............
........three and a half meter........	............साढ़े तीन मीटर........
	............sāṛhe tīn meter........
Please give me six more.	कृपया मुझे छः और दीजिए।
	kṛpayā mujhe chah aur dījie.
Please give two dozen bananas.	कृपया मुझे दो दर्जन केले दीजिए।
	kṛpayā mujhe do darjan kele dījie.

■ **The shopkeeper says to you:**

Yes please! / What would you like, please?	जी, कहिए! /आपको क्या चाहिए?
	jī, kahie! / āpko kyā cāhie?
May I help you, Sir?	मैं आपकी क्या सहायता कर सकता हूँ।
	maiṁ āpkī kyā sahāytā kar saktā hūṁ?
Are you being attended to?	कोई आपकी मदद कर रहा है?
	koī apkī madad kar rahā hai?

■ **You could say:**

Thanks. I am just looking.	धन्यवाद। मैं सिर्फ़ देख रहा/रही हूँ।
	dhanyavād. maiṁ sirf dekh rahā / rahī hūṁ.
I would like to buy a sari, a peticoat and a blouse	मैं एक साड़ी, पेटीकोट और ब्लाऊज लेना चाहता/चाहती हूँ।
	maiṁ ek sāṛī, ek peṭīkoṭ aur ek blāūz lenā cāhtā/ cāhtī hum.
Are there any sales/bargains?	कोई 'सेल–वेल' लगी है क्या?
	kyā koī sel-vel lagī hai.
Are there any discounts?	कोई छूट वगैरा मिल रही है क्या?

koī chūṭ vagairā mil rahī hai kyā?

Telling what one wants to buy:

I am considering buying a black suit.

मैं एक काला सूट ख़रीदने की सोच रहा/रही हूँ।
maiṁ ek kālā sūṭ kharīdne kī soc rahā/ rahī hūṁ

Also I would like to take a white blouse, a couple of neckties and and a pair of gloves.

मुझे एक सफ़ेद ब्लाऊज़, कुछ टाइयाँ और एक जोड़ा दस्ताने भी चाहिए।
muje ek safed blāūz, kuch ṭāiyāṁ aur ek joṛā dastāne bhīcāhie.

Asking about something other than what the shopkeeper showed to you.

1. Do you have something better than this?

   आपके पास कुछ और इससे बढ़िया होगा?
   āpke pās kuch aur isse baṛhiyā hogā?

2. Do you have something bigger than this?

   आपके पास कुछ और इससे बड़ा होगा?
   āpke pās kuch aur isse baṛā hogā?

3. Do you have something cheapter than this?

   आपके पास कुछ और इससे सस्ता होगा?
   āpke pās kuch aur isse sastā hogā?

Expressing Likes and Dislikes:

Do you like these shoes?

क्या आपको ये जूते पसन्द हैं?
kyā āpko ye jūte pasand haiṁ?

I detest this color.

मुझे इस रंग से घृणा है?
mujhe is raṅg se ghṛṇā hai.

I like this dress.

मुझे यह पोशाक पसन्द है?
mujhe yah pośāk pasand hai.

I very much like cotton dresses	मुझे सूती पोशाकें बहुत पसन्द हैं। mujhe sūtī pośākeṁ bahut pasand haiṁ.
He /She does not like cotton dresses.	उसे सूती वस्त्र/पोशाकें पसन्द नहीं। use sūtī vastra/ pośākeṁ pasand nahīṁ.
He/She likes it very much.	उसे यह बहुत पसन्द है। use yah bahut pasand hai.
We like denim.	हमें 'डेनिम' पसन्द है। hameṁ 'dainim' pasand hai.
They like those red shoes.	उन्हें वे लाल जूते पसन्द हैं। unheṁ ve lāl jūte pasand haiṁ.
Do you like the hat?	तुम्हें वह 'हैट' पसन्द है? tumheṁ vah haiṭ pasand hai?
He / She does not like shirts.	उसको कमीज़ें पसन्द नहीं। usko kamīzeṁ pasand nahīṁ.
I don't like this watch.	मुझको यह घड़ी पसन्द नहीं। mujhko yah ghaṛī pasand nahīṁ.
I absolutely don't like it.	मुझे यह बिल्कुल पसन्द नहीं। mujhe yah pasand nahīṁ.

■ Expressing Opinion

1. I like this book.	मुझे यह किताब अच्छी लग रही है। mujhe yah kitāb acchī lag rahī hai.
2. I find this sari very good.	मुझे यह साड़ी बढ़िया लग रही है। mujhe yah sāṛī baṛhiyā lag rahī hai.
3. I find this umbrella too expensive.	मुझे यह छाता बहुत महँगा लग रहा है। mujhe yah chātā bahut mahaṁgā

	lag rahā hai.
4. I find these gloves a bit too small.	मुझे ये दस्ताने कुछ छोटे लग रहे हैं। mujhe ye dastāne kuch choṭe lag rahe haiṁ.
5. I find these socks quite inexpensive.	मुझे ये जुराबें काफ़ी सस्ती लग रही हैं। mujhe ye jurābeṁ kafī sastī lag rahī haiṁ.

■ Something looks or doesnot look good on you:

It looks good on you (informal).	yah tumpar acchā lag rahā hai. यह तुमपर बहुत अच्छा लग रहा है।
It looks perfect on you (formal).	yah āppar bilkul ṭhīk lag rahā hai. यह आपपर बिल्कुल ठीक लग रहा है।
It does not look good on you(informal).	yah tumpar acchā nahīṁ lag rahā. यह तुमपर अच्छा नहीं लग रहा।
It suits /himher very well.	yah āppar bahut acchā lag rahā hai. यह उसपर बहुत अच्छा लग रहा है।

■ General comments:

It is good.	acchā hai.	अच्छा है।
It is horrible.	bilkul bekār hai.	बिल्कुल बेकार है।
It is too loud	bahut bhaṛkīlā hai.	बहुत ज़्यादा भड़कीला है।
It is narrow.	kam cauṛā hai.	कम चौड़ा है।
It is tight.	kasā huā	कसा हुआ है।
It is small.	choṭā hai.	छोटा है।
It is short.	kam lambā/ūṁcā hai.	कम लम्बा/ ऊँचा है।
	kuch ūṁcā hai.	कुछ ऊँचा है।
It is a bit too long.	zyādā lambā hai/nīcā.	ज़्यादा लम्बा/नीचा है।
	zyādā nīcā.	ज़्यादा नीचा है।
It is elegant and very practical.	yah bahut surucipūrṇ aur upyogī hai.	यह सुरुचिपूर्ण और उपयोगी है।

Shopping

I am looking for something less loud.	maiṁ kuch kam bhaṛkīlā cāhie.	मै कुछ कम भड़कीला चाहिए।
less expensive	kam mahaṁgā	कम महँगा
for party wear	dāvat meṁ pahnane ke lie	दावत में पहनने के लिए
for daily wear	roz pahnane ke lie	रोज़ पहनने के लिए

*** To specify color of your choice: see colors on pg 24**

INDEX

●●●●●